Massachusetts and Federal Employment Law Manual

Copyright © 2002 by American Chamber of Commerce Publishers. All rights reserved. No part of this publication may be reproduced or transmitted in any form or by any means, electronic or mechanical, including photocopy, recording, or any information storage and retrieval system, without the express written consent of American Chamber of Commerce Publishers.

The information in this guide is being provided by the authors and publisher as a service to the business community. Although every effort has been made to ensure the accuracy and completeness of this information, the authors and publisher of this publication cannot be responsible for any errors or omissions, or any agency's interpretations, applications and changes of regulations described in this publication.

"This publication is designed to provide accurate and authoritative information in regard to the subject matter covered. It is sold with the understanding that the publisher is not engaged in rendering legal, accounting or other professional service. If legal advice or other expert assistance is required, the services of a competent person should be sought."

- *From a Declaration of Principles jointly adopted by a committee of the American Bar Association and a Committee of Publishers and Associations.*

Published by
American Chamber of Commerce Publishers
100 Executive Way, Suite 101
Ponte Vedra Beach, Florida 32082
800-643-5999
www.hrcomply.com

0-923606-12-2
FT54-A0720B

Foreword

Objectives and Philosophy

This book is intended to provide a handy overview of the most important employment issues, from hiring and terminating through discrimination and electronic communications. It should help you make sense of the maze of federal and state laws that apply to all facets of the employment process and to help you determine if you are complying with fundamental employment laws and regulations. We have tried to do this by removing extraneous and less-relevant material and focusing on those things you need to know to do your job effectively and efficiently.

Even with some pretty heavy and, we hope, judicious pruning of the material, there is still a lot of material here—and it is not simple material. Law is, naturally, complex and often difficult even for experts to understand fully. For the most part we have tried to present federal and state law in standard English, rather than in the all-too-familiar "legalese" you know and love. Whenever possible we have rephrased especially obscure and confusing statements into something a bit more comprehensible. Where the legal language is particularly wordy and oblique we have tried to cut through the verbiage to find the germ of the section, the actual meaning lying beneath the often wordy and inflated prose. We have used as many bulleted lists as possible, presenting information in bite-size pieces in an easy-to-read and easy-to-remember format.

In some instances, however, we have kept portions of the actual law, not necessarily because those portions were especially clearly written but because they contained essential information that could best be said in the particular legal phrasings used. We make no apologies for this, since eliminating essential information because it may be a little difficult to understand is not useful economy.

So we make some assumptions here. One is that you are not a lawyer and do not care to wade through the full law in all of its obscurity and unnatural English to find out the best way to deal with on-the-job matters. A competing assumption, however, is that although you may not be a legal expert you are an intelligent and informed professional who is willing to do a little thinking to understand some important and complex material. Indeed some serious thought is required to really understand all facets of employment law as it currently exists—and considerable effort will be required to keep up with the law as it changes, which it is always doing.

Organization

In addition to removing some of the less-important material and rephrasing some of the remaining legal language, we have tried to provide in this document an organizational approach that will help you approach the material easily and find specific topics quickly.

We have tried to follow the same general pattern for each chapter, with some slight variation to accommodate the wide range of material covered. Each chapter has its own Introduction, indicating the specific topics treated under the general chapter topic. General information and federal law are always handled first, and the material is broken down into subheadings indicating the specific aspects being discussed. You can use the chapter subheadings to skim through the manual as you seek specific information.

Specific state law content is usually handled separately in the second part of the chapter, again with subheadings indicating specific aspects of the general law. Ordinarily, you can review the federal law—or the particular parts of it you need to review—and then go on to the state law or the parts of that you need to review.

Your Comments

Since a manual of this kind will always be a "work in progress," subject to constant updating, we urge you to share with us your reactions to it, how we could make it more helpful to you, what additional areas you would like to see covered. Please contact us by phone at 1-800-643-5999 or e-mail at Service@hrcomply.com.

About Jackson Lewis

For over 40 years, Jackson Lewis has placed a high premium on preventive strategies and positive solutions in the practice of workplace law. We partner with employers to devise policies and procedures promoting constructive employee relations and limiting disputes.

When complaints arise, we work with clients to take incisive action to effect solutions that minimize costs and maximize results. Whether we are counseling on legal compliance or litigating a complex case, we help our clients achieve their business goals and promote an issue-free work environment.

With offices in major cities throughout the U.S., Jackson Lewis combines a national perspective with an awareness of local business environments. Our clients represent a wide range of public and private businesses and non-profit institutions. We are experienced in all aspects of workplace law: employment litigation, affirmative action, race, gender and age discrimination, sexual harassment, preventive labor relations, union avoidance, strikes, collective bargaining, grievance arbitration, employee leaves, pension and benefit administration, immigration, wage and hour, independent contractors and contingent workers, occupational safety and health, substance abuse and drug testing, employee privacy, disability rights, workplace violence, restrictive covenants and non-compete agreements, and alternative dispute resolution.

When a client seeks counsel in any of these areas, we assign an experienced attorney to deliver the most effective representation. For clients with more than one location, we develop a multi-office team, which provides the advantages of local, as well as national, counsel. Heading the team is the "primary contact attorney" who is responsible for the overall coordination of services.

Employment Litigation

Federal and state equal employment laws impose legal obligations and their attendant risks on virtually every employer. The majority of Jackson Lewis attorneys devote their practice to defending management in employment-related lawsuits, the fastest growing area of civil litigation. We have litigated over 4,000 employment cases within the past five years, and we have substantial experience in evaluating, preparing and managing both individual and class action lawsuits. Our successful and cost efficient representation in every type of employment matter has earned us a reputation as a leader in the field.

Labor Relations

Jackson Lewis is deeply committed to the practice of preventive labor relations through issue assessment, supervisory training, policy development, and positive communications. The preservation of management rights is our goal, whether prior to a union offensive or during a union-organizing campaign. We have assisted many employers in winning NLRB elections or in avoiding union elections altogether. Our attorneys have handled thousands of matters before the National Labor Relations Board, state labor boards, and state and federal courts and have preserved management rights in contract negotiations, contract administration, grievance and arbitration proceedings, and work stoppages.

Employee Benefits

We assist our clients in administering benefit plans and identifying issues that may later develop into problem areas. When challenges arise, we defend employers against benefit claims and related litigation and provide counsel on all benefit issues occurring in the course of collective bargaining, corporate divestitures, acquisitions, business closures and reductions in force. We also design pension, profit-sharing, 401(k) and other types of retirement, deferred compensation and incentive compensation and welfare benefit plans.

Immigration

In an increasingly global economy, we help companies obtain temporary employment visas and immigrant visas authorizing unlimited employment with U.S. residence. We educate management about the visa system, facilitating long-term career planning for key employees and establishing in-house visa programs that ease transfers. We also advise about compliance with I-9 employment authorization verification requirements and, when necessary, litigate immigration matters in administrative and federal court proceedings.

Affirmative Action Plan Preparation and OFCCP Audit Defense

Many employers have contracts or subcontracts with federal, state or municipal governments that require implementation of affirmative action plans. Representing such employers requires a thorough understanding of affirmative action and equal employment opportunity laws. The team of attorneys and paralegals who make up our affirmative action practice annually prepare hundreds of affirmative action plans and have represented employers nationwide in "Glass Ceiling" and hundreds of routine affirmative action audits. In fact, our team regularly defends anywhere from one to four audits per month across the country. If you are audited by the Office of Federal Contract Compliance Programs, we will help you prepare for and defend the compliance review as your representative during the review or as a behind the scenes advisor.

Management Education

Employment, labor, immigration and benefits law is marked by constant change. We devote a significant amount of our resources to education. We train supervisors to comply with all applicable laws and regulations, avoid workplace disputes, resolve employee relations problems, and satisfy legitimate employee expectations. This preventive approach helps management pre-empt the filing of grievances, charges or lawsuits and avoid their costly defense and unproductive diversion of time and energy. We present seminars throughout the U.S. in our continuing effort to keep the management community fully informed and prepared for the workplace issues of today and the future.

Spanish Language Service

Se Habla Espanol: Jackson Lewis Offers Spanish Language Client Services

The Jackson Lewis Hispanic Practices Group is pleased to assist clients by providing Spanish language services. These services include the following:

- Preparation and English/Spanish translation of hiring materials, including job applications, arbitration agreements, employment contracts, employee handbooks, personnel policy materials, anti-harassment, vacation and sick leave, and FMLA policies, employee evaluations and counseling reports, separation materials, and other related documentation.

- Management and employee training in Florida and abroad (for U.S.-based clients), including anti-harassment policy training and promulgation, investigation of work-related harassment and employee disputes, guidance regarding equal employment opportunity (EEO) and other employment laws and regulations, and avoidance of work-related disputes.

- Litigation in Florida and abroad (for U.S.-based clients), including conducting interviews of Spanish-speaking management, employees, and other potential and/or expert witnesses, English/Spanish translation of personnel documentation, employee notes and memoranda and other potential discovery or documentary evidence, English/Spanish interpretation of witness statements, deposition and trial testimony, and pre-testimony preparation of Spanish speaking witnesses.

Regional Offices

Atlanta GA
1900 Marquis One Tower
245 Peachtree Center Avenue, NE
Atlanta GA 30303
Tel (404) 525-8200 | Fax (404) 525-1173
atlanta@jacksonlewis.com
Stuart Newman

Boston MA
One Beacon Street, 33rd Floor
Boston MA 02108
Tel (617) 367-0025 | Fax (617) 367-2155
boston@jacksonlewis.com
Thomas Royall Smith

Chicago IL
320 West Ohio Street, Suite 500
Chicago IL 60610
Tel (312) 787-4949 | Fax (312) 787-4995
Chicago@jacksonlewis.com
Peter R. Bulmer

Dallas TX
3811 Turtle Creek Blvd., Suite 500
Dallas TX 75219
Tel (214) 520-2400 | Fax (214) 520-2008
dallas@jacksonlewis.com
Christopher C. Antone

Greenville SC
2100 Landmark Building
301 North Main Street
Greenville SC 29601
Tel (864) 232-7000 | Fax (864) 235-1381
greenville@jacksonlewis.com
J. Steve Warren

Hartford CT
55 Farmington Avenue, Suite 1200
Hartford CT 06105
Tel (860) 522-0404 | Fax (860) 247-1330
hartford@jacksonlewis.com
William J. Anthony

Long Island NY
1000 Woodbury Road, Suite 402
Woodbury NY 11797
Tel (516) 364-0404 | Fax (516) 364-0466
longisland@jacksonlewis.com
Mark L. Sussman

Los Angeles CA
1888 Century Park East, Suite 1600
Los Angeles CA 90067
Tel (310) 203-0200 | Fax (310) 203-0391
losangeles@jacksonlewis.com
Lawrence H. Stone

Miami FL
200 South Biscayne Blvd., Suite 2600
Miami FL 33131
Tel (305) 577-7600 | Fax (305) 373-4466
miami@jacksonlewis.com
David E. Block

Minneapolis MN
150 South Fifth Street, Suite 2800
Minneapolis MN 55402
Tel (612) 341-8131 | Fax (612) 341-0609
Minneapolis@jacksonlewis.com
David J. Duddleston

Morristown NJ
60 Washington Street
Morristown NJ 07960
Tel (973) 538-6890 | Fax (973) 540-9015
morristown@jacksonlewis.com
Richard W. Schey

New York NY
101 Park Avenue
New York NY 10178
Tel (212) 697-8200 | Fax (212) 972-3213
newyork@jacksonlewis.com
Phillip B. Rosen & Gregory I. Rasin

Orlando FL
390 N. Orange Avenue, Suite 1285
Orlando FL 32801
Tel (407) 246-8440 | Fax (407) 246-8441
orlando@jacksonlewis.com
Diane E. Stanton

Pittsburgh PA
One PPG Place, 28th Floor
Pittsburgh PA 15222
Tel (412) 232-0404 | Fax (412) 232-3441
pittsburgh@jacksonlewis.com
Lynn C. Outwater

Sacramento CA
1215 K Street, Suite 1800
Sacramento CA 95814
Tel (916) 341-0404 | Fax (916) 341-0
sacramento@jacksonlewis.com
David S. Bradshaw

San Francisco CA
199 Fremont Street, 10th Floor
San Francisco CA 94105
Tel (415) 394-9400 | Fax (415) 394-9
sanfrancisco@jacksonlewis.com
Tyler A. Brown

Seattle WA
1420 Fifth Avenue, Suite 2000
Seattle WA 98101
Tel (206) 405-0404 | Fax (206) 405-4
seattle@jacksonlewis.com
Wayne W. Hansen

Stamford CT
177 Broad St. – P.O. Box 251
Stamford CT 06904
Tel (203) 961-0404 | Fax (203) 324-47
Stamford@jacksonlewis.com
Michael J. Soltis

Washington D.C.
1156 15th Street, NW, Suite 250
Washington D.C. 20005
Tel (202) 347-5200 | Fax (202) 223-85
washingtondc@jacksonlewis.com
Michael N. Petkovich

White Plains NY
One North Broadway, 15th Floor
White Plains NY 10601
Tel (914) 328-0404 | Fax (914) 328-18
whiteplains@jacksonlewis.com
Patrick L. Vaccaro

www.jacksonlewis.com
info@jacksonlewis.com

Chapter
Table of Contents

1. Snapshot 1
2. Compliance Thresholds 5
3. Job Descriptions 9
4. Recruiting and Hiring 13
5. Background Checks 29
6. Employee Screening and Lie-Detector Tests 33
7. Employee Handbooks 39
8. Non-Competition Agreements and Trade Secrets 43
9. Wages and Hours 51
10. Employment of Minors 71
11. Discrimination in Employment 81
12. Immigration 99
13. New Hire Reporting 107
14. Drug and Alcohol Testing in the Workplace 109
15. Employee Performance Evaluations 123
16. Discipline 131
17. Negligent Retention and Supervision 141
18. Termination 145
19. Plant Closings and Workforce Reduction 161
20. Payroll Taxes and Withholding 169
21. Healthcare Plans and COBRA 187

22.	HIPAA	205
23.	ERISA	219
24.	Employee Leave	225
25.	Retirement Plans	235
26.	Unemployment Compensation	241
27.	Workers' Compensation	251
28.	The NLRA and Labor Relations	271
29.	Alternative Dispute Resolution	285
30.	Independent Contractors	289
31.	Contingent Employment	301
32.	AIDS/Communicable Diseases in the Workplace	309
33.	Smoking in the Workplace	315
34.	Workplace Violence	323
35.	Safety in the Workplace	333
36.	Whistleblower Protection	361
37.	Privacy in the Workplace	371
38.	E-mail and Voicemail Systems	377
39.	Telecommuting	389
40.	Posting and Recordkeeping Requirements	395
Index		427

Table of Contents

Chapter 1
Snapshot 1

Chapter 2
Compliance Thresholds 5

Chapter 3
Job Descriptions 9
   Introduction 9
   Roles of Job Descriptions 9
      Disability Discrimination Cases 9
      Exemption From Wage and Hour Laws 10
      Performance Standard 10
   Preparation of Job Descriptions 10

Chapter 4
Recruiting and Hiring 13
   Introduction 13
   Advertising for Employees 13
   Employment Applications 13
   Pre-employment Inquiries 13
   Problem Areas and Possible Questions 14
      Age 14
      National Origin 14
      Race/color 14
      Sex 14
      Religion 14
      Disability 15
      Arrests/Convictions 15
      Education 15
      Military Service 15
      Organizations 15

Work Schedule 16
References 16
Photographs 16
Nondiscriminatory Practices 16
    Introductory Language 17
    Information Requested 17
        General 17
        Professional 17
Interviews 18
    Patterned Interview Form 19
    Things to Avoid 19
Offer Letters 19
INS I-9 Form 19
Notification of New Hires 20
Avoiding Negligent Hiring Claims 20
Contracts 20
    Collective Bargaining Agreements 21
    Express Contracts 21
        Express Written Contracts 21
        Express Oral Contracts 22
    Implied Contracts 22
        Employee Handbooks 23
    Promissory Estoppel 23
    No Contracts 24
        Employment for a Definite Term 24
        Employment for an Indefinite Term 24
Avoiding Employment Contract Claims 24
Employment Agreements 25
Some Final Suggestions on Hiring 26
    Employment-at-Will 26
    Definite Term of Employment 26
    Mandatory Arbitration 26
    Other Terms and Conditions 27

Chapter 5
Background Checks 29

Introduction 29
Information Sources 29
    Reports 29
    Consumer Reports 30
    Disclosure to Applicants or Employees 30
    Taking Adverse Action Against the Applicant or Employee 30

    Credit Checks 31
    Investigation of Criminal Records 31
    References 31
        Obtaining a Release 31
        Obtaining References 31
        Content of Conversation 31

Chapter 6
Employee Screening and Lie-detector Tests 33

    Introduction 33
    Federal Law 33
        Definitions 33
        Application 33
        Employee Polygraph Protection Act 33
            Exceptions 34
            Additional Exception 34
        Testing Procedures 34
        Prohibition Against Disclosure 35
        Enforcement 35
        Waivers 35
        Alternatives to Lie-detector Testing 35
    Final Cautions 36
    Massachusetts Law 36
        Provisions 36
        Exceptions 36
        Notice 36
        Enforcement 37
        Liability 37
        Waivers 37

Chapter 7
Employee Handbooks 39

    Introduction 39
    At-will Status 39
    Disclaimers 39
    Advantages and Disadvantages of Employee Handbooks 40
        Advantages 40
        Disadvantages 40
    Important Considerations When Preparing Employee Handbooks ... 40
    Commonly Asked Questions 41

Chapter 8
Non-competition Agreements and Trade Secrets 43

- Introduction 43
  - General Protections 44
  - The Duty of Loyalty 44
- Trade Secrets 44
  - What Is A "Trade Secret"? 44
  - Legal Tests 44
- Restrictive Covenants 45
  - Definition 45
  - What Do Restrictive Covenants Protect? 45
  - Restrictions on Non-compete Agreements 46
  - Enforcement 46
    - Additional Protection: Inevitable Disclosure Doctrine 47
    - Nondisclosure, No-solicitation, No-raid Agreements 47
    - Conflict-of-Interest Clauses 48
- Hiring a Competitor's Employees 48
- Summary 49

Chapter 9
Wages and Hours 51

- Introduction 51
- Federal Law 51
  - Covered Employers 51
  - Covered Employees 51
    - Exemptions to the FLSA 52
      - Salaried Employees 52
  - Fair Labor Standards Act (FLSA) Overview 52
    - Analysis of the Salary Basis Component of the Exempt Status Test 52
      - What Is the "Salary Basis" Prong of the Exempt Status Test? 52
    - Exemptions 56
      - Executive Exemptions 56
      - Professional Exemptions 56
      - Administrative Exemptions 57
      - Other Exemptions 57
    - Exceptions to Overtime 57
  - Compensation 57
    - Minimum Wage Requirements 57
      - Opportunity Wage 58

Exceptions for Student Learners	58
Exceptions for Disabled Individuals and Others	58
Timing of Wage Payments	58
Deductions from Pay	58
Required Deductions	58
Savings Bonds and Charitable Donations	58
Unions	59
Political Candidates	59
Wares, Tools, or Machinery	59
Wage Garnishments	59
Complying with a Garnishment Order	59
Employee Discharge Due to Excessive Garnishment	60
Child-Support Orders	60
Hours Worked	60
On-call Time	60
Training Time	61
Overtime Compensation	61
Computing Overtime Compensation	61
Unauthorized Overtime	61
Scheduling the Workweek	61
Regular Rate of Pay	62
Discrimination	62
Recordkeeping and Posting Requirements	63
Enforcement	63
Massachusetts Law	64
Covered Employers	64
Covered Employees	64
Compensation	64
Exceptions	65
Frequency and Method of Payment	65
Reimbursements and Benefit Payments	65
Termination	65
Discharged Workers	65
Employees Who Resign	65
Wage Statements	65
Deductions	66
Wage Assignment and Garnishment	66
Support Orders	66
Miscellaneous Deductions	67
Hours Worked	67
Overtime Payment	68
Exceptions to Overtime Pay	68
Regular Rate of Pay	68

Discrimination 69
Recordkeeping and Posting 69

Chapter 10
Employment of Minors 71

Introduction 71
Federal Laws 71
    Covered Employees 71
    Prohibited Employment 72
        Work Prohibited to All Minors 72
        Work Prohibited to 14-and 15-Year-Olds 72
        Work Prohibited to Children Under 14 72
    Punishment for Violations 72
    Hours of Employment 73
        Children Under 16 73
        Children 16 and 17 73
    Required Breaks 73
    Wages 73
    Records and Postings 73
Massachusetts Law 73
    Covered Employees 73
    Prohibited Employment 74
        Minors Under 21 74
        Minors Under 18 74
        Minors Under 16 74
        Minors Under 12 76
        Special Prohibitions 76
        Exclusions 76
    Hours of Employment 77
        Minors Between 16 and 18 77
        Children Under 16 78
        Exclusions 78
    Meal Periods 78
    Permits 79
    Records 79
    Postings 79
    Exceptions 79

Chapter 11
Discrimination in Employment 81

Introduction 81
Federal Law 81
    Protected Areas/Protected Status 81

Typical Discrimination Situations	82
Protected Conduct and Retaliation	82
Types of Discrimination Prohibited	82
Discriminatory Treatment	82
Discriminatory Impact	83
Laws Prohibiting Discrimination	83
Applications	84
Racial Discrimination	84
Discriminatory Treatment	84
Racial Harassment	84
Disparate Impact	85
Reverse Discrimination	85
National Origin Discrimination	85
English-only Rules	85
Harassment	86
Religious Discrimination	86
Sex Discrimination	86
Sexual Orientation	86
Sexual Harassment	87
Definition	87
Employer Liability	87
Same-sex Harassment	88
Pregnancy Discrimination	88
Age Discrimination	88
Hiring/Firing	89
Advertising	89
Mandatory or Involuntary Retirement	89
Benefits	89
Waiver of Rights	90
Enforcement	90
Discrimination Complaint Procedure	90
EEOC Investigations	90
Remedies	91
Damage Caps	91
Employer Defenses Against Discrimination Charges	91
Defenses Against Sexual-harassment Claims	92
Recordkeeping and Reporting Requirements	94
Recordkeeping	94
Reporting	95
Employer Information Report—EEO-1	95
Employer Information Reports—EEO-4, EEO-5, EEO-6	95

    Massachusetts Law 95
        General Prohibition Against Discrimination 95
        Equal Rights Act 96
        Religious Discrimination 96
        Sex Discrimination/Sexual Harassment 97
        Discrimination Based on Disability 97
        Age Discrimination 98
        Discrimination Based on Criminal or Mental Health Records 98
        Prohibitions Against Retaliation 98
        Recordkeeping and Reporting 98

Chapter 12
Immigration 99

    Introduction 99
    Documentation Requirements 99
    Anti-discrimination Enforcement 99
    Temporary Employment of Non-U.S. Citizens 100
        H-1B (Non-immigrants, Temporary Workers, or Trainees) 100
        H-2B (Lesser Skilled Workers) 101
        E-1 and E-2 (Treaty Trader and Investor Status) 101
        L-1 (Intracompany Transferee Status) 102
            Blanket Petitions 102
            Individual Petitions 102
        O (Extraordinary Ability Nationals) 103
    Permanent Employment of Non-U.S. Citizens (Green Cards) 103

Chapter 13
New-hire Reporting 107

    Introduction 107
    Information to Be Reported 107
        Employee Information 107
        Employer Information 107
    Means of Reporting 107
        Employers Operating in Two or More States 108
        Penalties 108
    Massachusetts New-Hire Reporting 108
        Employer Obligations 108
        Penalties 108
        Whom to Contact 108

Chapter 14
Drug and Alcohol Testing in the Workplace 109

- Introduction 109
- Testing Limits 109
  - Private At-will Employees 109
  - Union Employees 110
  - Nonunion Contract Employees 110
  - Public Sector Employees 110
  - Job Applicants 110
- Discipline and Discharge for Substance Abuse in a Union Setting 110
- Americans with Disabilities Act (ADA) 111
- Transportation Employee Drug and Alcohol Testing 112
  - DOT Drug Testing 112
    - DOT-required Drug Tests 112
    - Consequences for Violation of DOT Drug Testing Regulations 113
    - Additional DOT Drug Testing Requirements 113
  - DOT Alcohol Testing 113
    - Consequences for Violation of DOT Alcohol Testing Regulations 114
    - DOT-required Alcohol Tests 114
  - DOT Policy Requirement 114
- Drug-Free Workplace Act 114
  - Department of Defense Drug-Free Workplace Regulations 115
- Considerations When Implementing a Drug and Alcohol-testing program 116
  - Reasons to Implement a Testing Program 116
  - Employees to Be Tested 117
  - Types of Tests 117
  - Substance Testing 117
  - Testing Laboratory 118
  - Consequences of a Positive Test Result or Refusal to Take a Test 118
  - Other Features of a Good Testing Policy 118
  - State Law Considerations Concerning a Drug and Alcohol-testing program 119
- How Prevalent Is Drug Use Among Employees? 119
  - Drug and Alcohol Abuse—Performance Indicators 120
  - Do's and Don'ts for Supervisors When Confronting a Troubled Employee 120

Chapter 15
Employee Performance Evaluations 123

- Introduction 123
- Communication 123
  - Expectations 123
    - Job Description 123
    - Goals 124
  - Honesty 124
  - Presentation 124
  - Interaction 125
  - Confidentiality 125
- Procedure 126
  - Consistency 126
  - Content 126
  - Documentation 127
  - Self-evaluation 127
- The Post-evaluation Meeting 127
- Alternative Methods of Evaluation 127
  - Computer Assistance 128
  - Multi-rater Feedback Systems 128
- Conclusion 128
  - Performance Evaluation Checklist 129

Chapter 16
Discipline 131

- Introduction 131
- Creating and Implementing a Disciplinary System 131
  - Establishing the Rules 131
  - Enforcing the Rules 132
    - Investigation 132
    - Explanation and Imposition of Discipline 133
    - Appeal Process 134
  - Documentation 134
- Absenteeism—The Problem of the Invisible Employee 135
  - Establish an Attendance Policy 135
    - Incentive Plans 135
  - Chronic Absenteeism 136
    - Physician Certificates 136
    - Return-to-work Physicals 136
    - Absenteeism without Violation of Policy 136
    - Calculating Absenteeism 136
    - Discipline 137

Chapter 17
Negligent Retention and Supervision 141

Introduction 141
Negligent Retention 141
    Elements of Negligent Retention 141
    The Basis for Claims of Negligent Retention 141
        The Employer Knew or Should Have Known 142
        Appropriate Employer Action 142
Negligent Supervision 142
Negligent Training 143
Conclusion 143

Chapter 18
Termination 145

Introduction 145
Proper Termination 145
    Employment-at-will Employees 145
    Contractual Employees 145
    Guidelines for Proper Termination—Progressive Discipline 146
        Retain Employees When Possible 146
        Handle Discharges Correctly 147
Improper Termination 147
    Wrongful Discharge 147
    Laws and Regulations Restricting Employment-at-Will 147
        Federal Statutes Limiting Employment-at-Will 148
Constructive Discharge 149
        Avoiding Constructive Discharge Claims 150
Claims Employees May Bring After Termination 150
    Breach of Contract 150
    Interference with Contractual Relationships 150
    Constructive Discharge Claims 151
    Discharges in Violation of Public Policy 151
    Good Faith and Fair Dealing 151
    Intentional Infliction of Emotional Distress 152
        Reducing Liability for Emotional Distress Claims 152
    Fraud and Negligent Misrepresentation 152
    Defamation Suits 153
        Reducing Liability for Defamation Claims 153
    Invasion-of-Privacy 154
        Avoiding Liability for Invasion-of-Privacy Claims 154
General Techniques for Avoiding Liability for Wrongful Termination 155
    Perfect Your Hiring Techniques 155

- Review the Personnel Policy Manual 155
- Review Personnel Policies and Procedures 155
- Follow Progressive Discipline 156
- Adopt Specific Discharge Procedures 156
- Communicate the Final Decision Correctly 156
- Give the Employee Appropriate Termination Benefits 157
- Consider Separation Agreements 157
- Consider Arbitration Agreements 158
- A Termination Checklist 158
  - Termination for Poor Performance 158
  - Termination for Misconduct 158
  - Procedural 159
  - Legal 159
- Some Final Concerns 160
  - Unemployment Compensation 160
  - Replacing Terminated Employees 160

Chapter 19
Plant Closings and Workforce Reduction 161

- Introduction 161
- Workforce Adjustment and Retraining Notification Act (WARN) 161
  - Coverage 161
    - Part-time Employees 161
  - Legal Obligations 161
  - Relevant Term Definitions 162
    - Plant Closing 162
    - Mass Layoff 162
    - Employment Loss 162
    - Aggregation 162
    - Affected Employees 163
  - Exceptions to WARN Notice Requirements 163
    - Temporary Facility or Specific Projects 163
    - Strikes and Lockouts 163
    - Faltering Company 163
    - Unforeseeable Business Circumstances 164
    - Natural Disasters 164
  - Purchase and Sale of Facilities 164
  - Contents of a WARN Notice 164
    - For Affected Employees 164
    - For Employee Representatives 164
    - For State and Local Governments 165
  - Penalties for Violating WARN 165
  - Statute of Limitations 165

Massachusetts Law.. 165
    Notification of Plant Closings 166
    Re-employment Assistance Benefits 166
    Re-employment Assistance Programs 167
    Payment for Re-employment Assistance... 167

Chapter 20
Payroll Taxes and Withholding 169

Introduction 169
Who Is an "Employee"?... 169
    Employees vs. Independent Contractors... 169
    Common Law Employee Status 170
    IRS Common law Factors.. 170
        IRS Training Materials on Worker Classifications 171
        Federal Tax Penalties for Misclassification............................... 172
        Exceptions 172
            Taxable Independent Contractors:
            Statutory Employees 172
            Untaxed Employees 173
            Statutory Safe Harbor Relief from IRS
            Reclassification (Safe Haven Rule).............................. 173
            Taxes and Family Members... 174
    Employee Rights and Obligations 175
        Social Security Card 175
        Form W-4 175
        Tips.. 176
Wages... 176
    Exemptions.. 176
Withholding Period 177
Applicable Taxes 177
    Income Tax Withholding.. 178
    Social Security and Medicare Taxes 178
    Federal Unemployment Tax Act (FUTA) 178
    State Income Taxes.. 179
    State Unemployment Taxes 179
Paying the Taxes 179
    Employer Identification Number 180
    Federal Taxes 180
        Income Tax and FICA Tax... 180
        FUTA Taxes... 180
            Electronic Transfer of Funds 180
    State Taxes 181

Recordkeeping 181
   General Employment Tax Records 181
   Form 941 181
   Form 940 182
   Schedule H 182
   Form W-2 182
   Form 1099-MISC 182
   Caution 182
Massachusetts Law 182
   Definition of Employer 183
   Definition of Employee 184
      Exclusions 184
   Compensation 184
   Registering to Withhold 185
   Calculating Massachusetts Withholding Tax 185
   Filing and Paying Withholding 185
   Late Returns and Payments 185
   Correcting Withholding Payment Errors 186
   Recordkeeping 186

Chapter 21
Healthcare Plans and COBRA 187

Introduction 187
Healthcare Plans 187
   General Characteristics 187
   Other Required Benefits and Features 188
   State Law Regulations 188
COBRA Healthcare Continuation Coverage 189
   Background 189
   Covered Employers 189
      Counting Employees 190
   Covered Plans 190
      Exceptions 190
   Covered Employees and Beneficiaries 190
   Loss of Coverage and Qualifying Events 191
      Loss of Coverage Before a Qualifying Event 191
      Loss of Coverage After a Qualifying Event 192
      Coverage for Employees Terminated for Cause 192
      Reduction in Hours 192
   Nature of COBRA Coverage 192
      Employee Moves 193

Length of COBRA Coverage	193
Disability Extensions	193
Conversion Plans	194
Termination of COBRA Coverage	194
Notices of COBRA Rights	195
Electing COBRA Coverage	195
The Election Period	195
Coverage During the Election Period	195
Employee Revocation/Reinstatement	196
Multiple Beneficiaries and Separate Election	196
Paying for COBRA	196
Payment During the Election Period	196
Regular Payment for COBRA Coverage	196
Premium Increases	196
Payment Dates	197
Non-payment or Late Payment	197
Partial Payment	197
COBRA and Other Laws	197
Health Insurance Portability and Accountability Act	197
Family and Medical Leave Act	198
The Federal Government and COBRA Enforcement	198
Responsibility for COBRA Coverage	198
When a Business Is Sold	198
Massachusetts Regulations	199
Group Insurance Policies	199
Medical Health Coverage	199
Mental Health Coverage	200
Infant Health Coverage	200
Continuation Coverage	201
Hospital Service Contracts	201
Medical Health Coverage	201
Mental Health Coverage	201
Infant Health Coverage	201
Continuation Coverage	202
Medical Service Agreements	202
Medical Health Coverage	202
Mental Health Coverage	202
Infant Health Coverage	202
Continuation Coverage	203
Health Maintenance Organizations	203
Small Business Healthcare Continuation	203

Chapter 22
HIPAA 205

- Introduction 205
- HIPAA Requirements 205
  - Pre-existing Condition Exclusion 206
    - Creditable Coverage 206
  - Certification of Prior Plan Coverage 207
  - Health Status 208
  - Special Enrollment Periods 208
    - Loss of Coverage 208
    - Dependent Special Enrollment Period 209
  - Disclosure to Participants 209
  - The Mental Health Parity Act 210
  - Newborns' and Mothers' Health Protection 211
- Enforcement Provisions 211
- Conclusion 212
- HIPAA Questions and Answers 213
  - Certificate of Group Health Plan Coverage 216
    - Explanation of Model Form #1 216
      - Model Form #1: Certificate of Group Health Plan Coverage 216
    - Explanation of Model Form #2 217
      - Model Form #2: Information on Categories of Benefits 217

Chapter 23
ERISA 219

- Introduction 219
- Scope of ERISA's Coverage 219
  - ERISA-covered Plans 220
  - Pension Plans Subject to ERISA 220
  - Welfare Plans Subject to ERISA 220
- Reporting and Disclosure 222
  - Annual Reports (IRS Form 5500) 222
  - Summary Plan Descriptions 222
  - Other Disclosure Requirements 223
- Plan Administration 223
  - Plan Asset and Investment Requirements 223
  - Fiduciary Requirements 224
- Conclusion 224

Chapter 24
Employee Leave 225

- Introduction 225
- Family and Medical Leave Act of 1993 225
  - Covered Employers 225
    - Full time Instructional Employees 225
  - Eligible Employees 225
  - FMLA Requirements 226
    - Definitions 226
      - 12-month Period 226
      - Serious Health Condition 226
  - Medical Certification 226
  - Second Opinion 227
  - Recertification 227
  - Fitness-for-Duty Reports 227
  - Notification Requirements 227
    - Requirements for Employees 227
    - Requirements for Employers 228
  - Maintenance of Health Benefits 228
  - Restoration to the Same or Equivalent Position 229
    - "Key" Employees 229
  - Intermittent or Reduced-schedule Leave 229
  - Recordkeeping Requirements 230
  - Penalties and Enforcement 230
  - FMLA Summary 230
- Pregnancy Discrimination Act 231
- Other Leave Requirements Under Federal Law 231
- Massachusetts Law 231
  - Maternity Leave 231
  - School and Family Leave 232
  - Leave for Jury Duty 232
  - Voting Leave 232
  - Legal Holidays 232

Chapter 25
Retirement Plans 235

- Introduction 235
- Descriptions of Common Types of Retirement Plans 235
  - Defined Benefit Plans 235
  - Defined Contribution Plans 236

    Hybrid Plans 236
        Money-purchase Plans 236
        Profit Sharing Plans 236
        401(k) Plans 236
        403(b) Plans 237
    Stock Bonus Plans and ESOPs 237
Retirement Plan Requirements 237
    Participation 237
    Vesting 237
    Accrual of Benefits 238
    Spousal Protections 238
    Other Retirement Plan Rules 238
    Exemption for "Top-hat" Plans 239
Tax-qualification Rules for Retirement Plans 239
    Benefits of Tax-qualification 239
    Coverage Requirements 239
    Nondiscrimination in Benefits 240

Chapter 26
Unemployment Compensation 241

Introduction 241
General Considerations: Federal and State Law 241
    Who Must Pay? 242
    Computing the Tax 242
    State Tax Accounts and Experience Ratings 242
    Problems with UC Taxes 243
    Controlling Unemployment Costs 243
        Eliminating Employee Separations 243
        Independent Contractors and Unemployment Compensation 245
        Refusal of Suitable Employment 245
    Employment Separations 245
        Recording Separations 246
        Separation Terminology 246
    Documentation 246
        Contents of Documentation 247
Massachusetts Law 248
    Covered Employers 248
    Covered Employees 248
    Employee Wages 249
    Taxes or Contributions 249
    Returns and Reports 250
    Benefits and Eligibility 250
    Disqualification from Benefits 250

Chapter 27
Workers' Compensation and Massachusetts Law ... 251

- Introduction ... 251
  - Employers Affected ... 251
    - Massachusetts Requirements ... 251
  - Employees Affected ... 251
    - Massachusetts Requirements ... 252
  - Characteristics of Workers' Compensation Coverage ... 252
    - Employer-Financed Aspect ... 252
      - Massachusetts Requirements ... 252
      - Purchasing Coverage ... 253
      - State Fund ... 253
      - Providing Your Own Insurance ... 253
        - Massachusetts Restrictions on Self-Insurers ... 254
    - No-fault Aspect ... 254
      - Covered Injuries and Illnesses ... 254
    - Coverage Provided ... 255
      - Massachusetts Benefits ... 256
    - Penalties under Massachusetts Law ... 257
  - Advantages and Disadvantages of Workers' Compensation ... 257
  - Procedures in Benefit Claims ... 258
    - Employees' Responsibilities ... 258
      - Massachusetts Administrative Procedures ... 258
    - Employers' Responsibilities ... 259
  - Developing a Workers' Compensation Policy ... 260
  - Reducing Workers' Compensation Costs ... 261
    - Provide Education and Safety Programs ... 261
    - Investigate Claims Thoroughly ... 261
    - Monitor Each Case ... 261
    - Develop a Return-to-Work Program ... 262
    - Coordinate Workers' Compensation Benefits and Other Benefits ... 262
      - Retirement Plans ... 262
      - Medical Plans ... 262
      - Social Security ... 263
  - Workers' Compensation and the Americans with Disabilities Act ... 263
    - General Interactions ... 263
      - Interviewing and Hiring ... 264
      - Continuing Employment/Return to Work ... 265
    - Reasonable Accommodation and Workers' Compensation ... 267
  - Workers' Compensation and Other Federal Laws ... 269

Chapter 28
The NLRA and Labor Relations ... 271

- Introduction ... 271
- Federal Law: The National Labor Relations Act ... 271
  - NLRB Functions ... 271
  - Jurisdictional Limits ... 271
    - Non-retail Enterprises ... 272
    - Retail Enterprises ... 272
    - Other Enterprises ... 272
  - Areas Not Covered by the NLRA ... 273
  - Collective Bargaining under the NLRA ... 273
    - Selecting Bargaining Representatives ... 273
    - Types of Elections ... 274
      - The Representation Election ... 274
    - Conducting Elections ... 274
      - The Excelsior List ... 275
      - Election Challenges ... 275
      - Prohibited Pre-election Conduct on the Part of Employers ... 276
  - Unfair Labor Practices ... 276
    - Unfair Labor Practices by Employers ... 276
      - Duty to Bargain Over Plant Closings, Relocating, and Subcontracting ... 279
    - Unfair Labor Practices by Unions ... 280
  - Procedure in Unfair Labor Practice Cases ... 281
    - Filing of a Charge ... 281
    - Investigation and Disposition of Charge ... 281
    - Pre-hearing Procedures ... 281
      - Settlements ... 281
      - Grievance Arbitration Procedure ... 282
      - Injunction Proceedings ... 282
    - Hearing ... 282
    - Enforcement ... 283
      - Public Employees Excluded From the NLRA ... 283

Chapter 29
Alternative Dispute Resolution ... 285

- Introduction ... 285
- Types of ADR Solutions ... 285
  - Open-door Policies ... 285
  - Internal Mediation ... 286
  - Ombudsman ... 286

Peer Review 286
Arbitration 287
    Advantages of Arbitration 287
    Disadvantages of Arbitration... 287
    Arbitration to Avoid Civil Litigation 288
    Terms of Arbitration Clauses 288

Chapter 30
Independent Contractors 289

Introduction 289
Benefits of Independent Contractors 289
Legal Issues 289
Ways to Determine Employee/ Independent Contractor Status 290
    National Labor Relations Act: "Common Law Agency Test" 290
    The Fair Labor Standards Act: "Economic Realities Test"................. 291
    Unemployment Compensation Coverage: The "ABC Test" 292
        Liability.. 292
    Federal and State Income Tax 292
    Common law Employee Status 292
        IRS Common law Factors.. 293
        IRS Training Materials on Worker Classifications 294
        Federal Tax Penalties for Misclassification................................. 295
            Income Tax Withholding... 295
            Exceptions 295
    Taxable Independent Contractors: Statutory Employees 295
        Untaxed Employees... 296
        Statutory Safe Harbor Relief From IRS Reclassification
        (Safe Haven Rule) 296
    Important Forms 297
        IRS Form SS-8 297
        Form 1099 298
Independent Contractors and Discrimination and Safety Standards 298
    Federal Discrimination Statutes.. 298
    State Human Rights Act 298
    Drug and Alcohol Testing in the Workplace... 299
    Occupational Safety and Health Laws.. 299
Contingent Workers 299
Conclusion 299

Chapter 31
Contingent Employment 301

Introduction 301

What is the Contingent Workforce?	301
Temporary Workers	301
Contract Workers	301
Outsourced Employees	301
Independent Contractors	302
Leased Employees	302
Temporary Employees and Employment Laws	302
Discrimination	302
Workers Adjustment and Retraining Notification (WARN)	303
Family and Medical Leave	303
Immigration Reform and Control Act (IRCA)	304
The Fair Labor Standards Act (FLSA)	304
National Labor Relations Act (NLRA)	305
Occupational Safety and Health Act (OSHA)	305
Administrative and Financial Concerns	305
Income Tax Withholding	305
Conclusion	307

Chapter 32
AIDS/Communicable Diseases in the Workplace ... 309

Introduction	309
AIDS and HIV in the Workplace	309
AIDS as a Disability	309
Pre-employment Inquiries	309
Medical Examinations	310
Policy Statements on Risk of Transmission of AIDS or HIV	310
Protection for Applicants and Employees With HIV or AIDS Under the ADA	310
Reasonable Accommodation	311
Health Insurance Benefits	311
Confidentiality	311
Occupational Safety and Health/ Workplace Safety	312
Family and Medical Leave Act	312
Considerations for Employers When Drafting AIDS Policy	312
Commonly Asked Questions and Answers	313
For Further Information	313
Business and Labor Resource Service (formerly National AIDS Clearinghouse)	313
Centers for Disease Control	313
The American Red Cross	314
Job Accommodation Network	314

Chapter 33
Smoking in the Workplace 315

Introduction 315
Federal Laws... 315
    Workers' Compensation 315
    Americans with Disabilities Act... 315
    Rehabilitation Act of 1973... 316
    National Labor Relations Act 316
    The Occupational Safety and Health Act Standard 316
State and Local Regulations 317
Controlling ETS 317
    Smoking Bans 317
        Total Bans.. 317
        Partial Bans 318
    Engineering Controls 318
    Administrative Controls 318
    Workforce Screening 319
    Considerations in Implementing a Smoking Policy 319
Massachusetts' Smoking in the Workplace Law 320
    Basic Provisions 320
    Exceptions.. 320
    Employers' Requirements 321
    Penalties... 321

Chapter 34
Workplace Violence.. 323

Introduction 323
The Problem of Workplace Violence 323
Workplace Violence and Federal Regulations... 324
    Workers' Compensation 324
    Anti-discrimination Laws.. 324
        Catch 22: Restricting Employers' Access To Information 324
        Federal Protection of Potentially Violent Applicants
        and Employees 324
        State Law Issues.. 325
    OSHA Requirements 326
        OSHA's List of Potentially Dangerous Work Environments 327
Employer Obligations/Liabilities 327
    Negligent Hiring/Negligent Retention... 328
    Negligent Supervision.. 328
Anticipating Trouble 328
    Signs of a Troubled Work Environment 328

  Identifying Potentially Problematic Employees
  Before and During the Employment Relationship 329
    Dealing With the Violent Individual 329
 Ways to Avoid Incidents of Workplace Violence 330
  Anti-violence Policy 330
  Pre-employment Screening 331
  Informed Management 331
  Fair Treatment of Employees 331
  Education Programs 331
  Counseling 331
  Security 332
  Threat-assessment Team 332
  Aftermath Training 332

Chapter 35
Safety in the Workplace 333

 Introduction 333
 The Federal Government and Workplace Safety and Health 333
  AIDS and the Bloodborne Pathogen Standard 333
  Occupational Safety and Health Act 334
   Administration 334
   Enforcement 335
   Consultation Services 335
   Regulations and Standards 335
   Inspections 336
    Presentation of Credentials 336
    Reasonable Times 336
    Reasonable Limits 336
    Search Warrants 336
   Three Phases of OSHA Inspection 336
    Opening Conference 337
    Walk Around 337
    Closing Conference 337
   Citations and Penalties 337
   Appeals or "Contests" 338
   Recordkeeping Requirements 338
   Refusals to Work 338
   Employee Access to Exposure and Medical Records 339
   The OSHA Hazard Communication Standard 339
    Coverage 339
    Written Program 339
    Hazard Evaluation 339

                Labels and Other Forms of Writing 340
                Material Safety Data Sheets 340
                Employee Information and Training 340
            Trade Secrets 341
            Enforcement and Penalties 341
            OSHA Regulations on AIDS Virus
            and Other Bloodborne Viruses 341
                OSHA Personal Protective Equipment Standard 343
        Workplace Violence 343
        Whom to Contact 343
Guidelines for a Safe and Healthful Workplace—Developing a Program 344
    The Need for a Safety and Health Program 344
    Benefits of a Safety and Health Program 344
    Requirements of a Safety and Health Program 344
        Management Leadership 344
        Employee Involvement 345
        Individual Responsibility 346
            Importance of Job Descriptions 346
            Importance of Accountability 346
        Ample Safety and Health Resources 347
        Existence of a Written Policy Statement 347
            Contents of Policy Statement 347
    Implementing a Safety and Health Program 348
        Step 1: Clarifying Goals and Objectives 348
            Nature of Goals and Objectives 348
            Communication of Goals and Objectives 349
            Review of Objectives 349
        Step 2: Providing Safety and Health Training 349
            Training Design 349
            Specialized Training Programs 349
            Evaluating Training Programs 351
            Recordkeeping 351
        Step 3: Identifying Hazards 351
            Workplace Surveys 351
            Role of the Safety Professional 351
            Initiating a Survey 352
            Analyzing Potential Hazards 352
        Step 4: Preparing for Emergencies 353
        Step 5: Providing for Hazard Reporting 354
        Step 6: Correcting Hazards 354
        Step 7: Tracking Corrections 355
        Step 8: Investigating and Analyzing Accidents and Incidents 355
            Selecting the Investigator 355

        Seeking Information 355
        Identifying Patterns and Causes 355
      Step 9: Continuing Hazard Control and Equipment Upkeep 356
      Step 10: Designing a Medical Program 357
        Program Management 357
        Program Services 357
        Using the Program 357
  Program Evaluation 358

Chapter 36
Whistleblower Protection 361

Introduction 361
Federal Law 361
  OSHA's Anti-discrimination Provisions 361
  Protected Employees 362
    Employees Who Report Unlawful Activities 363
    Employees Who Participate in an Investigation or Hearing 363
    Employees Who Refuse to Follow an Unlawful Order 363
    Employees Who Report Healthcare Services Violations 363
  Protected Activities 364
  Protection Provided 364
    Federal Defense Contractor Whistleblower Statute 364
    Civil False Claims Act 364
    Environmental Acts 365
  Proving a Violation of Whistleblower Laws 365
Minimizing Whistleblower Complaints 366
Massachusetts Laws 367
  Statute 367
  Definitions 367
  Exclusions 368
  Enforcement 368
  Employer Obligation 369
  The Massachusetts Healthcare Whistleblower Law 369

Chapter 37
Privacy in the Workplace 371

Introduction 371
Investigative Methods 371
  Searches 371
  Surveillance 372
    Monitoring Telephone Conversations 372
    Monitoring E-mail and Computer Use 373

    Video Surveillance 373
    Drug and Alcohol Testing 373
  Polygraph Testing.. 374
  Honesty Testing 374
  Consumer Credit and Character Reports 374
 Recordkeeping 375
 A Note on Privacy and Employees' Private Behavior 375

Chapter 38
E-mail and Voicemail Systems 377

 Introduction 377
 General Issues and Federal Law 377
  Privacy Rights 377
    Fourth Amendment 378
    Federal Wiretapping Statutes 378
      ECPA Restrictions... 379
      Exceptions to ECPA Restrictions 379
      Access to Stored Communication 380
      Legislation Concerning Monitoring 381
  "On-line" Defamation, Slander, and Trade Libel 381
  Harassment and Discrimination Through Electronic Communication 382
  Trade Secrets and Confidential Information 382
  Copyright Infringement 383
  Union Solicitation by Electronic Communication 383
  Discovery of Stored Communication 384
  An Effective Company Policy 385
    Benefits... 385
    Characteristics 385
 Conclusion 387

Chapter 39
Telecommuting 389

 Introduction 389
 Benefits for Employers 389
 Jobs Adaptable to Telecommuting 390
 Concerns About Telecommuting 390
  Employee Concerns 390
  Employer Concerns 390
  Legal Concerns Regarding Telecommuting 391
    Occupational Safety and Health Act 391
    Workers' Compensation 391
    Fair Labor Standards Act.. 392

Americans with Disabilities Act 392
Insurance and General Liability Issues 392
Zoning 393
Telecommuting Written Agreement 393
Conclusion 393

Chapter 40
Posting and Recordkeeping Requirements 395

Introduction 395
Federal Recordkeeping 396
Table of Applicable Federal Laws 396
Age Discrimination in Employment Act (ADEA) 397
Mandatory Recordkeeping 397
Americans With Disabilities Act (ADA) 398
Mandatory Recordkeeping 398
Consolidated Omnibus Budget Reconciliation
Act of 1985 (COBRA) 399
Mandatory Recordkeeping 399
Optional Recordkeeping 399
Employee Polygraph Protection Act (EPPA) 400
Mandatory Recordkeeping 400
Employee Retirement Income Security Act of 1974 (ERISA) 401
Mandatory Recordkeeping 401
Employment Tax Laws—Federal
Insurance Contribution Act (FICA) 401
Mandatory Recordkeeping 401
Mandatory Recordkeeping 402
Optional Recordkeeping 402
Equal Pay Act (EPA) 403
Mandatory Recordkeeping 403
Fair Credit Reporting Act (FCRA) 403
Mandatory Recordkeeping 403
Fair Labor Standards Act (FLSA) 404
Mandatory Recordkeeping 404
I (Tipped Employees) 405
II (Trainees) 406
III (Students) 406
Family and Medical Leave Act of 1993 (FMLA) 407
Mandatory Recordkeeping 407
Health Insurance Portability and Accountability Act (HIPAA) 408
Mandatory Recordkeeping 408
Immigration Reform and Control Act (IRCA) 408
Mandatory Recordkeeping 408

Mental Health Parity Act (MHPA) 408
    Mandatory Recordkeeping 408
    Optional Recordkeeping 408
Newborns' and Mothers' Health Protection Act 408
    Mandatory Recordkeeping 408
Occupational Safety and Health Act (OSHA) 409
    Mandatory Recordkeeping 409
Title VII of the Civil Rights Act of 1964 411
    Mandatory Recordkeeping 411
Vietnam Era Veterans' Readjustment
Assistance Act (VEVRAA) 412
    Mandatory Recordkeeping 412
Women's Health and Cancer Rights Act (WHCRA) 412
    Mandatory Recordkeeping 412

Federal Posting Requirements 413
    Table of Federal Posters 413
        Required 413
        Recommended 413
    Private Employers, State and Local
    Governments, and Educational Institutions 414
    Government Contractors 416
    Recommended Posters 418

Massachusetts State Recordkeeping Requirements 419
    Table of Affected Subjects 419
        Benefits 419
        Discrimination 419
        Hiring 419
        Leave 419
        Pay 419
        Safety and Health 419
    Benefits 420
    Discrimination 420
    Hiring 421
    Leave 421
    Pay 421
    Pay (cont) 422
    Pay (cont) 423
    Public Works 424
    Safety and Health 424

Massachusetts State Posting Requirements 425

Index 427

Chapter 1
Snapshot

The following list of questions will provide a snapshot for you to use in determining whether or not you are complying with fundamental employment laws and regulations. You should know the answer to every one of these questions. Although a "No" answer does not necessarily mean you are in violation of any laws or regulations, you should understand why the answer is "No." The page number is provided for quick reference.

Yes	No		Page Reference
❑	❑	Do your employment application and your employee handbook contain a "disclaimer" statement of any promise of job security?	1
❑	❑	Do you know what drug-testing laws apply to your company?	109
❑	❑	Do you accommodate employees with AIDS?	309
❑	❑	Did you know to check your contracts with independent contractors against the tests used by the IRS to determine employment status?	293
❑	❑	Does your dress code potentially interfere with an employee's religious practices?	86
❑	❑	Do you have an employee handbook? If so, is it regularly updated and do you include a clear statement that continued employment is not guaranteed?	39
❑	❑	Do you know what questions you can't ask job applicants and which ones you should?	14
❑	❑	Do you give medical examinations to applicants only after the employment offer and are they given to all applicants in the job category?	16
❑	❑	Do you check all job and personal references before hiring?	29
❑	❑	Do you have a discipline policy, and do your supervisors understand it and apply it consistently?	131
❑	❑	Do you know when a company can be sued for negligent retention or supervision of an employee?	141
❑	❑	Do you pay required overtime compensation to nonexempt employees, which can include salaried employees?	61

Snapshot

☐	☐	Do you have a system for sending out COBRA notices within the required time limits?	195
☐	☐	Do you have a system for sending out HIPAA notices within the required time limits?	205
☐	☐	Do you have a written sexual harassment policy, and are your employees aware of it?	92
☐	☐	Do you have a procedure for investigating employee complaints about harassment?	93
☐	☐	Do you know what the exceptions are to the ADEA's prohibition of age discrimination?	88
☐	☐	Do you know if drug and alcohol abuse are considered disabilities under the ADA?	111
☐	☐	Do you know what "quid pro quo" sexual harassment is?	87
☐	☐	Do you know under what limited circumstances lie-detector tests are permissible?	34
☐	☐	Do you know what employers are covered by the Family and Medical Leave Act (FMLA)?	225
☐	☐	Do you know what constitutes a serious health condition under the FMLA?	226
☐	☐	Do you know what an I-9 form is? Do you know what the employer's responsibilities regarding this form are?	20
☐	☐	Do you know what form of documentation is required by the I-9?	99
☐	☐	Do you know whether it is safe to ask, "Have you ever been arrested?" in an interview or on an application?	15
☐	☐	Do you know if it is safe to ask, "Are you a U.S. citizen?" in an interview or an application?	14
☐	☐	Do you know if it is safe to ask, "What is your maiden name?" in an interview or on an application?	14
☐	☐	Do you know if it is safe to ask, "What is your age?" in an interview or on an application?	14
☐	☐	Do you know if it is safe to ask, "Do you have any physical or mental condition/disability which may affect your ability to perform the job applied for?" in an interview or on an application?	15
☐	☐	Do you know what "hostile environment" sexual harassment is?	87
☐	☐	Do you know if an employer can require job applicants to be screened for drugs?	112

Snapshot

- ❏ ❏ Do you use gender-neutral job titles when advertising position openings?................. 13
- ❏ ❏ Do you know if employee progress reviews are completed on at least an annual basis for each employee?... 126
- ❏ ❏ Do you know if adequate training has been given to supervisors on how to plan, organize and carry out effective progress reviews?... 129
- ❏ ❏ Do you know if human resources department reviews performance appraisals before final processing?.. 125
- ❏ ❏ Do you know if you have a written job description for all positions, and are the areas covered on each employee's performance appraisal related to it?... 10
- ❏ ❏ Do you know your state's child labor, minimum wage, overtime, and equal pay laws?... 71
- ❏ ❏ Do you know if all applicants are completing company application forms?............... 13
- ❏ ❏ Do you know if all interviews with applicants are conducted in a structured format?... 19
- ❏ ❏ Do you know if new employees are provided with copies of appropriate handbooks and benefits booklets, and are they required to sign handbook/booklet receipts?.. 39
- ❏ ❏ Do you know if new hires are informed of the "probationary period," if there is one?... 40
- ❏ ❏ Do you know if eligible full time new hires have been properly enrolled in all company group benefit plans?... 187
- ❏ ❏ Do you know federal/state laws concerning employees who serve jury duty?... 51
- ❏ ❏ Do you know the employee's federal right to notice of plant closings?................... 161
- ❏ ❏ Do you know that the Employee Polygraph Protection Act prohibits private employers from using lie-detector tests either for pre-employment screening or during the course of employment?... 33
- ❏ ❏ Do you know if human resources department reviews all involuntary terminations before they occur?.. 147
- ❏ ❏ Do you know if all objective guidelines are in place for evaluating all job applicants?.. 13
- ❏ ❏ Do you know if all questions concerning education and training are job related?.. 15
- ❏ ❏ Does the company distribute a written employee handbook and written employment policies and procedures to its employees?................................ 39

Snapshot

❏	❏	Does the company post applicable federal and state posters and notices regarding employment laws?	395
❏	❏	Does the company distribute to employees a written equal-employment-opportunity policy statement?	17
❏	❏	Does the company have a written family and medical leave policy?	225
❏	❏	Does the company have a non-discriminatory job application and interview process?	81
❏	❏	Does the company require applicants to prove they are legally authorized to work in the U.S.?	20
❏	❏	Does the company have written job descriptions?	9
❏	❏	Does the company regularly audit its compensation policies and practices to ensure they are in compliance with state and federal wage and hour laws?	51
❏	❏	Does the employer have a written procedure that covers work-force reductions, layoffs, termination of hours, or company reductions?	161
❏	❏	Does the company follow progressive discipline?	146
❏	❏	Does the company have a procedure whereby employees who are subjected to discipline or termination can file a complaint or grievance and appeal the disciplinary action to a higher management official or panel of officials?	134
❏	❏	Are terminated employees asked to sign a standard release or separation agreement?	157
❏	❏	Does the company conduct periodic surveys to determine if there are any health or safety problems in its facilities?	351

Chapter 2
Compliance Thresholds

The following list does not include all federal and state employment laws, but it does provide an overview of how many employees an employer must have to be covered under these most significant laws. Remember, however, that coverage for some of the laws also depends on requirements other than the number of employees. If the number places your business on the borderline, consult further in these materials for an explanation of those other requirements.

Federal Statutes	Minimum Employees
Age Discrimination in Employment Act of 1967 (29 U.S.C. §621)	20
Americans With Disabilities Act of 1990 (42 U.S.C. §12101)	15
Civil Rights Act of 1964—Title VII—Equal Employment Opportunities (42 U.S.C. §2000e et seq.)	15
Civil Rights Act of 1991 (42 U.S.C. §§1981-1996b)	15
Consolidated Omnibus Benefits Reconciliation Act (COBRA) (29 U.S.C. §1161 et seq.)	20
Consumer Credit Protection Act (15 U.S.C. §§1671-1677)	1
Drug-Free Workplace Act of 1988 (41 U.S.C. §701 et seq.)	1
Electronic Communications Privacy Act of 1986 (ECPA) (18 U.S.C. §§2510-2522)	1
Employee Polygraph Protection Act of 1988 (29 U.S.C. §2001 et seq.)	1
Employee Retirement Income Security Act (ERISA) (29 U.S.C. §1001 et seq.)	1

Compliance Thresholds

Employee Right-To-Know Laws (Hazardous Chemicals in Workplace) 1

Equal Pay Act (EPA) 1
(29 U.S.C. §206)

Executive Order 11246 (Affirmative Action) 1

Fair Labor Standards Act of 1938 (FLSA) 1
(29 U.S.C. §201 et seq.)

Family and Medical Leave Act of 1993 (FMLA) 50
(29 U.S.C. §201 et seq.)

Federal Income Tax Withholding 1

Federal Insurance Contribution Act (FICA) 1

Federal Unemployment Tax Act (FUTA) 1

Health Insurance Portability And Accountability Act of 1996 (HIPAA) 1

Immigration and Nationality Act 1
(8 U.S.C. §1101 et seq.)

Immigration Reform and Control Act of 1986 (IRCA) 1

Labor-Management Relations Act of 1947 National Labor Relations Act 1
(29 U.S.C. §141 et seq.)

Mental Health Parity Act of 1996 (MHPA) 2

Newborns' and Mothers' Health Protection Act of 1996 (NMHPA) 2

Occupational Safety and Health Act of 1970 1
(29 U.S.C. §651 et seq.)

Occupational Safety and Health Administration Compliance Assistance 1
Authorization Act of 1998
(29 U.S.C. 670d)

Older Workers Benefit Protection Act (OWBPA) 20
(29 U.S.C. §623)

Personal Responsibility and Work Opportunity Reconciliation Act of 1996 1

Pregnancy Discrimination Act (PDA) 2
(42 U.S.C. §2000e(k))

Uniformed Services Employment and Re-Employment Rights Act of 1994 (USERRA) 1
(38 U.S.C. §4301 et seq.)

Vietnam Era Veterans' Readjustment Assistance Act (VEVRAA) 1
(38 U.S.C. §§4211-4214)

Worker Adjustment and Retraining Notification Act of 1989 (WARN) 100
(29 U.S.C. §2101 et seq.)

Massachusetts Statutes	**Minimum Employees**
Age Discrimination Law Mass. Ann. Laws c. 149, Sections 24A-24J	6
Aids Testing Law Mass. Ann. Laws c. 111, Section 70F	1
Clean Air and Atmosphere Law Mass. Ann. Laws c. 111, Sections 31C &142A-M; Mass. Ann. Laws c. 29, Section 2Y	1
Employment and Training Contributions Mass. Ann. Laws c. 151 A, Section 14G	6
Equal Rights Law Mass. Ann. Laws c. 93, Section 102	1
Equal Rights For Elderly and Disabled Law Mass. Ann. Laws c. 93, Section 103	6
Fair Employment Practices Law Mass. Ann. Laws c. 149, Section 52D	6
Family and Medical Leave Mass. Ann. Laws c. 149, Section 52D	50
Hazardous Substances Disclosure Law Mass. Ann. Laws c. 111F, Sections 1-21	1
Occupational Health and Safety Law Mass. Ann. Laws c. 149, Sections 4-18G & 106-142F	1
Oil and Hazardous Material Release Prevention and Response Law Mass. Ann. Laws c. 21E, Sections 1-2	1
Labor Relations Law Mass. Ann. Laws c.150A	1
Maternity and Adoption Leave Law Mass. Ann. Laws c.149, Section 105D	6
Polygraph Testing Law Mass. Ann. Laws c. 149, Section 19B	1
Retaliatory Action Law Mass. Ann. Laws c. 149, Section 185	1
Healthcare Whistleblower Law Mass. G. Laws Ann. C.149, Section 187	1

Compliance Thresholds

Chapter 3
Job Descriptions

Introduction

Job descriptions play an important role in minimizing employee-related liability. Along with employment policies and employment contracts, whether individual or collectively bargained, job descriptions define the employment relationship. Job descriptions often become critical evidence in employment disputes. In particular, job descriptions play an important role in disability discrimination cases and the determination of which employees are exempt from the requirements of the wage and hour laws. Thus, employers need to take great care when preparing and updating job descriptions.

Roles of Job Descriptions

Disability Discrimination Cases

The disability discrimination laws protect only those disabled individuals who are qualified. Qualified individuals with disabilities are those who can perform the essential functions of a job, with or without reasonable accommodation. Virtually every disability discrimination case must look at the essential functions of the job to see if the complaining employee or former employee is protected as disabled under federal and state law. If the employer can show that the employee cannot perform any of the essential functions of the job even with accommodation, the employer wins. It is crucial to bear in mind, however, that one form of accommodation is reassignment to a vacant position for which the employee is qualified, with or without accommodation. Therefore, an employee with a disability who cannot be accommodated to perform all of the essential functions of a job may still be qualified if accommodated by reassignment to another vacant job the employee can safely and satisfactorily perform.

Determining the essential functions of the job can involve many factors, but job descriptions are an obvious starting point. The Americans with Disabilities Act (ADA) expressly recognizes that a written job description will be considered evidence of the essential functions of the job in ADA cases. Employers have won ADA cases where courts have held that an employee could not perform the essential functions of the job shown in the job description.

Conversely, other employers have lost ADA cases because their job descriptions did not include important job duties the employee could not perform. It is difficult for an employer to argue that a job duty is an essential function when that duty is not included in the job description prepared by the employer. These cases underscore the importance of carefully preparing job descriptions. As discussed below, job descriptions need to clearly state that the employee might be asked to perform duties not listed in the job description.

Exemption From Wage and Hour Laws

An employee's job description also plays a role in determining whether an employee is exempt from the overtime compensation and minimum wage requirements of the wage and hour laws. Even an employee who is paid a salary like an exempt employee is not exempt unless the employee has exempt duties involving the level of responsibility required by Department of Labor Regulations.

Just as in disability discrimination cases, a court or administrative agency likely will find that the employee's job description provides significant evidence of the employee's job duties. In Department of Labor investigations and court cases involving exemption issues, employees often minimize the importance of their duties so that they will be found to be nonexempt and be eligible for overtime compensation. Job descriptions may be the only written record available to an employer to refute the employee's statements, provided they are current and accurate.

Performance Standard

Almost any employment dispute where the employer has found the employee's job performance to be inadequate will require a similar determination of the employee's actual job duties. Judges and juries are much more likely to find in the employer's favor where the employee had clear notice of the job expectations, then failed to meet them. There is no better place to begin providing this notice than the job description. Employers who are unable to prove that the employee had notice of the employer's expectations may have a more difficult time resolving the dispute.

Preparation of Job Descriptions

To help minimize liability, your company should follow these guidelines in preparing your job descriptions:

- **Use the Employee.** No employer should let employees write their own job descriptions. However, obtaining an employee's input in writing the job description will make it very difficult for the employee to later allege that the job description does not accurately reflect his or her duties.

- **Update regularly.** Employees who do not review their job descriptions for a long time may allege that the job has changed. To avoid this problem, employers should periodically distribute job descriptions to employees. Employees should be required to identify any changes in their job duties since the descriptions were last reviewed. The employees might be asked to conduct this review as part of the performance-evaluation process.

- **Include essential information.** Employers need to maintain a balance between too much and too little information in job descriptions, yet should include as many job duties and expectations as possible. Employers should be particularly careful to include any physical requirements for the job such as lifting, standing, walking, working frequent overtime, working weekends, rotating shifts, and exposure to particular conditions such as weather and chemicals.

  The job description should also include unexpected job duties and should state that the employee may be asked to perform other duties as required by business needs.

  Employers should be careful not to include job duties that the employee will not perform. The more duties in a job description that the employee does not perform, the less likely the employer can persuade a judge or jury that the job description is a reasonable measure of the employee's job responsibilities.

Overall, job descriptions should reflect the reality of the employee's job as closely as possible. Business needs may also change on a daily basis, so job descriptions should specifically provide for this flexibility as well as in a properly drafted description.

- **Include special attendance requirements.** Employers covered by the Family and Medical Leave Act (FMLA) must provide employees with 12 weeks of leave per 12-month period for serious health conditions. It may be impossible for the company to function if certain positions are vacant for 12 weeks a year. If a particular job has unusual attendance requirements, the job description should include those requirements. However, an employee still might be entitled to be absent from work under the FMLA notwithstanding such requirements.

- **Include unusual job stress.** One common type of disability discrimination dispute involves job related stress. Job stress should be addressed in the job description so that job applicants and employees have advance notice of special circumstances they may be required to handle.

    Finally, include measures of satisfactory performance with regard to particular functions where applicable or state that a specific job task must be performed "safely and satisfactorily" in order to include quantitative and qualitative dimensions of job tasks.

- **Use descriptions in the application process.** Employers will benefit most from job descriptions if they use them at the earliest possible stage—in the application process. Applicants should be asked to review the job description for each job they are seeking and to certify by their signature that they are able to perform that job. This may prevent the employer from being surprised by an employee's disability. If the employee later asserts a disability that limits his or her ability to perform the job and the disability was known to the employee at the time of application, the employer may be able to assert that the employee falsified the application. Note, however, that termination of an employee for this reason should be carefully reviewed. Intentional falsification will not always be provable or even the real reason. Some employees who have performed similar work for another employer may honestly believe they can perform the present job as well only to discover there are some differences, not readily discernible from the job description that render them a bad fit for the job. For example, the job may require operating a truck, which it turns out, does not have an automatic shift, unlike the truck the employee used on a previous job. If the employee's disability precludes using the gearshift, the employee will not be able to do this particular job, but was not lying when he or she said it initially could be done.

Chapter 4
Recruiting and Hiring

Introduction

The hiring process is one of the most important activities an employer has. It is also a process full of traps for the unwary. Effective hiring policies and procedures will help avoid potential liabilities and improve the quality of an employer's workforce, thus improving productivity.

Advertising for Employees

Good advertising can help employers hire and retain the best employees and can protect against negligent hiring claims from applicants, employees, and others. Bad advertising can lead to lawsuits from applicants who were not hired and could result in a poorly qualified and unmotivated workforce.

Except when based on a bona fide occupational qualification (BFOQ), it is unlawful to print or publish a notice or advertisement for employment that suggests any preference, limitation, specification, or discrimination based on legally protected characteristics such as race, color, creed, religion, national origin or citizenship, sex or sexual orientation, marital status, disability, status with regard to public assistance, age, or any other protected category listed under federal, state or local law.

Employment Applications

The first step in the hiring process is the creation of an effective employment application. Applications and the application process make up a mutual introduction—the applicant gets a first impression of the company and the company gets to know something about the applicant. Applications allow employers and interviewers to compare applicants on some uniform basis, since all the applications are the same blank-form sort of document. Thus, all candidates should be required to complete applications even if they have submitted résumés.

Pre-employment Inquiries

Except when based on a BFOQ, it is unlawful for an employer, prior to employment, to require or request information from applicants, or from any source, pertaining to the applicant's race, color, religion, citizenship status, sex or sexual orientation, national origin, marital status, disability, status with regard to public assistance, age, or other protected status under any federal, states, or local law. This is true in employment applications as well as interviews.

Exception: The one exception to the prohibition on seeking this information is where an employer is required to maintain certain applicant information as part of an affirmative action plan.

Employers and employees involved in designing and reviewing applications, interviewing applicants, and hiring must be aware of the requirements of the law in this area. As a general rule, pre-employment inquiries, which relate to job qualifications, will be lawful while nonjob related inquiries could be relied upon to suggest unlawful discrimination.

Problem Areas and Possible Questions

The following list is a general outline of particularly difficult areas of pre-employment inquiry:

Age

- Any inquiry about an applicant's age must be limited to establishing that the applicant meets minimum age requirements.
- You **may not** ask the dates of attendance at elementary school, junior high school, or high school.

National Origin

- You **may** ask if the applicant can furnish proof of employment authorization that the applicant is eligible to work in the U.S. This proof must be in a form acceptable to the Immigration and Naturalization Service.
- You **may not** ask an applicant's place of birth or that of his or her relatives.
- You **may not** ask an applicant's national origin or that of his or her relatives.
- You **may not** ask about any foreign addresses, which might indicate national origin.
- You **may not** ask about languages spoken by the applicant, unless the question is job related.

Race/color

- You **may not** inquire into race or color or ask any questions that might reveal race or color.
- You **may not** ask questions particular to applicants of only one race or color.

Sex

- You **may not** ask questions that might reveal an applicant's sex.
- You **may not** ask questions applicable to only one sex, for example, "Do you plan on having children?"
- You **may not** ask about childcare arrangements.

Religion

- You **may not** ask about an applicant's religious denomination or his or her religious customs.
- You **may not** tell an applicant the employer's religion or religious preference.

Disability

- You **may** ask questions needed to determine an applicant's ability to perform specific essential job tasks. Questions in this area should be phrased positively:

    RIGHT: Are you able to lift a box weighing over 20 pounds with or without reasonable accommodation?

    WRONG: Is there any reason why you wouldn't be able to lift a box weighing over 20 pounds?

- You **may not** ask about disabilities or ask any questions that may reveal disabilities.
- You **may not** ask about workers' compensation history or claims.
- You **may not** ask about past or current medical conditions.

Arrests/Convictions

- Employers **may** ask whether an applicant has been convicted of or pled guilty to a felony. (Employers must make it clear that a "Yes" answer will not automatically disqualify the applicant from employment).
- You **may** ask about convictions of special crimes related to qualifications for the job applied for.
- You **may not** ask about any prior arrests.

Education

- Employers **may ask** about the nature and extent of an applicant's education to the extent such inquiry is job related.
- Employers **may** ask about an applicant's foreign language skills if the question is job related.
- Employers **may not** ask when an applicant graduated.
- Employers **may not** ask how an applicant acquired his or her foreign language skills.

Military Service

- Federal law says that employers **may ask** about service in the U.S. Armed Forces, when such service is a qualification for the job.
- Employers **may not** ask about foreign military service.
- Employers **may not** ask about the type of discharge an applicant received.
- Employers **may not** request military service records.

Organizations

- Employers **may** ask about job-related membership in professional organizations and positions held.
- Employers **may not** ask about membership in any organizations that would reveal the person's "protected status."
- Employers **may not** ask an applicant to name every organization to which he or she belongs.

Work Schedule

- Employers **may** ask whether an applicant is willing to work the required work schedule.
- Employers **may** ask whether the applicant is willing to work overtime.
- Employers **may not** ask if there is any reason why the applicant would not be able to work the required work schedule.
- Employers **may not** ask whether there are any religious holidays on which an applicant would be unable to work.

References

- Employers **may** ask for general personal and work references that do not reveal the applicant's "protected status."
- Federal defense contractors **may** make such inquiries as might be required by federal law or regulation for security purposes.
- Employers **may not** request references specifically from clergy.

Photographs

- Employers **may** require photographs after hiring for identification purposes.
- Employers **may not** require pre-employment photographs.

Nondiscriminatory Practices

Several exemptions in discrimination law specify that the following are **not** discriminatory practices:

- The protected classifications do not apply when an individual is employed by his or her parent, grandparent, spouse, child, or grandchild or in the domestic service of any person.
- It is lawful for religious organizations to consider religion where religion is a bona fide occupational requirement.
- It is lawful for an employer to observe a bona fide seniority or merit system provided it is not used as an excuse to discriminate unlawfully or there has not been a past pattern of discrimination.
- In accordance with the EEOC's equal-cost, equal-benefit regulations, it may be unlawful to reduce benefit levels for older workers, to the extent necessary to achieve approximate equivalency in cost for older and younger workers.
- It is lawful for a public entity to establish a maximum age for beginning employment as a peace officer or firefighter.
- It is lawful for an employer to require an applicant to undergo a physical examination to test the applicant's ability to perform essential job-related tasks, but only after the applicant has received a conditional offer of employment and only if all individuals who are conditionally offered the position are required to undergo the examination.

- It is lawful for an employer to administer pre-employment tests that measure essential job-related abilities if such tests provide an accurate measurement of these abilities and are required of all applicants for the same position.

Introductory Language

Certain information and disclaimers should be included either in the introduction to the job application or in an acknowledgement section the applicant must sign. These items can include the following:

- A statement that the employer is an Equal Employment Opportunity employer.
- A statement of nondiscrimination.
- A reminder that if the applicant is hired, it will be on an employment-at-will basis. This means that the employee may terminate his or her employment at any time for any reason with or without notice and that the employer may terminate the employee's employment at any time for any reason.

    Note: Exceptions to the employment-at-will concept are discussed briefly with contracts later in this chapter and in more detail in **Chapter 18, Termination**.

- A statement that the application is not a contract or guarantee of employment.
- An indication that by completing the application, the applicant represents that all information presented in the application is complete and accurate.
- A statement that if information in the application is found to be false or to have been intentionally omitted, adverse employment action, including termination, may occur.

Information Requested

Employers should seek information describing the applicant's qualifications for the job for which he or she is applying. The following suggested informational items are not all inclusive and may vary depending on the type of job you are trying to fill.

General

Basic information to be requested on all employment applications includes the following:

- Name.
- Address.
- Telephone number.
- Confirmation that applicant, at time of hire, will be lawfully eligible to work in the U.S.
- Identification of position sought.
- Identification of hours/shift sought if appropriate.
- Pay expectations.

Professional

Employers should ask for at least the following professional information from applicants.

- Work experience, including:
    - Current and previous employer's name, address, and telephone number.

- Dates of employment.
- Starting and ending wage/pay rate.
- Supervisor's name and title.
- Job title and duties.
- Reason for leaving.

♦ Educational background, including:
- School name.
- Last grade completed (not specific dates of graduation).
- Fact of graduation, but only if job related.
- Major or course of study, as it relates to position sought.
- Training and special skills.

♦ Other knowledge, skills, or abilities as required by the position, including:
- Equipment certification or experience.
- Licenses.
- Typing, computer, or other office skills.
- Professional affiliations and memberships.
- Languages.
- Other training and special skills (including military training).

♦ References:
- Do not require applicants to provide references from religious figures.

Interviews

Conducting interviews is a good way to improve recruitment and avoid potential liability. Interviews are, however, basically subjective predictors of how candidates will perform a job. Although an interviewer can assess the objective data provided by a candidate during an interview, often the interviewer will also rely on subjective indicators such as body language, tone of voice, mannerisms, and may fall into the trap of relying upon "gut feeling."

An interview is the appropriate time to review the job descriptions with the candidate to ensure that the candidate is aware of the job requirements and indicates that he or she is qualified to perform the job. If it is disclosed during the interview that the candidate may be unable to perform the job because of a known disability or religious beliefs, the interviewer should ask about any accommodation the candidate believes would permit him or her to meet the essential requirements of the job in order to perform the work. **The interviewer should make no decisions or assessment regarding the feasibility or reasonableness of a requested accommodation during the interview.**

Patterned Interview Form

An effective way to minimize potential liability based on interviews is to develop an objective, patterned interview form for each position. This forces the interviewer to remain focused on the essential job functions and to deal with each candidate in the same way. The form should be used as follows:

- Identify the job functions or goals based on information contained in the job description.

  Example: Word Processing Supervisor—Supervise and coordinate word processing staff to ensure timely processing of work orders.

- List the essential knowledge, skills, and abilities that will enable a successful candidate to effectively perform each job function.

  Example: Interpersonal skills, supervisory experience or training, ability to delegate tasks, and ability to work with required equipment.

- Develop interview questions that address knowledge, skill, or ability in a nondiscriminatory way. Focus on previous experiences or incidents that will serve as indicators of future on-the-job behavior. Be prepared to follow up each question with additional questions that look further into a candidate's answer.

  Example: In your previous job, what types of problems did your subordinates bring to you for resolution? How often? What decisions did you make regarding these problems? What types of decisions did you refer to your manager for resolution?

Things to Avoid

- Avoid excessive "chit chat" before and during the interview. This will help avoid topics that could cross over into unlawful areas (for example: age, marital status, etc.).

- Avoid interviewing from the application form. Take a moment to review the candidate's application before the interview and to frame questions based on the patterned interview.

Offer Letters

Employers may provide written offers of employment verifying the terms agreed to by the employer and the prospective employee. The offer letter usually outlines that the individual has accepted the offer for a particular position and will start work on a specific date. The offer letter also sets forth the agreed upon salary and describes any benefits. When writing an offer letter you should be careful to avoid making any promises of continued employment that might make it difficult for you to terminate the individual later. For example, an offer letter should never indicate that the individual will "always have a job with our company." Instead, the letter should clearly state that the employment is at-will, that is the employment may be terminated at any time by either the employer or the employee. If the applicant will be required to review and sign any policies or agreements, those can appropriately accompany the offer letter.

INS I-9 Form

Employers in the U.S. may not knowingly recruit, hire, or continue to employ an alien not authorized to work in the U.S. The U.S. Immigration Reform and Control Act of 1986 (IRCA) requires all employers to verify the immigration status of employees hired after November 6, 1986, and ensure that each employee is a U.S. citizen or an alien legally authorized to work in the U.S.

To accomplish this, employees must present documentation to their employer that establishes their identity and their authorization to work in the U.S. Employers must review the documents, check their validity, and fill out jointly with employees an Immigration and Naturalization Service (INS) I-9 Form within 3 days of hire. Employers are only required to ensure that the documents submitted by the employees reasonably appear to be genuine. Acceptable documents are listed on the I-9 Form. Employers who violate the IRCA are subject to civil and criminal penalties including imprisonment for up to six months.

Notification of New Hires

In an effort to improve collection of unpaid child support, state and federal regulations have been enacted that require employers to report new hires. Effective July 1, 1996, employers must report to state agencies the hiring or rehiring of employees—except for those hired for less than a two-month period or who will have gross earnings of less than $250 a month—who live or work in the state.

The report must be provided within 20 days of the hiring date and must include the following:

- The employer's name, address, and federal identification number.
- The employee's name, address, and Social Security number.
- The date of hire.
- The state of hire.

An employer may report the information by delivery, mail, fax, phone, or diskette or magnetic tape. The information may be included and delivered on an employee's W-4 or W-9 form, a printed list produced by the employer's computer system, or on a new-hire reporting form available from the state reporting agency. If the employer submits the employee's W-4 or W-9 form, the employee's date of birth can be added to the form.

Employers who do not comply may receive a written notice of noncompliance. Employers who incur additional violations may be fined up to $500 for each intentionally unreported employee.

Avoiding Negligent Hiring Claims

In recent years, there have been many claims related to the hiring and retention of employees. To guard against such claims, employers should review their standard applications, their interview procedures, and their pre-employment screening practices.

Courts will examine employers' actions and knowledge from the point at which the initial hiring decision was made. Thus, whether an employer failed to exercise reasonable care in hiring will be determined by examining the employer's actions **at the time of the hiring decision.**

Contracts

In centuries past, the law assumed that when an employer hired an employee, the employee was being hired for a full year, unless the employer and the employee reached a different agreement. Today, however, this assumption has changed and employment is ordinarily based on contractual relationships that are usually found to arise out of collective bargaining agreements, express written or oral contracts, or sometimes on implied contracts. Such contracts can restrict the employer's ability to discipline or discharge employees.

An employment relationship based on no contract at all or for a non specific period is known as *employment-at-will*. Either the employer or the employee may terminate such employment at any time for any reason. In other words, the job will last just as long as both parties want it to last and will end when either party wants it to end. The contractual sorts of employment listed above are exceptions to employment-at-will relationships. Additionally, many restrictions to employment-at-will exist, as we discuss in **Chapter 18, Termination**.

Collective Bargaining Agreements

Where a union has been recognized as the exclusive collective bargaining agent for employees, the respective rights and obligations of the employer and its employees are defined by the terms of the written contract between the employer and the union. Such contracts, called *collective bargaining agreements*, normally supersede individual contract rights or common law rights of employees covered by the agreement. They do not, however, supersede other rights provided by federal, state, or local laws, such as nondiscrimination laws or whistleblower laws.

Express Contracts

The terms and conditions of employment for employees not covered by collective bargaining agreements may be governed by written or oral individual employment contracts. Written contracts are most common with executive-level employees. Typically, individual contracts define current and deferred compensation arrangements, benefits, the period of employment, and the rights of the parties with respect to termination and resignation.

Express Written Contracts

Express written contracts can be, by definition, an exception to the employment-at-will understanding. In express written contracts, both the employer and the employee can indicate at the beginning of the employment that the employment will not be at-will.

Like any contract, express written contracts require the following:

- An offer by one party.
- Acceptance of the offer by the other party.
- Sufficient consideration (for example: salary, benefits, performance of work, etc.) to support the contract.

The terms of the contract may include as little as one or two concepts or a comprehensive and detailed description of the employment relationship.

The parties in such contracts generally intend to create an exception to employment-at-will because they perceive, at least at the time they enter into the contract, some advantage to abandoning the benefits of employment-at-will. An employer, for instance, may give up the right to fire the employee at any time for almost any reason because the employer feels it is more important to keep the employee for a fixed period (and, perhaps, to prevent the employee from going to work for a competitor after the term of employment) than it is to reserve the right to terminate at-will. Similarly, an employee in such a situation may decide that the extra salary in exchange for a promise to not resign is worth giving up the right to leave at any time.

Express Oral Contracts

Express oral contracts might create an exception to employment-at-will in certain jurisdictions in the event employees allege that they were promised a specific term of employment sometime during the hiring process. The lack of documentation of the parties' bargain makes it difficult to tell whether the parties have intended to form a contract and thereby create an exception to employment-at-will. As with express written contracts, the party alleging the existence of the contract must prove that there was intent to enter into a contract by demonstrating the existence of an offer, the acceptance of that offer, and some consideration sufficient to support the agreement.

For the employer, the most troublesome oral contracts arise out of employer statements made during the hiring process that the prospective employee perceives as promises about the terms of his or her employment. In such a situation, the prospective employee does not verbally accept these perceived promises but merely accepts employment with the employer. The employee then claims at termination that the contract for employment contained certain terms and conditions, which the employee accepted by coming to work for the employer. A court evaluating a claim of oral contract in such a situation might look at facts such as how definite was the promise and whether additional considerations, above and beyond an agreement, to forego other employment were supplied by the employee to support the alleged contract.

Whether an express oral contract has been formed in any given case is highly dependent upon the specific facts of the case. Employers should put procedures in place during the hiring process to minimize the chances that statements will be mistaken for offers regarding the particular conditions of employment. These procedures could include the use of a form signed by the employee acknowledging that the employment is at-will. Such a document would help to demonstrate that the parties did not intend to create an exception to employment-at-will. Similarly, the form can clearly disclaim any reliance on oral promises made during the application process.

Implied Contracts

Some courts have recognized certain "implied contract" rights governing the employment relationship, even when employers make no specific promises. In certain jurisdictions, courts sometimes restrict an employer's right to discharge an employee if, after examining the facts and circumstances of the employment arrangement, the court concludes that the parties intended a continuing employment relationship, terminable only for "just cause." Examples might include an implied right to certain disciplinary or evaluation procedures before termination, or a specified list of grounds for termination of employment.

In determining whether an "implied contract" existed and an employer had created a reasonable expectation that an employee would not be discharged, courts may consider facts and circumstances including the following:

- The nature and type of the employment.
- The custom or practice in the industry; (for example: treating employees fairly and discharging them only for a just cause).
- The employer's regular practice of only discharging employees for just cause.
- The course of dealing between the parties.
- The employer's personnel handbook or employee manual, especially statements about an initial probationary period.
- Statements appearing on the job application form.

- Oral representations made by the employer.
- Disciplinary policies that state employees will only be discharged for specific offenses.
- Progressive disciplinary policies that give employees chances to improve their performance, when such chances were not given an employee.
- Statements that special consideration will be given to employees because of longevity or seniority.
- An employee's work history that reflects regular merit raises, good performance evaluations, praise, and promotions.

Employee Handbooks

Employee handbooks may create binding contracts in some circumstances:

- The provisions of the handbook identified as the terms of the contract are definite.
- The terms are communicated to the employee.
- The employee accepts the offer.
- The employee furnishes adequate consideration by continuing to work while retaining freedom to quit.

As with interpretation of an express oral contract, the employee does not have to verbally reply to the terms of an offer made through an employee handbook. The employee may accept the offer simply by beginning and/or continuing employment. Therefore, whether an employee handbook creates an implied contract depends primarily on the definiteness of the terms of the handbook.

Unlike an express oral contract, there is not likely to be great dispute about the alleged terms of the contract implied by the employee handbook because those terms have been written down. Although this difference alone will not protect an employer from a court finding that the handbook has created a contract, it will probably turn the issue from a factual one to a legal one, thereby allowing the court to resolve the matter at a preliminary stage of litigation.

As with oral contracts, the easiest way to prevent forming a contract with the employee handbook is to include language that the handbook is not intended to be a contract, or to modify the employment-at-will relationship. Unlike the oral contract, the written handbook makes it easy for an employer to include such a disclaimer. For employers whose handbooks have no such disclaimers and have been distributed to employees, any risk that the handbook will create an implied contract can be reduced by distributing an amendment to the handbook, including the appropriate disclaimer.

Note: In situations where a handbook sets forth a policy on vacation days, a contractual obligation in effect is established, which cannot be disclaimed by an employer.

Promissory Estoppel

Although it cannot be used when a contract exists—again reinforcing the wisdom of a written offer of employment confirming that the employment is at-will—the courts can use the theory of promissory estoppel to determine that a contract has been made even when the parties do not intend to form such an agreement. Promissory estoppel exists in the following circumstances:

- A promise has been made.
- The person making the promise reasonably expected to induce an action in reliance on the promise.

- Action is actually taken in reliance on the promise.
- Failure to fulfill the promise would create an injustice, and/or economic harm.

This theory is used most often in cases where an employer extends an offer of employment to a prospective employee, and based on the offer, the prospective employee quits a current job or rejects another job offer. When the employer subsequently withdraws the offer or terminates the employee shortly after the employment begins, the employee can rely on this theory to establish a claim. For example, a court may hold that a hired-then-fired employee is entitled to damages reflecting a "reasonable" period of employment.

No Contracts

Employees who are subject to neither a collective bargaining agreement nor an individual employment contract, generally have only those rights to employment as are conferred by statute or recognized by common law. There may also be specific state statutes generally governing the employment relationship or prohibiting the discharge of an employee without just cause.

The nature of common law employment rights has been the subject of much recent court interpretation and expansion. Historically, common law has put employees without written contracts into one of two categories:

1. Those employed for a definite term.
2. Those employed for an indefinite term.

Employment for a Definite Term

Employees may be hired for a definite term, such as month-to-month, year-to-year, or until some specified date. These employees may only be terminated for "just cause" (for a good reason) until the expiration of the employment period. Employment for a definite term may commonly be handled by a written contract.

Either party may terminate the employment relationship at the end of the term. If the employment relationship is continued after the end of the term, unless otherwise specified, it is considered to be renewed for the same period as the original term. If there is a contract, and it requires notice before termination of employment, the contractual notice must be given or a breach of contract will exist. Courts will generally find the employer has the same notification requirements as the employee in terms of terminating and quitting.

Employment for an Indefinite Term

Employment for an indefinite term is the employment-at-will relationship discussed earlier in this chapter in which either the employer or the employee may terminate the employment relationship at any time for any or no reason. The employment-at-will relationship has all of the exceptions described above and all of the restrictions that will be noted in **Chapter 10, Employment of Minors**.

Avoiding Employment Contract Claims

While it is impossible to avoid all employment contract claims, employers may minimize the number of such claims and improve their ability to defend against these claims by taking some of the preventative measures in their policies and procedures listed below:

- Include in applications for employment a statement indicating that the employment is at-will and defining employment-at-will.

- Include in offer letters a statement indicating that the employment is at-will and defining the term.

- Include a similar statement in the employee handbook. Likewise, the employer can state in the handbook that it should not be construed as a contract of employment for any duration. Further, employee handbooks should also contain a carefully written section on discharge, specifying that an employee can be discharged at any time and with or without cause or notice.

- Train personnel involved in hiring not to make statements that can be construed as altering the employment-at-will relationship.

- Train supervisors to avoid such statements after hiring.

- Include an employment-at-will reminder in all significant employment documents (for example, performance reviews, performance improvement plans, warnings, etc.).

- Review all of the documents above with an attorney to ensure that contractual disclaimers are in place and effective and that the documents do not contain other language that might create a "for cause" employment relationship.

- Replace all older employee documents with newer versions and retrieve the older documents from employees.

These precautions will not guarantee victory in every employment contract case, but if followed they may help you defend yourself against contractual types of claims arising out of employment relationships.

Employment Agreements

Employers should consider using carefully written employment agreements to avoid employment contract and promissory estoppel claims and to gain valuable protections and benefits. In particular, employers commonly use employment agreements to implement non-competition restrictions, protections for confidential information and trade secrets, conflict-of-interest restrictions, and mandatory arbitration clauses. Additionally, some employers use employment agreements to eliminate uncertainty by specifically defining terms and conditions of employment, job duties, and compensation and benefits. To provide themselves with job security, applicants for professional or executive positions may sometimes require employment agreements setting forth specific lengths of employment or separating benefits as a condition of accepting an offer of employment.

To decide whether to use an employment agreement, consider the following factors:

- Employment agreements can establish certainty in the employment relationship by providing specifically agreed upon grounds and procedures for termination if the employment relationship deteriorates.

- Employment agreements can specifically define the employee's job duties, compensation, and benefits to clarify the employment relationship. Employment agreements let the employer specifically define terms and conditions of employment unique to a particular position.

- Confidentiality provisions and other restrictions defined in the employment agreement on the ability of former employees to compete with the employer can provide contractual protection to employers in highly competitive businesses that depend on customer goodwill and involves the use of confidential information.

- Employment agreements can provide mandatory arbitration or other alternative dispute-resolution methods to address potential discrimination, wrongful termination, and/or other employee claims. This helps employers manage litigation costs and expenses for employment related claims.

Although the benefits of employment agreements are considerable, employers who decide to use them must be willing to live with the terms they create. Employers must also decide if it is worthwhile investing the time and money necessary to draft and implement effective employment agreements and to enforce them if employees fail to abide by the terms of the agreement.

Some Final Suggestions on Hiring

Employment-at-Will

Where a particular position does not require a specified length of employment as a hiring condition, an employer may choose to hire an employee under an employment-at-will agreement, in which either the employer or the employee may terminate the relationship at any time and for any reason, with or without prior notice.

Definite Term of Employment

When an employee or employer requires the use of an employment agreement to specify the length of employment, the employer cannot use the employment-at-will doctrine to justify termination. Employment agreements defining an exact term of employment must be carefully written to express very specific, defined reasons and procedures for termination, along with any notification requirements. If the employment relationship breaks down, the employer must then follow the stated procedure for termination. It is, therefore, important to describe the grounds for termination in the most flexible way possible.

Mandatory Arbitration

Employers are increasingly implementing mandatory arbitration agreements with their employees as an effective and cost-saving alternative to litigation. Arbitration agreements can reduce the time needed to process and resolve a claim, minimize litigation costs, and eliminate the possibility of an unpredictable jury verdict. Arbitration agreements generally mandate that any potential claims by employees, including discrimination claims, be addressed by a panel of arbitrators rather than by a judge or jury. Most employment discrimination claims and other employment-related statutory claims as well as wrongful termination claims are now subject to jury trials, prompting many employers to implement arbitration agreements in an effort to avoid litigation. Although there is currently some conflict in the courts about which claims can be arbitrated, employers are increasingly implementing such agreements as effective strategic tools.

Employers who decide to include a mandatory arbitration clause in their employment agreements should list the specific types of claims that are subject to arbitration, including wages, contract, discrimination, employee benefits, and any other claims for violation of federal, state, or local law or ordinance. To avoid ambiguity, employers should also describe in the coverage clause the specific types of discrimination claims that are subject to arbitration. Employers should also specify applicable state law applying in an arbitration and whether the arbitration would be binding. Employers should not try to alter the established rights of employees in these provisions, such as by limiting the damages available, since such restrictions can invalidate the arbitration agreement.

Other Terms and Conditions

Employers can also use employment agreements to define other important terms and conditions of employment, including the job duties or expectations of the employee, and compensation and benefits such as stock options, bonuses, travel and entertainment expenses, and participation in employee-benefit plans. Employers may also use employment agreements to protect trade secrets and confidential information.

Chapter 5
Background Checks

Introduction

Employers have a number of tools with which to conduct pre-employment investigations. Pre-employment investigations are important to ensure that the applicant is the best-qualified individual and to provide another way to test the accuracy of the information provided by the applicant. A thorough pre-employment investigation is also a preventive measure that enables employers to determine if a candidate's background indicates a possible safety threat of injury to other employees.

If conducted with inappropriate planning and training, a pre-employment investigation can be a potential source of liability. Pre-employment investigations should not be used as fishing expeditions into an applicant's background. Therefore, when conducting pre-employment investigations, employers should consider the following general guidelines:

- Employers should use pre-employment investigation tools that are reasonable and appropriate for the position for which the applicant is applying.

- Pre-employment investigation should be used consistently with all candidates regardless of class or position.

- Pre-employment investigations should be conducted by persons with special training.

Information Sources

With these guidelines in mind, employers should consider which background checks are appropriate given the nature and scope of the position sought. For example, many employers request criminal background checks to be completed by an outside consumer reporting agency to reduce their exposure to negligent hiring claims. The company can internally conduct background investigations as well by contacting references provided by job applicants.

Reports

When appropriate and job-related, investigative reports obtained from third party consumer reporting agencies regarding an applicant's background and/or consumer credit information may be obtained and relied upon in making employment decisions. In general, background checks should be tailored to the type of position for which the applicant is applying. For example, when hiring for a bank teller position, an employer may want to conduct a credit check on the applicant to determine the applicant's credit history because the position will have access to money.

Federal and in some instances, state laws require certain steps to be followed prior to obtaining background information, including credit reports from third party consumer reporting agencies. In addition, if an employer is going to take an adverse action against an applicant because of information supplied in a consumer report, there are additional procedure requirements.

Consumer Reports

Consumer and investigative consumer reports covered by the law are supplied by a consumer reporting agency. A *consumer reporting agency* is an entity that regularly assembles or evaluates certain types of information for the purpose of providing consumer reports to third parties for a fee or on a cooperative nonprofit basis.

The federal Fair Credit Reporting Act (FCRA) and applicable state law requirements apply when an employer seeks to obtain a consumer or investigative consumer report that may be used for employment purposes, such as evaluating an applicant for employment, promotion, reassignment, or retention as an employee.

Disclosure to Applicants or Employees

The applicant or employee must give the employer written authorization to procure the report. Before obtaining a consumer report on an applicant or employee, the employer must certify to the consumer reporting agency that it has provided to the applicant or employee a "clear and conspicuous" written disclosure that a report may be obtained for employment purposes. The disclosure must appear in a "stand alone" document.

The employer must also certify to the reporting agency that before the employer takes any adverse action based in whole or part on the report, it will provide the applicant or employee with a copy of the report and provide a description of his or her FCRA rights (published by the Federal Trade Commission). The certification must include a statement that the information being obtained will not be used in violation of any federal or state equal employment opportunity law or regulation. There are additional disclosure requirements for employers who obtain investigative consumer reports, which usually involve some type of interviewing in addition to obtaining a background report.

Taking Adverse Action Against the Applicant or Employee

After receiving the consumer report—but **before** any adverse action is taken—the employer must provide the applicant or employee with the following: a copy of the report, containing the name and address of the consumer reporting agency making the report, and a description in writing of his or her rights under the law.

After taking adverse action based on the report, the employer must provide the applicant or employee with the following:

- An oral, written or electronic notice of the adverse action.
- The name, address and telephone number, either orally, in writing or electronically, of the consumer reporting agency that furnished the report.
- A statement that the consumer reporting agency did not make the decision to take adverse action and is unable to provide the applicant or employee with specific reasons why the adverse action was taken.

- An oral, written or electronic notice of the applicant's or employee's right to obtain a free copy of the complete consumer report from the reporting agency, if requested within 60 days, as well as information regarding the consumer's right to dispute the information with the reporting agency.

Credit Checks

One type of consumer report might be a credit history report. Employers should request credit checks only when such information is relevant to the position being filled. For instance, a credit check may be permissible when there is a close relationship between credit information and job performance. When conducting a credit check on a potential applicant, companies must be careful because neutral decisions, such as the rejection of an applicant solely on the basis of a poor credit rating, may have a disparate impact on minority groups.

Investigation of Criminal Records

An employer may investigate an applicant's criminal conviction record because the information might be job related and consistent with a business necessity. Before rejecting an applicant, the employer should consider the relationship between the conviction, the nature and number of convictions, the recentness of the crime, rehabilitation efforts, and the applicant's fitness for the job.

References

Employers may obtain references to confirm and supplement information in the applicant's résumé or application. You should seek confirmation of background data (dates of employment, salary, position and duties, education, professional licenses) and the applicant's competency with respect to certain job-related skills (attendance, dependability, judgment, initiative).

Obtaining a Release

When conducting a reference check, it is prudent to obtain a release from the applicant. A release signed by the applicant can be a useful tool to facilitate obtaining information from the applicant's former associates, former schools, and employers. A release should generally acknowledge that the information obtained by the prospective employer may not all be positive, and that the persons making statements about the applicant are discharged from any legal liability. The release may be included in the disclaimer language on the application or as a separate document.

Obtaining References

A reference check should consist of contacting people with knowledge of the applicant's actual work performance rather than a person in the company's general human resources department. If possible, an applicant's former supervisor should be contacted. Other individuals with knowledge of the applicant's work performance may include an applicant's associates, team members or peers, as well as any subordinates. Depending on the nature of the job, former clients or customers may also be knowledgeable sources of information about the applicant.

Content of Conversation

When conducting an interview of an applicant's references, employers should adhere to the following guidelines:

- Confirm the information provided on the application or résumé.

- Focus on work performance questions. These questions are crucial for obtaining the most useful information and include areas such as former job responsibilities, description of work performance, strengths and weaknesses of the applicant, reasons for leaving the job, and eligibility for rehire.

- Avoid questions that go beyond work performance and job-related issues. As with interviewing, questions regarding race, age, disability, or other protected characteristics should be avoided.

- Offer to mail or fax the reference form along with the release signed by the applicant if the reference giver is unwilling to discuss the former employee over the phone.

- Also, document non-responses such as, "Our company does not give references" or if the company only provides a "neutral" reference, confirming dates of employment.

Chapter 6
Employee Screening and Lie-detector Tests

Introduction

Congress and various state legislatures have regulated the use of polygraph tests in the workplace. Congress felt that employees and applicants should not be required to answer intrusive questions and that inaccurate test results would unfairly victimize honest employees and applicants. As a consequence, employers generally cannot use polygraph tests unless they meet certain narrow exceptions and follow a complex set of procedures. This chapter details the federal law on the use of polygraph and other types of tests used to determine individuals' honesty. Where appropriate, the chapter also reviews the relevant state law.

Federal Law

Although federal laws usually supercede state laws, the federal polygraph statute explicitly states that specific provisions of state polygraph laws must be adhered to if they are more protective of employees' and applicants' rights than the federal statute. Thus, employers must comply with both federal and state laws in this area.

Definitions

The federal statute includes not just actual polygraph tests, but also voice-stress analyses and other tests designed to determine honesty by measuring a person's physiological responses. Written tests generally are permitted. The federal statute also prohibits deceptographs and psychological stress evaluators, and any similar devices, whether mechanical or electrical, used to determine the honesty of an individual.

Application

The federal statute applies to almost all private employers. It exempts contractors for certain federal agencies and, to a limited extent, organizations whose business involves security services or controlled substances. The federal statute also exempts federal, state, and local government employers.

Employee Polygraph Protection Act

The Employee Polygraph Protection Act (EPPA) is the first federal statute to regulate truth verification in the employment setting. The EPPA prohibits most private employers from using lie-detector tests in pre-employment screening.

Exceptions

The EPPA allows lie-detector tests in the following very limited circumstances:

- **Governmental entities.** The U.S. government, any state or local government, or any political subdivision of a state or local government is exempt from the EPPA, if such an entity is acting in the capacity of employer.

- **Employers authorized to manufacture, distribute, or dispense controlled substances.** Employers authorized by the Drug Enforcement Agency to manufacture, distribute, or dispense controlled substances may administer polygraph tests to a prospective employee who, if hired, would have direct access to any controlled substance. In this context, *direct access* means contact with or direct involvement in manufacturing, testing, storing, distributing, selling, or dispensing controlled substances.

- **Employers providing security services.** Employers whose primary business is to provide security services may administer polygraph tests to prospective employees if the employees are being hired to protect "facilities, materials or operations having a significant impact on the health or safety of any State ... or the national security of the U.S." Employers in this category include armored car services, security protection, security alarm services, etc.

Additional Exception

Under the federal statute, an employer may, in some circumstances, request a polygraph test from a current employee during an investigation into a loss or injury to the employer's business. This is possible only under the following conditions:

- The employee had access to the property that is the subject of the investigation.
- The employer has a reasonable suspicion that the employee was involved in the loss or injury.
- The employer gives the employee a written statement detailing certain facts about the investigation before administering the test.

These requirements can be tricky. For example, the investigation must focus on a specific incident. The loss or injury must already have occurred—possible losses or contingent losses are not sufficient. The definition of economic loss or injury is, however, broad enough to cover non-tangible thefts such as the misappropriation of confidential information or trade secrets. In addition, employers must have a reasonable suspicion that the employee is responsible for the economic loss. Such reasonable suspicion requires "an observable, articulable basis in fact," which may include the employee's demeanor or behavior, information obtained from coworkers, or other types of information. The employee's access to the property, however, does not in itself establish reasonable suspicion unless only that employee had access to the property.

Testing Procedures

Even when polygraph tests are permitted, the federal statute requires employers to follow rigid procedures. All employers administering polygraph examinations under the EPPA must respect certain rights of the examinees as provided under the statute, including the right to terminate the test at any time and the right not to be asked degrading or unnecessarily intrusive questions or questions concerning religious or political beliefs or sexual orientation, or belief or opinions on racial matters or unions or labor organizations.

Before a polygraph test, an employer must give an employee a written notice of his or her legal rights, the nature of the investigation, and the specific questions that will be asked. During the test, the employer cannot ask certain questions and must allow the employee to terminate the test at any time. After the test, the employer must give the employee a copy of the written report, and the employer may not make any adverse employment decisions based solely on the results of the test.

Prohibition Against Disclosure

Federal law prohibits an individual from revealing the results of another person's polygraph test or even to disclose that a person has taken a polygraph test.

Enforcement

An employee or applicant may file a lawsuit to recover damages for any violation of the statute. If the employee or applicant wins, damages may include lost income or damages from emotional distress arising from the violation. In one case, a bank teller recovered $60,000 merely because she had nightmares and other emotional problems after her employer wrongfully administered a polygraph test to her. If a lawsuit is successful, the employee or applicant can also recover costs and attorneys' fees. These actions must be brought against employers within three years of the alleged violation.

In addition, the U.S. Department of Labor may file a lawsuit to prevent a planned polygraph test or to impose a civil penalty for any violation of the statute.

Waivers

An employer's potential liability under the federal statute cannot be completely avoided by a written waiver because this federal law specifically provides that the employee's federal rights cannot be waived unless the waiver is part of a settlement of a pending lawsuit.

Alternatives to Lie-detector Testing

The definition of lie-detector tests under the EPPA does not include written or oral tests, commonly referred to as honesty or personality tests. Therefore, under the federal statute, employers may consider alternative testing products marketed by many companies, which may be useful in evaluating honesty as it relates to job performance or in assessing a candidate's personality.

Honesty tests vary in form and content. Some are pen and paper examinations; others are computer administered or interactive examinations. Some tests pose questions that attempt to measure the test taker's attitudes toward honesty and dishonesty, while others pose fact specific examples and ask the test taker to identify what he or she would do under the circumstances.

Personality tests range from asking applicants to identify their personality traits to evaluations by trained psychologists.

Because a pre-offer test that identifies mental disorders or emotional impairments would violate the Americans with Disabilities Act and most state human rights laws, employers should use extreme caution when administering personality tests that also provide identification of mental or emotional impairments that are really psychological evaluations. Such tests should be administered only after making a conditional offer of employment. If a psychological test is considered a medical examination, the employer may only withdraw the job offer if the exclusion is "job related" and "consistent with business necessity and performance cannot be achieved with a reasonable accommodation." This may be a difficult standard to meet.

Employers should also be careful to ensure that the test does not contain inquiries regarding prohibited areas, such as indirectly inquiring about religious beliefs or sexual orientation.

There is, moreover, no guaranteed way to assess an individual's honesty or personality with complete accuracy. There are as many formulas for assessing honesty and personality as there are companies marketing the various tests. In selecting an honesty or personality test, certain guidelines may be useful:

- Beware of tests for which little or no validation research exists.
- Beware of test studies based on anonymously provided data or data not provided by real job candidates.
- Beware of tests whose validation studies have been designed, conducted, and published only by the test developer and not replicated by independent psychologists or agencies.

Final Cautions

Administering a lie-detector test to an applicant or employee is generally prohibited and, even when permitted, is very complicated. You should first decide whether your circumstances may be within the exceptions to the general prohibitions on lie-detector tests—if such exceptions exist. If they are, you should then determine whether the required procedures are worthwhile. Finally, if you still wish to administer a lie-detector test to an applicant or employee, you should contact an attorney to help you each step of the way to ensure compliance with the rigid requirements for a valid test.

Massachusetts Law

Use of lie-detector tests is covered in the Massachusetts General Laws Annotated, Part I, Title XXI, Ch. 149, Section 19B.

Provisions

The Commonwealth of Massachusetts includes in its definition of *lie-detector test* any test using a polygraph or any other device whose purpose is to help detect deception in an individual or to verify the truthfulness or honesty of an individual. For Massachusetts, unlike the federal government, the definition includes written examinations.

Under Massachusetts law, it is unlawful for any employer to require or request employees or applicants to take a lie-detector test, and they cannot make any kind of employment decision based on lie-detector tests.

Massachusetts' prohibition against lie-detector tests applies to all employment situations, including, for example, to applicants for police officer positions. It also applies to tests administered outside Massachusetts for employment within the state.

Exceptions

Massachusetts lists no exceptions to its law against use of lie-detector tests.

Notice

All applications for employment in Massachusetts must contain the following notice:

> "It is unlawful in Massachusetts to require or administer a lie-detector test as a condition of employment or continued employment. An employer who violates this law shall be subject to criminal penalties and civil liability."

Enforcement

Under Massachusetts law a person who violates any provision of the lie-detector statute shall be punished by a fine of not more than $1,000 nor less than $300 for the first offense. Subsequent offenses are punishable by a fine of up to $1,500 or by up to 90 days imprisonment, or both. Individuals who have been victims of violations of this statute have three years to bring charges.

Employees or applicants who are successful in their lawsuits may receive treble damages for any loss of wages or other benefits, with a minimum of $500 for each violation, as well as litigation costs and attorneys' fees.

Liability

The president or chief operating officer of a corporation—or any managerial or supervisory person allowing such a violation—is considered the responsible individual under the Massachusetts statute.

Waivers

Massachusetts accepts no waiver of the provisions of this law as a defense against criminal prosecution or civil liability.

Chapter 7
Employee Handbooks

Introduction

Employee handbooks—sometimes referred to as *personnel policies or statements*, *employee manuals*, and *personnel handbooks*—have formed the basis of express and implied contracts in some states limiting an employer's ability to discharge an employee without cause. Employers often use employee handbooks to outline company disciplinary policy, office procedures, evaluation procedures, or to list grounds for employee discharge. In addition to these company-generated policy statements, employers may use employee handbooks to inform employees of policies required by statute.

At-will Status

Most employees in the U.S. are considered to be employed at-will. Typically, being employed "at-will" means that in the absence of an express contract of employment, no contractual or similar obligation is implied or inferred from the employment relationship. Unless care is taken in drafting the language used in employee handbooks, they can be interpreted to create an implied contract. Although courts have traditionally been reluctant to alter the at-will employment relationship, specific representations and promises that employers make in employee handbooks can be viewed as contractual provisions if employees rely on the promises to their harm.

Disclaimers

Employers often insert disclaimer provisions into employee handbooks. Typically, *disclaimers* are worded and designed to inform employees that the employee handbook does not form an employment contract or alter the at-will employment relationship. Thus, disclaimers serve a useful purpose: if well drafted, they limit the scope and potential liability arising from representations made in an employee handbook. Employers must be careful, however, because poorly drafted or ambiguously worded disclaimers sometimes fail in litigation. Where there is ambiguity and inconsistency between the disclaimer and the contents of the handbook, courts have gone ahead, despite the disclaimers, to examine whether an employment contract existed between employer and employee. In many cases, contract liability arising from an employee handbook has been imposed even where a disclaimer was present because of a conflict with the disclaimers and other sections of the handbook.

Advantages and Disadvantages of Employee Handbooks

Advantages

- Information is distributed clearly to all employees.

- Supervisors can apply company policy more consistently.

- Supervisors have a definite plan of action allowing them to operate more confidently when issues arise.

- In litigation, a well-considered, carefully drafted employee handbook can provide an employer's best defense in showing that employees were treated consistently by company policy.

- A well-drafted employee handbook can help a company avoid unions.

Disadvantages

- If the employee handbook is not carefully drafted, it may support a claim that the employer created an express or implied contract modifying the employee's at-will status.

- Treating the employee inconsistently with the employee handbook may be evidence of disparate or discriminatory treatment.

- Losing track of when handbooks were revised, or specific policies were amended, can play havoc in litigation.

- A poorly drafted employee handbook can lead to employee dissatisfaction and encourage unionizing.

Important Considerations When Preparing Employee Handbooks

- Use clear and concise language. Avoid using phrases and terms that suggest a change in the at-will status, such as: "Upon completing the probationary period, you become entitled to all the rights and privileges of a permanent employee in reference to at-will employees in the handbook."

- Use positive language in policies to help employee morale.

- Have the employee sign an acknowledgment form stating that he or she has received the handbook and understands the at-will nature of his or her employment.

- In addition to the employee acknowledgment form, an employer should insert a disclaimer provision in the employee handbook. The disclaimer must be worded to convey the fact that the employee handbook does not form a contract or alter the at-will terms and conditions of the employment relationship.

- Place the disclaimer in a prominent place (such as the front page) in the employee handbook, set off by a border, contrasting print, or capitalized letters.

- The disclaimer should advise the employee that statements made by management or supervisors, especially those that contradict the employee's at-will status, are not binding on the employer.

- Employers should insert a provision in the disclaimer stating that the company reserves the right to alter, amend, or suspend the terms of the handbook at its sole discretion.

- After the employee signs the acknowledgment form and disclaimer, the employer should place a copy in the employee's personnel file.

- If a revised employee handbook replaces an older version, the employer should ensure that the employee is aware the revised version supersedes all previous versions. The employee should sign a statement acknowledging this fact.

- All employee handbooks should be dated and versions numbered where appropriate. The employer should keep dated or numbered versions of the handbook on file.

- Employers should inform their managers and supervisors not to make oral representations to employees having anything to do with permanent employee status.

- Employment law counsel should review employee handbooks before they are distributed and their policies implemented.

Commonly Asked Questions

Q. Does an employee handbook create an employment contract limiting an employer's right to discharge an at-will employee without cause?

A. Usually no. In most jurisdictions, unless the parties enter into an explicit employment contract, the employee handbook cannot be deemed to be a valid employment contract. However, some courts have interpreted "overly contractual" language, and inconsistent or ambiguous handbook language as an employment contract that may create limitations on an employer's right to discharge an employee.

Q. Must the employer follow the provisions of the employee handbook?

A. Lacking an express provision stating that the employer may exercise its discretion in implementing the employee handbook, courts have held that the employer must follow the provisions of the handbook.

Q. Is the employee bound by a second employee handbook if he or she refuses to sign the handbook, and writes on the handbook that he "does not agree with, nor agree to abide by the terms of the second handbook?"

A. In such cases, some courts have held that the first employee handbook is the one that governs if the employee continues in the employment relationship, because the first handbook is the one the employee assented to. Courts require that both the employee and employer agree on the employee handbook. However, if an employee refuses to be bound by the terms of a new employment handbook, the employer may be free to terminate the employment relationship.

Q. Does the disclaimer have to appear in the front of the employee handbook?

A. The disclaimer may appear anywhere in the employee handbook; however, it should be visible, conspicuous, and clear. The placement of the disclaimer should be noticeable to the average person. The most advantageous location is at the front of the handbook. Some jurisdictions demand placement at the beginning to accord full weight to the disclaimer.

Q. Does the employee have to read the employee handbook to be bound by its provisions and disclaimers?

A. An employee cannot escape the provisions of an employee handbook, especially the disclaimer provision, on the basis of not having fully read the handbook. Providing the employee a carefully drafted handbook should be enough. Careful employers, however, will take the extra step of obtaining a signed acknowledgment from the employee that he or she has received and read the handbook.

Chapter 8
Non-competition Agreements and Trade Secrets

Introduction

Whenever you bring on a new employee, you provide that person with access to your company's most valuable assets: its people, its customers, its way of doing business. Given that the average American will change jobs seven times over a work life, chances are high that some of that information will eventually find its way to a competitor. More frequently than ever, companies are trying to protect themselves and their assets from the damage that can result when employees depart to work for a competing business or set up a competing enterprise.

There is no easy way to prevent such conduct, especially if precautions have not been taken in advance. Require your employees to sign employment agreements wherein they agree to maintain the secrecy for all of the organization's trade secrets. Also, consider a covenant not to compete that has geographic, scope and duration limitations. Such terms should be included in an initial employment agreement entered into at the start of the employment relationship. While it may not be easy to go back and add these terms, because there must be adequate consideration in exchange for these post-employment obligations, if you will be paying the employee anything more than you absolutely legally owe him or her, you may be able to condition the "bonus" on his having signed an agreement to maintain the trade secret as confidential and to provide you with written assurances that he or she no longer has any proprietary or trade secret material.

Please note, however, that state law governs restrictive covenants, trade secrets, and other non-competition agreements discussed in this chapter. While many of the general legal principals set forth in this chapter apply universally, there can be significant differences among states. The most obvious distinction is that some states, notably California, prohibit restrictive covenants, which inhibit an employee's ability to find new employment. Other distinctions among the laws of various states may be less dramatic but, under certain circumstances, no less important. Such differences are particularly critical if the agreement is intended to apply to employees who may be located in different states, such as a sales force. The substance of individual state laws is beyond the scope of this chapter, which is intended to offer a general understanding of the concepts involved. Individual state laws should be reviewed before any agreement discussed in this chapter is drafted.

General Protections

Employers have certain recognized limited protections, recognized by the law under a variety of theories, against unfair competition, disloyal employees, and overreaching competitors. Turning legal theory into meaningful remedies requires attention to detail and an appreciation for conflicting public policies.

The Duty of Loyalty

A company's current employees are under a "duty of loyalty" to the company. Each state defines that duty a bit differently. In general, employees are not permitted to induce current customers, suppliers, or other employees to leave the company, nor are they allowed to operate a competing business while still employed by the company. When that duty is breached, the employer may be entitled to collect lost profits, punitive damages, and out-of-pocket costs incurred to train replacements. Offending employees may be forced to forfeit their salaries and to give up any profits they made as a result of the disloyal conduct. In addition, courts may issue injunctions forbidding the employees to engage in similar conduct for a specified period. Under the duty of loyalty, the law generally prevents an individual from using trade secrets or proprietary information of a current or former employer to the detriment of that employer.

An employer need not do anything special to create this duty, and the employee need not sign any agreement to be covered by it. The law recognizes the duty of loyalty and the value of proprietary information. When wrongful conduct has been proven, the law provides a remedy. It will, however, be up to the employer to prove in court that the information it seeks to protect meets standards for trade secrets and that it did everything it could to safeguard the secret nature of the information.

Trade Secrets

What Is A "Trade Secret"?

A trade secret can be any information that derives independent economic value from not being generally known or readily ascertainable. Among the things that can be trade secrets are a formula, pattern, compilation, program, device, method, technique, or process.

Among things courts have found to be "trade secrets" are machining processes, blueprints, and stock-picking formulae, customer lists, pricing information, and non-public financial data. On the other hand, information such as overhead rates and profit margins that help define a price may be found to be a trade secret even if the price itself is known.

Legal Tests

Forty-two states and the District of Columbia have adopted in whole or in part the Uniform Trade Secrets Act (UTSA). The UTSA codifies the basic principles of common law trade secret protection and may afford employers protection even in those states, like California, where restrictive covenants are generally not enforceable. UTSA protects an employer from misappropriation and misuse of actual trade secrets, which are defined as information, including a formula, pattern, compilation, program, device, method, technique or process, drawing, data or customer list that:

- Derives independent economic value, actual or potential, from not being generally known to, and not being readily ascertainable by proper means by, other persons who can obtain economic value from its disclosure or use.

- Is the subject of efforts that are reasonable under the circumstances to maintain its secrecy.

An employer must take reasonable measures to maintain the confidentiality of trade secrets. In determining whether reasonable steps have been taken, courts balance the costs and benefits on a case-by-case basis.

Even states that have not adopted the UTSA generally accord similar protection to trade secrets under the Restatement (Second) of Torts, §757.

To determine whether a piece of information is a trade secret, states following the Restatement will generally examine the following factors:

- Whether the information was known outside the company.
- The savings effected and the value to the holder in having the information as against competitors.
- The value of the information and the amount of money or effort spent to develop it.
- The efforts the employer made to limit the number of people having access to the information.
- What other efforts were made to keep the information secret.
- The relative difficulty required obtaining or duplicating the information using proper means.

Restrictive Covenants

Definition

Restrictive covenants, also known as non-competition/non-compete agreements, are contractual arrangements that restrict employees' rights to compete with their employers for a period of time following termination of employment. Once reserved for the highest-level executives, researchers, and outside sales personnel, non-compete agreements are being increasingly used with mid-level managers, technical staff, and any other employee whose departure could create a competitive disadvantage. Unlike the common law duty of loyalty, an agreement not to compete prohibits conduct that takes place after the employment relationship has ended and is not limited to "wrongful conduct," such as stealing client lists.

Such an agreement is referred to as a non-solicitation agreement. Through the use of non-compete, non-solicitation, and nondisclosure agreements, employers try to prevent employees from cashing-in on opportunities gained during the employment relationship.

What Do Restrictive Covenants Protect?

Restrictive covenants provide protection by preventing former employees from alienating long-standing customers and disclosing or using confidential information acquired from the employer.

Note, however, that with professionals such as doctors and accountants and certain others, where a personal relationship has developed, courts will frequently refuse to enforce a non-competition agreement that would result in patients not being able to see their own doctor, or clients not being able to use the accountant they have dealt with for years, etc.

Employers can protect confidential information that may be helpful to a competitor or to an employee who decides to go into business for himself or herself. Courts will enforce this protection if an employee has signed a restrictive covenant, and the covenant is reasonable in all other important aspects. This is distinct from the general provision provided by the law of trade secrets and is a way for employers to protect themselves against disclosure of information that may not otherwise qualify as a trade secret. An employer must, however, be able to show that the information was indeed treated as confidential.

Restrictions on Non-compete Agreements

Before embarking on a campaign to have employees sign non-compete agreements, companies should consider a few cautionary points. Considering these points will also help companies draft workable agreements.

Courts in all states dislike non-compete agreements and welcome the opportunity to limit or eliminate them. Their sentiment is largely based on a desire to allow individuals to earn a living in the field of their choice. Agreements that are too broad are likely to be tossed out or at least rewritten by a judge in those states that allow for such an option. As a general rule, courts will consider the following factors in determining whether to enforce a restrictive covenant:

- **Does the employer have a legitimate interest in being protected from this employee's competitive activity?** A court may refuse to enforce a restriction that is too broadly drafted even though the employer may be able to demonstrate a legitimate business interest worthy of protection.

- **Is the restriction reasonable in light of all the circumstances?** By reasonable, the courts would mean that the agreement is no more restrictive upon an employee than necessary to protect the employer's legitimate business interests.

- **Is the restriction reasonably limited in time and geography?** The agreement must contain a reasonable time restriction. Such a time restriction would be based on such factors as the time it would take to train a new employee and for customers to become familiar with this employee and eliminate the identification between the employer's business and the former employee. The geographical scope of the restriction must be limited to areas necessary to protect the employer's interests.

- **Will enforcing the restriction harm the public interest? Will any aspect of public policy be affected if the agreement is enforced?** This is usually not a particularly significant concern, because, for example, restrictions on which salespeople the public cannot buy from would not seem to have a major impact on the public interest as long as the public can buy the product from someone.

- **Was there reasonable consideration given in return for the restrictive covenant being signed?** Most states require an employee's agreement to non-competition restrictions to be in exchange for receiving something of value, such as the initial job offer or a raise or promotion or extra benefits upon leaving the company.

- **When will the non-competition restriction be triggered?** Some agreements apply automatically, whether the employee's termination was for cause, without cause, or as part of a layoff. Others apply only if the employee resigns or is terminated for cause. Others limit the period of restricted activity to the time severance benefits are being paid. In this leave the employee is free to forego severance payments to accept employment. Note that some employers include an agreed-upon fee that the employee will pay if he or she engages in the prohibited activity during the restricted period.

Enforcement

The best non-compete agreements are narrowly tailored to meet the most important needs of the company, judiciously applied to only individuals in sensitive positions, and vigorously invoked when violated. In many cases, merely having a non-compete agreement in place will discourage most employees from leaving the company. When an employee does leave, however, the agreement allows the employer to have some control over the timing, terms, and effect of the departure.

Companies must fight to enforce their non-compete agreements. If the potential harm is sufficient to justify a restrictive covenant, it is serious enough to do something about when that covenant is violated. Violation of non-compete agreements may allow employers to obtain, in addition to monetary damages, non-monetary relief such as a restraining orders and injunctions to protect the company's interests. Companies that fail to enforce their non-compete agreements often find that their former employees' attorneys can argue that there was no need for the restriction in the first place since the company has not bothered to enforce it in the past.

Additional Protection: Inevitable Disclosure Doctrine

In the past, the only way for employers to protect themselves from such trade secret flight was to seek enforcement of non-compete and confidentiality agreements. In the unfortunate absence of such an agreement, the employer had little protection. Now, employers have a new avenue for relief through a judicially-created doctrine known as "the doctrine of inevitable disclosure."

The inevitable disclosure doctrine applies to certain employees who accept jobs with a competitor of their former employer. Some former employees, because of the nature of the knowledge they acquired during their employ regarding the employer's strategies, processes, etc., will inevitably disclose that knowledge to the competitor in order to perform their new job. Under the inevitable disclosure doctrine, an employer can prevent a former employee from working for a competitor even when the employee was never asked to sign (or refused to sign) a non-compete agreement, and has never threatened to use or disclose trade secrets. Actual disclosure of trade secrets is not required.

Although the inevitable disclosure doctrine has not been applied in all states, the doctrine has been adopted in many courts and has not been discredited in any. Generally, an employer seeking an injunction under the inevitable disclosure doctrine should prove the following:

- The employee's new position is substantially similar to his previous position.
- The competitor for whom the employee now works uses processes or methods substantially similar to the former employer's.
- The employee had knowledge of the employer's specific strategies or processes that are unknown-and would be valuable-to the employer's competitors.
- The passage of time has not made the confidential information useless.

In order to defeat a claim of inevitable disclosure, the competitor will need only to disprove one of the above.

Nondisclosure, No-solicitation, No-raid Agreements

Employers can have employees sign even more limited agreements—for example, nondisclosure, no-solicitation, and no-raid agreements—which do not limit their ability to work in the field but do prevent them from causing harm to the old employer in their new job. These more limited agreements are usually more easily enforced than a true non-compete agreement. One difficulty with these agreements, however, is the difficulty of proving they have been violated.

A nondisclosure agreement can prevent an employee from using or disclosing an employer's confidential information in the new job. An advantage of this sort of agreement is that the employer can define confidential information so that more things are included than would qualify as trade secrets under common law. Also, such a signed agreement would prevent employees from pleading ignorance as an excuse for sharing confidential information. It would, of course, be difficult to prove a violation of this sort of agreement when the employer's confidential information could arguably be ascertained from sources other than the employee.

A *no-solicitation agreement* prohibits the employee from going after the company's customers or suppliers. A *no-raid agreement* prohibits the employee and his or her new employer from inducing other employees to leave the original employer to work for the new employer, at least for some specific time after the former employee leaves employment. While employee raiding is not recognized as a cause of action in most states, employers may be able to pursue a remedy for raiding of employees based on a claim of intentional interference with contractual relations or prospective economic advantage. These agreements tend to be viewed more favorably by the courts since they do not actually keep anyone from working.

Conflict-of-Interest Clauses

Many employers also include a conflict-of-interest clause in their non-competition agreements. This provision generally requires employees to devote their entire productive time and full attention to the employer as a condition of their employment. A conflict-of-interest clause may also contain an agreement by employees to refrain from directly or indirectly engaging in any outside employment, consulting, or other business activities while employed by the employer. Employees can additionally be required to agree to refrain from engaging in any outside employment without the written consent of the employer.

Hiring a Competitor's Employees

Employers often may find themselves in a position to hire a competitor's employees. In these cases, it is worthwhile to take some precautionary steps; because state courts may find that a new employer's interference with valid non-compete agreements constitutes "tortious interference" with the former employer's relationship with the employee.

You should first determine if the employee is subject to any restrictions. Do not be satisfied with a vague answer to your question whether the employee has any sort of restrictive agreement with the former employer. Have the employee sign a statement that he or she is not subject to any non-compete or other agreement. If you hire a competitor's employee knowing that the employee is subject to a restrictive covenant, your company could be sued for interfering with the previous employer's contractual rights, just as you could sue a company that hired one of your employees subject to such an agreement.

The key to lawsuits regarding violation of another company's restrictive covenant is the hiring company's knowledge of the restriction and its decision to employ the person in spite of this knowledge. This is why the first step in such a case may be the sending of a certified letter by the old employer to the new, putting the new employer "on notice" of the restriction. If, in fact, it can be proven that the nature of an individual's work for the new employer makes it virtually impossible for the individual not to use or disclose the old employer's confidential information, a court may be persuaded to restrain the employee from working for the competition at all.

If you learn that your new hire does have a restrictive covenant, get a copy of it and have legal counsel examine it. It may be that the prohibitive activity does not match the duties of the position you are filling. The agreement may also appear too broad. It may also be that there was no consideration in return for the agreement being signed.

Once you know how enforceable the agreement is, you can decide how to proceed. You may want to begin negotiations with the other employer in cases where the agreement seems especially strong. You should be especially cautious about hiring employees with non-competition agreements if your company requires such agreements of its employees. It will be very difficult to enforce your own agreements, based on what you argue is a legitimate reason for having your employees sign them, if you find it acceptable to violate another employer's agreements.

Summary

Employers are protected by common law from the misuse of their trade secrets by former employees. To ensure their confidential information is protected, employers must actually treat this information as confidential and restrict access to it, instituting restricted-access procedures and posting appropriate signs. Employees should be trained in the proper handling of confidential information.

In situations where employers fear that employees may leave and take customers with them or share crucial information with a new employer, employers should carefully draft appropriate restrictive covenants and have their employees sign them. Restrictive covenants must follow reasonable guidelines if there is to be any hope of their being enforced. They must protect a legitimate interest of the employer and they must be as narrow as possible, avoiding broad and lengthy restrictions.

While the Inevitable Disclosure Doctrine can be useful, it should not be relied upon as the sole means of protecting trade secret disclosure by former employees. Employers are encouraged to limit disclosure of confidential information in the workplace by:

- Requiring employees to sign reasonable non-disclosure agreements and non-compete agreements where possible;
- Disseminating information on a need-to-know basis;
- Restricting access to file drawers and offices containing proprietary information;
- Developing and maintaining a sensible document retention and destruction policy; and
- Conducting systematic inventories of confidential information.

Furthermore, upon the departure of an employee with access to trade secret information, a company should conduct an exit interview to obtain knowledge about the scope and duties of the employee's new position and to repossess or delete any trade secret information held by the employee (including his or her home files).

Likewise, employers interviewing candidates should also take certain precautions to ensure that new employees do not become the subject of an injunction based on their former positions. Employers should first investigate whether a particular candidate is bound by a non-compete agreement or a non-disclosure agreement. If such an agreement(s) exists, the employer should obtain a written representation from the new employee that he/she complied with all obligations set forth within the agreement(s). Employers also should be aware of a new employee's prior work product, which may be subject to "work for hire" limitations. Finally, employers should remember to use practical methods to avoid the appearance of impropriety such as creating a new position for employees hired from competitors or documenting new employees' activities in ways that show independent action.

Chapter 9
Wages and Hours

Introduction

While the overtime and minimum wage statutes are perhaps the most troublesome wage and hour laws for many employers, employers must also remember a number of other laws that govern employee wages and hours. These additional laws often relate to the timeliness of wage payments; the administration of wage garnishments and child-support orders; payment while on jury duty or military leave; and prevailing wages in public construction projects; and employment of minors.

The first section of this chapter reviews federal wage and hour laws, including the FLSA's definition of who is an employer, as well as exemptions from wage and overtime requirements. It also reviews discrimination concerns related to wage and hour laws, as well as recordkeeping and posting requirements and enforcement. The second section of this chapter provides an analysis of state laws. Employers should review both the federal and the state laws to ensure proper compliance.

Federal Law

The federal Fair Labor Standards Act (FLSA) and state minimum wage laws mandate payment of minimum wages and overtime compensation to most employees. These laws also impose various recordkeeping and posting requirements.

Covered Employers

The FLSA applies to those employers engaged in interstate commerce or the production of goods for commerce, and that have annual gross sales or business volume of $500,000 or greater. The FLSA also applies to all public agencies, most hospitals and other healthcare entities, and schools.

Covered Employees

The FLSA covers all individuals employed by a covered employer. Even if the employer is subject to the FLSA, certain employees may be exempt from some or all of the statutory requirements. In considering the possible exempt status of employees, employers and their attorneys must consider a lengthy list of exemptions. Some exemptions are common to both federal and state statutes (for example, the "white-collar" exemptions for executive, administrative, or professional employees, although definitions may vary) while others may appear in only one statute.

Individuals who are not employed by a covered enterprise may, nevertheless, be individually covered. Under individual employee coverage, employees are covered by the act in each week in which they are individually engaged in interstate commerce, produce goods for commerce, or work in activities that are closely related and directly essential to the production of goods for commerce.

Exemptions to the FLSA

Salaried Employees

The exemption for salaried white-collar employees is the most common overtime exemption. Payment on a salary basis generally is necessary for exemption as an executive, professional, or administrative employee. Employees are paid on a salary basis if they regularly receive a predetermined amount for their compensation in each pay period. Subject to limited exceptions, exempt employees must receive full salary for any week in which they perform any work, regardless of the number of days or hours they actually worked.

Fair Labor Standards Act (FLSA) Overview

As a general rule, the FLSA mandates that employees receive time and one-half of their regular hourly rate for working more than 40 hours in a workweek unless they are subject to a specific exemption from overtime pay eligibility. Because these exemptions deprive workers of a statutory benefit, the courts narrowly construe them. Consequently, it is the employer's obligation to prove that each employee classified as exempt truly is covered by a statutory exemption.

An exemption does not apply unless all of the statutory prerequisites have been satisfied. With respect to administrative, professional and supervisory staff, employers must show that the employee in question is **paid on a salary basis** and that his or her primary duty is administrative, professional, or supervisory in nature. Unless both prongs of the exempt status test are satisfied fully, the worker must receive overtime compensation after working more than 40 hours in a workweek.

Analysis of the Salary Basis Component of the Exempt Status Test

What Is the "Salary Basis" Prong of the Exempt Status Test?

To be exempt under the white-collar exemptions applicable to administrative, professional, or supervisory workers, an employee must be paid on a salary basis. A worker is considered to be paid on a salary basis only if he or she regularly receives each pay period on a weekly, or less-frequent basis, a predetermined amount constituting all or part of his or her compensation, which amount is not subject to reduction because of variations in the quality or quantity of the work performed. Subject to the exceptions provided below, the employee must receive his or her full salary for any week in which he or she performs any work without regard to the number of days or hours worked. This policy is also subject to the general rule that an employee need not be paid for any workweek in which he or she performs no work:

> **Q. If a salaried exempt worker reports to work late or leaves early, can his or her salary be reduced because of that lost work time?**
>
> A. No. Payment on a salary basis means that the employer has promised to pay, at least, a fixed amount for a predetermined period of time. Late arrival at work or leaving before the end of the workday cannot result in reductions of the worker's base salary. (Of course, appropriate disciplinary action may result from unreliable attendance or other misconduct.)
>
> **Q. If a salaried exempt worker takes an extended meal break, can his or her salary be reduced because of that lost work time?**
>
> A. No. Just like coming to work late or leaving early, missing part of a workday because of extended meal breaks cannot result in reduction in the worker's base salary. (While the FLSA does not mandate that lunch or dinner breaks be provided, various state laws direct that meal

breaks be given to certain workers, usually depending upon the number of hours worked in a day.)

Q. Can any deduction be made from an employee's salary because he or she misses part of a workday?

A. No. If a salaried exempt employee reports to work on a workday, he or she must be paid for the entire day.

Q. If the facility is closed because of a snowstorm or other inclement weather, must the salaried exempt employees be paid for that workday?

A. Yes. The salary of a salaried exempt employee cannot be reduced because of the quality or quantity of work performed in any given workweek. Thus, if work is not available because the store is closed (for whatever reason), then exempt workers must be paid their full salary for that workweek if any work has been performed during that week.

Q. Are there times when a salaried exempt worker's salary is subject to reduction because of lost work time?

A. Yes. Under very limited circumstances, the base salary of a salaried exempt worker can be reduced:

- An employee is absent for one or more days for personal reasons other than sickness or accident.

- An employee is absent for one or more days for sickness or accident and the deduction is in accordance with a bona fide sickness and accident plan, policy, or practice.

- An employee is absent due to service of jury or military duty (at which time there is an offset for military service or jury duty pay, rather than an actual salary deduction).

- Good-faith penalties for infractions of safety rules of major significance.

- An employee misses an entire week of work.

- Days not worked during the first or last week of employment.

- Intermittent leaves pursuant to the Family and Medical Leave Act (FMLA). The FMLA specifically provides that deductions for intermittent leaves of less than one day will not violate the salary basis test (but may result in loss of exempt status under state law).

Q. What constitutes an "infraction of a safety rule of major significance?"

A. Deductions from a salaried exempt worker's base salary for reasons other than full-day absences are so disfavored that any deduction will be examined closely. While deductions are permitted to penalize salaried workers who violate major safety rules, the Department of Labor or a court rarely will recognize "misconduct" as satisfying this exception to the "no docking" rule. Examples of violations of safety rules that may satisfy this standard are set forth in the Wage-Hour Administrator's regulations; for example, smoking cigarettes in an explosives factory or oil refinery. Thus, unless the infraction is of comparable magnitude (which probably will result in termination of employment, rather then a monetary penalty), docking should be avoided as a means of punishing violation of a work or safety rule.

Q. If an exempt worker reports to work and then leaves early because he or she is ill and then does not report to work on the following day, can a deduction be made from salary for all time missed?

A. No. Although it is permissible to make a deduction in an amount of a day or more for sickness or accident (so long as **bona fide** sick pay plan exists), it is not proper to make such a deduction

Wages and Hours

in an increment of **less than a day**. Thus, a full day deduction is permitted for the second day of the illness, but the employee must be paid for the entire day when he or she reported to work and then became ill. (However, if the employee is eligible for leave under the FMLA and the employee's healthcare provider has certified that it is medically necessary for the employee to take intermittent leave, a partial-day deduction may be permissible. Since this practice otherwise would violate the FLSA, any such deduction should be made with great care and after an in-depth analysis of these conflicting statutory provisions and state overtime law).

Q. **What if an employee has used up all of his or her paid sick days under the sick pay plan or is not yet eligible to participate in the plan and is absent for two days, can a deduction be made for these full-day absences?**

A. Yes. As long as a bona fide sick pay plan exists, then the employer is permitted to make deductions for full-day absences.

Q. **Can deductions be made from accrued paid time off if a salaried employee is absent for less than a complete workday?**

A. Yes. According to the Department of Labor, but not necessarily all courts, use of accrued paid time off to "make up" for absences of less than a full day is permissible. In an opinion letter issued by the acting Wage Hour Administrator in April 1993, the Department of Labor stated that "Where an employer provides bona fide vacation and sick time benefits, it is permissible to substitute or reduce the accrued benefits for the time an employee is absent from work, even if it is less than a full day, without affecting the salary basis of payment, if by substituting or reducing such benefits, the employee receives in payment an amount equal to his or her guaranteed salary." However, the Department of Labor goes on to state: "Where an employee has exhausted these benefits, deductions may be made in increments of full days only for absences for personal reasons or illness. Deductions from the salaries of otherwise exempt employees for partial day absences after they have exhausted their vacation or sick time benefits have never been permitted under the regulations...." Until the circuit court in your area of the country or the Supreme Court has ruled upon this issue, docking of accrued paid time-off when an exempt worker is absent for less than a full workday may expose the company to loss of exempt status.

Q. **If a salaried exempt employee were summoned for jury duty after working part of a workweek, must he or she be paid for that workweek?**

A. Yes. If the salaried exempt employee works at all during any workweek, then he or she must be paid the entire week's salary. An offset is permitted to account for any monies received from the court for that jury service.

Q. **If a salaried exempt employee is called upon to perform Reserve duty, to serve in the National Guard, or to participate in other military service, must he or she be paid for that time?**

A. Yes. If the salaried exempt employee works at all during the workweek when military service begins or ends, then he or she must be paid the entire week's salary. An offset is permitted to account for any monies received for military service.

Q. **What is the penalty if improper deductions are made?**

A. When an employer improperly docks an exempt employee's pay, courts and the Department of Labor conclude that the employer did not intend to compensate the employee on a salary basis. Consequently, exempt status would be lost for that worker and for all other workers considered to have been salaried exempt staff. (If the deduction resulted from inadvertence **and** is corrected promptly after discovery of the error **and** the employer demonstrates that it implemented pay practices designed to avoid repetition of similar errors, the exemption **may** be retained. Although the regulations provide for this "window of correction," deductions from salary due to partial day absences are contrary to the intent of the salary basis test and should be avoided! There is no assurance at all that a court will recognize an employer's acts as fitting within this limited defense to loss of exempt status because of wrongful deductions).

Q. **Under what circumstance will deductions from accrued paid time off result in the loss of exempt status?**

A. In *Abshire v. County of Kern,* the Ninth Circuit Court of Appeals found that otherwise exempt employees were entitled to overtime compensation because they were not paid on a salary basis. Under the County's pay practices, employees' base salaries were docked if accrued paid time off was exhausted; that is, after the employee had exhausted accrued paid time off (including compensatory leave), base salary would be docked. Because docking was mandatory, exempt status was lost and overtime pay was owed to this entire class of employees. This was found to be true even though none of the employees' salaries ever was docked because under the county's pay practice docking would result if accrued time-off were exhausted.

In *Bamer v. City of Novato,* the Ninth Circuit Court of Appeals retreated somewhat from its ruling in *Abshire* and held that "In the absence of an expressed policy subjecting an executive or administrative employee's pay to reduction for absences of less than one day, deducting accrued leave time is not conduct which puts the employee outside the applicable exemption."

Q. **What is the effect of the deductions made pursuant to the Family and Medical Leave Act for absences of less than a full workday, upon exempt status?**

A. As noted above, under the FMLA, an employer may be called upon to grant leave of absence under the FMLA on a partial-day basis (rather than an ongoing basis). The FMLA permits "The employer to make deductions from the employee's salary for any hours taken as intermittent or reduced FMLA leave within a workweek without affecting the exempt status of the employee …." The following quandary exists. If an employee's appointment stems from a serious health condition, the FMLA's provision permitting an employee to suffer a wage deduction did not result in loss of exempt status. In contrast, however, if the employee misses part of a workday for a condition not covered by the FMLA, and the employer made a deduction from the base salary, then loss of exempt status would result.

Q. **What liability will result if employees are wrongfully treated as exempt?**

A. If workers wrongly are classified as exempt, but are nonexempt, liability would include:

- Liability for all unpaid overtime compensation.

- Attorney's fees and costs if litigation were necessary to determine where the liability existed.

- Liquidated damages, which could equal the backpay, if the violation were found to be "willful" (that is, in reckless disregard of whether the pay program was in violation of the Fair Labor Standards Act).

- Potential imposition of civil money penalties (fines) of $1,000 per violation.

For nonexempt workers, compensation is required for the time an employee is suffered or permitted to work, even if not specifically asked to do so. As a general rule, all hours that the employee is required to be at work should be considered to be compensable work time, other than rest or meal breaks of 30 minutes or more (during which no duties are performed). Shorter rest periods, such as coffee or snack breaks, cannot be treated as a non-compensable meal periods; instead, rest breaks are compensable work time. When taking an unpaid 30-minute or longer meal break, the employee must be relieved of all duties, whether active or passive, and must be free to leave his or her post. Other examples of compensable work time are: participating in charitable work requested or controlled by the employer; participation in fire drills; being required to show up before one's shift begins to complete paperwork; and traveling from one work site to another.

When recording time worked by nonexempt employees, the employer must record, among other things, the total hours worked each workday and workweek. This will include signing/punching out at the end of the workday. All other hours worked, such as for compensable travel time, training time, and time spent doing paperwork, will have to be recorded. Since time records also will help your company defend against employee claims for unpaid overtime, you should consider requiring time records for those employees whose exempt status you question.

Exemptions

Payment by salary is not by itself sufficient to qualify for exempt status. The employer must be able to demonstrate that an employee meets the specific terms of one of the exemptions. The short tests for these exemptions, applicable to employees paid a salary of at least $250 per week, are broadly outlined below. Many court cases and administrative rulings apply these deceptively simple looking tests. Employers should consult an attorney when there is a question about an employee's exempt status.

Executive Exemptions

To qualify for the executive exemption, the following criteria must be met:

- The employee's primary duty must consist of the management of the enterprise in which he or she is employed or of a customarily recognized department or subdivision of the enterprise. The rule of thumb for determining a "primary duty" is whether 50 percent of the employee's time is spent on management duties.

- The employee customarily and regularly directs the work of two or more full-time employees or the equivalent (for example, two full-time employees or multiple part-time workers whose aggregate hours equal two full time equivalents).

Professional Exemptions

To qualify for the professional exemption, the following criteria must be met by a salaried worker:

- The employee's primary duty consists of one of the following:

  - Work requiring advanced knowledge in a field of science or learning customarily acquired by a long course of specialized intellectual instruction or study.

  - Work that is original and creative in a recognized field of artistic endeavor and the result of which depends primarily on the invention, imagination, or talent of the employee.

  - Teaching in a school system or educational establishment or institution.

  - Work that requires theoretical and practical application of highly specialized knowledge of computer systems analysis, programming, or software engineering. Such employees are exempt even if paid on an hourly rather than a salary basis, provided that they are paid on an hourly basis at a rate in excess of 6½ times the minimum wage requirement.

- The employee customarily and regularly exercises discretion and independent judgment.

Administrative Exemptions

To meet the administrative exemption, the following criteria must be met by a salaried worker:

- The employee's primary duty consists of the performance of office or non-manual work directly related to management policies or general business operations of the employer or the employer's customers.
- The employee customarily and regularly exercises discretion and independent judgment.

Other Exemptions

Examples of other exemptions are:

- Outside salespersons—employees who are regularly engaged away from the employer's place of business in
    - Making sales of goods and services, or
    - Obtaining orders or contracts for services or the use of facilities, and who spend 20 percent or less of their time in nonexempt work.
- Employees of amusement or recreational establishments meeting certain tests demonstrating the seasonal nature of their business.
- Certain agricultural employees.
- Employees of weekly or more frequent newspapers with a circulation of less than 4,000.
- Employees in the fishing industry.

Exceptions to Overtime

Some employees are exempt from the overtime compensation requirements of the FLSA, including:

- Certain employees of motor carriers subject to being regulated by the Department of Transportation.
- Announcers, news editors, and chief engineers of radio or television stations in small communities.
- Certain employees of automobile, truck, farm implements, trailer, boat, or aircraft dealers.
- Motion picture theater employees.
- Taxicab drivers.

Compensation

Work that requires theoretical and practical application of highly specialized knowledge of computer systems analysis, programming, or software engineering. Such employees are exempt even if paid on an hourly rather than a salary basis, provided that they are paid on an hourly basis at a rate in excess of $27.63 an hour.

Minimum Wage Requirements

The federal minimum wage is currently $5.15 per hour. Employers may pay $2.13 per hour to tipped employees. If the $2.13 plus tips does not equal at least the minimum wage, the employer must make up the difference to ensure that each tipped employee makes at least the minimum wage. Employers not covered by the FLSA must comply with state or municipal minimum wage laws.

Opportunity Wage

Employers may pay an "opportunity wage" of $4.25 per hour to employees under age 20 for the first 90 calendar days of employment. Employers may not discriminate against older workers to take advantage of the opportunity wage.

Exceptions for Student Learners

Student learners are students enrolled in cooperative, vocational education programs approved by a state board of education. Learners must be employed on a part-time basis at no less than 75 percent of the employer's regular minimum wage. A special student-learner certificate shall be effective for a period not to exceed the length of one school year unless a longer period is found to be justified by extraordinary circumstances. It should be noted that Department of Labor regulations distinguish between student-learners and other types of learners, messengers, and apprentices.

Exceptions for Disabled Individuals and Others

State and federal laws authorize employers to pay less than the minimum wage to individuals whose earning capacity is impaired by physical or mental deficiencies or injuries. To do so, employers must first obtain a license from the U.S. Department of Labor (and an authorized state official under state law).

Under such a license, the employer must pay a rate commensurate with the rate paid to non-handicapped workers for essentially the same type, quality, and quantity of work. Certain learners, apprentices, messengers, and student workers may also be paid subminimum wages with a license issued by the Department of Labor.

Timing of Wage Payments

Under state law, failure to pay wages promptly may possibly subject the employer to liability for unpaid wages and additional damages. A written contract between the employer and the employee may provide for other methods of payment, or the custom of the industry may prevail. As there is little guidance about what constitutes a custom justifying variance from the statutory rule on prompt payment, employers are cautioned to consult with counsel regarding this issue.

Deductions from Pay

Required Deductions

Employers are required to make deductions for contributions and applicable local, state, and federal income taxes, Social Security and Medicare taxes. The employer must submit the amounts withheld to the appropriate governmental agency.

Employers may make deductions to correct errors, such as overpayment.

Employers who make deductions from the wages of exempt-status employees, however, run the risk of losing the exempt status of those employees. Additionally, deductions for shortages, debts to the employers, uniforms, and uniform maintenance generally are found to destroy exempt status.

Savings Bonds and Charitable Donations

Employees may authorize deductions from their paychecks for various reasons, including purchasing savings bonds or making charitable donations. Employers should only make such deductions after first having obtained the employee's written authorization for such discretionary deductions.

Unions

Employers are not generally required to deduct employees' union dues. However, a negotiated collective bargaining agreement with dues check off clause may require the employer to deduct such dues.

Political Candidates

With the written authorization of the employee, and depending on state law, employers also may deduct from wages voluntarily designated by employees for the support of political candidates, political action committees, political parties, or ballot issues. The employer may either absorb the administrative costs of such deductions or may deduct its administrative costs from the amount deducted before transmitting the balance to the designated recipient. While not a federal wage/hour issue, employers should be careful to apply the same policy for all deductions, regardless of the candidate or the issue.

Wares, Tools, or Machinery

Subject to state law, any deductions an employer makes from wages for wares, tools, or machinery destroyed or damaged must be authorized in writing by the employee. Making such deductions from an exempt employee's salary may be destructive of exempt status.

Wage Garnishments

If an employee's creditor obtains a court judgment against him or her, the creditor may collect the judgment by garnishing the employee's wages. Under this procedure, the creditor obtains a court order directing the employer (the garnishee) to withhold a certain amount from the employee's wages and pay that amount directly to the court. Garnishment proceedings may not be instituted until the creditor has first given the employee an opportunity to make voluntary payment and the employee has failed to do so.

Complying with a Garnishment Order

An employer first learns of a garnishment proceeding when it receives an *Order and Notice of Garnishment and Answer of Employer* form. This notice sets forth the obligations of the employer. Employers must complete the form and return it to the court along with the garnished wages. The payment must be accompanied by a complete *Interim Report and Answer of Garnishee* form. That is, unless the garnishment has been satisfied to the extent required by law, in which case the employer shall submit a completed *Final Report and Answer of Garnishee* to the court. State and federal law limit the amount of money subject to garnishment. A step-by-step procedure for calculating the amount that may be garnished is contained in the form.

If the employee is no longer employed at the time the employer receives the notice, the employer should so indicate on the form and return it.

A continuing garnishment order remains in effect unless one of the following occurs:

- The amount described in the garnishment order is paid in full.
- The judgment creditor files notice that the judgment is paid in full or otherwise satisfied.
- The court's continuous order is stayed by a bankruptcy court or because a trustee has been appointed.
- A garnishment order of higher priority under state or federal law, for example a child-support order or a tax levy, is issued to the garnishee from a different judgment creditor with respect to the same debtor.

State law may impose other requirements or limitations.

Employee Discharge Due to Excessive Garnishment

Although complying with garnishment actions may be burdensome to employers, employees may not be discharged solely because of one successful garnishment by a creditor in a 12-month period. However, two or more successful garnishments by separate creditors within the same 12-month period are valid grounds for discharge, unless the employer is otherwise prohibited from discharging the employee. Employers adopting a policy of discharging employees for multiple garnishments should be careful that such a policy does not have a discriminatory impact on any protected group of employees and does not violate state laws, which may be more protective.

Employers discharging employees in violation of the garnishment laws are subject to criminal penalties.

Child-Support Orders

Courts may order employers to make regular payroll deductions for the collection of child-support payments as the result of divorce or support proceedings. Child-support payments are given priority over other garnishment or wage-withholding orders. The amount to be deducted is fixed by court order and the employer should treat such a deduction as it would any payroll tax, paying the deducted payments regularly to the proper agency.

An employer may not discipline, discharge, or refuse to hire an individual because of a withholding order for child support. An employer violating these provisions may be liable both for statutory penalties and subject to a civil suit for wrongful discharge.

Hours Worked

Nonexempt workers are entitled to compensation based on the number of hours worked. Hours for which employees should be compensated include the following:

- Time during which an employee is required to be on duty or on an employer's premises or at a prescribed workplace.

- Time during which an employee is allowed to be actually working, whether or not required to do so, even though performed away from the employer's premises, away from the job site, or at the employee's home. Thus, an employer must compensate its employees for unauthorized work that, even though prohibited, is performed with the knowledge on acquiescence of management.

- Time spent in idleness or on-call if the employee is "engaged to be waiting"—that is, required to be engaged in these activities as part of the employee's job and is not completely relieved from duty for a period of time long enough to effectively use the time for the employee's own purposes.

- Time spent in incidental activities before or after work such as preparing for work or cleaning up if the activities are an integral and indispensable part of the employee's principal activities.

- Rest periods of 20 minutes or less.

- Meal periods during which the employee is required to perform duties.

- Required attendance at training programs.

- Certain travel time (that is not in-town commuting time).

On-call Time

Some employers wish to have their employees ready to work in the event of an emergency or other occurrence. This is known as *on-call time*. Many employers—for example, ambulance services—have been sued in recent years by employees seeking compensation and overtime compensation for time during which they are subject to being called to work.

Although each case depends on its own particular circumstances, generally, employees must be compensated for on-call time **only** if they cannot effectively use the time for their own personal benefit.

Example: If an employee is subject to being called in on the off-shift and is actually called numerous times each day, the employee's on-call time might not be used for his or her own benefit. In that case, the employee would be entitled to overtime pay for the on-call time.

Employers requiring significant compensable on-call time should note that they may pay less for the on-call time as long as the on-call rate equals or exceeds the minimum wage.

Training Time

Generally, attendance at training programs does not constitute "hours worked" if all four of the following conditions are met:

1. Attendance is outside normal working hours.
2. Attendance is voluntary.
3. The training is not directly related to the employee's job.
4. The employee performs no work of value for the employer during the training time.

Overtime Compensation

Federal and state law requires covered employers to pay nonexempt employees for hours worked in excess of 40 hours in one workweek at a rate of one-and-one-half times the employee's regular wage rate. Note, however, that the FLSA is full of special rules and exceptions that **may** also be incorporated into state law. For example, a hospital employer may pay overtime after hours worked in excess of 80 hours in two weeks. Employers with employees who work fluctuating hours should consult an attorney regarding specially permitted methods of paying overtime compensation that may save overtime costs.

Computing Overtime Compensation

Overtime must be computed separately for each workweek. If an employee works 30 hours one week and 50 the next, the employer must pay the employee overtime compensation for 10 hours for the second week regardless of the "short" prior week. An employer is not required to include paid time off (for example, sick days, vacation, paid holidays) in hours worked for purposes of computing overtime. Thus, if holiday pay, sick pay, or any other type of pay for hours not actually worked is included in the weekly pay, the overtime rate does not have to be paid until the hours **actually** worked exceed 40 hours.

Unauthorized Overtime

Even when an employee does not have specific permission to work overtime, his or her extra hours will count toward the total hours worked and thus be included in overtime as long as the employer knew or should have known that the employee was working extra hours and permitted the employee to do so. The employer may discipline an employee for working unauthorized overtime but may not refuse to count the hours worked for purposes of determining overtime.

Scheduling the Workweek

Employers are free to set the day and hour when the seven-day workweek starts and ends, but it must be a fixed time. A change may be made later, but it must be intended to be permanent. The employer cannot attempt to minimize overtime payments by juggling the workweek to respond to changes in the pattern of hours worked.

Regular Rate of Pay

The rate of pay for overtime hours is one-and-one-half times the employee's regular rate of pay. In determining the employee's regular rate, an employer must include the hourly wages and any bonus, shift premium incentive, or longevity pay plus any commissions the employee receives. Even if the employee will not receive a bonus until later—for example, a quarterly production bonus—if the employee has a contractual right to receive that bonus, the payments must be included in the overtime compensation computation. This may require retroactively adjusting the overtime pay computation when the amount of the bonus is determined.

The regular rate for salaried employees may be determined by calculating the weekly salary and dividing by the number of hours worked during the workweek.

Two methods are permissible for determining the regular rate for an employee who works at more than one rate of pay during a single workweek. The usual method is to calculate the regular rate for that week by determining the weighted average of the two rates. The regular rate is determined by dividing the total amount of compensation by the total number of hours worked.

Example: If an employee works 30 hours of production work at $7.00/hour and 20 hours of custodial work at $6.00/hour, the employee's regular rate would be determined as follows:

Total compensation	=	(30 hrs x $7.00/hr) + (20 hrs x $6.00/hr)
	=	$210.00 + $120.00 = $330.00
Total hours	=	50 hours
Regular rate	=	$330.00 ÷ 50 = $6.60/hour
Overtime premium	=	$3.30/hr
Overtime hourly rate	=	$9.90/hr
Overtime premium for hours worked over 40	=	10 hrs x $3.30/hr = $33.00
Total compensation	=	$330.00 + $33.00 = $363.00

Alternatively, an employee who performs two or more different kinds of work for which different straight time hourly rates are established may agree with his or her employer in advance of the performance of the work that he or she will be paid during overtime hours at a rate not less than one-and-one-half times the hourly non-overtime rate established for the type of work he or she is performing during overtime hours.

Such an agreement should be in writing. This method would reduce overtime compensation costs when an employee's overtime hours are typically spent on the lower paying of two job functions, as the custodial work in the example above. Extra overtime compensation for any additional pay—for example, bonuses—would still need to be computed and paid.

Discrimination

The Equal Pay Act (EPA), enacted in 1963 as an amendment to the FLSA, prohibits employers from discriminating in wages between male and female employees. Pursuant to the EPA, an employer cannot pay lower wage rates to employees of one sex than to those of the other when the work that they do requires equal skill, effort, and is performed under similar working conditions. However, individuals who perform roughly equivalent work under similar conditions may be paid at different rates when the payment is made under one of the following bona fide conditions:

- A seniority system.
- A merit system.
- A system that measures earnings by quality and quantity of production.
- Any other nondiscriminatory factor, such as job performance or qualifications.

Violations of the Equal Pay Act subject employers to recovery of damages. Employers are prohibited from discriminating against any employee in retaliation for the employees having made a complaint to the employer, the Department of Labor, or a state agency that he or she has not been paid proper wages.

Recordkeeping and Posting Requirements

The FLSA requires employers to maintain three general categories of records for at least three years:

- Payroll records, including name, address, date of birth (if under 19), sex and occupation of the employee, daily and weekly straight time and overtime earnings, additions to or deductions from earnings, time of day and day of week on which the employee's workweek begins, regular hourly rate of pay for any workweek in which overtime compensation is due, hours worked each work day and total hours worked each workweek, total wages paid each pay period, and the date of payment and the pay period covered by the payment.
- Certificates, agreements, plans, and notices, including collective bargaining agreements, trusts, employment contracts.
- Sales and purchase records (total volume).

The FLSA requires employers to maintain the following record for at least two years:

- Basic employment and earnings records including time and earning cards or sheets.
- Wage rate tables.
- Order, shipping, and billing records.
- Records of additions to or deductions from wages paid.

Employers must also maintain summaries of federal and state minimum wage and overtime laws and regulations and post them in a conspicuous and accessible location in the workplace.

Enforcement

The Department of Labor investigates and determines compliance with the FLSA. Investigators must be allowed to enter any place of business to inspect the books, payrolls, or other records that relate to wages, hours, and conditions of employment and to question employees about whether their employer is complying with the act.

The Secretary of Labor, or an individual employee or group of employees, may sue an employer to collect past-due wages. If the FLSA violation is willful, employees also may recover liquidated damages in an amount equal to past-due wages plus interest and attorneys' fees and costs.

Generally, a two-year statute of limitations applies to FLSA suits. In the case of a willful violation, however, the suit may be brought up to three years after the violation occurred.

Massachusetts Law

The Massachusetts minimum wage is currently $6.75 an hour, $1.60 for agricultural and farm labor. Boston employers who receive more than $100,000 in assistance from the city must pay their employees $7.80 an hour.

Covered Employers

Massachusetts wage laws are generally applicable to all employers.

Covered Employees

Massachusetts law provides a list of exceptions to the minimum wage laws. These include the following:

- Employees performing professional service.
- Individuals doing agricultural or farm work.
- Individuals being rehabilitated or trained under rehabilitation and training programs in charitable, educational, or religious institutions.
- Members of religious orders.
- Individuals doing outside sales work who regularly sell a product away from their employer's place of business and who do not make daily reports or visits to the office or plant.

Massachusetts law includes the same exemptions for salaried executive, professional, and administrative employees as does the federal law. Salaried employees with positions requiring management, supervision, or other forms of authority, and requiring considerable discretion and/or specialized expertise gained only through considerable education are exempt both from the minimum wage laws and the overtime pay requirements.

Massachusetts further explains the salary requirement. For each week of work the employee must receive a predetermined salary that is not subject to reduction based on the quality or quantity of the work performed. The salary may not be subject to partial-day docking under any circumstances. Docking the salary of an employee sent home for a half day, for example, could jeopardize the exemption, as could docking salaries for absences because of jury duty.

With the caveat that the duties, not the title, are what determine whether an employee is exempt, Massachusetts provides the following examples of exempt positions:

- Executive — production supervisor, department director, office manager or shift supervisor, plant or factory manager or superintendent.
- Professional — registered nurse, physician, chemist, engineer, teacher, accountant, attorney, psychologist, social worker, physical therapist, artist.
- Administrative — director of marketing and marketing representative, personnel or human resources director, comptroller, treasurer, buyer, affirmative-action coordinator, public relations director, wholesale sale employee, financial or budget analyst.

Compensation

As we noted at the beginning of this section, the Massachusetts' minimum wage is currently $6.75 per hour, with a higher living wage paid to Boston employees. Massachusetts statute precludes agreements between employers and employees to work for less.

Exceptions

Massachusetts allows for subminimum wages to be paid to the following:

- **Employees with impaired earning capacity.** The Commissioner of Labor and Workforce Development may issue special certificates authorizing employment of employees whose earning capacity is impaired by age, physical or mental deficiency, or injury, or who are certified as "handicapped" at wages below minimum wage.
- **Student learners.** The commissioner may issue a school, college, university, summer camp, hospital, laboratory, or educational institution a license permitting them to employ students for not less than 80 percent of the minimum wage if the students are enrolled in the institution or in a formal training program.
- **Apprentices and learners.** Certificates can be obtained to employ apprentices and learners at no less than 80 percent of the minimum wage in approved training programs. In retail, merchandising, or laundry establishments the subminimum scale applies only to the first 80 hours of work.
- **Tipped employees.** Employees who receive tips must receive the minimum wage but this can be made up by a combination of tips plus wages paid. The employer may take credit for the employee's tips only up to 40 percent of the minimum wage. Employers are specifically forbidden to demand from employees tips as a condition of employment or to keep from employees any tips or gratuities given to the employer for the employees.

Frequency and Method of Payment

Under the Massachusetts Wage Payment Law, wages must be paid weekly or biweekly in cash or by checks or drafts that can be cashed without charge. Casual workers who work for fewer than five days must be paid within seven days of the end of their pay period. Salaried employees may be paid biweekly or, by agreement, monthly. Agricultural workers may be paid monthly. Manufacturing employers of more than 100 persons must pay their workers on the day chosen before the end of regular working hours.

Reimbursements and Benefit Payments

An employer that requests or requires an applicant or employee to undergo a medical examination as a condition of employment must reimburse the individual for the medical expenses. Employers that have agreed to make payments into a benefit fund for an employee, either a medical, health, hospital, pension, or some other fund, must provide for the required payments as agreed.

Termination

Discharged Workers

Discharged workers must be paid in full on the day of discharge or, in Boston, as soon as the laws requiring payrolls, bills, and accounts to be certified have been complied with.

Employees Who Resign

An employee who resigns or quits must be paid in full on the following regular payday or, in the absence of a regular payday, on the following Saturday. Employees absent on payday must be paid on demand.

Wage Statements

An employer must furnish a suitable pay slip, check stub or envelope showing the name of the employer, the surname of the employee, the date, the number of hours worked, the hourly rate, and the amounts of deductions or increases for the pay period.

Employees on piecework must receive notification either while on the job or before the next payroll calculation of the basis for remuneration and the amount of pay earned in addition to any other pay to which he or she may be entitled.

Deductions

Massachusetts stipulates that employers may not withhold, deduct, or divert any part of an employee's pay unless the employer is empowered to do so by state or federal law or the employee has so authorized the employer in writing. Massachusetts specifically excludes withholding of the following from employees' wages:

- Bad checks from customers.
- Improper use of credit cards by customers.
- Customer "walk outs."
- Cash or register shortages.
- Damage or breakage costs.
- Machinery stoppage, unless the workers are allowed to leave the mill while the machinery is being repaired.
- Tardiness, except for the wage that would actually have been earned during the time lost.

Massachusetts law specifies that employers must furnish each employee a suitable pay slip notifying the employee of the amount of each deduction or contribution. New employees must be notified in writing of the nature of deductions and contributions and employees must be notified in writing of any new deductions or contributions.

Wage Assignment and Garnishment

Massachusetts acknowledges that an employer may be required to pay part of an employee's wages to the employee's creditors either through a voluntary wage assignment, a garnishment, or a support order. Employers must make the required payments or be held liable for the debt.

A wage assignment is a written document signed by the employee and given to the creditor, authorizing the creditor to claim part of the employee's wages. Unlike a garnishment, no court order is involved.

Support Orders

An order from the court or a child-support enforcement agency has priority over all other orders of assignment, income withholding, etc. from whatever source and compels an employer to withhold child-support payments from an employee's wages. The Uniform Interstate Family Support Act is in effect in Massachusetts and orders issued in other states may be sent directly to Massachusetts employers without going through the courts. Such orders are treated the same as if they were issued by Massachusetts courts.

When they receive a child-support order, employers must provide a copy to the employee and immediately begin withholding and distributing the funds as directed in the order. Payments are made to the agency designated to receive payments. Employers are directed to withhold and distribute medical support costs for the child, any related costs for the enforcement agency, payments on interest on arrearages, processing fees, etc. If the employee has not enrolled the dependent child in available health-insurance coverage, the employer is empowered to enroll the child in the insurance program.

The income withholding is to begin on the first payment of income that occurs more than three days after the employer is notified of the withholding order and will continue until the employee leaves employment or the employer is notified by the appropriate agency that the withholding should be terminated. Employers are required to submit the required payments of the appropriate agency within three business days of the date the employee is paid.

When an employee is terminated or leaves the employer, the employee is required to notify the subsequent employer of the child-support order and the relevant agency of the new employment. If the employee has no employer, these steps must be taken as soon as employment is gained.

Miscellaneous Deductions

Massachusetts specifies the deductions employers may take from employees for board and lodging. The lodging limits are $30 a week for a one-person room, $25 for a two-person room, and $20 for a three-person room. Employers may deduct $1.00 for breakfast and $1.75 each for lunch and dinner. Written consent of the employee is required before these deductions may be taken. Massachusetts does not allow for any deductions for uniforms or for the cleaning of uniforms.

Hours Worked

For Massachusetts, *working time* includes all time, except meal time, during which an employee is required to be on an employer's premises or to be on duty or to be at the prescribed workplace, and any time worked before or after the normal shift to complete the work. In general, according to Massachusetts law, time spent primarily for the benefit of the employer is compensable, while time spent primarily for the benefit of the employee is not.

Some specific assessments, under Massachusetts law, of whether specific times are to be compensated include the following:

- ♦ **Rest periods.** These are considered primarily for the benefit of the employer and are thus to be compensated.

- ♦ **Meal periods.** A meal period of at least 30 minutes is not compensable if the employee is not required to do any duties during that time.

- ♦ **Medical attention.** Time spent waiting for and receiving medical attention during working hours is compensable.

- ♦ **Physical examinations.** Time spent receiving a required physical examination is compensable.

- ♦ **Travel time.** Time spent on required travel outside of normal hours is compensable and all travel costs must be reimbursed.

- ♦ **On-call time.** As with federal law, if the employee is not free to do as he or she chooses during on-call time, the time is compensable. If the employee only has to leave a telephone or beeper number, the time is not compensable.

- ♦ **Training time.** Generally, attendance at courses, lectures, meetings, and the like is not compensable if attendance is outside of normal hours, is voluntary, and not directly related to the employee's present job.

- ♦ **Attending school.** Even if courses taken at an independent school are relevant to an employee's job, the time spent taking the courses is not compensable if the course are taken on the employee's own initiative.

- **Uniform changing.** Time spent changing into or out of a uniform is compensable only if the changing is required to be done at work.
- **Civil and charitable work.** If an employee is directed by an employer to work for a civic or charitable purpose, the time working is usually considered compensable.

Massachusetts lists the following additional requirements for hours worked:

- Under no circumstances may a non-exempt employee work without pay, not even for a few minutes before punching in.
- Employees who report to work on time as requested must be paid for a minimum of three hours of work, four for employees working in funeral homes, doctors' offices, and other places where emergencies may be expected. This is also true for workers who must be on call for nighttime work.

Overtime Payment

Any employee not exempt under the Massachusetts minimum wage statute who works more than 40 hours in a workweek must be paid for the overtime at one-and-one-half the regular wage. Massachusetts calculates the overtime rate exactly as does the federal law, with overtime required to be paid for each workweek and with hours not actually worked not being counted towards overtime.

Exceptions to Overtime Pay

In addition to the employees excluded from minimum wage provisions listed under **Covered Employees** (salaried executives, administrators, professionals, agricultural workers, workers being rehabilitated or trained, members of religious orders, and outside salespeople), Massachusetts overtime law provisions do not cover the following workers:

- Janitors making less than $30 a week.
- Golf caddies, news carriers, child actors.
- Persons employed in fishing.
- Truck drivers and others covered by the Interstate Commerce Act.
- Workers in seasonal businesses.
- Restaurant, garage, hotel, and amusement park workers.
- Workers in nonprofit schools or colleges.
- Workers in hospitals, sanatoriums, nursing homes, etc.

Regular Rate of Pay

Massachusetts calculates overtime on the employee's regular rate of pay, which is defined exactly as with the federal law—including bonuses and commissions. Massachusetts lists the following exclusions from the regular rate of pay:

- Gifts, including Christmas bonuses.
- Paid leave for vacations, holidays, illnesses, etc.
- Expense reimbursement.

- Discretionary bonuses.
- Benefit plan contributions.
- Premium payments for overtime work.

As with the federal statutes, all overtime work must be compensated, even if unauthorized. Comp time may not be used to make up for overtime work. Massachusetts allows employers to require employees to work overtime and allows them to discipline or terminate employees who refuse to do so. Required overtime must also be compensated at one-and-one-half the regular rate of pay.

Discrimination

As with federal wage-and-hour laws, Massachusetts laws prohibits any sort of discrimination in employment-related decisions. Specifically, the state law precludes sex-related discrimination:

> An employer may not pay lower wages, refuse to hire or employ, bar or discharge from employment or discriminate in terms, conditions or privileges of employment because of the sex of an employee.

Massachusetts wage-and-hour laws also warn against any sort of retaliation against employees because of an income withholding order and specifies that no employee may be discharged because of having been "trusteed" or because he or she has had enforced child-support payments withheld.

Recordkeeping and Posting

Under Massachusetts statutes, employers must keep a record of each employee (name, address, Social Security number, occupation) including hours worked and amount paid each pay period. These records must be kept for two years and be open to inspection by state authorities.

Employers must keep a copy of the Massachusetts minimum fair wage order posted in a conspicuous place in every room where people are employed. Employers must also post a copy, provided by the commissioner, of the wage rate established for the particular occupation in question and any related regulations.

Chapter 10
Employment of Minors

Introduction

Federal and state laws closely regulate the employment of minors, imposing special restrictions on the terms and conditions of their employment. These laws also impose additional administrative duties on employers. If a minor is injured while working illegally, his or her employer may be subject to criminal penalties, civil liability, and a substantial penalty under workers' compensation statutes. Accordingly, it is crucial that employers comply fully with employment-of-minors laws. This chapter reviews the federal laws regarding employment of minors and, where appropriate, looks at the state law in some detail. The following specific areas are treated:

- Prohibited employment.
- Employment restrictions on each age group.
- Limitations on hours minors may work.
- Required recordkeeping and postings.

Federal Laws

Covered Employees

Child labor laws generally cover all employees under age 18. However, minors who satisfy one of the following criteria are not subject to the laws:

- Have a high school diploma or a certificate of attendance or high school equivalence.
- Are heads of households or parents contributing to the support of children.
- Are employed by their parents in occupations not prohibited to minors.
- Are participating in a vocational program approved by the State Department of Education.
- Are employed delivering newspapers, mowing residential lawns, shoveling snow on a casual basis, acting or performing in motion pictures or theatrical productions or in radios or television productions, wreath making, and loading scrap balers or paper box compactors (if certain requirements are met).

Certification and recordkeeping requirements do not apply to minors who perform volunteer work for a nonprofit organization. The FLSA, generally, permits the employment of children under 16 years of age in agricultural work, provided that certain conditions are met. Nevertheless, hazardous agricultural work may not be performed by minors under age 16, except where such minors are enrolled in certain vocational training programs. The rules governing child labor in agricultural occupations allow 14-and 15-year-olds to be employed on farms outside of school hours, except in occupations designated as hazardous.

Prohibited Employment

The Department of Labor has adopted detailed regulations prohibiting the employment of any minor in occupations potentially hazardous or detrimental to the minor's health. (Readers should consult state laws and regulations for additional restrictions).

Work Prohibited to All Minors

No minor can work in any of the following areas:

- Roofing.
- Wrecking and demolition.
- Railroad work.
- Maritime and longshore work.
- Excavation.
- Logging.
- Sawmill work.
- Mining.
- Operating certain dangerous machines.
- Jobs involving manufacture of, storage of, or exposure to explosives or radioactive substances.

Work Prohibited to 14-and 15-Year-Olds

Children ages 14 and 15 are, additionally, prohibited from the following:

- Manufacturing, mining, or processing occupations.
- Occupations involving the operation of hoisting apparatus or power-driven machinery other than office machines.
- The operation of motor vehicles or service as helpers on such vehicles.
- Public messenger service.
- Occupations declared hazardous for minors between 16 and 18 years of age (see above).
- Occupations in connection with the transportation of persons or property; warehousing and storage; communications and public utilities; construction.

Work Prohibited to Children Under 14

Employers may not employ children under 14 unless they are specifically permitted, as detailed under **Covered Employees** above.

Punishment for Violations

A violation of federal regulations concerning prohibited employment of minors subjects an employer to substantial monetary penalties. A violation leading to a serious injury or death of a minor is now punishable by a fine of up to $10,000 under federal law. Additional sanctions may be imposed under state law for violation of state restrictions.

Hours of Employment
Children Under 16
No one under 16 may be employed during school hours except as part of certain vocational training programs. People under 16 may only be employed three hours a day and 18 hours a week when school is in session. They may be employed up to eight hours a day and 40 hours a week when school is not in session. During the school year, people under 16 may not work more than three hours in a day between the hours of 7 a.m. and 7 p.m. During vacations lasting five or more days and from June through August, people under 16 may work until 9 p.m.

Children 16 and 17
Teens aged 16 and 17 are permitted more extended hours. They are prohibited from working:

- Before 7 a.m. Monday through Friday.
- Before 6 a.m. Saturday and Sunday in any week school is in session.
- After 11 p.m. on days before school days.

Required Breaks
No minor may be employed for more than five consecutive hours without a rest period of at least 30 minutes.

Wages
Minors are covered by the minimum wage laws applicable to adults. Overtime compensation should not be a concern since virtually all minors are prohibited from working more than 40 hours a week.

No employer may withhold from a minor's pay any amount due to negligence, breakage, or failure to observe work rules or meet production standards. No employer may demand a deposit or other security from a minor to cover such losses.

Records and Postings
In addition to compliance with recordkeeping and posting obligations imposed by the FLSA, employers should consult with legal counsel to confirm compliance with state law obligations regarding the employment of minors, if applicable.

Massachusetts Law
Massachusetts provides substantial amplification of federal employment-of-minors regulations in Massachusetts Annotated Laws Ch. 149. The following section summarizes the Massachusetts law, with appropriate subsections within Ch. 149 indicated.

Covered Employees
In addition to the federal regulations outlined above, applying to minors under 18, Massachusetts law addresses employment of minors under 21, specifically in regard to work in saloons, barrooms, and "any

Employment of Minors

disorderly house or house of prostitution…" Massachusetts law also addresses children under 12 and children 9 and above in regards to street trades.

Prohibited Employment
Minors Under 21

Massachusetts law (Ch. 149, Sec. 64) forbids employers to employ anyone under 21 in, about, or in connection with any saloon or bar room where alcoholic liquors are sold. Additionally, an employer cannot take or send anyone under 21 to "any disorderly house or house of prostitution or assignation or other immoral place of resort or amusement."

Minors Under 18

Under Massachusetts law (Ch. 149, Sec. 62), no one under 18 can be employed in the following areas or jobs:

- In or about blast furnaces.
- Operating or managing hoisting machines.
- Oiling or cleaning hazardous machinery in motion.
- Operating or using any polishing or buffing wheel.
- Tending railroad switches.
- Tending railroad gates.
- Repairing railroad track.
- As a brakeman, fireman, engineer, motorman, or conductor on a railroad or railway.
- As a fireman or engineer on any vessel.
- Operating motor vehicles of any description except in the course of employment in an automobile repair shop.
- In or about establishments where gunpowder, nitroglycerine, dynamite, or other dangerous explosive is manufactured or compounded.
- Manufacturing white or yellow phosphorus or phosphorus matches.
- In any distillery, brewery, or other establishment where alcoholic beverages are manufactured, packed, wrapped, or bottled.
- In the parts of hotels, theatres, concert halls, places of amusement, or other establishments where intoxicating liquors are sold.
- At 30 feet above ground or water level, as the case may be, or 30 feet above floor level in any room or subdivision of a building.
- In operating or managing any type of elevator.

Minors Under 16

Massachusetts excludes the following types of work or places of work for minors under 16:

- Factories, workshops, manufacturing or mechanical establishments.
- Mercantile establishments, barber shops, bootblack stands, stables (other than of farms).

- Garages, brickyards, lumberyards.
- Telephone exchanges, telegraph or messenger offices.
- Places of amusement.
- Construction or repair of buildings.
- Radio broadcasting stations except as talent.
- Operating and helping to operate any of the following machines:
  - Circular or band saws or silage cutters.
  - Wood shapers.
  - Wood jointers.
  - Planers.
  - Machines used to pick wool, cotton, hair, or other material.
  - Paperlace machines.
  - Leather burnishing machines.
  - Job or printing presses operated by any power other than foot power.
  - Stamping machines used in sheet metal and tinware or in paper or leather manufacturing or in washer and nut factories.
  - Steam boilers.
  - Corrugating rolls such as those used in corrugated paper or in roofing or in washboard factories.
  - Dough brakes or cracker machinery of any description.
  - Wire or iron straightening or drawing machinery.
  - Rolling mill machinery.
  - Power punches or shears.
  - Washing or grinding or mixing machinery.
  - Calendar rolls in paper or rubber manufacturing or other heavy rolls driven by power.
  - Laundering machinery.

Additionally, children under 16 may not do the following:

- Work upon or in connection with any dangerous electrical machinery or appliances.
- Adjust or help adjust any hazardous belt to any machinery.
- Oil or clean hazardous machinery.
- Work near unguarded belts, machinery, or gearing while the machinery is in motion.
- Work on scaffolding.
- Work in the building trades.
- Work in stripping, assorting, manufacturing, or packing tobacco.

- Work in a public bowling alley, pool, or billiard room.
- Work in moving motor vehicles in any capacity.
- Work in any gasoline service establishment except to dispense gas and oil and to provide courtesy service outside the service bay area.

Minors Under 12

Massachusetts excludes children under 12 from selling magazines, periodicals, or other articles of merchandise of any description. This section also prohibits children under 12 from exercising the trade of bootblack or scavenger or any other trade in any street or public place.

Special Prohibitions

Massachusetts allows the Attorney General to determine whether a particular occupation or manufacturing process in which minors are not forbidden by law to work is, in fact, sufficiently dangerous or injurious to the health or morals of minors under 18 to justify minors being excluded. Massachusetts provides an overriding general exclusion which states that no minor under 16 or 18 shall be employed or permitted to work in any trade, process or occupation thus determined to be dangerous or injurious to such minors, respectively.

Exclusions

Massachusetts law provides many exclusions to the employment prohibitions on minors detailed above:

- Children under 16 may take part on the stage for a limited period in a play or musical comedy in a theatre that does not give more than two performances a day nor more than eight performances in a week. The attorney general would have to be satisfied that the supervision of such children is adequate, their living conditions are healthful, and that their education is not being neglected in order for this exception to be approved.
- Children under 15 may participate in fashion shows if they are accompanied by either parent.
- Children from 14 to 16 may voluntarily perform services in a nonprofit hospital after regular school hours and up to 8 p.m. Children aged 13 may perform such voluntary services up to 5 p.m. Children performing volunteer services in a nonprofit hospital must be provided with an orientation by the hospital and be supervised while they perform the services.
- Minors under 16 related by blood or marriage to the owner or operator of the farm where they are employed may work with circular or band saws or ensilage cutters on the farm.
- Minors may be employed in drug stores and retail food stores.
- Minors with a driver's license who are working on a farm may operate any truck, tractor, trailer, or self-propelled agricultural instrument registered by the farmer on the farm or within 10 miles of the farm. If the vehicle is not registered, minors with licenses may operate such a vehicle if the vehicle is used exclusively for agricultural purposes.
- Minors over 14 may operate or help operate small power equipment, such as that used by home gardeners, and they may operate a farm tractor on a farm if they have been certified by the Department of Education as having completed a training program in vocational agriculture.
- The prohibitions prohibiting the employment of minors in certain occupations do not apply to graduates of trade or vocational schools, provided these minors are employed in the occupation they were trained for in school.

- Minors over 16 may work in the occupations excluded above if they are enrolled in a course of study and training in a co-operative vocational training program under a state or local authority. Such minors must be employed under written agreements, and the work must be incidental to their training. Additionally, the work must be intermittent and for short periods, and it must be done under the supervision of a qualified person. The minors must receive safety instruction as part of their on-the-job training.
- Minors nine or older may be employed in the sale or delivery of newspapers if the publisher or distributor of the newspaper provides the minor with written policies regarding the duties and responsibilities of the minor and the employer. The employer must provide a training program for the minor before he or she takes on responsibility for newspaper sales or delivery, and the minor must provide a written statement of permission from a parent or guardian who has reviewed the newspaper's sales and delivery policies.

Note: Under Massachusetts law, before minors under 16 may sell newspapers in a street they must obtain a badge from the appropriate official indicating they have complied with all legal requirements concerning school attendance. The badge may not cost more than 25 cents.

Hours of Employment

Massachusetts lists many exceptions to the hours-of-employment limitations.

Minors Between 16 and 18

The basic Massachusetts law states that a minor under 18 cannot be employed more than nine hours in any one day in a variety of places and occupations, including the following:

- Factory work/workshops.
- Manufacturing, mercantile, mechanical establishments.
- Telegraph, telephone, express, or transportation offices.
- Private clubs.
- Offices, letter shops, financial institutions.
- Laundries, hotels, hairdressers, weight-reducing salons.
- Cinemas, theatres, or other places of amusement.
- Garages.
- Hospitals.
- Elevators.
- Domestic service.

This list also includes farms, radio stations, stables, lumberyards, etc. Basically, the rule covers all occupations or places of employment. Minors under 18 may not work more than six days a week nor more than 48 hours a week. This restriction also applies to nonprofessional workers in nursing or convalescent homes, rest homes, or charitable homes for the aged.

Minors between 16 and 18 are restricted from working before 6 a.m. or after 10 p.m. except for those working in telephone or telegraph offices who may work until 11 p.m. Minors between 16 and 18 may work in restaurants and racetracks until midnight on Fridays and Saturdays and during school vacations,

Employment of Minors

except for the last day of vacation. Minors employed as messengers or delivery-persons for telegraph or telephone companies or messenger companies may begin work at 5 a.m. They may not work after 10 p.m.

Children Under 16

Massachusetts law restricts the employment of children under 16 to no more than eight hours in any one day, six days a week, 48 hours maximum. They may not work before 6 a.m. nor after 7 p.m., except from July 1 through Labor Day, when evening hours may be extended to 9 p.m. If the work performed by a minor under 16 in one day is not continuous but is divided into two or more periods, it must still fall within a nine-hour period.

Note: In addition to the restriction on hours, minors may not be employed in street trades (selling newspapers, etc) during the hours that the public schools in that town are in session. Additionally, minors under 14 are prohibited by Section 56 from working on farms more than four hours a day or 24 hours a week unless they are related by blood or marriage to the owner or operator of the farm.

Exclusions

Massachusetts law provides a complicated series of exclusions to the basic nine-hour, six-day restriction on the employment of minors between 16 and 18:

- In establishments where the attorney general determines the employment to be seasonal, such as hotels and places of amusement, and in situations in which the minor's work is broken up into periods, such as serving meals, the work may be spread over 10 consecutive hours.

- In mercantile establishments the work period may be extended to 11 and one-half hours up to seven days in any one year, of which six must be within the four weeks before Christmas and the seventh the Saturday before Easter.

- In establishments where the principal source of income of some employees is tips, the attorney general may extend the work period to 12 consecutive hours if 60 percent of the employees petition for this in writing.

- In manufacturing establishments or hotels where employment is seasonal, the workweek may extend beyond the usual 48-hour maximum to 52 hours, but only in June, July, August, September, and October. The average number of hours worked per week over a one-year period must not, however, exceed 48.

- The attorney general may grant permission for some office workers to work more than nine hours in any day, but not over 48 hours in a week.

- Minors under 18 may make up time lost on a previous day of the same week if the lost time was the result of the machine on which the person was working stopping for more than 30 minutes. The attorney general must be notified of such stoppage if overtime work results.

- The attorney general may grant authority for employees of hospitals, nursing or convalescent homes, or rest homes and charitable homes to be employed for more than nine hours a day or 48 hours a week in emergency situations.

Meal Periods

Massachusetts stipulates that a person cannot be required to work more than six hours in a day without at least a 30-minute interval for a meal. This requirement does not, however, apply to iron works, paper mills, letterpress establishments, print works, bleaching works, or dyeing works, and other jobs where the continuous nature of the process—or some special consideration such as collective bargaining agreements—makes the exception seem, in the opinion of the attorney general, necessary.

Permits

No Massachusetts employer may employ a child under 16 without obtaining a permit from the superintendent of schools (unless the minor has already been granted such a permit from the superintendent of schools who has determined that it would be better for the child to work). Permits may not be issued to minors under 16 to work in manufacturing or mechanical establishments, factories or workshops.

Massachusetts requires children under 14 who are pupils in co-operative courses in public schools to obtain permits for their co-operative employment, and children between 14 and 16 employed in domestic service or on farms must also secure a permit.

Records

Employers must keep the permits on file, accessible to supervisors of attendance, agents of the Department of Education, and agents of the Department of Labor and Industries, and they must keep a complete list of the names and ages of minors employed. When a minor's employment is terminated the permit must be returned to the office or individual issuing the permit within two days of the termination. Employers who fail to do this are subject to a fine of from $10 to $100.

Postings

Massachusetts requires that everyone employing any minor in a mercantile establishment, barber shop, stable, garage, brick or lumber yard, place of amusement, construction/repair work, telephone or telegraph office, or radio station must post, in a conspicuous place, a printed notice containing the following information:

- The number of hours the minor is permitted to work each day.
- The total hours per week the minor is permitted to work.
- The time work begins and ends.
- The time meal breaks begin and end.

Employing minors during times other than stated on the posted notice is considered a violation, and the posted times cannot be changed after work begins on the first day of the week without the written consent of the attorney general.

Note: Printed forms for lists and notices are available from the attorney general.

This posting requirement provides an exclusion for "employers of persons in domestic service in the employer's home." For other employers the notice must be posted in every room where minors are employed. For employers furnishing public service or in any business in which it is determined that minors must be employed in shifts during different parts of the day, the posted notice must state separately the hours for each shift and the amount of time allowed for meals. Employers must keep a list of the employees, indicating the shift each is employed on, for inspection by enforcing officers.

Exceptions

Cases of extraordinary emergency or public requirement may warrant a variance from the requirements above, but only with a written report of the day, hour, and length of the occurrence demanding a variance.

Chapter 11
Discrimination in Employment

Introduction

Under federal and state anti-discrimination laws, employers may not base adverse employment decisions on the protected status or protected conduct of employees or applicants. Under the federal law portion of this chapter, we describe the various types of prohibited discrimination and protected conduct, outline the penalties associated with losing discrimination claims, consider possible employer defenses against discrimination claims, and suggest ways to avoid discrimination in employment decisions. Under the section on state anti-discrimination law, we review any state laws against specific forms of discrimination.

Federal Law

Although this section is titled *Federal Law* and emphasizes federal statutes against various forms of discrimination, it should be noted that state anti-discrimination laws generally agree with the federal law. Some local laws provide even further protections; for example, against discrimination based on an individual's sexual orientation.

Protected Areas/Protected Status

Federal and state law prohibit discrimination based on the following:

- Race/skin color.
- Sex (including pregnancy).
- National origin and citizenship.
- Religion.
- Age (over 40).
- Disability.
- Military status.

Typical Discrimination Situations

Discrimination claims most frequently arise out of the following situations:

- The application and interview process.
- Failing to hire an applicant.
- Preselecting an employee for a position or promotion.
- Failing to promote an employee.
- Challenges to job qualifications or requirements.
- Terminations or reductions in workforce.
- Sexual harassment.
- Racial harassment.
- Working conditions so difficult and unpleasant that an employee is forced to resign (constructive discharge).
- Performance evaluation and disciplinary measures.

Protected Conduct and Retaliation

In addition to the protected areas or status listed above, the law prohibits employers from retaliating against employees for engaging in *protected conduct*; that is, exercising their rights guaranteed by law. In general, employers are barred from retaliating against an employee for:

- Participating in an investigation or proceeding involving a claim of discrimination, or
- Opposing an unlawful discriminatory practice.

The following are examples of protected conduct:

- Filing a charge of discrimination with the Equal Employment Opportunity Commission (EEOC) or with the state civil rights agency.
- Testifying on behalf of another employee in connection with a charge of discrimination.
- Requesting a reasonable accommodation for a disability.
- Requesting leave under the Family and Medical Leave Act.
- Filing an internal sexual harassment complaint against another employee in good faith.

Types of Discrimination Prohibited

The law forbids two types of discrimination—discriminatory treatment and discriminatory (or disparate) impact.

Discriminatory Treatment

Discriminatory treatment occurs when an individual is treated differently from other applicants or employees who are similarly situated because of that individual's protected status. For example, replacing a 45-year-old employee with an equally qualified 25-year-old would be discriminatory if no legitimate business reason can be shown for the action.

Discriminatory Impact

Discriminatory (or *disparate*) *impact* occurs when an employment policy or practice adversely affects a protected group and no legitimate business reason can be shown for the policy or practice. For example, a minimum height requirement, not necessary for job performance that tends to exclude women and members of certain ethnic groups would be discriminatory. Any job requirement not necessary for effective performance that has a significant and adverse impact on a protected group is unlawful (for example, a high school diploma for custodians).

Laws Prohibiting Discrimination

The following are the major federal anti-discrimination laws:

- **Title VII of the Civil Rights Act of 1964 (Title VII).** Title VII is probably the best known of the federal anti-discrimination laws. It governs the employment practices of most public and private employers, prohibiting employment discrimination based on race, color, religion, sex (including pregnancy), and national origin.

    Title VII applies to private employers and governmental agencies with 15 or more employees for each working day in each of 20 or more calendar weeks in the current or preceding calendar year. Individual supervisors and managers are not considered liable under Title VII and thus cannot be held personally liable for their own discriminatory acts. They may, however, be liable under state law.

- **The Civil Rights Act of 1866 (Section 1981).** The Civil Rights Act of 1866, sometimes known as Section 1981, generally requires equal treatment for all persons without regard to race or color. In some cases, it has been held to prohibit discrimination based on ethnicity or citizenship. It does not apply to discrimination based on sex, religion, age, or disability.

    Section 1981 has generally been interpreted to be consistent with the requirements of Title VII, but there are some differences between the two laws:

    - Unlike Title VII, Section 1981 does not require a charge to be filed with and investigated by the EEOC before a lawsuit can be filed. Employees can immediately pursue their claims against the employer under this statute in federal court.

    - Cases under Section 1981 are not restricted by the short statute of limitations contained in Title VII. Federal courts have held that the statute of limitations for cases under Section 1981 is determined by state law.

    - Compensatory and punitive damages under Section 1981 are not subject to the damage caps of Title VII.

    - Unlike Title VII, which applies only to employers of 15 or more employees, Section 1981 applies to all employers.

- **Americans with Disabilities Act (ADA).** The ADA is a federal law prohibiting employment discrimination against people with disabilities who are able to perform a job with or without reasonable accommodation. The ADA applies to employers with 15 or more employees.

- **Rehabilitation Act of 1973.** The Rehabilitation Act of 1973 is similar to the Americans with Disabilities Act. It applies to all federal agencies and employers doing business under certain federal contracts.

- **Age Discrimination in Employment Act (ADEA).** The ADEA prohibits employment discrimination against people 40 years of age or older. The ADEA prohibits discrimination against those over 40 in favor of younger people and it prohibits discrimination within the over-40 age group. The ADEA applies to private employers with 20 or more employees for each working day in 20 or more consecutive calendar weeks in the current or preceding calendar year. The U.S. Supreme Court has held the ADEA inapplicable to state and local governments.

- **Older Workers' Benefit Protection Act (OWBPA).** The OWBPA amends the ADEA. It gives older workers protection with respect to waiver and release agreements and prohibits discrimination in the administration of employee benefit plans. The OWBPA applies to any benefit plan established or modified after October 16, 1990, (the effective date) for private employers and after October 16, 1992, for governmental employers. It also applies to any conduct of an employer occurring more than 180 days from the effective date.

- **Equal Pay Act (EPA).** The Equal Pay Act is an amendment to the Fair Labor Standards Act that prohibits paying different wages to employees of different sexes who perform equal work under similar conditions.

- **Uniformed Services Employment and Re-employment Rights Act.** This federal statute prohibits employment discrimination against individuals because of their service in the armed forces of the U.S. Leave may be unpaid but cannot affect the employee's right to vacation, sick leave, and other normal benefits. Usually an employee returning from active military service must be restored to the position the employee would have attained had the employment relationship continued without interruption with the appropriate seniority, status, and pay unless business conditions have so changed as to make the employee's being restored to his or her former position impossible. Employers are prohibited from discharging certain re-employed veterans, in the absence of just cause, for up to one year.

Applications

This section considers some of the laws outlined above in more detail, as they apply to specific discriminatory practices.

Racial Discrimination

Discriminatory Treatment

Title VII forbids discrimination on the basic of race and on immutable characteristics—such as skin color—associated with race. Treating an employee less favorably because of his or her race is illegal. Disciplining an African-American differently from Caucasian employees for the same rule violation would be an example of discriminatory or disparate treatment based on race. Title VII also includes a prohibition against discrimination based on association with others of a different race, as in an interracial marriage.

Racial Harassment

Employers are prohibited from engaging in racially motivated harassment or from tolerating a racially hostile work environment. Hostile environment harassment occurs when unwelcome, severe, and repeated racial comments or acts unreasonably interfere with an individual's job performance or create an intimidating, hostile, or offensive working environment. A racially hostile environment can be created when a group of employees tells racial jokes and refers to employees of other racial groups in racially derogatory terms. In such situations, a few key points should be noted:

- The intent of the harasser does not matter—the test for harassment is from the viewpoint of a reasonable person.

- Employers will generally be liable for the acts of their employees if the employers knew or should have known that such acts occurred.

- Hostile environment harassment must be severe and pervasive. One incident is unlikely to create liability.

Disparate Impact

Certain employment practices can have a disparate impact on minority applicants and employees and lead to disparate-impact discrimination claims. The following are examples of such practices:

- Requiring employees to be clean-shaven. Some African-American men suffer from a skin condition called *pseudo-folliculitis barbae,* which is aggravated by daily shaving. Employers should make accommodations for employees with this condition, unless a beard interferes with an employee's use of a respirator required by the job.

- Rejecting applicants on the basis of arrest records rather than conviction records. Minorities may be more likely to be arrested than whites, and an arrest does not prove an individual committed a crime.

- Using aptitude or intelligence tests unrelated to job skills. Tests have been challenged on the grounds that members of some racial groups consistently perform worse on them than members of other racial groups.

- Requiring a high school diploma when this level of education is not necessary to perform a job.

Reverse Discrimination

Reverse discrimination is a term used to describe a situation in which a majority group member, such as a white individual, receives less-favorable treatment than a member of a minority group because of that individual's race. Title VII also protects whites from discrimination based on race and men are protected from discrimination based on sex.

National Origin Discrimination

Title VII prohibits discrimination on the basis of national origin. This prohibition also includes discrimination on the basis of characteristics associated with national origin such as the following:

- Marriage to a person of a particular national origin.

- Participation in organizations identified with a particular national origin.

- Having a name associated with a particular national origin.

Section 1981 of the Civil Rights Act of 1866 does not explicitly prohibit national origin discrimination, but the Supreme Court has held that the law prohibits discrimination based on ancestry or ethnic characteristics. These need not be physical characteristics. For example, the Supreme Court has held that an individual of Arabian ancestry could bring a discrimination claim under Section 1981 if he could show discrimination based upon the fact that he was born an Arab.

English-only Rules

The EEOC has held that English-only rules are presumed to violate Title VII when they require that English be spoken at all times in the workplace. Employers may, however, adopt rules requiring English in situations where they can show that the rule is justified by business necessity, such as where safety is a concern or because the job requires communication with the public. Employers must notify applicants and employees of an English-only policy.

Harassment

Employers may be open to charges of discrimination if they allow their employees to direct ethnic slurs at other employees and fail to take disciplinary action against those who are making the ethnic comments, thus creating a hostile work environment.

Religious Discrimination

It is illegal for employers to discriminate against applicants or employees because of their religion. For purposes of this law, *religion* includes religious observance and practice as well as belief. It also includes individual moral and ethical beliefs sincerely held with the strength of traditional religious views.

Employers must make reasonable accommodations for the religious beliefs of their employees unless an accommodation would cause undue hardship on the employer. Factors such as the size of the company, the nature of the employee's job, the feasibility of transferring job duties or changing work schedules, and the amount of employee cooperation affect the reasonableness of an accommodation.

Some reasonable accommodations and limits on accommodations might be the following:

- Whenever possible, an employer should try to accommodate an employee's request to take time off for religious holidays. This could be done by allowing the employee to use vacation time, a day off without pay, using "floating holidays," or allowing employees to swap shifts.

- An employer should try to accommodate an employee's scheduling needs for certain days or shifts to accommodate the employee's religious practices or beliefs. This could be done by having a flexible work schedule or by allowing employees to swap shifts. However, employers are not required to accommodate a scheduling request if the change would conflict with a seniority system established in a collective bargaining agreement. An employer also is not required to make accommodations that would involve more than minimal cost, such as by hiring another employee or paying premium wages to other employees as substitutes.

- An employer should try to accommodate an employee's religious practices with respect to the way the employee dresses. However, the employer need not do this if the particular mode of dress would create a safety hazard. For example, an employer could ban loose clothing around machinery or require employees to be clean-shaven if their job requires the use of a respirator. An employer may also enforce dress and grooming policies for employees whose jobs require extensive contact with the public.

Note: Employers do not have to accommodate religious beliefs until employees have requested such accommodation. Employees have no right to a particular type of accommodation; employers may offer reasonable accommodations different from what the employees propose.

Sex Discrimination

Employers are prohibited from discriminating against applicants and employees on the basis of sex. For example, female employees must be treated the same as male employees for disciplinary purposes. Title VII also protects males from discrimination based on sex; that is, reverse discrimination—a situation in which a male employee, because of his sex, receives less-favorable treatment than a female employee.

Sexual Orientation

Title VII does not protect individuals from discrimination based on their sexual orientation and courts have refused to recognize these claims. Some state and local laws, however, prohibit such discrimination and employers should find out if such laws exist and if so whether the laws apply to them.

Sexual Harassment

Sexual harassment is one of the most familiar aspects of Title VII's prohibition against sex discrimination. It is also one of the most frequently litigated areas. Although sexual harassment is not specifically mentioned in the Civil Rights Act of 1964 (that is, Title VII) or its legislative history, it is now a complex and often misunderstood—but thoroughly established—cause of action under sex discrimination law.

Definition

The EEOC defines *sexual harassment* as unwelcome sexual advances, requests for sexual favors, and other verbal or physical conduct of a sexual nature constitute sexual harassment when:

- Submission to such conduct is made either explicitly or implicitly a term or condition of an individual's employment, or

- Submission to or rejection of such conduct by an individual is used as the basis for employment decisions affecting the individual, or

- Such conduct has the purpose or effect of unreasonably interfering with an individual's work performance or creating an intimidating, hostile, or offensive working environment.

Courts have traditionally recognized two general types of sexual harassment:

- Quid-pro-quo harassment.
- Hostile environment harassment.

Employer Liability

The Supreme Court has established the standard for employer liability for sexual harassment by supervisors. For purposes of liability for sexual harassment, a *supervisor* for whose acts an employer may be held liable is an individual who has the authority to recommend tangible employment decisions affecting the employee or someone who has the authority to direct the employee's daily work activities. The Supreme Court reached the following decisions for employer liability:

- Employers without disseminated sexual-harassment policies and complaint procedures will be automatically or "vicariously" liable for harassing conduct of supervisors regardless of whether the harassment is of the quid pro quo or the hostile-environment variety.

- Employers will be vicariously liable for sexual harassment by supervisors, regardless of the existence of a sexual-harassment policy, if the harassment results in a "tangible employment action." The court defines *tangible employment action* as "a significant change in employment status, such as hiring, firing, failing to promote, reassignment with significantly different responsibilities, or a decision causing a significant change in benefits."

- For purposes of imposing liability on an employer, the traditional sexual harassment categories are less important than whether or not the harassment by the supervisor results in a tangible employment action. If it does, the employer is vicariously liable. If it does not, an affirmative defense—described later in this chapter under **Employer Defenses Against Discrimination Charges**—is available.

- Employers are liable for sexual harassment by non-supervisors—for example co-workers, customers, vendors, independent contractors, etc.—based on a negligence standard that applies if the employer knew or should have known of the harassment and failed to take corrective action.

♦ Employers with a disseminated sexual harassment policy containing clearly outlined complaint procedures may not be liable if an employee claiming sexual harassment, but suffering no tangible job detriment, unreasonably failed to make use of the existing policy.

Same-sex Harassment

The Supreme Court has held that same-sex harassment claims—in which an employee claims harassment by another employee of the same sex—are actionable under Title VII. The court reasoned that harassing conduct need not be motivated by sexual desire. As in all sexual harassment cases, however, an individual claiming same-sex harassment must show that the behavior was severe and pervasive and was offensive to a reasonable person in the particular context where it occurred.

Courts have defined sexual harassment very broadly to include conduct that is discriminatory based on the victim's gender. A manager's demeaning or otherwise mistreating persons of one gender but not the other could be considered sexual harassment even if no sexual misconduct is involved. The EEOC has released the document *Guidance on Vicarious Employer Liability for Unlawful Harassment by Supervisors* that says it applies not only to sexual harassment but also to other forms of unlawful harassment, including harassment based on race, color, religion, national origin, age, disability, or protected activity.

Pregnancy Discrimination

The Pregnancy Discrimination Act of 1978 (PDA), an amendment to Title VII, prohibits discrimination because of pregnancy, childbirth, or related medical conditions. For the most part, women incapacitated by pregnancy, childbirth, or medical conditions related to pregnancy or childbirth must be treated the same as individuals incapacitated by other disabilities, including receiving benefits and being allowed to perform "light-duty" work.

Employer policies, including general leave policies, must be applied the same way to pregnant employees as they are to other employees requiring leave because of a temporary disability. Requiring an employee to be employed for at least six months before becoming eligible for leave, if applied equally to all employees, has been found not to discriminate against pregnant women. The FMLA, however, may require granting a leave.

Pregnant employees must be allowed to work until they are medically unable to do so. Employers who pressure pregnant employees to begin leave before leave is medically necessary are liable for unlawful discrimination.

Employers may not use pregnancy or maternity leave as an excuse for terminating employment. If some legitimate business necessity, such as a business downturn, causes the position of a pregnant woman or of a woman on maternity leave to be eliminated, an employer is justified in discharging the woman or refusing to reinstate her at the end of her leave. This would be one instance in which an employer could lawfully discharge such an employee. If an employer has been tolerating poor performance or poor attitude from an employee and then fires her when she takes pregnancy leave, discrimination could be found. If the employer would have continued to accept the poor performance or poor attitude and would not have fired the employee had she not taken leave, the pregnancy leave was the impermissible factor leading to the discharge.

Age Discrimination

The ADEA sets forth a number of specific prohibited practices. The act is supplemented by the Older Workers Benefit Protection Act.

Hiring/Firing

An employer cannot refuse to hire, cannot discharge, or otherwise discriminate regarding compensation, terms, conditions, or privileges of employment against any individual 40 years of age or over because of the individual's age. Although this law protects individuals over 40 from being treated differently, an important consideration in determining if age discrimination exists is the actual disparity in ages. If a 55-year-old employee is replaced by a 40-year-old one, discrimination may well be found. If, on the other hand, a 60-year-old employee is replaced by an employee 55 or so, there is less likely to be a finding of discrimination. This would be true even though the ADEA prohibits discrimination within the over-40 group.

The ADEA prohibits limiting or classifying employees over 40 in any way that might deprive them of employment opportunities or affect their employment status.

Exceptions: In some circumstances, employers are allowed to consider age:

- In situations where age preference is necessary in the operation of a business, employers may claim a BFOQ (bona fide occupational qualification).
- Age can be considered in following a bona fide seniority system or benefits plan.
- Job requirements that may affect employees over 40 may be set as long as they are based on some factor other than age, such as a physical requirement for doing a job.

Advertising

The ADEA also prohibits the use of employment advertising that in any way discriminates against older individuals or indicates a preference based on age. This prohibition does not only apply to advertisements that state an age below 40 for potential candidates but to any indication of a preference for one age group over the group protected by the act. Examples of prohibited phrasings include the following:

- "Recent college graduates" should be simply "college graduates."
- "Young professional."
- "Age 50 or over"—this discriminates against those 40 to 49 in the protected group.

Mandatory or Involuntary Retirement

The act forbids mandatory or involuntary retirement except for certain military personnel and executives who meet the following criteria:

- They have been in executive or high policy-making positions for at least the two years before their retirement.
- They are at least 65 years old at the time of retirement.
- They must be entitled to an immediate, non-forfeitable annual retirement income of $44,000.

Benefits

Employers may not use age as a basis for discontinuing contribution or, accrual of retirement benefits or, for reducing the rate of contribution or, accrual under a retirement plan. However, a plan is lawful if it limits the total contribution or benefits or number of years of service, provided those limits are not based upon age. A retirement plan may require participation for at least five years for benefit eligibility but cannot exclude participation because an employee is too old.

The Older Workers Benefit Protection Act amends the ADEA to further protect older workers' benefits.

The OWBPA allows for the following:
- The actual amount of the benefits paid or the cost incurred by the employer for benefits provided to older workers may not be less than that paid or incurred on behalf of younger workers.
- When implementing a reduction in force, limited "voluntary early-retirement incentive plans" targeting older workers meeting age and service requirements are permitted in the following circumstances:
  - The plan is created for legitimate business reasons.
  - The plan is accurately presented to employees without intimidation.
  - The employee is given at least 45 days to consider the plan.
- Set-offs for severance pay for pension benefits received by older workers upon termination are allowed.

Waiver of Rights

Under certain circumstances, laid down by the OWBPA, older workers may waive their rights under the ADEA if they do so knowingly and voluntarily. Minimum standards for such a waiver are the following:

- The agreement must be in writing and understandable to the average person.
- The agreement must specifically refer to ADEA rights or claims arising under the ADEA.
- The employee must be given a benefit, such as a sum of money, which would otherwise not be made available to the employee in return for the employee's waiver of ADEA rights.
- The employee must be given 21 days to consider the agreement before signing (45 days in cases of group termination).
- The employee must be advised in writing to seek the advice of an attorney before signing the agreement.
- The agreement must provide for a seven-day period after signing during which the employee may revoke the agreement.
- Information regarding selection criteria and employees affected must be provided to those who are discharged in a group termination.

Enforcement

The Equal Employment Opportunity Commission enforces federal anti-discrimination laws. In cases where a discrimination charge is proceeding simultaneously at the state and federal levels, the EEOC must defer its investigation for at least 60 days to allow the state agency to pursue its case. The EEOC is not bound by the state's findings but generally gives them strong weight.

Discrimination Complaint Procedure

A discrimination charge must be filed within 180 days of the alleged wrongful acts. The filing period is extended to 300 days for charges filed with a state fair-employment agency.

EEOC Investigations

After its investigation, the EEOC determines whether there is probable cause to support the charge of discrimination. The following are the possible results of the EEOC investigation:

- The EEOC may find probable cause. In this case, it must attempt to conciliate the charge, to reach a voluntary agreement with the employer to remedy the charge of discrimination. If conciliation is unsuccessful, the EEOC must either sue in federal court or issue a right-to-sue letter allowing the individual to sue the employer in federal court.

- If the EEOC finds no probable cause, it will dismiss the charge and issue a right-to-sue letter allowing the employee to sue the employer in court.

- The employee may request a right-to-sue letter before the EEOC has completed the investigation.

After receiving a right-to-sue letter the employee has 90 days in which to sue in federal court. The employee may request a jury trial, creating more liability risk for employers.

Remedies

Employees who win their discrimination suits are entitled to various remedies, including the following:

- Compensatory and punitive damages.
- Backpay and benefits.
- Being hired, reinstated, promoted, or upgraded.
- Front pay (in cases where the employee is not reinstated).
- Liquidated damages if the discrimination was intentional (under the Equal Pay Act or the ADEA).
- Interest on back wages.
- Attorneys' fees and costs.
- Cease and desist orders.
- Affirmative action by the employer to correct discriminatory practices.
- Posting of compliance notices.

Damage Caps

Federal law limits compensatory and punitive damages by the size of the employer, as follows:

- $50,000 for employers with between 15 and 100 employees.
- $100,000 for employers with between 101 and 200 employees.
- $200,000 for employers with between 201 and 500 employees.
- $300,000 for employers with more than 500 employees.

Employer Defenses Against Discrimination Charges

The best defense employers have against discrimination claims is to show that there is a legitimate business reason for taking the disputed employment action. In some cases, in fact, a legitimate business reason defense is valid even when there has been intentional discriminatory treatment of a protected group or when employment practices had an adverse impact on members of a protected group. Examples of valid defenses of this type include the following:

- **Bona fide Occupational Qualifications**—Employers are not liable for intentional discrimination on the basis of sex, religion, national origin, or age if the discrimination is the result of a BFOQ. A BFOQ is a specific job requirement for a particular position reasonably necessary to the normal operation of the business. For example, sex-based BFOQs may be recognized for some attendant jobs in prisons or mental institutions. Sex-based BFOQs have, however, been rejected as a hiring basis for nursing home aides.

- **Business Necessity**—Employers may defend against disparate-impact claims on the basis that the practice that led to the discriminatory impact was job related and consistent with business necessity. This protection will not work, however, if an employer knows of but does not use a different available practice that would accomplish the same result without being discriminatory.

- **Bona fide Seniority or Merit Systems**—Title VII permits employment practices based upon a legitimate seniority or merit system even if the practice adversely affects members of a protected group. The purpose of the practice must be to reward employees for such things as longevity or merit, not to discriminate. A seniority system that protects more senior employees in the event of layoffs at the expense of employees from protected groups would be an example of this type of practice.

In all cases, defenses against discrimination claims must be supported by appropriate documentation showing, for example, that an employment action on which a claim of discriminatory or disparate treatment was based was taken for a legitimate business reason and not a pretext for discrimination. In discriminatory impact cases the employee must prove disparate impact by producing relevant statistics showing the effects of the employer's business practice. In disparate impact claims, it need not be proven that the discrimination was intentional, just that it occurred.

Defenses Against Sexual-harassment Claims

Because of the serious implications of sexual-harassment claims, employers would be wise to follow the EEOC's suggested procedures for avoiding sexual harassment in the workplace. The suggestions below will help you comply with EEOC guidelines for avoiding charges of sexual harassment. They will also help you avoid charges of any form of harassment in the workplace.

- **Develop, implement, publicize, and distribute an anti-harassment policy.** This policy should do the following:

  - Prohibit **any** form of harassment in the workplace, but especially sexual harassment.

  - Encourage employees to report any unwelcome sexual conduct or other forms of sexual harassment, or other harassment.

  - Specify clear ways for employees to voice complaints—ideally to someone other than their immediate supervisors—about possible harassment.

  - Assure employees of a prompt and effective investigation.

  - Assure employees that retaliation for voicing a complaint will not be tolerated.

- **Educate and sensitize the work force about sexual harassment issues**:

  - Remind employees about the anti-harassment policy.

  - Advise employees that those who violate the anti-harassment policy will be subject to corrective action.

  - Warn employees that certain kinds of conduct (jokes, touching) may be viewed as harassment.

  - Train supervisors to recognize and respond to observed problems and to handle harassment complaints properly.

♦ **Develop and implement a fair and effective procedure for thoroughly investigating all complaints of harassment.** Assign responsibility for investigating harassment complaints to individuals who are trained to be objective, thorough, and sensitive to the concerns of the victim, the alleged harasser, and the witnesses.

Prompt and adequate investigations are critical in preventing or minimizing liability for harassment. Various interests must be considered:

- The interest of the complainant in not having to endure unwelcome conduct at work.
- The interest of the alleged harasser in not losing a job or reputation on the basis of an accusation that turns out to be mistaken, false, or trivial.
- The interest of other employees who may have witnessed harassment or may be exposed to harassment in the future.

Guidelines for Investigating a Harassment Complaint:

- Interview the Complainant:

  After reassuring the complainant of protection for reporting the harassment, and of the company's commitment to take appropriate action, and of the company's intention to maintain confidentiality as much as possible, the investigator should obtain from the complainant the following information:

  - A complete description of all offensive conduct.
  - A list of all potential witnesses.
  - A detailed chronology of incidents.
  - Any allegations of retaliatory conduct by the alleged harasser.

- Interview the Alleged Harasser:

  Employers should inform the alleged harasser of the company's duty to investigate and of the alleged harasser's corresponding duty to cooperate fully and truthfully with the investigation. The alleged harasser should be warned against retaliation. The alleged harasser also may be entitled to have a co-worker present during the interview if a proper request is made, and the employee has reason to believe the investigative interview may result in discipline. Investigation of the alleged harasser should obtain the following:

  - A detailed response to each charge.
  - Information on whether the complainant may have a motive to fabricate or exaggerate the charges.

- Interview the Witnesses:

  Employers should question potential witnesses without identifying the complainant or the alleged harasser except to the extent necessary to frame an understandable inquiry. The witnesses should be reminded of the need to keep the investigation confidential.

- Conclude the Investigation:

  When the investigation is complete, you should reach one of three conclusions:

  - **Misconduct occurred.** In these cases employers must ensure that any discipline imposed is severe enough to satisfy the legal duty to take effective remedial action. The employer must also consider the harasser's rights under any employment contract, employment discrimination statute, or common law principles that protect privacy and reputations. Note that it is often possible to conclude that the company's anti-harassment policy has been violated and that discipline is appropriate without concluding that unlawful harassment has occurred. Many companies forbid, for example, even isolated or ambiguous conduct that may give the appearance of unlawful harassment.

- **Misconduct did not occur.** In cases where the investigator concludes that no harassment occurred—either because the alleged incident did not occur, the allegedly unwelcome incidents were actually welcome, or because the incidents were actually harmless and could not reasonably be interpreted as harassment—the parties should still be informed of the results of the investigation. The complainant and the alleged harasser should be reminded of the importance of keeping the investigation confidential and about the company's policy against retaliation for making reports of harassment.

- **Results are inconclusive.** There is insufficient evidence to reach a conclusion. In such cases both parties should be told of the results, why no conclusion could be reached, and be reminded of the company's no-retaliation policy.

In all cases, you should reinforce the employer's prohibition of harassment with all involved.

- **Take prompt remedial action when necessary:**
  - Determine what corrective action is necessary, if any, to end the harassing conduct.
  - Discipline the harasser as appropriate.
  - Report results of the investigation to the complainant, including the steps taken to prevent further harassment, if applicable.
  - Assure the complainant that no retaliation for making the complaint will be tolerated.
- **Follow up on your investigation to prevent retaliation.**
- **Document all steps taken in response to the complaint.**

Recordkeeping and Reporting Requirements
Recordkeeping

Employers covered by federal anti-discrimination laws must keep for at least one year from the date they were made, personnel and employment records concerning the following:

- Hirings.
- Promotions.
- Demotions.
- Transfers.
- Layoffs.
- Terminations.

- Rates of pay.
- Selections for training and apprenticeship programs.

Covered employers are generally advised to keep such records for six years or more.

Note: Discrimination and retaliation issues arising under other than Equal Employment Opportunity statutes are addressed in chapters dealing with those laws.

Reporting

Employer Information Report—EEO-1

The EEOC requires all employers with more than 100 employees, private employers with fewer than 100 employees who are owned by or affiliated with another company to make up an enterprise totaling 100 or more employees, and most federal contractors to annually file an Employer Information Report known as the EEO-1. This report must include statistical information about the number of minority-group employees in the total workforce. Employers must keep the latest copy of the report and make it available to an EEOC representative upon request.

Employer Information Reports—EEO-4, EEO-5, EEO-6

Public employers with more than 15 employees must file an Employer Information Report EEO-4 annually. Public school systems or districts must file an EEO-5 report biannually, and all public or private institutions of higher learning must file an EEO-6 report biannually. The requirements for these reports are similar to those for Employer Information Report EEO-1. Forms for these reports are available from the EEOC's Washington, D.C. office: (202) 663-4900. For more information, contact EEOC at www.eeoc.gov.

Massachusetts Law

Massachusetts provides a substantial number of laws to supplement the federal laws against discrimination. It also provides an extensive glossary of terms basic to the interpretation of the laws. The Massachusetts law does not apply to individuals employed by their parents, spouses, or children nor individuals employed in domestic service. It does not cover employers with fewer than six employees and it does not cover social or fraternal clubs, associations, or corporations, if such club, association or corporation is not organized for private profit.

General Prohibition Against Discrimination

Massachusetts law provides one basic overriding prohibition against discrimination. Employers and their agents cannot refuse to hire or employ nor may they bar or discharge from employment or discriminate against in compensation or terms and conditions of employment any individuals based on any of the following considerations, unless the employment action is based on a bona-fide occupational qualification:

- Race or color.
- National origin or ancestry.
- Religion or creed.
- Sex or sexual orientation (unless the individual's sexual orientation involves minor children as the sexual object).

- Disability.
- Age.
- Arrest, detention, or disposition record not resulting in conviction.
- Mental illness.

Massachusetts law also forbids any form of advertising or employment inquiries that directly or indirectly express any limitation, specification, or discrimination based on any of the protected areas listed above.

The Massachusetts law also contains the provision that the requirements to avoid discrimination in the areas above do not suggest a corresponding requirement to grant preferential treatment to any individual or group in any of the protected categories listed above because of an imbalance in an employer's workforce.

Equal Rights Act

Massachusetts provides the following summary Equal Rights Act to preclude several forms of discrimination:

> All persons within the commonwealth, regardless of sex, race, color, creed or national origin, shall have, except as is otherwise provided or permitted by law, the same rights enjoyed by white male citizens, to make and enforce contracts, to inherit, purchase, to lease, sell, hold and convey real and personal property, to sue, be parties, give evidence, and to the full and equal benefit of all laws and proceedings for the security of persons and property, and shall be subject to like punishment, pains, penalties, taxes, licenses, and exactions of every kind, and to no other.

The same provisions are specifically provided for the elderly and the disabled under a separate equal rights act.

Religious Discrimination

Massachusetts prohibits employers from requiring employees to do anything that violates their creed or religion in order to obtain or retain employment. Employers must make reasonable accommodations for the religious needs of employees, including their observance of the Sabbath or holy days and reasonable travel time for religious occurrences. *Reasonable accommodation* here means accommodation that would not cause undue hardship for the employer. Situations where the health or safety of the public would be jeopardized by an employee's absence, where the employer could not provide services required by law, where the employee's presence is essential to the orderly transaction of business, or where emergency conditions exist are considered to place undue hardship on the employer.

Massachusetts law requires employees to give 10 days notice for absences for religious purposes and stipulates that the time must be made up at some mutually convenient time if at all possible. Employers do not need to pay employees for time taken for religious observance. If required, employees must provide proof of the need to take time off from work for religious purposes.

For purposes of this section, Massachusetts defines *creed* or *religion* to mean any sincerely held religious beliefs. They do not need to be the familiar, approved, and established beliefs of traditional churches and other religious institutions or organizations.

Massachusetts excludes from this aspect of the anti-discrimination law religious or denominational institutions or organizations operated by religious institutions. These entities may give preference in hiring and in other employment decisions to members of the same religion.

Sex Discrimination/Sexual Harassment

Massachusetts law provides for the same general protections for equal treatment of the sexes as does federal law:

> No employer shall discriminate in any way in the payment of wages as between the sexes, or pay any person in his employ salary or wage rates less than the rates paid to employees of the opposite sex for work of like or comparable character or work on like or comparable operations.

Salary differences based on seniority are, however, prohibited. Violators of this provision are subject to unpaid wages and liquidated damages plus attorneys' fees and court costs.

Note: With the one exception noted—sexual orientation involving minor children—Massachusetts law, unlike federal law, prohibits discrimination based on an individual's sexual orientation as well as on the individual's sex.

Massachusetts law requires all employers, employment agencies, and labor organizations to promote "a workplace free of sexual harassment." According to the law this can be achieved if employers establish an appropriate policy against sexual harassment containing the following:

- A definition of sexual harassment.
- Examples of sexual harassment.
- A statement indicating that sexual harassment in the workplace is unlawful.
- A statement that it is unlawful to retaliate against an employee for filing a sexual-harassment complaint or for cooperating in a sexual-harassment investigation.
- A statement of the consequences of violating the sexual-harassment policy.
- A description of the process for filing internal sexual-harassment complaints, including the work addresses and telephone numbers of the people to whom to complain.
- The identity of state and federal employment discrimination enforcement agencies and information on how to contact these agencies.

Employers must distribute a written version of this policy annually to all employees and to each new employee at the beginning of employment. The Massachusetts Commission Against Discrimination provides a model policy and supporting posters to help employers comply with this law.

The Massachusetts law warns that compliance with this law in and of itself will not protect an employer from liability for sexual harassment of any current or former employee or applicant. Failure to comply will not automatically make an employer liable in actions alleging sexual harassment).

Massachusetts further states that employers and labor organizations are encouraged to conduct education and training programs for new employees and members. These training programs should include at least the information required to be in employers' sexual-harassment policies. Supervisors and managers should, according to the Massachusetts law, receive additional training, covering—in addition to the basic sexual-harassment policy information—the specific responsibilities of supervisors and managers and the methods they should take to address sexual-harassment complaints.

Discrimination Based on Disability

Massachusetts prohibits discrimination against qualified handicapped persons capable of performing the essential functions of a position with reasonable accommodation, unless the employer can prove an undue hardship. Factors to be considered in determining whether an undue hardship would be imposed include the following:

- The overall size of the employer's business.
- The type of operation involved.
- The nature and cost of the accommodation needed.

The law requires that the physical and mental job-qualifications listed be functionally related to the specific job. Employers may not make pre-employment inquiries about the existence or severity of a handicap.

Age Discrimination

Massachusetts law precludes basing any employment decision—hiring, firing, compensating, etc—on an individual's age, unless the decision is based on a bona fide occupational qualification. The Massachusetts prohibitions against age discrimination do not apply to farm laborers.

Requiring the compulsory retirement of individuals over 65 who have been employed in executive positions for at least the two preceding years is not unlawful if these individuals are eligible for retirement benefits of at least $44,000. Individuals working at independent institutions of higher learning may be required to retire at 70.

Discrimination Based on Criminal or Mental Health Records

Under Massachusetts law employers cannot discriminate against individuals based on their arrest records in cases which did not result in conviction. Employers may also not discriminate against individuals with a first conviction for any of the following: drunkenness, simple assault, speeding, minor traffic violations, affray or disturbing the peace. Additionally, individuals whose conviction or completion of a period of incarceration occurred more than five years before the date of application for employment may not be discriminated against based on their previous record.

Individuals who have been discharged from any facility for the treatment of the mentally ill and who have certification that they are mentally competent to perform the jobs for which they are applying may not be discriminated against.

Prohibitions Against Retaliation

The Massachusetts law provides for penalties for employers who retaliate against employees who make claims under any of the discrimination laws or against employees who testify in any investigations into alleged discriminatory behavior of the employer.

Recordkeeping and Reporting

All employers, employment agencies, and labor organizations must make and keep records relating to race, color, and national origin to show compliance with the law. Massachusetts specifies that any federal recordkeeping requirements must also be adhered to. Massachusetts employers must also keep records of the age of all employees and provide these records to the commissioner or a representative when required. A fine of from $25 to $100 is provided for each day of failure to keep these records or of failure to furnish requested copies of them.

Chapter 12
Immigration

Introduction

Under legislation and rules issued by the federal Immigration and Naturalization Service (INS), employers may legally hire workers only if they are citizens of the U.S. or aliens authorized to work in the U.S. This chapter addresses the federal rules that govern documentation of eligible employees, anti-discrimination enforcement and aliens, and temporary and permanent employment of foreign nationals.

Documentation Requirements

All employers are required to verify the employment eligibility of individuals hired after November 6, 1986. Employers must require applicants to show proof of their employment eligibility and complete the required I-9 Form (Section I must be completed when the employee begins work and Section II must be completed no later than the hired day of employment.) The employer must then examine the appropriate documentation establishing the identity and employment eligibility of each new hire and must so indicate on the form. Forms for all current employees (other than those employed on or prior to November 6, 1986) must be kept on file and made available for inspection by government officials. The employer may dispose of I-9 Forms relating to terminated employees, after the longer of:

- Three years from the date of hire.
- One year after employment of the individual has ended. One way of avoiding problems with this confusing rule is to keep all Forms I-9 until three years after an employee has been terminated.

Employer penalties range from $100 to $11,000 for each employee for which the I-9 Form is not properly completed, retained, or made available for inspection. An employer who engages in a practice of hiring illegal foreign nationals may also be subject to imprisonment for up to six months. The INS is authorized to enforce the requirements on employment eligibility verification.

Anti-discrimination Enforcement

The Department of Justice's Office of Special Counsel and the INS are authorized to enforce the anti-discrimination provisions of the law. Employers with three or more employees are prohibited from discriminating in hiring or promoting on the basis of national origin citizenship status. The responsibility for investigating and prosecuting claims of discrimination resides with the Department of Justice. An employer may be required to hire, promote, reinstate, pay back salary, and/or attorneys' fees to a successful discrimination complainant. In addition, the employer may be assessed a civil penalty of up to $11,000 per offense. These enforcement efforts are generally paired with Office of Federal Contract Compliance Program or Wage and Hour Division inspections.

Temporary Employment of Non-U.S. Citizens

H-1B (Non-immigrants, Temporary Workers, or Trainees)

Primarily, the H-1B visa provides temporary admission to the U.S. for aliens who are professionals in specialty occupations.

H-1B non-immigrant visas are limited to employees in specialty occupations who are coming to the U.S. temporarily. A *specialty occupation* is an occupation that requires theoretical and practical application of a body of highly specialized knowledge and at least a bachelor's degree in the specific specialty as a minimum for entry into the occupation. For example, in 1999 there was an increased demand by employers for H-1B professionals to assist with Year 2000 (Y2K) issues.

The H1-B visa will be granted for an initial term of three years and can be renewed for an additional three years. An H1-B alien does not have to maintain a separate residence abroad during his or her temporary stay in the U.S. Employers are required to offer benefits to H1-B employees on the same basis as similarly employed U.S. workers.

The American Competitiveness in the Twenty-First Century Act, signed into law in late 2000, increased the number of H1-B visas available. For the three fiscal years below (a fiscal year begins on October 1 and ends on the following September 30), the H1-B visas availability was and will be:

- 2001—195,000
- 2002—195,000
- 2003—195,000

Only 65,000 H1-B visas per year will be available for fiscal years 2004 and beyond.

Before filing the *H-1B Non-immigrant Visa Petition* employers will need to file a *Labor Condition Application* with the Department of Labor that certifies the following:

- The employer is offering the position at the higher of the actual wage or the prevailing wage and with working conditions that will not adversely affect similarly employed U.S. workers.
- There is not a strike or lockout involving the position at the place of employment.
- The employer has provided notice of the petition to any bargaining representative or has posted notice of the petition in conspicuous locations at the place of employment if there is no bargaining representative.

The Department of Labor (DOL) has established procedures for receipt, investigation, and disposition of complaints filed by injured persons or organizations. If the DOL finds the complaints to be justified, it may sanction the employer in the following ways:

- Impose a civil monetary fine of $1,000.
- Bar the employer from having H-1B petitions approved for one year.
- Impose possible reinstatement and back-pay awards for similarly situated employees.

H-2B (Lesser Skilled Workers)

H-2B status is available when the following are met:

- An employee has a residence in a foreign country that he or she has no intention of abandoning.
- An employee is coming to the U.S. to perform temporary services or labor in a temporary position.
- Qualified persons willing to perform such service or labor at the prevailing wage cannot be found in the U.S.

The total number of employees who may be issued H-2B visas may not exceed 66,000. This limitation applies only to principal aliens, not to the spouses or children of such employees.

Employers submitting H-2B petitions must consider available U.S. workers for the temporary services or labor to be performed and must offer terms and conditions of employment which are consistent with the nature of the occupation, the activity, and the industry in the U.S. H-2B workers may not displace U.S. workers capable of performing such services or labor, or adversely affect the wages and working conditions of U.S. workers.

In order to qualify for H-2B classification, the job must be temporary in nature; that is, seasonal or a one-time need. As a general rule, the period the petitioner is needed must be one year or less, although there may be extraordinary circumstances in which the temporary services or labor might last longer than one year.

An *Alien Labor Certification* must be filed with the Job Service Office of the DOL within the area of intended employment. This certification, which is issued by the Secretary of Labor, demonstrates that qualified workers in the U.S. are not available and that the alien's employment will not adversely affect wages and working conditions of similarly employed U.S. workers.

An approved H-2B petition is valid for up to one year. Employers can apply for extensions in one-year increments for a maximum of three years if the employer still needs emergency temporary labor. Seasonal workers and employers spending six months or less per year in the U.S. are not subject to this three year limit.

E-1 and E-2 (Treaty Trader and Investor Status)

The requirements for traders or investors from a country with a treaty of commerce and navigation or equivalent agreement with the U.S. to conduct business in the U.S. are as follows:

- Nationals of the foreign country must have majority ownership and control of the business.
- Each employee or principal of the company who seeks entry into the U.S. under the treaty must hold citizenship of the same country as the majority owners of the company.
- Such person must be considered an E-1 Trader or an E-2 Investor:
  - An *E-1 (Trader)* is one who enters solely to carry on substantial trade, including trade in services or in technology, principally between the U.S. and the foreign state of which the trader is a national.

    No set amount determines what is "substantial" trade, but cases with a steady flow and high number of transactions will be given greater consideration.

Immigration

- An *E-2 (Investor)* is one who enters solely to develop and direct the operations of an enterprise in which he or she has invested or is in the process of actively investing a substantial amount of capital.

  No set amount determines "substantiality." New businesses must show the investment is an amount normally considered necessary to establish a viable enterprise of the nature contemplated. Ongoing businesses must show the investment is an amount sufficient to cover operating expenses.

♦ A foreign employee of treaty investors must be employed in a responsible capacity. He or she must assume a managerial position or be a highly trained or specially qualified person.

L-1 (Intracompany Transferee Status)

The Intracompany Transferee Visa requires the transferring company, the receiving company, and the transferred individual to satisfy certain conditions.

Blanket Petitions

Requirements for a Blanket L-1 petition are as follows:

♦ The company and each of the entities must be engaged in commercial trade or services.

♦ The company has an office in the U.S. that has been doing business for one year or more.

♦ The company has three or more domestic and foreign branches, subsidiaries, or affiliates.

♦ The company has:

- Obtained approval of petitions for at least 10 "L" professionals during the previous 12 months.
- U.S. subsidiaries or affiliates with combined annual sales of at least $25 million, or
- A U.S. workforce of at least 1,000 employees.

Individual Petitions

Requirements for an individual petition are as follows:

♦ The employer abroad and the petitioning U.S. company must be properly related; for example, enjoy parent-subsidiary, sibling, joint venture, or affiliate relationships.

♦ The transferee must have worked in a managerial, executive, or specialized knowledge capacity for the employer abroad for at least one continuous year within the three years immediately preceding his or her entry into the U.S.

♦ The transferee must be coming to work for the U.S. employer in a managerial, executive, or specialized knowledge capacity for a temporary period.

♦ In addition, to obtain an L-1B visa for specialized personnel continuing employment with an international firm or corporation, the employer must justify its need for the transferee's specialized knowledge in the U.S.

The L-1 visa category will permit executives and managers to have a visa validity term of up to seven years. This longer term does not apply to transferees with "specialized knowledge." Specialized knowledge employees are limited to a visa term of five years.

O (Extraordinary Ability Nationals)

A new visa became available October 1, 1991, for foreign nationals with extraordinary ability in the sciences, arts, education, business, or athletics. An O-1 visa may be granted only after consultation by the INS with peer groups in the area of the foreign national's ability. Thus in the case of a person seeking entry for a motion picture or television production, consultation shall occur with the appropriate union representing the occupational peers and with the management organization in the area of the ability of the applicant. Regarding the O-2 visa, consultation shall occur with the labor organization with expertise in the skill area of the applicant.

The statutory requirements of O visas are as follows:

- O-1. To be eligible for this type of O visa, a foreign national must have the following:
  - Extraordinary ability in the sciences, arts, education, business, or athletics as demonstrated by sustained national or international acclaim or a demonstrated record of extraordinary achievement.
  - Achievements recognized in the field through extensive documentation.
  - Desire to enter the U.S. to continue work in the area of extraordinary ability.
  - Work that will substantially benefit the U.S.
- O-2. To be eligible for this type of O visa, a foreign national must:
  - Desire to enter the U.S. temporarily for the purpose of accompanying and assisting the artistic or athletic performance by a foreign national admitted under an O-1 visa for a specific event.
  - Be an integral part of the actual performance of the O-1 visa holder.
  - Have critical skills and experience with such O-1 foreign national that are not of a general nature and cannot be performed by others or are critical based upon a pre-existing long-standing working relationship.
  - Have a foreign residence that the foreign national does not intend to abandon.

The O visa is issued for the duration of the event in which the alien is participating. In no circumstances may the initial O visa term exceed three years. There after, one-year extensions of O status may be obtained.

Permanent Employment of Non-U.S. Citizens (Green Cards)

Five employment-based immigration classifications are currently available, with 140,000 visas available per year for the following:

- **Priority workers ("First Preference").** There are three subcategories of priority workers, and a maximum of 40,000 visas will be issued in the following categories:
  - Aliens with extraordinary ability.
  - Outstanding professors and researchers.
  - Certain multinational executives and managers.

- **Advanced degree or exceptional ability aliens ("Second Preference").** Qualified employee immigrants must be members of the professions holding advanced degrees (or the equivalent) or have exceptional ability in sciences, arts, professions, or business that will substantially benefit the national economy of the U.S. The requirements of a job offer and labor certification may be waived if a determination is made that it would be in the national interest to admit an applicant for lawful permanent residence.

- **Skilled workers, professionals, and other workers ("Third Preference"):**
  - *Skilled workers* are defined as aliens capable of performing a job requiring two or more years of experience or training.
  - *Professionals* are defined as immigrants who hold baccalaureate degrees (for example, bachelors degrees in engineering, computer science, or economics) and are members of a profession.
  - *Other workers* are defined as immigrants petitioning for classification as unskilled labor that requires less than two years of training or experience. A limitation of 10,000 visas per year has been placed on this particular subcategory.

- **Special immigrants. This category includes the following:**
  - Special ministers and religious workers who were members of a qualifying religious organization (with a proven non-profit status) for the immediate two years prior to entry in such status and who worked in a particular vocation or occupation for those two years. They must seek to enter the U.S. to do the following:
    - Be a minister of religion.
    - Work for the religious organization in a professional capacity.
    - Work for a bona fide religious organization affiliated with a religious denomination.
  - Overseas employees of the U.S. government, consulate, and embassy offices.
  - Former employees of the Panama Canal Company and their families.
  - Foreign medical graduates.
  - Retired employees of international organizations and their family members.

- **Investors.** To qualify for this employment-based preference category, a foreign investor must establish a new commercial enterprise and invest $500,000 (in areas of high unemployment) or $1 million (in areas of normal unemployment) in the new enterprise. The new investment must create at least ten full time jobs for U.S. workers, excluding the investor and immediate family members.

  Targeted areas. Only $500,000 is required for investment in targeted high unemployment areas to encourage investment. One-third of the visas available for investors have been allocated for these particular types of investments.

The second and third preferences for (1) advanced degree or exceptional ability aliens and (2) skilled workers, professionals, and other workers require labor certification before a permanent visa can be issued. An employer must submit appropriate original forms in duplicate to the employment security office in the location where the alien is to be employed. Supporting documentation of the alien's qualifications and the employer's recruiting efforts must be provided with the application. Wages paid to the alien must be the prevailing wage for that occupation and all job requirements must be reasonable and minimum.

The employer must adhere to the following recruitment requirements:

- A job order must run for a minimum of 30 days through the National Employment Service job bank system.
- The employer must conspicuously post the job opening on the premises for at least 10 days.
- There must be an advertisement once in a professional publication or for three consecutive days in a local newspaper, depending on the position to be filled.
- The new expedited reduction-in-recruitment (RIR) version of labor certification requires the employer to advertise in a newspaper of general circulation once a month for one to three months, depending upon the requirements of the regional DOL office.

If a union represents for the company's employees in the occupational classification and geographical areas for which aliens are sought, the law requires employers to notify a union representative or bargaining agent that such alien labor certification application has been filed. If no such bargaining agent or representative exists, the employer must post a notice conspicuously on its premises informing its employees that an alien labor certification application has been filed.

Chapter 13
New-hire Reporting

Introduction

To help locate individuals for purposes of establishing paternity; establishing, notifying, and enforcing child-support orders; and detecting fraud in any program administered by the Department of Human Services, all employers other than the federal government must report the hiring, rehiring, and return to work of paid employees. This chapter reviews federal and state law on new-hire reporting.

Information to Be Reported

Information reported includes that in the lists below.

Employee Information

- Name.
- Address.
- Social Security number.
- Date of hire, rehire, or return to work.

Employer Information

- Name.
- Address.
- Employer identification number.

Means of Reporting

Reports may be made by, submitting any of the following items:

- A copy of the employee's W-4 form, or an equivalent form.
- Any other hiring document or data storage device or mechanism authorized by state law.

Employers Operating in Two or More States

An employer that has employees in two or more states and transmits reports magnetically or electronically may make the report to a designated state in which they operate. However, in order to be in full compliance with state law, the employer must do the following:

- Notify the state agency and the U.S. Secretary of Health and Human Services in writing the designated state to which the employer will transmit the report.
- Transmit the report to that state in compliance with federal law.

Penalties

An employer who fails to make a report as indicated above may be liable for up to $25 for each failure to make a report. Additionally, if the failure to make a report is the result of a conspiracy between the employer and the employee not to supply the report or to supply a false or incomplete report, the employer will be required to pay a fee of up to $500 for each such failure.

Massachusetts New-Hire Reporting

Massachusetts' new-hire provisions are found in the Massachusetts General Laws Annotated, c.62E, §2.

Employer Obligations

Massachusetts law defines *employer* as the person for whom an individual performs service of any nature as the employee of that person. If the person for whom the individual performs the service does not have control of the payment of wages, the term refers to the person having control of the payment of the wages. Every employer must notify the Department of Revenue of the hire of any new employee. Massachusetts defines *employee* to as officers, employees, or elected officials of the United States, a state, any political subdivision, the District of Columbia, or any agency or instrumentality of any governmental agency.

The timing and the form of such notification will be dictated by the Commissioner of Revenue and some employers, including governmental agencies and labor organizations, may be required to report on magnetic media or other machine-readable form if they are otherwise subject to this type of reporting.

Federal and state agencies performing intelligence or counterintelligence functions are not required to notify the department of the hiring of an employee if they determine that such notification could endanger the employee's safety or compromise an ongoing investigation or intelligence mission. An agency head who has made such a determination must, however, notify the commissioner that some employees have not been reported.

Penalties

Employers who fail to submit new-hire reports as required will be liable for a penalty assessed by the Department of Revenue for up to $25 per employee if the failure is the result of inaccuracy. Employers become liable for a fine of up to $500 per employee if the failure to report is the result of a conspiracy between the employer and the employee not to submit the report or to submit a false report.

Whom to Contact

Telephone: 1-800-332-2733
Web site: www.baystatebiz.com.

Chapter 14
Drug and Alcohol Testing in the Workplace

Introduction

Drug use on the job and the job-related effects of drug and alcohol use off the job have become important concerns for employers. As a result, drug and alcohol-testing programs have been widely implemented in both the private and public sectors.

Most states do not provide mandatory regulation of substance-abuse policies, although a significant number do. However, even in the absence of state regulation, these policies are subject to scrutiny on several levels. For example, testing and searches can give rise to common law invasion-of-privacy claims. Adoption of a policy is subject to an employer's duty to bargain with a union. Further, discipline and discharge for substance abuse may be attacked under nondiscrimination laws and in court or arbitration under wrongful discharge theories.

In recent years, the federal government has drafted employers to help in its war on drugs. Thus, defense contractors must strive for a drug-free workforce. Federal contractors and grantees have drug-free workplace obligations. Transportation employers such as railroads, merchant mariners, airlines, motor carriers, and pipeline operators must develop and implement applicant and employee drug and alcohol-testing programs.

This chapter reviews federal regulations concerning drug and alcohol testing, discusses the Drug-Free Workplace Act and related regulations, and details procedures for employers planning to implement a drug and alcohol-testing program. Where appropriate, any state laws are reviewed.

Testing Limits

Everyone can be tested within reason. For certain classes of employees, however, there are established limits as to how far employers may go. Those limits depend upon the nature of the employment relationship, as well as federal, state, and local laws.

Private At-will Employees

At-will employees have brought claims of invasion-of-privacy when employers have engaged in random testing, and defamation claims when reports of false positive results have been circulated to others. At-will employees also have sued for breach of contract based upon information about drug testing in the employee handbook.

Union Employees

Courts, interpreting the National Labor Relations Act, mandate that employers bargain collectively with unions about substance abuse-testing programs. This prevents an employer from unilaterally implementing drug testing for union employees, unless there has been a clear and unmistakable waiver by the union of its right to bargain over these issues. The National Labor Relations Board generally disfavors finding such a waiver.

The National Labor Relations Board does not require employers to bargain over pre-employment testing programs, except in situations such as hiring halls, where the union has become a participant in the hiring process.

Nonunion Contract Employees

A drug-testing program need not necessarily be contained within an employment contract in order for it to be valid. However, to avoid breach-of-contract lawsuits, employees should agree, in writing, to comply with all personnel policies implemented by management before or during employment, and should argue specifically to abide by the employer's substance-abuse testing program.

Public Sector Employees

Federal, state, and local government employees have Fourth Amendment constitutional protection generally not enjoyed by their private sector counterparts. Drug tests initiated by public employers are subject to prohibitions against unreasonable search and seizure. Random testing should be limited to employees who work in safety-sensitive positions.

Job Applicants

Applicants have fewer privacy rights than employees. Employers often make offers of permanent employment conditioned upon successful completion of a drug test. The Americans with Disabilities Act does not consider such a pre-employment test for illegal drugs to be an unlawful pre-employment medical examination. However, no such exclusion is provided for pre-employment alcohol tests and they are often regarded as being of questionable value, since applicants can easily abstain from drinking for the short period needed to obtain a negative result.

Administering drug tests before an offer of employment is made can prove problematical; any information gathered in a drug test about a person's medical condition or history cannot be considered before a job offer. Consequently, employers should delay drug tests until they have extended a conditional offer of employment. Thus, the employer does not have pre-offer knowledge of real or apparent disabilities revealed by test results and cannot be accused of basing a decision not to hire because of the applicant's actual or perceived disability.

Discipline and Discharge for Substance Abuse in a Union Setting

Employer attempts to enforce a drug and alcohol policy within a union workforce will most likely result in challenges through the grievance and arbitration process. Arbitrators have varying attitudes about the circumstances under which alcoholism or drunkenness is cause for discharge. Some arbitrators will sustain discipline based solely upon employee performance without regard to any explanations for shortcomings. Others consider alcoholic employees to be victims of a disorder who should be offered an opportunity to recover, complete with leaves of absence and appropriate treatment.

While arbitrators tend to view alcoholism as a treatable disorder, there is considerable resistance to the concept of rehabilitating an employee with a drug-related problem. Most drug offenses carry a taint of criminality and, therefore, arbitrators are more inclined to look with disfavor on drug users.

Generally, an employee's activity on his or her own time and off the employer's premises is regarded by arbitrators as being of no concern to the employer, unless the employer can demonstrate that the off-duty activity caused the following:

- Damaged the company's reputation or product.
- Interfered with the employee's work attendance or performance.
- Resulted in a fellow employee's reasonable refusal, reluctance, or inability to work with the employee.

Arbitrators tend to uphold the discharge and discipline of employees who test positive for drugs or alcohol when the employer has done the following:

- Defined a drug-testing policy that clarifies possible consequences.
- Applied its policy reasonably and consistently.

Americans with Disabilities Act (ADA)

The Americans with Disabilities Act excludes current users of illegal drugs from its protection. Such current users need not be accommodated and may be discharged (or not hired) for testing positive. *Illegal drugs* are defined as controlled substances not being taken under the supervision of a licensed healthcare professional or otherwise in accordance with federal law.

The ADA does, however, protect former drug users who have successfully completed treatment, former users who are participating in treatment, and persons erroneously regarded as illegal drug users. Persons who are legally using prescribed drugs are also protected. Given the distinction between legal and illegal drug use under the ADA, employers should use a physician as a Medical Review Officer to verify test results and separate illegal drug users from persons lawfully taking prescribed medications.

Alcoholism is treated differently from illegal drug use under the ADA. Alcoholism is considered a protected disability under the ADA. The ADA also protects former alcoholics and persons erroneously regarded as alcoholics. Moreover, tests for alcohol use are "medical examinations" under the ADA. Accordingly, alcohol tests must be job related and consistent with business necessity and, if given to applicants, may be administered only after conditional offers of employment are extended. As a practical matter, however, such pre-employment alcohol tests are of questionable value. Note, however, that the ADA specifically allows employers to prohibit the on-the-job use of alcohol and to prohibit employees from being under the influence of alcohol while in the workplace.

There is a split among federal courts about whether employers may hold alcoholics to the same standards of performance as non-alcoholics where the performance problems are caused by alcoholism. Some federal courts have held that an employer may hold an alcoholic employee to the same performance and behavior standards as other employees, even if the unsatisfactory performance is related to alcoholism.

Persons dependent upon legally obtained medications also are protected by the ADA. Tests to determine whether employees or applicants are using prescribed drugs must be job related and consistent with business necessity. Employees who receive positive results on such fitness for duty tests may be entitled to reasonable accommodation under the ADA. Because the ADA increases the legal risks involved in testing for such drugs as pain relievers and tranquilizers, the risks of testing for legal drugs probably outweigh the benefits except in safety-critical jobs or cases where a substance abuse professional has authorized follow-up testing after an employee has returned to work from treatment for drug abuse.

The ADA allows employers to perform any testing required by Department of Transportation, Defense, or Energy regulations. It also allows employers to prohibit employees from using or being under the influence of illegal drugs in the workplace and from violating the Drug-Free Workplace Act.

Transportation Employee Drug and Alcohol Testing

Federal law requires various forms of drug and alcohol testing by employers in the following transportation industries:

- Motor carrier.
- Railroad.
- Aviation.
- Maritime.
- Mass transit.
- Pipeline.

Employers in these industries are required by the Department of Transportation (DOT) to implement highly specific drug-testing programs conforming to detailed DOT regulations. Under the regulations, all employees who need a commercial driver's license (CDL) to perform their work are subject to drug testing. The regulations apply to any employer who has even a single CDL employee. Additionally, all employers should regard the Department of Transportation rules as an important yardstick against which their testing programs will be measured.

DOT Drug Testing

The following is a general summary of the existing DOT federal drug testing regulations for transportation employees. Because the regulations vary from one transportation agency to another, guidelines should be obtained from each agency with jurisdiction over an employer and legal counsel should be consulted.

DOT-required Drug Tests

- **Pre-employment testing.** Applicants for employment in covered positions must successfully complete a drug test before performing a safety-sensitive function.
- **Random testing.** For 2001, DOT employers in the motor carrier and mass transit industries must conduct a number of random drug tests each year equal to 50 percent of the number of covered positions. (Different random testing rates may apply to employers in the DOT-covered industries). Such tests must be spread throughout the year. Employees can have no advance warning of random tests and must have an equal chance of being tested each time selections are made. Employers may wish to join consortiums or to contract with third party administrators to reduce some of the administrative problems involved in scheduling random tests.

- **Post-accident testing.** Testing is required within a specific number of hours after serious accidents or rule violations. Employees who may have contributed to the accident must be tested after receiving any necessary medical attention. Truck drivers should be tested after reportable accidents if they receive a citation for a moving violation arising out of the accident or if someone dies as a result of the accident.

- **Reasonable suspicion testing.** Tests for reasonable suspicion must be based on specific, contemporaneous, articulable observations by a trained supervisor or supervisors concerning the employee's appearance, behavior, body odors or speech.

- **Return-to-duty testing.** Employees who violate DOT drug testing regulations must undergo a return-to-duty test with a verified negative result before performing a safety-sensitive function.

- **Follow-up testing.** Employees who violate DOT drug testing regulations and have a drug problem, as diagnosed by a substance-abuse professional, are subject to random follow-up testing for one to five years after returning to duty.

Consequences for Violation of DOT Drug Testing Regulations

Employees who receive verified positive test results or otherwise violate the regulations must be immediately removed from safety-sensitive positions. Such employees may not return to duty until after they undergo evaluation and treatment or pass medical tests. Such employees are then subject to random follow-up tests.

Employees who refuse to be tested or engage in conduct that clearly obstructs the testing process are subject to the same consequences as employees who test positive.

DOT regulations neither mandate nor forbid the imposition of additional disciplinary consequences (such as discharge) by an employer for violating DOT rules. Employers are free to impose additional consequences on their own authority, subject to the legal obligations and limitations discussed above.

Additional DOT Drug Testing Requirements

The DOT regulations also require and authorize the following:

- Testing only for marijuana, cocaine, opiates, amphetamines, and PCP.

- Testing only by labs certified by the Department of Health and Human Services (DHHS).

- Test results must be reviewed by Medical Review Officers (MROs) who are required to determine whether there may be a legitimate explanation for positive tests and whether lab results are scientifically reliable.

- Employers must use the split-sample method of urine testing. Under this method, the urine sample provided at the testing site is divided into a primary sample and a split sample. Employees and applicants who receive verified positive results or verified adulterated or substituted results, on the primary sample may request that the split-sample be sent to another certified lab for testing.

DOT Alcohol Testing

All employers covered by the DOT drug testing regulations are also required to have an alcohol-testing program complying with DOT standards.

The alcohol rules provide for breath testing using trained technicians and evidential breath-testing devices. The breath-testing devices must be federally approved. The regulations allow the option of using saliva tests or non-evidential breath-testing devices for screening tests only. Confirmation tests must be conducted with evidential breath-testing devices.

Consequences for Violation of DOT Alcohol Testing Regulations

Employees with a confirmation test result indicating a blood alcohol concentration (BAC) of 0.04 or greater or who otherwise violate the DOT alcohol regulations must be immediately removed from performing safety-sensitive duties. They may not return to such duties until they are evaluated by a substance-abuse professional and undergo a successful return-to-duty test. Such employees are also subject to follow-up testing and must successfully complete any prescribed treatment program. Employees who refuse to be tested or obstruct testing are subject to the same consequences as employees testing 0.04 BAC or above. As with DOT drug testing, employers may impose additional discipline subject to the other legal obligations and limitations discussed above.

Employees with a BAC of 0.02 or greater but less than 0.04 are not deemed to be in violation of the regulations, but must be removed from safety-sensitive duty for 24 hours or until the employee's next shift, whichever is later.

DOT-required Alcohol Tests

The DOT regulations generally require covered employers to conduct the following types of tests for alcohol:

- Post-accident.
- Reasonable suspicion.
- Return to duty.
- Follow-up.
- Random.

For 2001, the regulations presently require that random alcohol testing be conducted at an annual rate of 10 percent of the number of covered employees (except in the gas pipeline and maritime industries).

DOT Policy Requirement

Employers are required to prepare and distribute to all covered employees a policy explaining the requirements of the DOT regulations. Each covered employee must sign a statement certifying receipt of the policy.

Drug-Free Workplace Act

Direct recipients of federal grants and most federal contractors holding contracts under the Federal Acquisition Regulations that exceed $100,000 must comply with the Drug-Free Workplace Act. The act applies to employees and facilities engaged in directly performing work under such contracts and grants. It does not apply to subcontractors or second-tier recipients of pass-through grants, nor does it apply to companies that hold multiple small contracts of less than $100,000 each.

Covered employers must have a policy and a drug-free awareness program. The policy must notify employees performing work under the contract or grant of the following:

- That they may not manufacture, distribute, dispense, possess, or use controlled substances in the workplace.

- That they must report any criminal convictions for manufacturing, distributing, dispensing, possessing, or using controlled substances in the workplace to the employer within five days.

- Of the penalties for such convictions.

With respect to employees who report such convictions, employers have 30 days to take appropriate disciplinary action, up to and including discharge, or to require satisfactory participation in an assistance/rehabilitation program. The act gives contractors and grantees discretion to decide what action to take. Contractors must also report any employee convictions for workplace drug crimes of which they have been notified to the contracting agency within 10 days.

The act also requires contractors and grantees to establish drug-free awareness programs informing employees of the employer's drug-free workplace policy, the adverse effects of drug abuse, the penalties that will be imposed for workplace drug violations, and any available drug counseling, rehabilitation, or assistance programs. It does not, however, require that any particular rehabilitation program be provided.

Under the act, drug testing, employee assistance programs, and supervisor training are optional. Such options and the ways unionized employers choose to exercise their discretion under the act are subject to collective bargaining. Thus, such employers may have to bargain over whether treatment will be offered and whether employees will be reassigned to jobs that do not involve the performance of federal contract work, instead of being fired.

Grantees and contractors should maintain a current list of the facilities and departments performing federal contract work and have operable programs within 30 days of receiving contracts or grants. Any government audits may include a review of Drug-Free Workplace Act compliance programs.

Department of Defense Drug-Free Workplace Regulations

Certain Department of Defense (DOD) contracts involving classified information and national security contain a drug-free workforce clause. DOD contracts should be reviewed individually to see whether they contain such a clause. Ordinarily, contracts to deliver commercial products and contracts to be performed outside the U.S. are not covered. The clause requires prime contractors to institute and maintain a drug-free workforce program. Such programs must include the following:

- An employee-assistance program emphasizing high-level direction, education, counseling, rehabilitation, and coordination with available community resources.

- Supervisory training to identify and address illegal drug use by employees.

- Provisions for self-referrals, and supervisory referrals to treatment, with maximum respect for confidentiality consistent with safety and security.

- A means of identifying illegal drug users, including drug testing of employees in sensitive positions.

- The removal of identified drug users from sensitive positions. Contractors who are subject to the clause may not allow employees who use drugs illegally to remain on duty or perform in a sensitive position until the contractor determines that they may properly perform in the position.

Sensitive positions are positions involving access to classified information, national security, health or safety, or requiring a high degree of trust and confidence.

The rule provides that the criteria for testing shall be determined by the contractor based on such factors as the nature of the contract, the employee's job duties, and the risks to health, safety, or national security that could result from an employee's failure to perform his or her job adequately. Testing is limited to marijuana, cocaine, opiates, PCP, and amphetamines.

In addition, contractors may test for the following reasons:

- When there is reasonable suspicion of use.
- When an employee is involved in an accident or unsafe practice.
- As part of treatment, or follow-up to rehabilitation.
- As part of a voluntary testing program.

Contractors may also test applicants.

Contractors who are subject to the clause may not allow employees who use drugs illegally to remain on duty or perform in a sensitive position until the contractor determines that they may properly perform in the position. Contractors must also adopt appropriate personnel procedures to deal with employees who use drugs illegally.

Considerations When Implementing a Drug and Alcohol-testing program

Employers must consider a variety of factors when implementing a drug and alcohol-testing program. The employer should determine the following:

- The reason the program is being implemented.
- The employees to be tested.
- The types of tests will be given.
- The substances to be tested for.
- The test administrator.
- The consequences of a positive test.

Reasons to Implement a Testing Program

Testing programs may be implemented for the following reasons:

- To comply with federal requirements. These include requirements for certain Department of Defense contractors, employers subject to the Nuclear Regulatory Commission, and employers subject to Department of Transportation testing programs.
- To save money. Studies have shown employers lose between $60 and $100 billion annually because of drug abuse among employees. That the cost results from lost productivity, increased absenteeism, drug-related accidents, medical claims, and theft.
- To control insurance costs.
- To reduce workers' compensation premiums.

- For employee safety.

- To discourage drug-users from applying for employment. When an employer has a pre-employment drug-testing program, potential applicants who are drug-users may be more likely to apply to other employers who do not have such a program.

- To avoid negligent hiring and retention claims. An employer with a drug-and-alcohol-testing program in place may be able to avoid claims of negligence for hiring or retaining employees who the employer knew or should have known had a substance-abuse problem.

Employees to Be Tested

Employers must decide which employees will be tested. The options are to test applicants only, all employees, or merely those employees in safety-sensitive or security-sensitive positions. Employers may also decide to test only those employees they reasonably suspect are under the influence of alcohol or are using illegal drugs.

Types of Tests

The types of drug or alcohol tests that can be given include the following:

- **Pre-employment.** Testing is given before employment to determine if the applicant is using illegal drugs. Most employers do not give pre-employment alcohol tests.

- **Reasonable suspicion.** Any employee the employer has a reasonable basis to suspect is using drugs or is at work under the influence of alcohol can be tested.

- **Post-accident.** Testing is given after an employee is involved in an accident. Such testing is generally given if provided for in the employer's policy and there is any personal injury involved or damage to property estimated at a minimal level.

- **Random.** Testing is given on an unannounced basis and employees are selected for testing on a random basis.

- **Follow-up.** Testing is given on a scheduled or random basis when an employee returns to work after completing rehabilitation or counseling for substance abuse.

- **Periodic.** Testing is given at specified times. This may be used for employees who have been returned to the workforce after testing positive or generally for employees who are in safety-or security-sensitive positions. For example, drivers may be required to submit to an annual test in addition to being subjected to random testing.

Substance Testing

An employer can elect to test for the following types of substances:

- Alcohol.

- The five-drug panel required for DOT testing—cocaine, opiates, amphetamines, PCP, and marijuana.

- Eight-drug panels or as many substances as a laboratory can test.

- Abused prescription drugs.

The common drugs of abuse are those contained in the five-drug panel required for DOT testing. For an employer to test beyond those drugs is likely an unnecessary expense.

Testing Laboratory

Care should be taken in the selection of a laboratory to analyze the tests. Employers required to test employees under federal drug-testing programs must use laboratories certified for those programs. Even when not required by law, it is preferable to have a laboratory that is certified to do drug testing in federal programs.

It is important to have a reputable laboratory, experienced and knowledgeable in the proper methods of handling and analyzing urine samples and breath alcohol tests. A good chain of custody is essential to ensure unadulterated samples have been analyzed and that there can be no question as to whose sample has been analyzed.

The laboratory should have the highest quality-control standards. A screening test should be used for samples with a confirming test for positive results. The most reliable confirming test is considered to be Gas Chromatography/Mass Spectrometry. Laboratory personnel must be willing to defend results and testify in arbitration or court hearings.

Employees should be given notice of test results and an opportunity to establish a legitimate explanation for positive drug-test results to a Medical Review Officer (MRO). Positive drug test results should be verified by the MRO before being reported to the employer.

Consequences of a Positive Test Result or Refusal to Take a Test

Any drug-and-alcohol policy must have a clear statement as to the consequences of a positive result or for the refusal by an employee to take a required test. The consequences for refusing to be tested should be similar to the penalties for failing a test so employees will have an incentive to cooperate. If an Employee Assistance Plan (EAP) is part of the policy, one element should include referral to the EAP. In developing a policy, an employer must consider the following questions in determining how it will respond to positive test results:

- Will there be an opportunity for rehabilitation?
- Is the program to be a one-, two-, or three-strike program?
- If there is more than one strike before an employee will be terminated, will the employee be required to complete or merely enroll in a rehabilitation program before being permitted to return to work?
- Will the employee be required to enter into a last-chance agreement?
- Will there be a disciplinary suspension or a suspension until the employee is drug-free?
- If the employee is in a safety-sensitive or security-sensitive position, will there be a transfer or demotion after a positive test?
- Will the transfer or demotion be for a specified period of time or indefinitely?

Other Features of a Good Testing Policy

A good testing policy will do the following:

- Clearly describe the prohibited conduct and the consequences for such conduct.

- Clearly communicate the policy and program to employees and supervisors. Employees should be required to separately sign the policy even if they are already required to sign a general acknowledgment of receipt of a policy handbook.
- Ensure adequate training for supervisors and education for employees.
- Consider whether to create an Employee Assistance Plan.
- Require consent forms for all tests and make clear that refusal to comply will be considered a violation of the policy.
- Ensure that employee privacy is protected in the testing process and in the dissemination of test results.
- Document all performance inadequacies.

State Law Considerations Concerning a Drug and Alcohol-testing program

Employers who are not covered by federal laws or regulations still must consider whether there are any state or local laws or regulations concerning drug and alcohol testing. Some states have mandatory laws governing the conduct of drug and/or alcohol testing. For example, Maine requires employers to submit their drug and alcohol-testing policies to the Maine Department of Labor for approval prior to implementing such policies. Minnesota, Rhode Island, Vermont and Boulder, Colorado, prohibit breath testing when testing for alcohol. Some states and localities such as San Francisco, California, and Boulder, Colorado, prohibit random drug and alcohol testing; other states prohibit random testing unless the employee being tested is in a "safety-sensitive" position, because of the right of privacy recognized in their state constitution or laws.

In addition, states including Maryland, Minnesota, Louisiana, Oklahoma and North Carolina, among others, have requirements concerning the procedures to be followed in drug and alcohol testing.

Some states have voluntary drug- and alcohol- testing laws. Employers who elect to comply with the requirements of these voluntary laws may be eligible for a reduction in workers' compensation premiums, or be entitled to raise an "intoxication causation" defense in workers' compensation proceedings or a "misconduct" defense in unemployment insurance proceedings.

Therefore, where substance abuse testing is not mandated by federal regulations, employers should inquire whether state or local laws restrict their ability to test or offer incentives for certain testing programs.

How Prevalent Is Drug Use Among Employees?

A survey released in 1996 by the Department of Health and Human Services suggests drug-testing programs may be having a positive effect. The results of the survey indicate that use of illegal drugs by full time workers has decreased by more than 50 percent since 1985. The survey also indicated, however, that 7 percent of the nation's full time workers continue to use illegal drugs. The survey also indicated the following:

- Thirteen percent of workers surveyed reported participating in a mandatory workplace drug test in the past year.

- Illegal drug use is highest in the construction and restaurant industries, and lowest among police, teachers, and childcare workers.

- Heavy alcohol use is highest among construction and restaurant workers, light truck drivers, and laborers, and lowest among clerical workers.

- Unmarried workers reported twice the rate of illegal drug and heavy alcohol use as married workers.

- Persons who changed jobs two or more times in the past five years were twice as likely as others to use illegal drugs.

Drug and Alcohol Abuse—Performance Indicators

Changes in job performance and in behavior on the job may be indicators that an employee has a problem with drugs or alcohol. It is vital for employers to objectively and carefully document such changes. Some performance indicators that may indicate an employee has a drug or alcohol problem are the following:

- Frequent tardiness or absences for implausible reasons.
- Long lunch, coffee, or bathroom breaks.
- Frequently missed deadlines.
- Disruption of fellow employees.
- Withdrawal from interaction with fellow employees.
- Overreaction to constructive criticism.
- Frequent mistakes related to poor judgment.
- Decreased productivity.
- Great variations in productivity from day to day.
- Inability to concentrate on work.

Do's and Don'ts for Supervisors When Confronting a Troubled Employee

The following are actions an employer **should** take in the event an employee is suspected of drug or alcohol abuse on the job:

- **Do** establish expected levels of work performance.
- **Do** document.
- **Do** be consistent.
- **Do** be firm.
- **Do** be prepared to deal with the employee's resistance, denial, defensiveness, and hostility.

- **Do** base confrontation on job performance, and/or on specific, observed behavior including, for example, slurred speech, stumbling gait, bloodshot eyes, smell of alcohol on breath, etc.
- **Do** be direct.
- **Do** provide the information and make appropriate referral according to company policy.
- **Do** take the responsibility to intervene.
- **Do** continue to monitor and document.

The following are actions an employer **should not** take in the event an employee is suspected of drug or alcohol abuse on the job:

- **Do not** be a diagnostician or counselor.
- **Do not** make value judgments.
- **Do not** moralize.
- **Do not** allow the employee to play you against higher management or the union.
- **Do not** make idle disciplinary threats.
- **Do not** discuss drinking unless it occurs on the job.
- **Do not** treat employees differently.
- **Do not** ignore the problem.

Chapter 15
Employee Performance Evaluations

Introduction

The most stressful decisions made by managers often involve employee performance evaluations. Performed correctly, an evaluation facilitates communication between the employer and the employee and provides helpful data for salary increases, bonuses, promotions, demotions, or terminations. Conversely, poorly planned evaluations can result in unnecessary legal complications.

The two most important aspects of a successful evaluation system are:

- Communication—including accurate communication of expectations, honesty, effective presentation techniques, open interaction with employees, and confidentiality.
- Procedure—including consistency, content, documentation, and the use of self-evaluations.

This chapter examines these factors and attempts to provide a legal and commonsense approach to conducting successful evaluations.

Communication

Communication, one important aspect of a successful evaluation process, includes the accurate communication of expectations, honesty, presentation techniques, interaction with employees, and confidentiality.

Expectations

Essentially there are two components to clear communication of expectations. The first is a properly constructed job description that can serve as the basis of the evaluation. The second is a compilation of employer and employee goals for the upcoming evaluation period. After the initial evaluation, the goals can be monitored to chart an employee's progress.

Job Description

The initial step of any successful performance evaluation process must be to establish the legitimate expectations of the employer. The best method for accomplishing this task is to incorporate an accurate job description into the evaluation process. Properly designed job descriptions focus employees on the essential purpose and functions of their jobs, preventing them from becoming sidetracked by inconsequential tasks. A current and well-prepared job description can also be critical in defending a wrongful termination or other lawsuit, since it ensures that the employee knew in advance what was expected and how performance would be measured.

Goals

The performance evaluation should also include a description of the employee's goals for the coming year. This should include goals established by the employer as well as goals set by the employee. Goals may include working on specific projects, improving character traits, or meeting particular quota requirements.

Example: ABC Corporation requires managers to evaluate employees once a year and to meet with employees to discuss their performance. Mary, an employee, received an evaluation encouraging her to keep up the good work. However, the manager never explained to Mary what he liked about her work specifically or what she might improve upon. Mary enjoyed the positive reinforcement but could have benefited from a discussion with her employer regarding shared goals for the coming year.

Honesty

The largest problem encountered by employers using formalized evaluations is the reluctance of the evaluator to be candid with the employee. Fear of hurting feelings or creating an uncomfortable work environment results in inaccurate and problematic evaluations. Although some managers have been known to be unduly harsh, the problem usually is misguided praise.

An employer's failure to include justifiable criticism in an employee's evaluation may have legal repercussions. A poorly or marginally performing employee who is terminated may rely on positive evaluations as evidence of adequate performance. After years of good or even glowing evaluations, the logical inference is that the employer terminated the employee for a reason other than performance, the employers stated reason for the dismissal perhaps an unlawful one. Non-critical performance evaluations can also result in an employee's eligibility for undeserved pay increases or job promotions.

Example: John, an ABC employee, should receive an "inadequate" rating for productivity but instead receives a "satisfactory". Mary, a good employee who unfortunately was disabled temporarily during the winter, also receives a "satisfactory". John is terminated six weeks later because of poor productivity. John, relying on his evaluations, thought his productivity was acceptable and took no steps to improve. John files a sex discrimination suit against ABC alleging female employees with similar absenteeism records were not discharged. As evidence, John compares his productivity evaluation with Mary's.

Presentation

Managers and supervisors must be aware that an evaluation is a very stressful event for the employee. Employees listen very carefully to the manner and content of the employer's message. Care must be taken to avoid any miscommunication or misperceptions. Employers should be particularly careful not to use inflammatory words. Informing an employee that you are not satisfied is never easy, but careful wording can reduce stress for both you and the employee without reducing the effectiveness of the message.

Employers must avoid using tactless language during an evaluation. For example, an employer can say an employee "lacks interpersonal skills"; however, the employer should not say that the employee "needs a course in charm school." Juries are seldom amused by such comments.

You also should bear in mind that the language used in one employee's evaluation can lead to a legal claim by another employee. For example, if you refer to a new vice-president as providing "new blood," an older employee who did not receive the job could use this choice of words in a subsequent age discrimination claim. Even if the comments were not meant to intentionally harm another employee, such statements can create legal problems for the employer.

Example: John is an older branch manager with ABC. The manager evaluates John's performance by stating that one "can't teach an old dog new tricks." John is ultimately replaced with a younger employee. The employer's inconsiderate and stereotypical comment is used as evidence in John's subsequent age discrimination claim.

Interaction

Communication is a two-way street. An evaluation should not be considered an opportunity to preach to the employee. Rather, the employee should have the opportunity to comment on the evaluation and should be encouraged to place written comments on the evaluation form. Allowing feedback lets the employee feel that he or she is part of the evaluation system and adds enhanced validity to the process. Even when an employee disagrees with the substance of the evaluation, providing the employee an opportunity to speak may lessen the employee's potential hostility or resentment.

Allowing the employee to provide an oral or written response to an evaluation is beneficial to the employee *and* the employer. Perceptive employers can learn a great deal from feedback provided by employees. Consistent employee dissatisfaction within the same section or department may indicate that a manager or supervisor is unduly harsh or perhaps discriminatory. Similarly, a pattern of unjustified complaints by a particular employee should warn the employer of a potential problem.

Example: A supervisor consistently gives female employees lower evaluations than male employees. Without employee comments this might have been overlooked. However, employee comments from several female employees state their evaluations are undeserved and overly harsh. This should cause the perceptive employer to look closely at the supervisor for possible discriminatory conduct.

Confidentiality

Evaluations are confidential. Access to an employee's evaluations should be strictly limited. Only persons with a legitimate reason to know their contents should have access. Employers are reasonably protected from defamation and other causes of action stemming from an evaluation by qualified immunity. Therefore, distributing the evaluation information only to persons involved in the evaluation process (such as managers and human resource personnel) would be protected by qualified immunity, while sharing the information with others outside of the process would not be protected and could be a source of liability. Also, going beyond statements of opinions about an employee's work performance in a evaluation report and making specific statements of fact—statements capable of objective proof—about what an employee did and did not do (for example, saying that a hospital worker changed the strength of radiation doses prescribed by a physician, misplaced radiation sources so as to endanger other employees, and lied in an effort to cover up these errors), if erroneous may be a basis for a defamation claim where state law permits.

Example: A manager at ABC made the mistake of telling Mary, a recent non-supervisory hire and good friend, about his demoralizing evaluation of John. The manager told Mary how John's drinking problem was preventing him from performing adequately. Mary, shocked by the news, repeats the information to her friends at lunch. This could lead to potential claims of discrimination, defamation, or intentional infliction of emotional distress. Since Mary had no reason to learn the content of John's evaluation, it was improper for her manager to discuss it with her.

Procedure

Procedure, another important aspect of the evaluation process, includes the consistency, content, and documentation of employee evaluations, as well as the use of employee self-evaluations to further involve employees in the process.

Consistency

A process should be in place to evaluate all employees on a regular basis—a minimum of once a year. The evaluation procedure should indicate which manager or supervisor is responsible for each employee's evaluation. Issues of inconsistency occur when an employer's evaluation process is not formalized. The failure to give a specific employee a timely evaluation possibly can serve as possible evidence of discriminatory conduct. The evaluation system should include firm dates by which evaluations must be completed.

Example: ABC is a growing company with no formal evaluation procedure. Mary is a foreman at ABC but is performing below expectations. ABC decides that in order to create a paper trail Mary will be evaluated next week. Even though the evaluation will be truthful when it states that she is a poor performer, Mary might use the inconsistent timing of the evaluation in subsequent litigation.

Content

An evaluation form—even if honest, consistent, and timely—is only beneficial if it evaluates the correct information. Too often evaluation forms contain little useful information. For instance, neither the employee nor the employer will gain significant insight from a purely numerical system of evaluation. Words capture a sense of employee performance better than raw numbers. Thus, if you choose to use a numeric scale, it is important to assign a cogent explanation for each potential choice so that the numbers will be meaningful and there is consistency across evaluations.

Although avoiding liability is important, the main goal of the evaluation process is to create an accurate and current record of the employee's overall performance. Specificity is important. This is particularly true when dealing with generalized character traits such as leadership or knowledge. Additionally, evaluators should also be encouraged to use the entire spectrum of the evaluation and should avoid the temptation to group employees together in the middle range. While it is certainly easier to distinguish higher-performing employees from lower-performing employees, it is just as important to draw finer distinctions among employees performing between those extremes. In drawing these distinctions, employers should consider what actually distinguishes each performance level from the other.

Example: A successful evaluation occurs when employees are informed about their employer's expectations. An evaluation form is helpful if it has a legend similar to the following:

Unsatisfactory	=	Consistently below expectations
Needs Work	=	Sometimes below expectations
Satisfactory	=	Consistently meets expectations
Excellent	=	Sometimes exceeds expectations
Outstanding	=	Consistently exceeds expectations

(However, even these ratings should be accompanied by comments of the evaluator addressing particular elements of the employee's work).

Documentation

An evaluation is of little use if it is not properly documented. In addition to providing a record of the substance of an employee's evaluation, the form should also indicate the time and date of the evaluation as well as any comments, complaints, or suggestions made by the employee during the course of the evaluation. Particular attention should be paid where a manager performing the evaluation may not be the employee's immediate supervisor. A standardized evaluation form is helpful in ensuring that all relevant information is discussed and also provides a level of consistency among various evaluators.

The employee should sign the evaluation form. The signature block should clearly indicate that the employee's signature is only an indication the employee has reviewed and understood the rating received. It should not indicate that the employee agrees with the substance of the evaluation.

Example: A manager at ABC completes an evaluation form and meets with an employee, John, to discuss performance. During the meeting, John tells the manager that he is interested in a transfer to another department because he cannot get along with his immediate supervisor. The manager should ask the reasons for the conflict, consider how they might affect the evaluation, and document the discussion in a comments section after the evaluation is complete.

Self-evaluation

Employers may want to include employee self-evaluations as part of the evaluation process. Employees should complete self-evaluations on the same form used by the employer and should submit the self-evaluation in time for the employer to include it with the supervisor's evaluation. Self-evaluations provide a way to gain employee participation in the evaluation process.

The Post-evaluation Meeting

After completion of the evaluation it is important to convey the content of the evaluation clearly and in accordance with the following procedures:

- Hold the meeting in private.
- Conduct the meeting in a professional manner.
- Be specific.
- Do not threaten.
- Explain any consequences thoroughly.
- Encourage dialogue.
- Listen carefully.
- Document the meeting by adding a written summary to the file.

Alternative Methods of Evaluation

Much like the ever-changing business environment, new and supposedly improved methods of evaluations are constantly appearing.

Computer Assistance

Not surprisingly, computer software is now available that leads managers through the evaluation process while looking out for dangerous vocabulary on the evaluation. This is designed to make the evaluation process more consistent and to help employers avoid unintentional legal problems.

Multi-rater Feedback Systems

Multi-rater feedback systems are also known as *360-degree evaluations*. This method relies on information collected from an employee's direct reports and peers as well as his or her supervisors. Some employers widen the evaluation process even further and include feedback from customer and clients. This is referred to as a *540-degree system*.

For employers to successfully use a multi-rater feedback system they must:

- Ensure that people provide honest feedback.
- Ensure that the data remains confidential.
- Verify that the data provided is accurate.
- Ensure that subjects can use the data to improve their performance.
- Understand how the system will affect the overall organization and make any necessary adjustments.

There are some drawbacks to the 360-degree system. For instance, employers should not use peer evaluations as a basis for bonuses or other compensation programs, since there is a possibility that peers may falsify input to the detriment of their co-workers for their own benefit. Further, some managers may find it difficult to share the evaluation process with other employees or to be evaluated by their subordinates.

Example: Mary receives an evaluation from her supervisor but disregards it because she believes the supervisor does not like her. A year later ABC implements a 360-degree system, and Mary gets similar reviews from her peers. Mary places more credibility in the peer review and begins to improve in targeted areas.

Conclusion

Employers need to understand the various elements of effective employee performance evaluations, including the need for effective communication and orderly procedures. The performance evaluation checklist that follows will provide a helpful outline as you design and implement your employee performance evaluation system.

Performance Evaluation Checklist

- [ ] Maintain a current and accurate job description for each position that will be evaluated.
- [ ] Ensure that employees have access to the job description for their positions, so they are aware of the essential job duties and performance objectives for their jobs as well as the means by which their performance will be measured and evaluated.
- [ ] Understand that the job of conducting a proper and effective performance evaluation is difficult, and only choose persons who will have the honesty, clarity of judgment, personal fortitude, and interpersonal skills necessary to conduct a proper and effective evaluation.
- [ ] Ensure that persons selected to serve as evaluators are properly trained. Evaluators must thoroughly understand the job that they are evaluating, as well as the importance of a timely, honest, fair, and confidential performance evaluation.
- [ ] Evaluators should be provided with clear instructions regarding the manner in which the company would like all performance evaluations to be conducted so there is consistency in the procedures and rating of employees.
- [ ] After an evaluation has been completed, review its form and content with representatives of the human resource department and/or upper management before sharing it with the employee. Problems can be remedied before they create difficulties, legal or otherwise, and consistency can be maintained in the application of company evaluation procedures.
- [ ] Be sure that employees are formally reviewed on a regular basis but no less than once a year. This should be done in a face-to-face evaluation conference.
- [ ] After the employer shares feedback, allow the employee to state his or her reaction to the content of the evaluation verbally and in writing.
- [ ] Require every employee to sign his or her performance evaluation acknowledging that he or she has seen the evaluation. Note that this signature should not suggest the employee agrees with the contents of the evaluation, only that he or she has read it.
- [ ] Maintain the confidentiality of every employee performance evaluation to the maximum extent possible.
- [ ] Regularly review and assess the effectiveness of the current evaluation system including evaluation forms, evaluation procedures, evaluator training, and evaluator neutrality. Make any changes that are necessary.

Chapter 16
Discipline

Introduction

In spite of an employer's best efforts to avoid hiring people who will be difficult employees, the employer will not always be successful. When a difficult employee is hired, the employer needs to take appropriate disciplinary action. Handling the situation well can mean the difference between ultimately terminating the difficult employee and helping him or her become a productive worker.

An effective and manageable disciplinary system is an integral part of any successful company. This chapter addresses the first two of the three components of a total disciplinary system. The first component involves the creation and implementation of an effective disciplinary policy. The second component is concerned with the unique problem caused by excessive employee absenteeism. The final component of an effective disciplinary system is a useful evaluation system.

Creating and Implementing a Disciplinary System

An effective disciplinary policy consists of several interrelated components:

- Establishing a fair system of work rules and expected standards of behavior and performance.
- Ensuring discipline is applied consistently.
- Requiring for detailed documentation.

Consistency and documentation are the foundation of an effective disciplinary policy. No matter how good the company's work rules are if they are not applied consistently they will lead to disputations in labor/management relations. A wise and consistent disciplinary policy that does not provide for adequate documentation will be of little value to an employer forced to defend its disciplinary decisions in an arbitration, administrative procedure, or court. Each component must be designed with the individual company's needs and capabilities in mind.

Establishing the Rules

The logical first step in a disciplinary system is making known to the employees what actions or inactions will constitute grounds for discipline. Because of the many differences that exist among employers and their operations, disciplinary policies are varied. Nevertheless, a few general rules may be gleaned from these divergent approaches.

The cardinal rule for drafting an effective disciplinary policy is to know the operation. Disciplinary rules should not be adopted uncritically from another employer; a borrowed policy will cause unnecessary problems and require constant amendment. Rather, a disciplinary policy should be suited to your specific operation. Seek input from each level of supervisory personnel, and then draft a policy that addresses your particular concerns.

Employers with nonunion workforces should exercise caution to ensure their disciplinary policy does not contain language that must be construed as a promise altering the employment-at-will relationship. Courts are reluctant to alter the at-will relationship. The disciplinary policy should include such qualifying language as:

- All employment at [company] is employment-at-will. Nothing contained in this disciplinary policy is intended to create a contract of employment or change the at-will nature of this employment.

- Nothing in this disciplinary policy restricts the employer from terminating employees for reasons unrelated to discipline so long as not contrary to law.

- The following list of offenses is not exclusive. This list is only intended to provide an example of offenses warranting discipline or discharge. The employer fully reserves the management right to discipline employees for misconduct not specifically referenced in this list, up to and including discharge.

Statements of this nature prominently displayed in the disciplinary policy will significantly reduce the risk of inadvertently altering the at-will relationship.

Enforcing the Rules

Once the rules are determined, a process must be established for initiating disciplinary action whenever the rules are broken. Normally, the process will include three steps:

1. An investigation.
2. A decision, explanation, and imposition of discipline.
3. An appeal process.

Investigation

Once an employer becomes aware that a possible infraction of the rules has occurred, an appropriate management official should immediately conduct a preliminary investigation. An appropriate official can be a supervisor, a human resources department professional, or someone in authority who is completely removed from the incident. The only essential requirement is that the person conducting the investigation must be capable of objectively evaluating the facts and the persons involved. A related consideration is whether the person conducting the investigation will be perceived by the employees involved as someone who is fair and objective. If the employees do not have confidence in the objectivity of the person conducting the investigation, the result of the investigation will not provide the finality necessary for the resolution of the problem. The official investigating the incident should determine:

- Whether misconduct occurred.

- Which employees were involved in the misconduct?

- Who witnessed the misconduct?
- What was the specific misconduct involved?
- What the consequences of the misconduct were (injury, hindered production, etc.)?

As soon as possible after the event, an interview should be conducted with the employee suspected of the misconduct. The employee's supervisor or another appropriate representative of management should conduct the interview in private, away from other employees. If the misconduct is serious, the person conducting the interview should consider having another management representative present in case a witness is needed to verify what occurred during the interview.

The employee should be given a chance to explain what happened and why it happened. The employee should be encouraged to identify any other employees who may have knowledge of the incident. At the conclusion of the interview, the employee should be told that he or she will be contacted again when the investigation is complete. If serious misconduct is involved, the employer may suspend the employee with or without pay during the course of the investigation. The interviewer must keep detailed and accurate notes of the interview. Under recent National Labor Relations Board case law, even nonunion employees who are subject to investigative interviews that they reasonably believe may result in disciplinary action are entitled to consult with another employee prior to the interview. They are also entitled to have the employee present during the interview, if they so request and if compliance with such a request will not unduly delay the investigation.

Interviews should be conducted with all of the witnesses as soon as possible after the incident. Interviews with witnesses should be conducted separately and detailed notes should be taken. If the misconduct involved is serious, the interviewer should get signed statements from each witness. In some cases, such as those involving alleged harassment, it may be preferable to interview other witnesses identified by a complainant before conducting an interview with the suspected perpetrator.

Explanation and Imposition of Discipline

The personnel department or management staff should review the information obtained from the investigation. At least one person in the decision-making process should be familiar with past disciplinary actions taken relevant to the group of employees involved. The personnel file of the employee should be reviewed to identify circumstances that would support either increasing or reducing the discipline imposed.

If it is decided that the employee should be disciplined for misconduct, the employee's supervisor must complete a written disciplinary form. The employee's name, job classification, department, and supervisor should be identified on the form. In describing the nature of the misconduct, the following information should be provided:

- The date and time of the offense.
- A brief description of the events surrounding the incident.
- All of the rules or policies violated by the misconduct.
- The effective date and nature of the discipline to be administered. If the discipline is a final warning, it should be clearly stated that future offenses will result in discharge.

It may be advisable to devise a standardized *Disciplinary Action Form*. In addition to the *Disciplinary Action Form*, in cases of serious misconduct a complete factual account of the incident should be maintained in the employee's personnel file. (Since fair employment practice agency charges and complaints constitute only allegations, however, they should be maintained separately from personnel files).

The employee should be allowed to review the *Disciplinary Action Form* at the time the offense and the corresponding disciplinary action are clearly explained. In addition, the employee must understand exactly what action the company will take if another violation of company rules occurs. Finally, the employee should be asked to sign the *Disciplinary Action Form*. If the employee refuses to sign, an attempt should be made to have him or her sign a notation on the document stating, "Employee refused to sign." If the employee still refuses the supervisor should indicate on the document that the employee refused to sign, and if possible have a management witness verify this fact.

As with previous steps it is important to keep detailed notes of this meeting and to have another person present to serve as a witness. The management official must at all times retain his or her composure. Do not argue with the employee. Be willing to listen to the employee but do not apologize for taking disciplinary action.

Appeal Process

An appeal process should be part of the procedure, particularly in instances of serious misconduct. The appeal should be made to a high-level management official who was not involved in the disciplinary process. The appeal process can be initiated verbally; however, at some point the issues and outcome of the appeal should be reduced to writing. The person considering the appeal should review the detailed notes of the investigation and compare the disciplinary action with discipline imposed in previous cases. In short, the reviewing official is to ensure that the discipline is fair and consistent with past practice. The appeal process should be timely, requiring no longer than a week to complete. (Under some union contracts, an employee's time to grieve discipline resulting from misconduct may be expressly limited. If the employee or union does not exercise this right to appeal in a timely manner, the matter may be deemed settled.) Alternative dispute resolution (ADR), such as peer review, mediation, or arbitration may also be used in these circumstances.

Documentation

The best-designed disciplinary policy can be rendered useless by the failure to maintain adequate documentation. Upholding any disciplinary action will require the employer to show the action is consistent with the employer's normal disciplinary policy. Without proper documentation, an employer will have difficulty ensuring disciplinary actions are consistent and assuring a third party of that consistency.

Ideally, a separate file should be maintained for each company rule or policy. Any time an employee receives discipline for violating a company rule or policy, a copy of the *Disciplinary Action Form* should be placed in the corresponding offense file. This way, all discipline imposed on employees for insubordination, for example, will be in one file for easy reference and comparison. If more than one company rule or policy is violated by an employee's misconduct, one copy of the *Disciplinary Action Form* should be placed in each corresponding offense file.

It is also a good idea to keep a record of policy or rule violations where no disciplinary action is taken. For example, if an employee breaks a company rule but the investigation reveals reason to support a reduced discipline. In such circumstances, a memorandum should be placed in the offense file indicating that a violation of the rule or policy was excused for a particular reason. This filing system should not replace the company's personnel filing system. It is an additional system designed to help supervisors administer consistent discipline.

Absenteeism—The Problem of the Invisible Employee

In almost every company absenteeism is the most prevalent disciplinary problem. Absenteeism results in inefficiency and decreased productivity as employers reassign workers and rearrange schedules to cover for absent employees. Employers pay a heavy price when employees fail to report to work consistently.

Establish an Attendance Policy

The first step in combating absenteeism is for the employer to establish an attendance policy that encourages and rewards attendance and discourages absenteeism. A formalized plan provides an objective goal for the employee and a framework for uniform implementation that ensures equal and just treatment for all employees.

Incentive Plans

A comprehensive attendance policy should have elements of both the "carrot" and the "stick." The carrot can take the form of a reward for exemplary attendance. Many employers offer additional time off for employees who do not use sick days. For instance, for every six-month period during which an employee has not used a sick day, the employee earns a personal day.

There is no requirement that the incentive take the form of extra days. Some employers offer cash incentives, awards, prizes, or even dinners to employees who achieve exemplary attendance. An effective incentive program offers a reward worth achieving within a reasonable timeframe. Quarterly incentives are often more effective than yearly incentives, which may often seem unreachable to an employee. (Note, however, that OSHA has criticized incentive plans which discourage employees from fully reporting occupational injuries and illnesses, such as those which offer rewards based on having the fewest lost work time accidents).

The stick component of the attendance plan can be as varied as the carrot portion. Such a policy can take the form of a traditional plan distinguishing between excused and unexcused absences or it can be a no-fault plan. Both types contain progressively severe penalties for increased absenteeism. Traditional plans usually share several features. Most importantly, they provide absent employees with an option, distinguishing between excused and unexcused absences. Such plans also typically allow employers to take special circumstances into account and provide for progressive discipline. The result is a plan in which supervisory personnel exercise significant discretion.

No-fault plans diminish supervisory discretion by eliminating the excused/unexcused distinction and informing employees that a certain number of absences will result in a definite disciplinary action. Typically such a plan also seeks to foster consistent attendance by maintaining a rolling tally where points drop off with the passage of time, or by returning the absenteeism tally to a blank slate after a certain period of perfect attendance. However, despite having a no-fault policy, some arbitrators still require an employer to take into account all relevant factors in determining whether to discharge an employee. Furthermore, in large organizations, prompt enforcement of such plans may prove difficult, since there often will be a day between the time the employee incurs a triggering absence and the time the human resources officials calculate the running total and direct disciplinary action. This could give rise to the appearance of inconsistent treatment.

In developing a no-fault plan, the employer must assess any Family and Medical Leave Act absences and not count them. It is unclear how courts will treat an Americans with Disabilities Act claim under a no-fault plan. However, government investigators looking into allegations of unlawful retaliation for the exercise of protected rights under various labor and employment laws may view with skepticism an employer's reliance on a lock-stop policy to explain a suspect termination, especially where it is not enforced with a high degree of consistency. In particular, employers should be mindful of the requirements of the Family and Medical Leave Act, the Americans with Disabilities Act, and similar state and local laws in applying any policies or practices discussed in this section.

Chronic Absenteeism

Physician Certificates

An important component of any successful attendance policy provides for verification and reintegration of absent employees returning to work. Employees absent for more than a few days should be required to provide medical verification of their condition. The number of days used to trigger this requirement should range from between three to five workdays. Accordingly, an employee who calls in sick for more than five days should be required to provide a physician's note verifying the existence of an injury or illness and releasing the employee to return safely to the workforce. Such a policy protects the employee who may try to return to work too soon after a serious illness, protects other employees who may be subjected to an infectious illness, and protects against employees using sick leave for unauthorized purposes. A policy may also be developed that requires a physician's note if a sick day is taken in conjunction with other forms of leave or in conjunction with weekends. A good policy will allow the employer to request a physician's note whenever the employee is suspected of abusing sick leave.

Return-to-work Physicals

A comprehensive attendance policy should also allow the employer to require an employee returning to work after a long illness or injury to undergo a physical examination to ensure the employee is fit to return. This examination should be limited to ensuring that the employee is able to meet the legitimate physical requirements for the position (subject to any appropriate accommodation).

Absenteeism without Violation of Policy

Regardless of the type of plan used, a company may still be concerned that a chronically absent employee, who does not technically violate the basic attendance policy, is having a negative effect upon the productivity of the workplace. Arbitrators recognize the right of employers to ensure their operations do not experience productivity declines and inefficiency resulting from chronic absenteeism, even if the absenteeism results from illness or other legitimate reasons. Regular attendance is a basic requirement and an employer cannot maintain efficiency and productivity without consistent attendance from employees.

In cases of chronic absenteeism, the employee can be disciplined and even discharged even though he or she has not directly violated the absenteeism policy. The key in such cases is to first determine what constitutes excessive chronic absenteeism, and then to develop a method for disciplining such an employee that meets a just-cause standard.

Calculating Absenteeism

Often a statistical approach is used to determine what constitutes excessive absenteeism. For example, the number of days missed can be divided into the number of days scheduled to obtain a simple percentage, which can then be compared to rates throughout the employer's facility.

Employers also should consider not only the gross number of absences, but also their frequency. For example, it is well-accepted that an employee who is out for a single 36-day period for surgery or another medical problem causes much less disruption than an employee who randomly misses work an average of three times per month, even though both employees have a yearly absenteeism rate of 13.8 percent.

Discipline

Once an employee has been identified as being chronically absent, the employer should construct a system for disciplining the absent employee that takes into account the following factors:

- How frequently has the employee been absent?
- Of what duration were the absences?
- Over what period of time?
- What are the reasons for the absences or tardiness?
- Did the employee provide timely notice and required documentation?
- Has progressive discipline or other corrective action been taken?
- Has the employee been notified of attendance requirements?
- How does the employee's record compare to other employees' records?
- Have employees in similar situations been treated the same way?

Particular attention must be paid to special leaves of absence. Leaves of absence protected by the Family and Medical Leave Act (FMLA) may not be counted against an employee's attendance record. Also, the Equal Employment Opportunity Commission (EEOC) has taken the position that an extension of leave beyond that authorized by company policy may constitute a reasonable accommodation under the Americans With Disabilities Act. Leaves of absence because of on-the-job injury can be counted against the employee's record if other absences are treated in a similar manner. With these considerations in mind, an employer may discipline or discharge a chronically absent employee even though no violation of the basic attendance policy was committed.

Discipline

Disciplinary Action Form

(You should be able to answer "Yes" to each of these questions before you take the action specified.)

Yes No

Before determining if discipline is appropriate, have you:

❑ ❑ Determined that the employee knew of the rule or performance standard that he or she violated?

❑ ❑ Determined that the rule or standard is reasonable, and that its enforcement would be reasonable under the circumstances?

❑ ❑ Reviewed all relevant materials including employee handbooks, contracts, policy statements, the employee's disciplinary history, evaluations, and attendance records?

❑ ❑ Interviewed all employees or third parties who may know of or were involved in the misconduct?

❑ ❑ Taken accurate notes from interviews/investigations about who, what, where, when, and why?

❑ ❑ Confronted the employee about the misconduct?

❑ ❑ Given the employee a fair opportunity to explain/deny the misconduct?

❑ ❑ Concluded that you are confident, based upon your interviews, records, etc., that you know all the necessary facts (who, what, when, where, why, and how)?

Before disciplining the employee, have you:

❑ ❑ Reviewed the proposed disciplinary action to ensure accuracy, consistency, and completeness?

❑ ❑ Determined that the disciplinary action is consistent with how other employees have been disciplined for the same or similar misconduct?

❑ ❑ Determined that the disciplinary action is the proper corrective measure under applicable policies and the employee's disciplinary history?

❑ ❑ Checked to make sure that the discipline notice/memo is accurate and complete? Be sure that it includes:

  ○ The date of the violation.
  ○ The specific rule violated.
  ○ The number of prior warnings.
  ○ A detailed description of misconduct.
  ○ The corrective action/penalty.
  ○ The date and signature of the employee's supervisor.

❑ ❑ Had the proposed disciplinary action been approved by personnel?

❑ ❑ Arranged to have a reliable management witness present if you are concerned about how the employee may react?

During a private conference with the supervisor or management representative and the employee:

☐ ☐ Has the supervisor reviewed the disciplinary notice/memorandum with the employee?

☐ ☐ Has the supervisor reviewed the facts with the employee?

☐ ☐ Has the supervisor explained:

- ○ The misconduct?
- ○ Why it is unacceptable?
- ○ The penalty given?
- ○ What penalty will result if the misconduct is repeated?
- ○ How the employee may improve his or her performance/conduct?

☐ ☐ If the employee is to be discharged has the supervisor given the employee written notice (a copy of which should be kept in the employee's personnel file) of the effective time and date of discharge?

After the disciplinary conference:

☐ ☐ Has the supervisor immediately made the necessary entries in the personnel file and other applicable records?

Chapter 17
Negligent Retention and Supervision

Introduction

The recommendations discussed in **Chapter 4, Recruiting and Hiring,** relate primarily to the pre-employment process. Employers should also pay close attention to behavior and information gained about employees **after** the hiring decision has been made. In particular, given the frequency of negligent retention claims involving allegations of sexual harassment, employers should document and respond decisively to any indication that an employee has engaged in harassing conduct or potentially violent behavior. This chapter looks at problems—grouped under the categories of negligent retention and negligent supervision—associated with employers' failure to monitor their employees closely.

Negligent Retention

The negligent retention theory arose out of *fellow servant law*, which imposed a duty on employers to select employees who would not endanger their fellow employees by their presence on the job. The theory evolved from one designed to protect employees to one designed to protect employees and the general public. Thus, the doctrine of negligent retention involves the employer's continued employment of an unfit individual.

Elements of Negligent Retention

To establish a claim for negligent retention, an individual must generally meet the following requirements similar to those found in the negligent hiring context:

- The employer retains an employee who is incompetent or unfit for the job.

- The employer knew, or should have known, that the employee presents an unreasonable risk of harm to others.

- The employee commits an intentional or negligent act, which results in injury to a third party.

- The third party's injuries are proximately caused by the employer's retention of the employee.

The Basis for Claims of Negligent Retention

Negligent retention claims may arise even when the employer has conducted an extensive investigation into an employee's background at the time of hire. During the course of employment, the employer may become aware of problems with an employee that indicate unfitness. A claim of negligent retention will arise when an employer becomes aware of problems with a particular employee but fails to take further action such as investigating, disciplining, discharging, or reassigning the employee. In such cases, the employer has a duty to take appropriate action to protect other employees and the public. This duty is not limited to actions occurring on the employer's premises.

The Employer Knew or Should Have Known

Negligent retention claims often focus on whether the employer *knew or should have known* of the employee's unfitness for duty. This question is often very fact-specific, but the courts have identified a number of factors that may be relevant to such a determination:

- The employee's overall work record.
- Whether the employer had received any complaints about the employee.
- The degree to which the employee's negative activities were related to the job.
- Whether any managers or supervisors witnessed the alleged negative activities.

Appropriate Employer Action

A second and related issue that often arises in the negligent retention context concerns the nature of appropriate employer action. Even if an employer learns of an employee's negative activities, the employer will only be held liable for negligent retention if it fails to take appropriate action to address the activities. Appropriate action may include:

- Disciplining the employee.
- Removing the employee from a position in which he or she could harm other employees or members of the public.
- Exercising closer supervision over the employee.
- Terminating the employee.

Negligent Supervision

Another claim recognized in the employment context is negligent supervision. To establish a claim of negligent supervision an individual generally must demonstrate the following elements:

- The employer knows that the employee is engaging in wrongful conduct.
- The employee's wrongful conduct is substantially certain to cause injury to a third party.
- The employee's conduct, through either intentional or negligent action, results in injury to a third party.
- The third party's injury was a reasonably foreseeable consequence of the employer's lack of supervision.

Negligent supervision claims are brought most often in the context of sexual harassment lawsuits. An employee may allege that poor supervision by the employer of another employee allowed the harassing conduct to continue. In these circumstances, the success of the negligent supervision claim may depend on the following circumstances:

- Whether the employee/victim reported the harassment to the employer.

- Whether the employer otherwise knew or should have known about it.
- Whether the employer took prompt action to prevent further harassment.

Negligent supervision claims also arise when injuries occur to non-employees through the conduct of an employee. For an employer to be found liable, courts generally require that the harmful conduct must have occurred on the employer's property or with something belonging to the employer (for example, an automobile). Courts sometimes examine whether the conduct occurred while the employee was working or on duty. Thus, a negligent supervision claim might be successful if the employee's conduct occurred while he or she was subject to the supervision or control of the employer. But even then, employers generally must have had some reason to anticipate the harmful conduct by the employee before they may be held liable for failing to prevent the harm through properly supervising the employee.

Claims for negligent supervision are still fairly new in most states, but the number of such claims is likely to grow. A claim that an employer failed to take proper care in supervising its employees fills the gap between a claim for negligent hiring and a negligent-retention claim. The best way for an employer to avoid negligent-supervision claims is to pay close attention to the conduct of employees after they are hired, to take prompt action if observation indicates that a particular employee may be behaving inappropriately, and to clearly document such actions and observations as they occur.

The success of a claim for negligent supervision or negligent retention may also depend on whether the employee or injured individual has brought claims under the state anti-discrimination laws. Taking advantage of such state law remedies may nullify the employee's claims for negligence.

Negligent Training

Employees may also raise claims of negligent training arising out of facts similar to their claims of negligent supervision and negligent retention. Many state courts have not yet addressed the issue of negligent training but the trend to recognize such claims is growing.

Conclusion

Employees are raising claims of negligent retention, supervision, and training with increasing frequency. Employers should document inappropriate behavior by current employees and take prompt and appropriate steps to respond to such conduct. Following the guidelines below can help employers reduce their exposure to negligent retention, supervision, and training claims while improving the quality of their workforce:

- Document all complaints about current employees and supervisors, especially complaints regarding sexual harassment and/or potentially violent behavior.
- Investigate all complaints promptly and document the results of the investigation.
- Exercise closer supervision over offending employees.
- Remove offending employees from positions in which they could harm other employees or members of the public.
- When appropriate, transfer offending employees to another shift or workstation.
- Document all disciplinary action taken against employees.
- Have employees sign forms acknowledging the disciplinary actions taken against them.

- Discharge offending employees, if necessary.
- After complaints of harassment, disseminate or redistribute anti-harassment policies to all employees.
- Adopt policies or employee handbook provisions that require employees to report any inappropriate conduct by co-employees.
- Conduct supervisory training regarding workplace harassment and/or violence and other common types of allegations in negligent hiring and supervision cases.

Chapter 18
Termination

Introduction

Termination is when an employee is:

- Fired.
- Laid off.
- Suspended for an unreasonably long period.
- Constructively discharged.

Most employment-related lawsuits follow an employee's termination. Employers can reduce their exposure to wrongful-termination lawsuits and damage awards by deciding carefully whether, when, and how to terminate an employee and by implementing and following effective strategies and procedures for hiring, evaluating, and disciplining employees, as discussed in previous chapters.

This chapter reviews proper versus improper termination, looks closely at types of wrongful discharge, and considers some ways to avoid liability for improper termination.

Proper Termination

Employment-at-will Employees

When an employee is hired under an employment-at-will relationship, he or she may be terminated at any time with or without a reason, and the employer need not follow any particular procedure in discharging the employee. Therefore, an employer is at liberty to discharge an at-will employee unless the termination violates a statute, is constitutionally impermissible, or breaches an express limitation in a contract of employment. The precise contours of the at-will doctrine vary from state to state. Employers should consult with an employment law attorney prior to terminating the employment of an employee presumed to be at-will.

Contractual Employees

Employees who are not hired under an employment-at-will relationship are promised some type of job security. Employees working under a union contract, for example, can usually only be fired for "just cause." In addition, employees hired for a definite period of time often may be terminated only for "just cause." *Just cause* may include, but is not limited to, the following:

- Misconduct, including:
  - Theft.

Termination

- Workplace violence.
- Intoxication on the job.
- Bringing firearms to work.
- Engaging in serious racial or sexual harassment.
- Insubordination.

♦ Unsatisfactory performance, including:
- Excessive absenteeism.
- Poor quality of work.
- Failure to meet numerical production standards.

Serious misconduct often subjects an employee to immediate dismissal even under a union contract. However, unsatisfactory job performance often may not result in discharge for cause until the employee has received a series of warnings and failed to improve.

Guidelines for Proper Termination— Progressive Discipline

An effective discharge procedure is generally based on progressive discipline. Although there are situations that require varying from progressive procedures, a progressive approach is based upon a presumption that employees, by nature, do not wish to engage in misconduct and if allowed a chance will correct their behavior. Such a system recognizes that discharge is generally a last resort.

The following section outlines procedures for properly dealing with employee termination and avoiding wrongful-discharge claims.

Retain Employees When Possible

Obviously, retaining employees precludes the possibility of wrongful-discharge problems. Whenever possible, employers should try to retain their employees. Consider the following before discharging an employee:

- ♦ Establish fair and reasonable work rules, related to valid business interests, and apply them uniformly to all employees. Fair and reasonable rules foster good employee morale since employees know what is expected of them.

- ♦ Always investigate thoroughly before disciplining an employee.

- ♦ Respond to inappropriate employee behavior or performance with appropriate disciplinary or corrective procedures. The degree of the penalty should relate to the seriousness of the offense. Factors to be considered in this determination include the need for corrective action, the employee's past record, the employee's length of service, whether the employee knew the conduct would result in discipline, and whether management contributed to the misconduct.

- ♦ Progressive discipline systems generally involve a three- or four-step approach before an employee is discharged. For example, an employee may initially be given a verbal warning for an offense, followed by a written warning for the same offense, and then a short suspension from one to five days for a third offense. The fourth offense may result in discharge.

    Note: Progressive discipline systems vary from employer to employer. Consult with an employment law attorney prior to adopting any specific procedure.

- While rules must be enforced consistently, a disciplinary system should maintain some degree of flexibility in both procedure and substance.

Handle Discharges Correctly

Sometimes discharge is unavoidable. Sometimes, discipline or performance problems are so severe that discharge is the only viable option. However, employers will minimize their liability and help maintain the dignity of their employees if they take the following steps:

- Termination should be done in person. Have two managers or a manager and a human resources representative present at firings.
- Do not discharge someone before birthdays, holidays, or the like.
- Make certain the individuals communicating the termination are prepared to be calm, concise, and factual as to the reason for the employer's action.
- Do not encourage the employee to feel the termination is the end of his or her career.
- Maintain control over the situation. Be compassionate yet firm. Employees should not feel they control the outcome.
- Consider providing job counseling for terminated employees.
- Collect keys and other security-sensitive property.
- Make any severance package consistent with what other employees have been offered.
- Consider a general release of all claims and/or prospective claims in appropriate cases.
- Ensure that the final decision to discharge is made by the executive in charge, based on recommendations of lower management and human resource executives.
- Conduct an "exit interview" even though the termination is involuntary. Assess the employee's attitude about the employer and cover pay, benefit matters, final checks, and insurance options.
- Consult with an employment counsel.

Improper Termination

Wrongful Discharge

Terminating employment-at-will employees for an illegal reason or terminating contractual employees without following proper procedures or without just cause may be examples of wrongful discharge.

Laws and Regulations Restricting Employment-at-Will

The most commonly recognized restrictions on employment-at-will are the specific rights provided by federal and state laws and regulations. These laws and regulations state that employers may not fire at-will employees because they are members of a statutorily protected group. These classifications include, but are not limited to:

- Race.
- Creed.

- Color.
- Sex/Gender.
- National origin.
- Religion.
- Age.
- Marital status.
- Disability.
- Union activity.
- Sexual orientation.
- Parental status.
- Military status.
- Whistleblower activity.
- Serving on a jury.
- Filing a workers' compensation claim.
- Assisting in a government investigation.

Employees fired for any of these reasons may sue for wrongful discharge. Many federal and state statutes exist to protect employees from being terminated for discriminatory reasons, greatly restricting employment-at-will. In addition, many statutes prohibit employers from retaliating against employees who have exercised their rights under the statutes.

States (and some localities) have their own statutes prohibiting discrimination in employment and otherwise prohibiting employment actions based on certain grounds. For example, many states' laws prohibit disciplining or discharging employees for engaging in whistle blowing activity, filing workers' compensation claims or serving on jury duty.

Federal Statutes Limiting Employment-at-Will

- **Age Discrimination in Employment Act** (29 USCA §621)—prohibits employment discrimination against workers 40 years old or older, bars retaliation against people exercising their ADEA rights.

- **Americans with Disabilities Act** (42 USCA §12101)—prohibits employment discrimination against qualified individuals with disabilities, bars retaliation against those exercising the ADA rights.

- **Bankruptcy Code** (11 USCA §525)—prohibits employers from discriminating against or terminating an employee solely because the person has filed for bankruptcy.

- **Civil Service Reform Act of 1978** (5 USCA §7513a)—permits removing federal civil service employees only for efficiency-related reasons.

- **Civil Rights Act of 1964, Title VII** (42 USCA §§2000e-2, 2000e-3a)—prohibits discharge based on race, color, religion, sex, or national origin and prohibits reprisal for exercising rights under the act.

- **Clean Air Act** (42 USCA §7622)—prohibits firing employees who assist in any proceeding under the act.

- **Consumer Credit Protection Act** (15 USCA §1674a)—prohibits firing employees because of garnishment of wages for any one indebtedness.
- **Employee Retirement Income Security Act of 1974** (29 USCA §§1140, 1141)—prohibits terminating employees to prevent them from obtaining vested pension rights.
- **Energy Reorganization Act of 1974** (42 USCA §5851)—prohibits firing employees who assist in any proceedings under the act.
- **Fair Labor Standards Act** (29 USCA §§215(a)(3), 216b)—prohibits discharge for exercising FLSA rights.
- **Family and Medical Leave Act of 1993** (29 USC §250 et seq.)—prohibits discharge for exercising rights under the act; bars retaliation against those exercising FMLA rights.
- **Federal Water Pollution Control Act** (33 USCA §1367)—prohibits firing employees who assist in any proceeding under the act.
- **Immigration Reform and Control Act of 1968** (8 USCA §1324b)—prohibits employment discrimination against individuals, except unauthorized aliens, because of national origin and against U.S. citizens or aliens eligible for citizenship because of citizenship status.
- **Judiciary and Judicial Procedure Act** (28 USCA §1875)—prohibits firing employees for service on grand or petit juries.
- **National Labor Relations Act** (29 USCA §§158(a)(1), 158(a)(3), 158(a)(4))—prohibits termination for union activity, protected concerted activity, or filing charges or giving testimony under the act.
- **Occupational Safety and Health Act of 1970** (29 USCA §651 et seq.0)—prohibits firing employees for exercising OSHA rights.
- **Railroad Safety Act** (45 USCA §§441a, 441(b)(1))—prohibits firing employees who assist in any proceeding under the act.
- **Rehabilitation Act of 1973** (29 USCA §§793, 794)—prohibits federal contractors or any program or activity receiving federal financial assistance from discriminating against persons with disabilities.
- **Uniformed Services Employment and Re-employment Rights Act** (38 USC §§4301-4333)—requires reinstatement of and protects returning veterans for a limited time against discharge without just cause.

Constructive Discharge

Sometimes employees quit, but they do not do so voluntarily. When employees are forced or coerced into quitting, it may be considered a *constructive discharge*. For example, an employee who is victimized by her supervisor's constant sexual harassment may feel compelled to quit. The employee's leaving might be considered a constructive discharge.

Generally, a discharge is considered "constructive" if the following apply:

- The employer deliberately created or condoned working conditions for the employee that a reasonable person in the employee's position would find intolerable.
- Any reasonable employee would quit rather than endure the situation.

Employees may be constructively discharged for a number of reasons including, but not limited to, the following:

- Discrimination.
- Dangerous duties.
- Hazardous situations.
- Harassment.
- Demeaning or malicious assignments.
- An employer's failure to give the employee any work to do.

Avoiding Constructive Discharge Claims

When an employee quits after complaining of intolerable work conditions, the employer should immediately investigate to verify the employee's claim and, if appropriate, to remedy the situation. The employer may wish to consider offering the employee unconditional and immediate reinstatement. The employer should assure the employee that the intolerable conditions have been corrected. This approach can reduce potential liability and severely undercut an employee's claim of constructive discharge. If an employee who raised a complaint of discrimination or similar violation of law is reinstated, however, great care must be taken in dealing with the employee to avoid claims of retaliation.

Claims Employees May Bring After Termination

This section reviews the sorts of claims terminated employees might bring against employers. We also outline some procedures to help employers protect themselves from liability resulting from these claims.

Breach of Contract

In the most common wrongful termination lawsuits, plaintiffs claim that their discharge breached a contract—whether formal or informal, express or implied—not to terminate employment except for "good cause." Consequently, employers must structure employment documents and policies carefully and precisely in case a terminated employee later sues for alleged breach of contract. If possible, seek the advice of an employment law counsel prior to executing an employment contract. Doing so may help avoid future litigation or provide a successful defense of a future breach of contract claim.

Both express written and oral contracts and implied contracts, such as employee handbooks and disciplinary procedures (as discussed in **Chapter 4, Recruiting and Hiring**), are enforceable in many states. Juries have often treated informal oral statements such as those made by a supervisor to an employee, a series of positive performance evaluations, or offer letters as binding contracts.

Interference with Contractual Relationships

This type of claim alleges that individual supervisors or managers interfered with the contractual relationship between an employee and his or her employer. An example of such a claim is where a supervisor knowingly communicates false information about an employee to higher management and that information results in the employee's termination. These claims are normally brought against supervisors or managers who are acting maliciously outside the scope of their employment.

Constructive Discharge Claims

Employees who are forced to quit as a result of constructive discharge may claim that their resignation was not voluntary but rather the result of an employer's actions or the employer's failure to correct an intolerable working environment. In such situations, the employees may sue for wrongful discharge.

Discharges in Violation of Public Policy

In certain states, a separate public-policy exception to employment-at-will exists if the reason for terminating an employee is contrary to clearly established public policy. This is known as *wrongful discharge in violation of public policy.* While the elements of such a claim vary by state and statute, the discharged employee must usually prove that he or she was discharged under circumstances that would jeopardize public policy and for reasons motivated by conduct damaging to public policy rather than for overriding legitimate business reasons.

Examples of conduct that may be protected include, but are not limited to:

- Whistleblowing—reporting unlawful activities by an employer to law-enforcement officials. This may also be something as simple as complaining to another employee or to the media.
- Filing a workers' compensation claim.
- Refusing to perform illegal, unethical or unsafe activities on behalf of an employer.
- Fulfilling a legal duty, such as serving on a jury or attending court when subpoenaed as a witness, or for taking time off to vote.
- Cooperating in a governmental investigation involving the employer.
- Many statutes also prohibit employers from taking retaliatory action against an employee who engages in such activities.

Under some whistleblowing laws, employees must first report the alleged unlawful activities to the employer who has a certain time period to correct or initiate a reasonable good faith effort to correct the unlawful activities. If the employer makes no reasonable effort to correct the problem, the employee may report the conduct to the prosecuting authority of the county, a peace officer, an appropriate inspector general, or other appropriate officials or agencies. Employers may take no retaliatory action against employees who follow this procedure.

Employers must be aware of public policy discharge cases because they are often treated like personal injury cases; that is, plaintiffs may actually recover compensation for mental anguish and punitive damages as well. Punitive damages "punish" the defendants by awarding damage amounts that are often much greater than the actual economic damages of lost wages and benefits.

Under the Federal False Claims Act, employees may file suit against their employers for suspected fraud against the government. This law entitles employees to recover a percentage of any amounts recovered by the government. Employers doing business with the government need to be aware that disgruntled employees have this option open to them. The act prohibits retaliation against an employee who files an action, testifies, or otherwise helps the government in an investigation under the act.

Good Faith and Fair Dealing

Many state courts have held that contractual employment relationships contain an implied promise or covenant of good faith and fair dealing. In theory, one party to the contract must not act in bad faith and deprive the other party of the benefits of the agreement. Such cases may involve the following:

- Terminating an employee to avoid paying a sales commission.

- Retaliating against an employee who refuses to become romantically involved with a supervisor.
- Retaliating against an employee who publicizes a wrongdoing on the part of the employer.

Intentional Infliction of Emotional Distress

Intentional infliction of emotional distress is defined as the actions of one party, who by extreme and outrageous conduct, intentionally or recklessly causes severe emotional distress to another party. The law in this area varies from state to state. Under some circumstances, at-will employees may accuse their former employers of intentionally inflicting emotional distress during the termination of employment. This type of claim may include allegations of intentional and extremely abusive discharge of the employee. The employee also may claim his or her discharge was conducted in a degrading and humiliating manner. Furthermore, allegations of sexual harassment may amount to intentional infliction of emotional distress.

To win in this claim, the employee must show that the following occurred:

- The employer intended to cause severe emotional distress, or knew or should have known that the actions taken would result in severe emotional distress.
- The employer's conduct was extreme or outrageous. (In many states, this requires the plaintiff to show that the alleged outrageous conduct so transcends the bounds of decency as to be regarded as atrocious and intolerable in a civilized society.)
- The employer's actions proximately caused the employee's severe emotional distress.
- The mental anguish the employee suffered was serious.

If the employee is successful in the claim, the employer may be liable for the emotional distress as well as for any bodily harm—if any—that results from it.

Reducing Liability for Emotional Distress Claims

Employers are not liable for any resulting emotional distress when they have merely exercised their legal rights to terminate an employee. However, the mere fact that an employee's termination was done lawfully will not necessarily preclude a claim for intentional infliction of emotional distress.

To reduce the chances of liability for causing emotional distress, employers should do the following:

- Avoid anger in administering discipline.
- Require review of any contemplated disciplinary decisions by another supervisor or manager who has no personal bias against the employee.
- Use common sense and avoid embarrassing the employee in front of others.
- Document, sign, and date every critical incident.

Since the type and degree of behavior that amounts to "outrageous conduct" varies by state, employers should consult with an employment law counsel when faced with such a claim or potential claim.

Fraud and Negligent Misrepresentation

A terminated employee may also bring a fraud claim against an employer, alleging that the employer made false assurances of job security or benefits either in writing or orally. It may be that the employee has discovered that the job is not all it appeared to be during the pre-employment interviews. The job duties may be different, the bonuses may be difficult to earn, or the boss is more difficult to work with than expected. Under these circumstances, the employee may claim to have accepted the job offer because the employer made statements that seemed sincere but were actually statements the employer knew or should have known were not true. This is especially likely to happen when the discharged employee was in a highly compensated job.

In addition, an employee may claim that during the hiring process the employer knowingly made false representations about the future to induce the employee to join the employer.

To succeed in a fraud claim, the employee generally must show the following:

- The employer made a representation.
- The representation was significant to the transaction.
- The representation was made falsely.
- The representation was made with the intent to mislead.
- The employee relied on the misrepresentation.
- The employee's reliance on the misrepresentation was justified.
- The representation proximately caused an injury to the employee.

Employees who can demonstrate the existence of these elements can recover damages for their losses and possibly receive punitive damages for the employer's conduct.

Defamation Suits

Defamation claims are often linked to wrongful termination. An employee or former employee may sue his or her current or former employer based upon alleged false or defamatory statements of fact communicated to another person that purportedly injured the employee's reputation. Statements by an employer that an employee was guilty of or had any of the following could lead to potential defamation claims:

- Gross misconduct, theft, embezzlement, or falsifying records.
- Using or abusing drugs.
- Professional incompetence.
- Criminal convictions or arrests.
- A communicable or venereal disease.

Defamation claims may be based on oral or written statements communicated to individuals inside or outside the company. Any derogatory statements can be the basis for a defamation action. In some states, statements made by the terminated employee himself have been considered compelled" self-defamation."

Employers have a right to make truthful statements about employees, even if they are viewed as derogatory. Additionally, employers have a *qualified privilege* right to communicate derogatory statements about employees to others within and outside the company who share a common interest in the information. When there is a legal requirement to make the derogatory statements—as in judicial or quasi-judicial proceedings—this is known as *absolute privilege* and no defamation exists.

Reducing Liability for Defamation Claims

Employers can avoid defamation claims by acquiring and applying a basic understanding of the law in this sensitive area and by following a few simple precautions:

- Discuss an employee's alleged misconduct, poor performance, or termination only with those who need to know. Caution those with whom the information is shared to be discrete.

- Investigate and document incidents of employee misconduct before imposing discipline.
- Keep medical data, especially drug-test results, strictly confidential.
- Respond to reference requests only by providing such objective facts as dates of employment and position held.
- Obtain a signed release from employees before releasing any employment data.
- Provide adverse information only if it is factually based and verified as true.
- Balance discussion of weaknesses with discussion of strengths.
- Distinguish opinion from assertions of fact and denominate it as such.

Truth is a complete defense to a defamation suit since it defeats an essential element of the suit—the claim that a false statement was made. True statements, even if damaging to an employee's reputation, may not give rise to a legal claim.

Consent is another defense against defamation claims. An employee's agreeing to the publication or communication of the alleged defamatory statements also serves as a complete defense and is recognized by the courts.

The **statute of limitations** can provide another complete defense to a defamation claim. If the employee does not bring a claim within the statutorily defined period (which often is short, such as one year), the claim is lost and cannot be initiated.

Invasion-of-Privacy

Employees also have raised invasion-of-privacy claims in employment litigation. Invasion-of-privacy claims often accompany defamation suits. These claims may be based on one of the following theories:

- Unreasonable intrusion into an individual's personal affairs.
- Publication of an individual's private affairs, including embarrassing and private facts, which the public has no right to know.
- Publishing facts that are literally true but that give a false and negative impression of an individual.

Invasion-of-privacy claims are most likely to come out of such employment-related situations as the following:

- Checking references.
- Testing for drug use.
- Disclosing employee records.
- Disclosing reports on discipline or misconduct.
- Searching employees' persons or belongings.
- Transmitting data electronically.

Since the viability and elements of invasion-of-privacy claims vary significantly from state to state, employers should consult with employment law counsel when faced with such a claim or potential claim.

Avoiding Liability for Invasion-of-Privacy Claims

Employers can avoid liability for invasion-of-privacy claims by simply removing the expectations of privacy if doing so is permitted under the law. Employers can establish, distribute, and post policies stating that personal items, lockers, purses, and automobiles are subject to search and that drug testing may be required under certain circumstances during employment. Employers may consider the following after consulting with an employment law counsel:

- Inform employees with e-mail access that e-mail is not private and may be read by anyone having access to the system, including the employer.
- Obtain consent to provide employment references, search employee person and property, or perform drug testing.
- Protect the confidentiality of employee performance evaluations, medical records, and disciplinary records.
- Limit undercover investigations to workplace surveillance.

General Techniques for Avoiding Liability for Wrongful Termination

Employers can limit liability arising from certain wrongful termination claims by explicitly stating in employee handbooks, policy manuals, offer letters, and application forms the following:

- The employment offered, if accepted, is employment-at-will.
- No contract or other enforceable obligation is intended.
- Only a few specified managers or administrators can alter the at-will employment relationship.

Employers can minimize termination claims by reviewing all aspects of the employment relationship and using appropriate techniques throughout the relationship. For example:

Perfect Your Hiring Techniques

- Review all writings, offer letters, contracts, and employment applications to ensure they specify employment-at-will.
- Provide training to interviewers and recruiters so they make no statements that will cause problems for the employer.
- Adopt a checklist of what interviewers should cover and what they should avoid.

Review the Personnel Policy Manual

- Should it deal with termination at all?
- To whom should it be addressed?
- Should there be more than one version?
- Should there be a disclaimer?
- Have you reserved the right to terminate at-will?
- Have you reserved the right to change the manual at any time?
- Should there be "training periods" rather than "probationary periods"?
- Is the manual current with changes in law or circumstances?

Review Personnel Policies and Procedures

- Remove references to job security, just cause or good cause, or other promises to employees.

- Maintain documentation.
- Base documentation on fact, not opinion.
- Review documentation with employees.
- Give employees a chance to respond in writing.
- Be consistent in application.
- Delete policies not being followed or enforced.
- Develop a procedure for deleting out-dated materials in personnel files that is consistent with record retention laws and litigation requirements.
- Put performance appraisals, criticisms, and warnings about the employee in writing.
- Ensure that performance appraisals reflect warnings given to an employee to avoid inconsistency.

If you consider evaluations during termination decisions, you must verify the quality of the evaluation. Evaluations must be done right or not at all. If employee evaluations were considered, make sure they were based on actual performance as indicated by the job title, job description, and the actual duties the employee performed. Additionally, you should ensure that the evaluations were done when required by company policy, provided information about significant performance or behavioral problems, and provided a plan or mechanism for correction.

Follow Progressive Discipline

- Make the discipline appropriate.
- Treat employees fairly and provide them with due process.
- Let employees know what is expected of them.
- Give employees warnings of the consequences of their actions.
- Give employees time to correct or lessen their deficiencies.
- Be uniform and consistent in applying discipline.

Adopt Specific Discharge Procedures

- The discharge procedure should include progressive discipline, although room should be left for exceptions.
- The procedure may include a list of "capital offenses." Any list should contain language such as "or similar offenses" to indicate that the list is not exhaustive.
- A grievance procedure may be included in the discharge procedure (an employment law counsel should be consulted on establishing any alternative dispute resolution procedure).
- Care should be taken not to create inconsistencies with the general employment at-will rule.

Communicate the Final Decision Correctly

Communicating the termination decision is an important part of the process. The employee should understand the company's reasons for the decision to discharge. Some techniques for effectively communicating the termination are the following:

- Try to lessen the severity by making the news not unexpected. In many situations, for example, the employee will be on probation or possibly expecting termination.

- Make the termination notice brief and candid. Do not apologize.
- Treat the employee with dignity and respect.
- If the employee is to leave the premises immediately, carry out the discharge at the end of the day, after co-workers have left.

Give the Employee Appropriate Termination Benefits

A terminated employee is entitled to the following:

- The payment of all wages actually earned, such payment to be made on or before the next regularly occurring payday.

  Note: State laws often regulate such payment and may impose penalties for non-payment or late payment of final pay.

- Vacation pay if such vacation is earned and vested in accordance with the employer's policies about unused vacations.

  Note: State laws vary regarding the handling of vacation time.

- Severance pay as provided in the employer's policies, by practice, by contract, or by plan.
- Group health insurance at the employee's own expense, according to the requirements of COBRA.
- Sixty days' advance notice of termination if such termination results from plant closings or mass layoffs according to the requirements of WARN. Employees are entitled to full pay and benefits during these 60 days.
- Such additional benefits as may specifically be required by an employee's employment contract, company policy, or a collective bargaining agreement.

Consider Separation Agreements

Especially in cases where employers have reason to believe discharged employees may file lawsuits, employers and employees may enter into separation agreements that may include extra severance benefits for the employee in exchange for the employee's general waiver of all claims and prospective claims against the employer. A non-coerced, written waiver or release of claims (covenant not to sue) may effectively prevent an employee from later suing an employer. If the waiver includes a waiver of age discrimination claims under the Age Discrimination in Employment Act (ADEA), the statute requires, among other things, that:

- The release must be written in ordinary language the employee can understand.
- The release must specifically refer to employee rights and claims under the ADEA.
- There can be no waiver of claims arising after the date the release is executed.
- There must be additional consideration of value given for the release, such as paid benefits or cash. Such consideration must be in addition to that the employee would have received had there been no separation agreement.
- The employer must advise the employee to consult an attorney.
- The employer must give the employee at least 21 days to consider the release. An employee must be given 45 days if the waiver is part of group termination procedure.
- The employee must have at least seven days to revoke the release after signing it.

- Additional statistical information must be given to employees terminated as part of a group termination program.

According to recent rulings by the U.S. Supreme Court, if a separation agreement does not meet these requirements the release is ineffective and the employee may still sue the employer under the ADEA, while still keeping the benefits paid by the employer. Employers must be certain the release identifies specifically what claims the employee is agreeing not to pursue and must specify the employer's rights if the employee fails to follow the agreement.

Employers should always consult with an employment law attorney prior to entering into a severance agreement and/or general release of claims with a former employee.

Consider Arbitration Agreements

Employers may substantially reduce the costs and risks of employment litigation by directing formal disputes to final and binding arbitration.

A Termination Checklist

A central authority should review all individual terminations to confirm that all procedures have been followed and that the discharge is consistent with prior treatment of other employees. Indeed, before any final decision is made to discharge an employee, the personnel department or human resources department should become involved. The human resources manager should review the termination decision. It is **not sufficient** for a department head to review a supervisor's decision. The human resources department should check for oversights, ensuring uniform and consistent treatment of all employees.

You should develop a checklist of things to be reviewed for each proposed termination, along the lines of the one detailed below:

Termination for Poor Performance

- If the termination is for poor performance, is the termination consistent with the employee's performance appraisals?
- Were performance standards and expectations communicated to the employee? Was the employee told how to improve and when he or she needed to meet expectations?
- Is the deficiency capable of objective assessment (for example, "bad attitude" vs. "employee refused to assist customer")?
- Is the action **consistent** with prior incidents of a similar nature?
- Was the employee given a notice of poor performance? If there has been a sudden drop in the employee's performance, can it be justified?
- Was the employee given an opportunity to improve?
- Is the articulated reason for discharge the real reason?
- Was the employee ever told that his or her failure to improve could result in termination?

Termination for Misconduct

- If the termination is for misconduct, was the rule the employee violated published? Can you document where and when it was published?

- Did the employee receive a written copy of the work rules? You should distribute employee handbooks upon hiring and have all employees sign an acknowledgement of receipt specifying they have read and understood the content of the document.
- Was the event triggering disciplinary action thoroughly investigated?
- Did the employee have an opportunity to explain his or her actions?
- Are the witnesses credible?
- Did the employee receive warnings and an opportunity to correct the behavior?
- Was the employee notified of the possible results of such conduct?
- Was progressive discipline tried?
- Have rules been applied consistently? Have other employees been terminated for the same or similar conduct?
- Are there previous documented violations of the same rule or standard of conduct?
- Does the degree of discipline imposed on the employee reflect the seriousness of the proven offense?
- Is there proper documentation of the misconduct, including names of witnesses?
- Have you considered the extent, if any, to which the company contributed to the problem?
- Was the information regarding the infraction obtained lawfully (for example, drug or alcohol test, private investigator, body search)?

Procedural

- Has the supervisor complied with all provisions of personnel policies or the employee handbook?
- Would this termination be consistent with the company's actions in the past?
- If they exist, were contractual procedures followed?
- Have alternatives to termination—for example, last-chance agreements, demotion, option to resign, settlement agreements—been considered?
- Have you considered the employee's length of employment?
- Has human resources checked to see that all relevant requirements have been met?
- Will the interview be conducted in private with a witness?
- Have you made every effort to make the termination as humane as possible?
- Has a checklist been prepared of what the employee needs to return to the employer?
- Have appropriate steps been taken to ensure confidentiality?
- Has the final paycheck and other pay, such as, accrued vacation, been taken care of?
- Have COBRA benefits, notifications and paperwork been prepared?

Legal

- Taken as a whole, does this case appear to be an example of fairness, honesty, and good faith?

- Are there potential legal problems? Do the circumstances suggest discrimination, unjust discharge, or violation of any other laws?

- Is there evidence this employee has been singled out and treated differently?

- If the employee is a member of any protected group, has that employee been treated the same as members of other groups?

Terminating employees who may claim discrimination—for example, pregnant employees, older employees, minority employees, and disabled employees—is especially sensitive. With these types of employees, the potential problem of a subsequent claim or lawsuit is obvious. You should take special care with these employees during termination procedures not to make any reference to anything that could be considered discriminatory. The termination interview should never contain references to sex, age, race, religion, national origin, disability, etc.

- Has the employee filed any kind of claim against the company—workers' compensation, benefits pay claim, etc.—or filed a discrimination charge? Could the termination be seen as reprisal and therefore be open to a retaliatory discharge claim?

- Has the employee complained about company policies or activities the employee considered illegal or immoral? Could the termination be seen as reprisal for whistleblowing?

- Have you consulted with an employment law counsel?

Some Final Concerns

Unemployment Compensation

Employers should handle unemployment compensation claims carefully and meticulously. Often an employee will state a different reason for termination than that given by the employer. An unemployment compensation hearing provides a useful opportunity to learn the former employee's position. An unemployment compensation decision favoring the employer may help persuade the employee not to pursue matters further. It may also help convince the Equal Employment Opportunity Commission (EEOC) or a court that any claim an employee may make is not valid. See **Chapter 26, Unemployment Compensation,** for further discussion of this topic.

Replacing Terminated Employees

Employers should replace terminated employees carefully. Obviously, you should seek the most qualified employees.

Chapter 19
Plant Closings and Workforce Reduction

Introduction

This chapter reviews federal law relating to workforce reduction, defining relevant terms and considering the provisions of the Worker Adjustment and Retraining Notification Act (WARN). State law on plant closings is briefly addressed.

Workforce Adjustment and Retraining Notification Act (WARN)

Coverage

WARN covers employers who employ:

- 100 or more employees, excluding part-time employees, or
- 100 or more employees (full time and part-time) who, in the aggregate, work at least 4,000 hours per week, excluding overtime.

For purposes of the 100-employee threshold, the number of employees working at different sites is combined. Employees on leave or layoff who have a reasonable expectation of recall also count as employees for purposes of the act. Local, state, and federal governments are not covered by WARN.

Part-time Employees

The term *part-time employees* is defined in WARN as employees who work an average workweek of fewer than 20 hours, or who have been employed for fewer than six of the 12 months preceding the date on which WARN notices would be required.

Legal Obligations

WARN requires that a covered employer provide at least 60 days written notice before a plant closing or a mass layoff. The notice must be given to the following:

- The union representative of the affected unionized employees, or where there is no union who represents the affected employees, to each affected employee.

- The state dislocated worker unit in the state where the closing or layoff will occur.
- The chief elected official of the local government where the closing or layoff will occur.

Relevant Term Definitions

Plant Closing

A *plant closing* is a permanent or temporary shutdown of a single employment site, or of one or more operating units or facilities within a single employment site if the shutdown results in an employment loss for 50 or more employees, excluding part-time employees, during any 30-day period. This 30-day period is extended by the requirement that layoffs be aggregated during a rolling 90-day period. WARN analysis under both plant closings and a mass layoff scenarios, may involve determining whether an employer's multiple locations can be considered a single site for the purpose of determining whether 50 or more employees are affected.

Mass Layoff

A *mass layoff* is a reduction in force that results in an employment loss of at least 33 percent of the workforce at a single site of employment during any 30-day period. The reduction is not due to a plant closing and must affect at least 50 employees, excluding part-time employees. If 500 or more employees (excluding part-timers) suffer an employment loss, notice is required even if the affected number of employees at the site is less than 33 percent of the workforce.

Employment Loss

The term *employment loss*, as used in WARN, means:

- An employment termination other than a discharge (for cause), voluntary departure, or retirement.
- A layoff for more than six months.
- A reduction in hours of individual employees of more than 50 percent during each month of any six-month period.

Employment Transfer Not an Employment Loss

No employment loss occurs when the closing or layoff results from the relocation or consolidation of all or part of the employer's business if, before the closing or layoff, either of the following occurs:

- The employer offers to transfer the employee to a different employment site within a reasonable commuting distance with no more than a six-month break in employment.
- The employer offers to transfer the employee to any other site of employment, regardless of distance with no more than a six-month break in employment and the employee accepts the offer within 30 days of the offer, closing, or layoff, whichever is later.

Aggregation

In determining whether a plant closing or mass layoff will trigger WARN's notice requirements, the employer may be required to total employment losses over a rolling 90-day period within a single site of employment. All employment losses at a single site of employment that occur within a rolling 30-day period must be added together, regardless of their cause and regardless of whether the reduction of one group alone constitutes a plant closing or mass layoff. All employment losses at a single site of employment that occur within a rolling 90-day period must be added together unless an employer can show that one of the sets of employment losses alone was a plant closing or mass layoff or unless the employer can show that the employment losses were for separate and distinct causes and their timing did not show an attempt to evade WARN's requirements.

Affected Employees

The term *affected employees* includes any employees who may reasonably be expected to suffer an employment loss as a result of a planned plant closing or mass layoff. It includes employees who may lose their jobs because of bumping rights. The term does not include consultants or contract employees who are separately employed and paid by another employer or who are self-employed. While part-time employees are not included in the calculation to determine whether a WARN notice must be issued, if a WARN covered event occurs they must receive appropriate WARN notice.

Exceptions to WARN Notice Requirements

There are some exceptions to the WARN notice requirements, which follow below.

Temporary Facility or Specific Projects

A WARN notice is not required if the facility closed is a temporary one or the layoff or closing is the result of a specific project's being completed if the affected employees were hired with the understanding that their employment was limited to the amount of time the facility existed or to the duration of the project.

Strikes and Lockouts

WARN does not apply to a plant closing or mass layoff if that action constitutes a strike or lockout, and is not intended to avoid the requirements of WARN occurring in the normal course of collective bargaining. However, non-striking employees at the site who experience employment losses as a result of the strike may be entitled to notice, as are all employees who experience employment losses, which are not the result of the strike or lockout. The duty to notify the non-striking employees may be somewhat modified by other exceptions, such as the company's faltering or unforeseeable business circumstances, described below.

Faltering Company

A company may give fewer than 60 days notice of a plant closing (not a mass layoff) if the company is faltering and the following are true:

- The company was actively seeking capital or business at the time the notice would have been required.

- There was a realistic opportunity to obtain the financing or business sought.

- The company could have avoided or postponed the closing if the capital or business had been obtained.

- The company reasonably and in good faith believed that giving notice would have prevented the company from obtaining the additional capital or business.

The faltering-company exception refers to the entire company, not just a single site or particular facility. The employer's actions will be reviewed in a company-wide context. Companies relying on this exception are still required to give as much notice as possible and to explain in writing why the notice period was reduced.

Unforeseeable Business Circumstances

Fewer than 60 days notice may be permitted when a plant closing or mass layoff is the result of unforeseeable business circumstances. *Unforeseeable business circumstances* means circumstances that are caused by some sudden, dramatic, and unexpected action or condition outside the employer's control.

Natural Disasters

Fewer than 60 days notice may be permitted when a plant closing or mass layoff is the result of a natural disaster, including floods, earthquakes, droughts, storms, tidal waves, tsunamis, and similar events. The plant closing or mass layoff must be the direct result of the natural disaster.

Purchase and Sale of Facilities

A sale, in and of itself, does not give rise to a WARN notice obligation. If a plant closing or mass layoff occurs in connection with the sale, notices are required. The seller is responsible for providing notices if layoffs occur for workers who will be terminated before the date of the sale. The buyer is responsible for notifying workers whose employment will be terminated after the date of the sale. For purposes of WARN coverage only, an employee of the seller is considered to become an employee of the buyer at the time of the sale.

The buyer may authorize the seller to give notice of a plant closing or mass layoff on the buyer's behalf prior to the sale.

Contents of a WARN Notice

The Department of Labor has issued regulations specifying what must be included in a WARN notice. The information differs according to whether the notice is for the affected employees, employee representatives, or representatives of state and local governments.

For Affected Employees

Notices sent to affected employees must contain the following:

- Name and phone number of the company official to contact for information.
- Expected date of closing or layoff.
- Anticipated date of, or 14-day window period, for the individual's separation.
- Indication of whether bumping rights exists.
- A statement as to whether the planned action is permanent or temporary.
- A statement as to whether the entire plant will be closed.

For Employee Representatives

Notices sent to employee representatives (of local and international unions) must contain the following:

- Name and address of the employment site where the action will occur.
- Nature of planned action (closing or layoff, temporary or permanent).
- Expected date of first employee separation and anticipated schedule for separations.
- Job titles of positions to be affected and names of workers holding these jobs.
- A statement as to whether the planned action is permanent or temporary.

- A statement as to whether the entire plant will be closed.
- Name and telephone number of the company official to contact for further information.

For State and Local Governments

Notices to representatives of state and local governments must contain the following:

- Name and address of the employment site where the action will occur.
- Name and phone number of the company official to contact for information.
- Date of first separation and anticipated schedule for separations.
- Job titles of positions to be affected and number of affected workers holding these jobs.
- The name and address of each union, which represents the affected employees.
- The name and address of the chief elected officer of each union.
- An indication of whether bumping rights exists.
- A statement whether the action is temporary or permanent and whether the entire plant will be closed.

The notice to governmental officials may be abbreviated as set forth in 20 C.FR §639.7(f) of Department of Labor regulations as long as more specific information is maintained by the employer and made available to governmental representatives upon request.

Penalties for Violating WARN

Employers violating WARN are liable to each employee suffering employment loss for backpay and benefits, including possible out-of-pocket medical costs for each day of violation. This liability may be reduced by wages paid, by other voluntary and unconditional employer payments, and by benefit premiums paid for the employee and pension credit given to the employee.

An employer violating WARN by failing to notify a local government may also be liable for a civil penalty up to $500 for each day of violation, unless the employer pays each affected employee fully within three weeks of the closing or layoff. The amount of the penalty may be reduced if the employer is determined to have acted in good faith and had reasonable grounds for believing its conduct was not a violation of WARN.

Affected employees or local governments may sue to enforce WARN and may be awarded attorneys' fees if successful.

Statute of Limitations

The WARN Act does not contain a specific statute of limitations period for filing claims. The U.S. Supreme Court has left open this issue. Some federal courts have held that the proper statute of limitations period is determined by reference to the state's breach-of-contract limitations period.

Massachusetts Law

Massachusetts law relating to plant closings and workforce reduction focuses on four areas:

- The requirement to inform the state officials of any plant closing and the subsequent certification by that official of the closing.

- The determination of re-employment assistance benefits (eligibility, amount, length of coverage), including health-insurance benefits.
- The creation and management of re-employment assistance programs.
- Payment for the costs of these benefits and training programs.

Massachusetts also includes a list of definitions of relevant terms to help in the interpretation of its laws. Summary definitions of key terms are provided under the appropriate topics in this section.

Notification of Plant Closings

Under Massachusetts law, every employer closing a facility must report to the commissioner (the Director of the Department of Labor and Workforce Development), providing any information needed to determine employees' re-employment assistance benefits. For purposes of this requirement, Massachusetts defines *facility* as a plant, factory, commercial business, hospital, institution or other place of employment in the commonwealth that had fifty or more employees during any month in the six-month period prior to the date of certification.

The commissioner, once notified, will determine if a plant closing did occur. Under Massachusetts law, a plant closing will have occurred if 90 percent of the employees of a facility have been or will be permanently separated within the six-month period before the date of certification. It is also up to the commissioner to identify *partial closings*, defined by Massachusetts law as a permanent cessation of a major discrete portion of the business conducted at a facility, which results in the termination of a significant number of employees, and which affects workers and communities in a manner similar to that of plant closings.

If the commissioner determines that a plant closing or partial closing did take place, the commissioner will inform the employer, any appropriate labor union, and other interested parties. Any interested party may appeal the decision of the commissioner in a fair hearing.

Re-employment Assistance Benefits

Employees who have lost their jobs because of plant closings or partial closings are eligible under Massachusetts law for specific re-employment assistance benefits. For this purpose, Massachusetts defines *employee* as an individual who has worked full time or part time for the employer for four quarterly periods and who is otherwise eligible for unemployment benefits. This definition excludes seasonal employees. To receive re-employment assistance benefits employees must participate in the re-employment assistance programs discussed in the next section.

Specific re-employment assistance benefits include the following:

- Payment of an amount equal to the difference between the weekly unemployment benefit amount and 75 percent of the employee's average weekly wage, provided that a certain maximum, calculated on the yearly increase in the unemployment benefit, is not exceeded.
- Payment of this amount for a maximum of 13 weeks, less any weeks of advance notification the employee received or any weeks of separation pay the employee received.
- Receipt of health-insurance benefits during the eligibility period (that is, 13 weeks from the date of notification of closing or the date of certification of closing, whichever is earlier). To receive this health-insurance benefit the individual must have been covered by an individually purchased health-insurance plan at the time of termination and must not be able to be covered under a health-insurance plan of a family member.

Re-employment Assistance Programs

As part of its efforts to assist employees that are terminated due to plant closings, Massachusetts specifies that appropriate governmental representatives and agencies will establish a re-employment assistance program. The program will provide counseling, placement, training, and any other services deemed necessary to lead to the employees' re-employment. These re-employment services are to be held at a plant-closing site, at local offices of the Division of Employment and Training, or at sites provided by other agencies.

Terminated employees must participate in these re-employment assistance programs to be eligible for re-employment assistance benefits.

Payment for Re-employment Assistance

Massachusetts requires that at the end of each month the commissioner will bill the employers of each certified plant closing or partial closing 100 percent of the costs of re-employment assistance benefits. These payments must be made within 30 days and late penalties are subject to interest and penalties.

Chapter 20

Payroll Taxes and Withholding

Introduction

This chapter reviews the complex topic of payroll taxes. We define employee for payroll deduction purposes and review the responsibilities of employers regarding taxes and withholding. You are cautioned not to take this as the full and complete text on payroll taxes and withholding. We urge you to consult the many IRS and other documents available on the topic. The IRS's Circular E, *Employer's Tax Guide,* which outlines the rules and regulations for payroll deductions and deposits, is just one such document available to help with this topic. It can be obtained by calling 1-800-829-3676.

Who Is an "Employee"?

Employees vs. Independent Contractors

Employers must be able to identify their "taxable workers." You only have to withhold and pay taxes for those workers properly classified as employees. If you have even one employee, you will most likely have to withhold federal income tax from that employee's wages, and Social Security tax as well. You may also be subject to federal unemployment tax. Remember that once a worker is deemed an employee for tax purposes, the fact that he or she works only part time, on a temporary basis, or is a minor ordinarily will not remove the need to withhold and pay taxes on that employee's wages.

Although there is some variable interpretation of the term *employee*, it basically means an individual who performs services for you under your direct control of when, where, and how the work is done. For payroll tax purposes, the IRS and state tax agencies rely on common law rules to determine who is an employee. If you have the legal right to control the activities of your workers, they are employees under the common law definition, even if they have much discretion in determining exactly how they will do their work. Employers must be especially careful here to realize that it is the *actual* employment relationship that is important in making the decision about whether your workers are employees. What you call them, possibly in a misguided effort to avoid payroll tax obligations, is irrelevant to the common law definition.

The status of an individual as an independent contractor or an employee for purposes of the federal tax laws (and state income tax laws) is determined, with few exceptions, under the common law tests for determining whether an employment relationship exists.

Common Law Employee Status

The Federal Employment Tax Regulations (FICA taxes, FUTA taxes, and income tax withholding) provide that an individual generally is an employee if, under the usual common law tests, the relationship between the individual and the person for whom he performs services is the legal relationship of employer and employee. Such a relationship generally exists if the person for whom the services are performed "has the right to control and direct the individual who performs the services, not only as to the result to be accomplished by the work but also as to the details and means by which that result is accomplished. That is, an employee is subject to the will and control of the employer not only as to what shall be done but [also] how it shall be done."

The regulations state that the determination is to be based upon the particular facts in each case and warn that the designation or description of the relationship by the parties will not be determinative where the facts prove otherwise.

IRS Common law Factors

Over the years, the IRS developed a list of 20 common law factors to be used as guidance in assessing whether sufficient control exists to establish an employer-employee relationship. According to the IRS, the presence of the following factors tends to indicate that an individual is an employee:

1. The worker must comply with the employer's instructions about the work.
2. The worker receives training from or at the direction of the employer.
3. The worker provides services that are integrated into the business.
4. The worker provides services that must be rendered personally.
5. The worker hires, supervises, and pays assistants for the employer.
6. The worker has a continuing working relationship with the employer.
7. The worker must follow set hours of work.
8. The worker works full time for the employer.
9. The worker does work on the employer's premises.
10. The worker does work in sequence set by the employer.
11. The worker must submit regular reports to the employer.
12. The worker receives payments of regular amounts at set intervals.
13. The worker receives payments for business or traveling expenses.
14. The worker relies on the employer to furnish tools and materials.
15. The worker lacks a major investment in facilities used to perform services.
16. The worker cannot make a profit or suffer a loss from services.
17. The worker works for only one employer at a time.
18. The worker does not offer services to the general public.
19. The employer can fire the worker.
20. The worker may quit work at any time without incurring liability.

The IRS guidance states, however, that some of the common law factors do not apply to certain occupations and that the degree of importance to be given to any factor may vary in a particular case. The IRS guidance also states that any single fact or small group of facts will not necessarily establish conclusive evidence of employee or independent contractor status.

As a result, the application of these factors is extremely subjective and the IRS itself has acknowledged that "in many cases, applying the common law test in employment tax issues does not yield clear, consistent, or satisfactory answers, and reasonable persons may differ as to the correct classification." In sum, even the IRS apparently acknowledges that the factors do not provide reliable practical guidance in assessing the status of the workers for employment tax purposes.

IRS Training Materials on Worker Classifications

Because of the difficulty in applying the 20-factor test and because business trends have changed over the years, the IRS recently has begun using a new approach with respect to worker classification. See *Internal Revenue Service Training Materials on Worker Classifications for Tax Purposes as Independent Contractors or Employees* (issued 3/4/1997). Rather than listing items of evidence under the 20 factors, the approach now is to group the items of evidence into the following three main categories: behavioral control, financial control, and the relationship of the parties.

1. **Behavioral Control**
   Evidence in this category includes facts regarding whether the business has the right to direct and control how the worker performs the specific tasks for which the worker is hired. Facts that show behavioral control include the type and degree of instructions given to the worker and the training the business gives the worker.

2. **Financial Control**
   Evidence under this category includes facts regarding whether there is a right to direct and control how the business aspects of the worker's activities are conducted. Facts that show financial control include whether the worker has a significant investment or incurs significant expenses in the business and whether the worker provides services to the relevant market.

3. **Relationship of the Parties**
   Evidence under this category includes facts that illustrate how the parties perceive their relationship. Relevant facts include those which show the intent of the parties with respect to their relationship and whether the parties were free to terminate their relationship at-will. The permanency of the relationship between the worker and the business is also relevant in assessing the relationship.

Employers can request an IRS determination by filing Form SS-8, *Determination of Employee Work Status for Purposes of Federal Employment Taxes and Income Tax Withholding*. This form is supplemented with additional information about the employment relationship between the employer and the worker(s), for example, a description of the nature of the supervision and method of payment.

Payroll Taxes and Withholding

Federal Tax Penalties for Misclassification

The Internal Revenue Code generally limits an employer's liability for federal employment taxes with individuals who have been misclassified as an independent contractors. The liability is as follows:

Tax Category	Employer Liability
Income Tax Withholding	1.5% of wages per year
Social Security Tax—Employer plus Employee Portion	7.44% of wages (up to maximum Social Security wage base) per year *Plus* 1.74% of wages (no maximum wage base) per year
FUTA Taxes	$434 per worker per year

In addition, the IRS has established several audit settlement programs under which the IRS, depending on the circumstances, may reduce or eliminate an employer's liability for the employment taxes for misclassified workers.

Exceptions

To add to the problem of distinguishing employees from independent contractors are the following considerations:

- Some independent contractors who perform certain types of duties are taxable as employees.
- Some individuals may be statutorily exempted from federal employment withholding taxes.
- The employer may be exempt under the "safe haven rule" from withholding taxes for individuals who normally would be classified as employees.
- Employed family members are exempt from certain taxes as employees.

Taxable Independent Contractors: Statutory Employees

Employers will be required to withhold FICA taxes in certain circumstances for independent contractors who are considered *statutory employees*. These are individuals performing the following services:

- Deliver specified products as agent-drivers or commission drivers. This includes individuals who operate their own trucks or trucks of the persons for whom they perform services, serve customers designated by their employer as well as customers they solicit on their own, make wholesale or retail sales, and are paid commissions on their sales for the products or services they sell or earn the difference between what they charge their customers and what they pay their principals for the products or services. This includes drivers who distribute beverages, meat, vegetables, fruit, or bakery products, and drivers who pick up and deliver laundry or dry cleaning. It does not include drivers who distribute milk.

- Work full time for an employer as traveling salespersons. This includes individuals who remit orders for items that will be resold or used as supplies in their businesses from customers who are retailers, wholesalers, contractors, or operators of hotels, restaurants, or other furnishers of food and lodging.

- Perform work at home on a contract or piecemeal basis. This would include individuals hired as word processors who do their work on their home computers.

- Work full time selling life insurance primarily for one insurance company.

Ordinarily, these individuals are considered independent contractors and employers would not have to withhold income taxes from their pay. However, if the following conditions exist, employers must withhold and pay FICA taxes:

- The contract requires the individual to perform most of the work personally (in other words, he or she is not free to hire someone to do the job).
- The individual has invested little in equipment and property other than the necessary vehicle.
- The services are performed on a continuing basis.

Employers must withhold FICA taxes on all wages they pay individuals working at home if the individuals are paid more than $100 in a year. Additionally, if the conditions above exist in the cases of drivers and salespeople, employers must pay federal and state unemployment taxes as well.

Untaxed Employees

Employers may be relieved of all taxes for two types of employee salespersons—real estate agents and direct sellers (that is, individuals who sell consumer products to consumers or to buyers for resale at a place that is not a permanent retail establishment)—if the following are true:

- Substantially all of the compensation these individuals receive is directly related to sales or other output, rather than to the hours they work.
- The salespeople are subject to written contracts indicating that they will not be treated as employees for federal income tax purposes.

Statutory Safe Harbor Relief from IRS Reclassification (Safe Haven Rule)

The Safe Haven Rule under Section 530 of the Revenue Act of 1978 protects an employer from liability for federal employment taxes.

- **Requirements for Safe Haven Rule**

    The employer must have a reasonable basis for not treating the individual as an employee. The Safe Haven Rule provides that a reasonable basis exists where an employer relies on anyone or more of the following safe havens:

    - Judicial precedent or published rulings whether or not relating to the employer, or IRS technical advice or letter ruling issued with respect to the employer.
    - Past IRS audit of the employer in which there was no assessment of employment taxes attributable to the treatment of workers holding positions substantially similar to the position held by the individual in question. (The audit need not have been conducted for employment tax purposes.)
    - Long-standing recognized practice of a significant segment of the industry.
    - An employer who fails to meet any of the three "safe havens" may still be entitled to the Safe Haven Rule if it can demonstrate, in some other manner, a reasonable basis for not treating the individual as an employee.

The employer must consistently treat the individual, and any other individual holding a substantially similar position, as an independent contractor at all times. For this purpose, consistency is determined by whether the employer has timely filed Form 1099s for all tax periods; and the employer has not withheld federal income taxes or FICA taxes for any tax periods, and filed federal employment tax returns for any tax periods.

- **Burden of Proof**

    The IRS has the burden of proving that a taxpayer is not entitled to relief under the Safe Haven Rule with respect to an individual, if:

    - The taxpayer establishes a prima facie case that it was reasonable not to treat the individual as an employee.
    - The taxpayer has fully cooperated with reasonable requests from the IRS.

- **Effect of the Safe Haven Rule**

    - The Safe Haven Rule terminates an employer's liability for federal employment taxes attributable to the erroneous classification of an individual as an independent contractor.
    - The Safe Haven Rule prevents retroactive employment tax assessments against the employer.
    - As long as the requirements of the Safe Haven Rule are met, the IRS is prevented from making future employment tax assessments against the employer with respect to such individuals.
    - The Safe Haven Rule applies solely for federal employment tax purposes.
    - It does not prevent an individual's classification as an employee for all other purposes under the code; for example, an individual may be treated as an employee for purposes of the tax qualification requirements applying to retirement plans and various other employee benefit nondiscrimination requirements under the code.

A few reminders: If your treatment of workers is based on something similar to the provisions above, you may still qualify for the Safe Haven Rule. You would not qualify, however, if you treat some workers as independent contractors and others in similar positions as employees, nor would you qualify if you try to convert a worker you have treated as an employee any time since 1977 to independent contractor status. If your workers do not satisfy the requirements of the safe haven, the common law test of their employment status is applied.

Taxes and Family Members

Employing one's family members may save payroll taxes, although if they are common law employees they are subject to the same payroll taxes as any employees. In some situations, however, there may be some savings in FICA taxes and unemployment taxes if the business is not run through a corporation or partnership (except for husband/wife partnerships). Some basic rules apply to employing relatives:

- Employers are not required to withhold and pay Social Security and Medicare taxes for their children who work for them until the children reach age 18. If the children's services are for work other than in a trade or business—such as domestic work in the parents' home—taxes do not have to be paid until the child reaches 21.

- Employers have to pay FICA taxes—but not FUTA taxes—for spouses they employ in a trade or business. No taxes are paid if the work is for other than a trade or business.

- The wages of parents employed by their children are subject to income tax withholding and Social Security and Medicare taxes. Social Security and Medicare taxes do not apply if the service is in other than a trade or business unless it is for service caring for a child under age 18 or that requires care for more than four hours a day because of a mental or physical condition. Wages paid to a parent by a child are never subject to FUTA taxes.

- Employers have to pay the same payroll taxes on siblings and other relatives they pay for any employees.

Employee Rights and Obligations

Social Security Card

Employees, including resident and nonresident aliens, are required to have Social Security numbers so you can enter them on your W-2 Forms. An employee is required to show the card to the employer if the card is available. Employees without a Social Security card can get one by completing Form SS-5, *Application for a Social Security Card* available from a Social Security Administration office or by calling 1-800-772-1213. Once an employee receives a card, a corrected wage and tax statement (Form W-2c) should be submitted. It is also up to the employee to ensure that the name is correct on the card.

Employers must record Social Security numbers for resident and nonresident aliens also. Aliens who are not eligible for a Social Security card may request an IRS individual taxpayer identification number (ITIN) for tax purposes but employers cannot accept an ITIN in place of a Social Security number for employment.

Employers may verify Social Security numbers by telephone for up to five names (1-800-772-6270) or by calling their local Social Security office for up to 50 names. The Social Security Administration's website has information on verifying more than 50 names and numbers. The website is www.ssa.gov/employer.

Form W-4

A newly hired employee has to fill out a Form W-4, telling the employer how many withholding allowances to use when deducting federal income taxes. The more withholding exemptions an employee claims, the less taxes an employer will have to withhold. Employees may claim fewer exemptions than they are entitled to, in an effort to reduce later tax obligations. They may even ask employers to take additional money from their wages if they anticipate a larger tax bill. The IRS provides Pub 505, *Tax Withholding and Estimated Tax,* and Pub 919, *How Do I Adjust My Withholding?* to help employees fill out the form.

Employees may not claim more exemptions than they are entitled to. They may claim one for themselves, (unless they can be claimed as a dependent by another taxpayer), one for their spouse if the spouse is not claiming his or her own exemption on a W-4 Form, and they may claim one exemption for each child or other dependent claimed on their tax return.

Some employees may qualify for a no-tax-liability exemption, thus relieving the employer of having to withhold federal income taxes (but not FICA taxes). To qualify for this, the employee must have had no tax liability for the previous year, is not being claimed as a dependent on someone else's tax return, and must have under $250 in nonwage income and under a specified income ($750 in 2001). Employers must send the IRS copies of W-4 Forms of employees making over $200 a week who are claiming complete exemption from withholding.

It is the employee's responsibility to identify his or her exemptions. Employees who submit W-4 forms that result in less tax being withheld than properly allowable are subject to a $500 fine. Employers are under no obligation to confirm the validity of the exemptions, although if they discover that an employee has improperly claimed an exemption they must inform the IRS, request a new W-4 Form from the employee, and send the IRS a copy of the invalid form. Employers must also send the IRS copies of W-4 forms on which more than 10 exemptions are claimed.

Tips

Employees who make more than $20 in tips in any month are required to report the amount they receive to their employers. This must be in the form of a written report submitted by the tenth day of the following month. Employees who receive under $20 in tips in any month are not required to submit a report but they must include such tips on their tax return. Service charges added to bills are considered wages and not tips.

Wages

The employer has a considerably more complex responsibility in the tax process, beginning with exactly what constitutes wages for income tax purposes. Obviously, wages subject to federal employment taxes include all pay for services performed. This includes salaries and such "supplemental pay" as vacation allowances, bonuses, commissions, and fringe benefits and may be paid in cash or in other forms. The IRS Pub 15-A, *Employer's Supplemental Tax Guide,* provides information on other forms of compensation that may or may not be taxable. Most awards and gifts are taxable unless clearly unrelated to employee performance (for example a wedding gift). Christmas gifts or cash are taxable (turkeys are not). Paid vacation time is considered taxable, as is any form of time-off pay. Wages in the form of property are taxable and present the special problem of withholding the taxable amount.

Employers are responsible for withholding taxes on tips employees receive from customers. Employees report the tips on Form 4070, *Employee's Report of Tips to Employer,* or a similar statement showing their name, address, and Social Security number. Employers must collect income tax, Social Security tax, and Medicare tax on the tips either from wages or other funds the employee makes available. Employers who operate large food or beverage establishments (more than 10 employees on a customary day) are not required to withhold income, Social Security, or Medicare taxes on allocated tips (tips allocated according to hours worked, gross receipts, or good-faith agreement).

Exemptions

Certain types of payments are exempt from withholding taxes:

- **Business expense reimbursement.** Employees who have incurred deductible expenses while performing services as an employee, have accounted to their employers for these expenses, and have been paid for their expenses are not subject to income tax withholding or payment of Social Security, Medicare, and FUTA taxes for the reimbursement—as long as they return any excess payment within a reasonable amount of time (usually within 120 days). Employees who are not required to account for and substantiate their expenses are subject to Social Security, Medicare, Unemployment and income withholding taxes. Employees who are paid on a per-diem rate are considered to have accounted for their expenses if they have stayed within federal guidelines. This is further clarified in Pub 535, Ch. 16.

- **Noncash payments.** Noncash payments for household work, agricultural labor, and service not in an employer's trade or business are not subject to Social Security, Medicare, and FUTA taxes. Payment "in kind" for work done within an employer's trade or business is taxable.

- **Moving expenses.** Reimbursed and employer-paid qualified moving expenses need not be included in an employee's income unless the employer knows the employee previously deducted expenses on his tax return. Pub 521, *Moving Expenses,* explains this further.

- **Meals and lodging.** The value of meals is not taxable income if the meals are furnished for the employer's convenience and on the employer's premises. This is also true of the value of lodging furnished for the employer's convenience, on the employer's premises, and as a condition of employment.

- **Health insurance plans.** Payments to employees' accident or health insurance plans are not taxable as income unless the employee owns more than 2 percent of a "Subchapter 5" corporation paying the cost of the insurance.

- **Medical saving accounts.** Employer contributions to employees' medical savings accounts are not taxable if there was expectation they would not be included in income. Employee contributions are, however, taxable.

- **Medical care reimbursements.** Medical care reimbursements paid for under an employer's self-insured medical reimbursement plan are not taxable. Sick pay paid to an employee unable to work because of illness or injury is subject to FICA and FUTA taxes for a period up to six months after the last calendar month the employee last worked for the employer. After six months, sick pay is exempt from FICA and FUTA taxes.

- **Fringe benefits.** Ordinarily, fringe benefits (cars, company-provided air travel, service discounts, club memberships, tickets, etc.) are taxable as income. However, services that do not cost the employer anything, minimal value fringes (local transportation benefits, parking, etc.), and such services as tuition reduction and the use of on-premise athletic facilities are not considered income.

- **Casual labor.** Employers are not required to withhold federal taxes and most state income taxes or to pay federal and state unemployment taxes for cash payments of less than $50 in a calendar quarter if the employee was engaged in casual labor fewer than 24 different days during the quarter.

To calculate withholding on fringe benefits, employers may add their value to regular wages for a payroll period and figure withholding taxes on the total or they may figure the tax on the flat 28 percent supplemental-wage rate of the estimated value of the fringe benefits.

Withholding Period

You withhold taxes for each *payroll period*—that period of service for which you usually pay wages—even if an employee does not work for the full pay period. Employers without a payroll period should withhold the tax as if they paid wages for a daily or a miscellaneous pay period. For commissions paid on completion of a sale and other wages unrelated to a specific number of days, taxes are calculated based on the number of days back to the last payment or the date employment began (if during the same calendar year) or back to January 1, whichever was most recent.

Applicable Taxes

Once you know which workers you are required to collect and pay taxes on and on what income and how often you are required to collect these taxes, you need to know exactly which taxes to collect.

Income Tax Withholding

Income tax must be withheld from an employee's wages, as previously defined, for each payroll period. Income tax withholding is based on the Form W-4 filled out by each employee. The IRS Circular E provides valuable information for employers on handling these W-4 forms. Basically, however, the amount of income tax withholding is based on an employee's marital status and withholding allowances. Some employees may claim an exemption from withholding based on having no income tax liability last year and on the expectation of having none for this year. This employee's wages are still subject to Social Security and Medicare taxes.

In general, employers have to withhold income tax from the wages of nonresident aliens, but Pub 515, *Withholding of Tax on Nonresident Aliens and Foreign Corporations,* and Pub 519, *U.S. Tax Guide for Aliens,* present exceptions to this general rule.

Employers must withhold income tax from each pay period. The IRS provides wage-bracket tables to help employers calculate withholding tax. These are easy-to-use tax tables similar to those used to calculate taxes owed on the standard Form 1040. The IRS also supplies percentage-method tables based on the particular pay period an employer uses (weekly, biweekly, etc.), which are slightly more complicated to use. Employers who wish to use a method other than the wage-bracket or the percentage method should consult a tax specialist. Note that whatever method is used, employers may not withhold less than the prescribed amount.

Part-time and temporary workers are treated the same as full time workers for purposes of income tax withholding.

Advanced Earned Income Credit Payment: An employee who is eligible for the EIC and has a qualifying child is entitled to receive EIC payments with his or her pay during the year. The employee must give a completed Form W-5 to the employer to receive these payments. Employers are required to make advance EIC payment to employees who provide them with a completed and signed Form W-5. The W-5 form remains in effect until the end of the calendar year unless revoked by the employee.

Social Security and Medicare Taxes

The Federal Insurance Contribution Act (FICA) is intended to provide a system of old age, survivor, disability, and hospital insurance. The first three of these are financed by the Social Security tax, the hospital insurance by the Medicare tax. The taxes are reported separately.

Both employees and employers are responsible for paying these taxes. Employers withhold and pay the employees' share and pay a matching amount. The amount the employer pays is the same as the employee's tax, with the Social Security tax limited to the wage base limit ($80,400 for 2001). Thus, both employees and employers must pay a tax of 6.2 percent on the first $80,400 of an employee's salary, for a total of 12.4 percent. Both employees and employers must pay 1.45 percent for Medicare **on all covered wages**, for a total of 2.9 percent.

Part-time employees, temporary employees, and employees with more than one job are all treated the same as full-time employees for purposes of Social Security and Medicare taxes. IRS publication 15-A explains the part-year-employment method of figuring taxes or the same method as used for full time workers may be used.

Federal Unemployment Tax Act (FUTA)

Employers with one or more employees other than farm or household workers or their own children are subject to FUTA if the wages amount to $1,500 in any calendar quarter in the current or previous calendar year or if they employ workers for at least one day in each of 20 calendar weeks. Employers are subject to FUTA for household workers only if they paid total cash wages of at least $1,000 for all household employees in any quarter of the current or previous year. Employers who paid more than $20,000 in cash wages to farm workers during any calendar quarter of 1999 or 2000 or who employed 10 or more farmworkers during at least part of a day during any 20 or more weeks in either 1999 or 2000 are also subject to FUTA. FUTA wages are the same as for income tax withholding.

FUTA tax is computed on the first $7,000 of wages paid to each employee each year, with the tax rate varying by state. The federal FUTA tax rate is 6.2 percent of the first $7,000, the federal wage base. The state wage base may be different and employers can generally take a credit—up to a maximum of 5.4 percent—against the FUTA tax for amounts they pay to the state unemployment fund. Only the employer pays FUTA. It is not deducted from an employee's wages.

State Income Taxes

Some states—all but Alaska, Florida, Nevada, New Hampshire, South Dakota, Tennessee, Texas, Washington, and Wyoming—impose a personal income tax and employers doing business in those states must withhold that tax along with the federal taxes. Employers can usually use the same methods to calculate state income taxes they used to calculate federal ones and most states have their own equivalent to the federal Form W-4.

In some cities, employers may have to withhold local income taxes in addition to federal and state income taxes. Multi-state employers may have to withhold taxes for several states when employees live and work in different states. Again, the services of a tax specialist are highly recommended as these situations become more complex.

State Unemployment Taxes

Most states require employers to pay part of the first $7,000 to a state unemployment fund, to fund the benefits for former employees terminated without cause after working for at least 20 weeks. A company's liability is based on the prior year's claims experience. Companies are required to register with the state and file quarterly tax returns. The state unemployment tax rate will be adjusted to ensure the company maintains a minimum balance relative to its experience rating.

Paying the Taxes

It is probably unnecessary to include a series of warnings about the need for the accurate withholding and timely payment of the various taxes we have described, so we shall just list a few reminders:

- Failure to pay over taxes withheld may subject business owners to an obligation for the tax withheld plus interest and penalties. Individuals responsible for payroll are liable for the taxes withheld portion of payroll taxes due, and bankruptcy does not protect someone from this obligation.

- Deposits of less than the required amounts may subject employers to penalties, unless the shortage is less than the greater of $100 or 2 percent of the required amount and the shortage has been made up by the dates specified in Circular E.

- Failure to deposit income tax and FICA by the due date results in a 2 percent penalty for deposits one to five days late, a 5 percent late-payment penalty for deposits made six to 15 days late, and up to a 15 percent penalty for deposits unpaid more than 10 days after an IRS notification.

Payroll Taxes and Withholding

- Employers must pay federal payroll taxes with the appropriate financial institution on at least a monthly basis.
- State tax payments must be sent to the administering agency on a quarterly basis.
- Employers must notify employees of payroll taxes withheld.

Employer Identification Number

To file the various tax returns, employers need an employer identification number (EIN). Every employer except a sole proprietor with no employees needs an EIN. Employers can obtain their EIN by filing Form SS-4, available at most Social Security Administration and IRS offices. The number can be obtained by mail, fax, or by phone (1-800-829-1040). If the organization or ownership of a business changes, an employer may have to apply for a new EIN.

Federal Taxes

Income Tax and FICA Tax

Withheld income taxes and Social Security and Medicare taxes, less any advance Earned Income Credits, must be deposited by mailing or delivering a check, money order, or cash to an authorized financial institution or Federal Reserve Bank. These deposits are usually made monthly (by the 15th of the following month) or semiweekly (within the next week), as the IRS determines for the individual employer.

The frequency of deposits is based on an employer's total taxes, as reported on Form 941 in a four-quarter "lookback period" beginning July 1 and ending June 30. Taxes of less than $50,000 are usually deposited monthly. Taxes of over $50,000 are deposited semiweekly. New employers deposit taxes monthly for their first calendar year, although there is an exception to this—the $100,000 Next-Day Deposit Rule— explained in Circular E. Employers who incur a tax liability of $100,000 or more on any day during a deposit period must deposit the tax by the next banking day, whether they are on a monthly or semiweekly depositing schedule. Taxes of less than $1,000 for a quarter may be paid directly with the quarterly return, rather than being deposited.

FUTA Taxes

Federal unemployment tax is usually deposited quarterly, on the last day of the month that follows the end of each quarter. Thus payments are due by April 30, July 31, October 31, and January 31. Employers with a FUTA liability of less than $100 do not have to deposit the tax but may carry it forward and add it to the liability of the next quarter to see if a deposit must be made. Form 8109, *Federal Tax Deposit Coupon*, which the IRS supplies when it supplies your EIN, must accompany deposits of federal payroll taxes. This is how the IRS credits your tax account. The authorized financial institution or Federal Reserve Bank cannot accept payment without a deposit coupon.

Electronic Transfer of Funds

As of January 1, 1999, larger employers have been required to use electronic transfer of funds to pay their taxes. Circular E indicates that for 2001, employers whose total of all federal tax deposits— employment tax, excise tax, corporate income tax, etc.—in 1999 was more than $200,000 or who were required to use electronic transfer in 2000 **must** use electronic transfer rather than FTD coupons. Employers who paid less than the minimum may participate voluntarily. Employers with a FUTA tax liability of more than $50,000 must use electronic transfer of funds. Larger employers must use the Electronic Federal Tax Payment System or they will be assessed a penalty. Publication 966 explains the use of the system.

State Taxes

State income taxes withheld and employer payments for state unemployment taxes will have to be submitted to the appropriate state agency at least quarterly, although some states, notably California, have special requirements.

Recordkeeping

Employers are not relieved of their tax responsibility once the taxes are withheld and deposited. They must also comply with elaborate recordkeeping requirements.

General Employment Tax Records

Employers should keep the following employment tax records for at least four years from the due dates of the relevant returns or from the dates the taxes were paid:

- Amounts and dates of wages paid and tips reported.
- The fair market value of noncash wages.
- The names, addresses, Social Security numbers, and job titles of all employees.
- The dates of all employees' employment.
- The rate of pay of each employee.
- Copies of Form W-4 showing each employee's withholding allowances.
- Duplicate copies of Forms 940 and 941 filed.
- The dates and amounts of all tax deposits.
- Canceled checks or check stubs for all wages paid and deposits made.
- Undeliverable W-2 Forms.

These records must be kept in such a way as to allow them to be easily accessed by the IRS or by state authorities.

Form 941

All employers who are not farmers who pay wages subject to income tax withholding or Social Security or Medicare taxes must file Form 941, *Employer's Quarterly Federal Income Tax Return*. Even if they have more than one location or division, employers must only file one Form 941 per quarter—January–March, April–June, July–September, and October–December. The form is due by the end of the month following the end of the quarter. Employers who qualify may file the form by phone using TeleFile (call 901-546-2690 for information), or electronically in the cases of reporting agents filing for groups of taxpayers. A final Form 941 is required for employers who go out of business. Agricultural employers file an annual return, Form 943.

Form 941 reports wages paid, tips employees have received, federal income tax withheld, Social Security and Medicare taxes withheld, the employer's share of Social Security and Medicare taxes, and advance earned income credit payments. An adjustment line is available to correct the Social Security and Medicare taxes employers were unable to collect on employees' tips or for Social Security and Medicare taxes withheld from employees' sick pay from a third party, such as an insurance company. The income tax withheld is added to the Social Security and Medicare taxes on the form, and any advance earned

Payroll Taxes and Withholding

income credit payments, are subtracted. The remainder is the employer's employment tax bill for the quarter. Employers with a tax of more than $1,000 must complete a special portion of Form 941 or Schedule B (Form 941).

When there are discrepancies between the Forms 941 filed with the IRS and the W-2 and W-3 forms filed with the Social Security Administration, employers will have to resolve the discrepancies. Employers should reconcile the amounts on all the forms, comparing the W-3 forms with the quarterly 941 forms. Employers must use an adjusted Form 941 to resolve discrepancies, following instructions on the form and on Form 941c.

Form 940

Employers may also have to file a federal unemployment tax return, Form 940 or 940-EZ, by January 31 of each year if they paid more than $1,500 in wages in any calendar quarter in 1998 or 1999 or had at least one employee work for some part of a day in any 20 different weeks in 1998 or 1999. This includes regular, temporary, and part-time workers.

Agricultural employers will have to file Form 940 or 940-EZ if they paid more than $20,000 in cash wages in any quarter of 1998 or 1999 or employed 10 or more workers for at least part of a day in each of 20 weeks in 1998 or 1999.

Schedule H

Employers who do not report employment taxes for household employees on Form 941 or 943 must report FUTA taxes for those employees on Schedule H of Form 1040.

Form W-2

Employers who are required to file a Form 941 are required to inform their employees how much they withheld from the employees' wages for federal and state income taxes and FICA taxes. This reporting is done by, supplying each employee with a Form W-2, *Wage and Tax Statement*, by January 31 of the month following the reporting year. Employees who were terminated before the end of the year may request the W-2 form earlier, and the form must be furnished within 30 days of the request. Copies of the W-2 forms must be filed with the Social Security Administration by the end of February.

Form 1099-MISC

Independent contractors who have been paid more than $600 for their services receive a copy of the federal information return form (Form 1099-MISC) that employers must file with the IRS. The form must be received by the independent contractor by January 31 and by the IRS by February 28.

Caution

This material is intended solely as an introduction to a very complex topic. We urge you to read the suggested IRS publications and to consult additional publications, as well as your tax professional, to help you understand this very complicated subject.

Massachusetts Law

Under Massachusetts law, withholding tax is considered a *trustee tax*, which is one that employees are trusting their employers to remit to the commonwealth. Employers are required by law to withhold

Massachusetts personal income tax from the wages of residents for services performed within or outside Massachusetts. Employers are also required to withhold the tax from the wages of nonresidents for services performed within the state.

Massachusetts' tax documents emphasize the importance of withholding taxes to the commonwealth and reinforce this importance by providing easy-to-use tax forms, helpful tax guides, and helpful customer service for taxpayers, with all of this accompanied by ongoing enforcement efforts. Massachusetts tax forms can be obtained by calling the Massachusetts Department of Revenue at (617) 887-MDOR. Tax forms may also be obtained via the DOR website (www.dor.state.ma.us/) or through the fax-on-demand system at (617) 887-1900, using the handset and keypad of your fax machine.

Definition of Employer

In the Massachusetts tax documents, an *employer* is a person, corporation, partnership, estate, trust, association, or joint venture or other unincorporated organization for which an individual performs a service as an employee. This definition does not exclude educational, charitable, and social organizations. Under Massachusetts law, tax-exempt organizations such as religious and government organizations must withhold income tax from their employees.

Employers are required to register with the DOR and to do the following:

- Obtain from each employee a completed *Employee's Withholding Allowance Certificate* (Form W-4) and *Massachusetts Employee's Withholding Exemption Certificate* (Form M-4).

- Submit to the department (Department of Revenue, PO Box 7032, Boston, MA 02204 or by fax to (617) 887-5049) a completed copy of the W-4 form from all newly hired or returning personnel and all independent contractors within 14 days of their beginning work.

- Withhold state income taxes from employees who live or work in the state.

- Remit withheld taxes to the commonwealth in a timely manner, along with the appropriate forms.

- Provide each employee with a *Wage and Tax Statement* (Form W-2) showing wages paid and taxes withheld by January 31 of the following year. Employees whose employment terminates before the end of the year must receive their W-2 form within 30 days of the termination of employment. Failing to provide this form or providing a false form makes the employer liable for a fine of up to $1000 and/or imprisonment for up to one year. Employers with 250 or more employees who file W-2 forms with the IRS must also provide the DOR with these forms on magnetic media by the last day of February of the following year. Employers with fewer than 250 employees are encouraged to do the same.

- File quarterly reports of gross wages paid to each employee who lives or works in the state using an *Employer's Quarterly Report of Wages Paid* (Form WR-1) or by filing on tape or cartridge mailed to Department of Revenue, PO Box 7030, Boston, MA 02204. DOR will send registered employers the form quarterly. This form is intended to verify eligibility for programs such as Welfare, Medicaid, unemployment compensation, and workers' compensation and to help track down employees owing child support. Failing to provide this form or Form W-4 above could result in penalties of up to $100 per employee. Employers may get information on wage reporting by contacting DOR's Wage Reporting Group at (617) 887-5030.

Employers are also responsible for paying state unemployment security taxes as well as federal income and Social Security and Medicare taxes.

Definition of Employee

Under Massachusetts law, an *employee* is anyone who performs services for another person or organization under the direction or control of that person or organization. To fall within this definition, the person performing the service must be under the control of the employer as far as the details and manner in which the service is to be performed.

For taxing purposes, Massachusetts includes under the term *employee* anyone who performs a service in the state, whether or not the individual lives in Massachusetts. Employees who are not residents of Massachusetts would file a nonresident income tax return in the state. Massachusetts residents who work in another state are still required to pay Massachusetts income taxes, including the difference between income tax paid to another state and the amount that would be owed to Massachusetts. The DOR's Directive 91-4, *Multiple State Withholding Requirements*, provides further information on handling the taxes of individuals who live in Massachusetts but work in another state.

Employers keep employee information—full name, address, Social Security number, total number of exemptions, any additional withholding amounts requested—on Form W-4 *(Employee's Withholding Allowance certificate)* and Form W-4 *(Massachusetts Employee's Withholding Exemption Certificate)*. Employees need to complete both forms to ensure accurate withholding and they may file a new form any time the number of exemptions increases. They must file a new form within 10 days of a decrease in exemptions. Employees holding more than one job may only claim exemptions with their major employer. Employees may request employers to withhold additional money to pay taxes due on income not covered by withholding.

Exclusions

Massachusetts excludes the owner of a sole proprietorship from its definition of *employee* and such an individual does not have to withhold taxes on his or her own wages. If, however, the individual expects to pay more than $200 in Massachusetts Income Tax on business income, he or she would have to make individual estimated tax payments. More information may be found in the department's Form 1-ES instructions.

Employers do not need to withhold Massachusetts tax from the wages of employees who are not subject to federal income tax withholding, such as domestic employees, although they may do so to relieve their employees from having to pay estimated federal and state taxes. Additional information may be found in the department's *Household Employment Tax Guide*.

Massachusetts notes that complex definitional questions regarding withholding taxes must be resolved in accordance with federal law.

Compensation

Under Massachusetts law, all compensation to an employee for services performed is taxable. This includes wages, salaries, tips (employees must report tips of over $20 a month to employers), commissions, bonuses, fees, or any item of value given to an individual for services as an employee. This would also include pension and annuity payments to Massachusetts residents who have not elected to be exempt from federal income tax withholding. Also considered under compensation are lump sum and eligible rollovers subject to federal withholding. This is further explained in several documents—TIR 98-8 and TIR 93-3—available from DOR's Rulings and Regulations Bureau.

Massachusetts provides a special form, Form TA-1, *Massachusetts Trustee Tax Application for Original Registration*, for trustees or administrators of a pension or annuity plan to use to register with the DOR. Recipients of payments from these pension or annuity funds must register to pay taxes on these payments using Form M-4P, *Massachusetts Withholding Exemption Certificate for Pension, Annuity and Other Periodic and Nonperiodic Payments.*

Registering to Withhold

Employers must file a *Massachusetts Trustee Tax Application for Original Registration* (Form TA-1) before collecting Massachusetts withholding. The TA-1 booklet contains important information including filing schedules and instructions for completing the form. Once DOR has processed the form it will mail the employer a booklet of preprinted tax forms. Businesses that are required to file annually will not receive the forms until December of the year for which they are filing.

Calculating Massachusetts Withholding Tax

Massachusetts withholding is based on an employee's taxable wages and the number of exemptions the employee claims. Calculation is done using tax tables available from DOR, which factor in employee wages plus number of exemptions and additional withholding requested, or by using the percentage method. Both methods are explained in the department's *Circular* and may be done daily, weekly, biweekly, or monthly. Massachusetts allows additional reductions in withholding tax for employees filing as head of household or who claim the blindness exemption. Businesses with automated payroll systems generally use the percentage method of figuring Massachusetts withholding

Filing and Paying Withholding

Massachusetts specifies different filing schedules according to the amount of withholding tax employers collect a year:

- Employers with a projected annual withholding tax collected of $100 or less must file annually by January 31 of the following year, using Form M-941A.

- Employers with a projected annual withholding tax collected of $101 to $1,200 file quarterly, on or before the last day of the month after the end of the quarter, that is April 30, July 31, October 31, and January 31, using Form M-941.

- Employers with a projected annual withholding tax collected of $1,201 to $25,000 file monthly by the 15th of the following month except for the payments for March, June, September, and December, which are due by the last day of the following month. These employers use Form M-942.

- Employers with a predicted annual withholding collected of more than $25,000 file quarterly, as with the second group above, using Form M-941D.

For the first three groups above, payment is due with the return. For the over $25,000 category, when Massachusetts tax withheld is at least $500 by the 7th, 15th, 22nd, and last day of the month payment is due within three business days using Form M-941W for each payment. Note that employers with an annual tax liability of $250,000 or more must make weekly payments through Electronic Funds Transfer [(617) 887-5020]. In all categories a form should be filed even when no tax is due for a period (enter zero in the appropriate places on the form) for DOR's recordkeeping purposes.

Late Returns and Payments

Employers that fail to file a return by the due date will be fined 1 percent of the balance due per month or fraction of a month up to 25 percent of the tax due. Employers who fail to pay withholding taxes on time will be charged interest at the federal short-term rate plus 4 percentage points, compounded daily.

Businesses with annual withholding liabilities over $25,000 who fail to make timely withholding tax deposits are liable for a 5-percent penalty on the amount of underpayment (that is, the portion of the tax payment or weekly deposit that was not paid on time).

Employers found guilty of willfully failing to collect and pay over taxes are guilty of a felony punishable by a fine of up to $10,000 and/or imprisonment for up to five years.

Correcting Withholding Payment Errors

Employers who make errors in withholding payments can take the following steps:

- For adjustments to underpayments for the period immediately before in the same calendar year, adjustments must be made in Item 2 of the employer's current form and submitted with payment for the additional amount.

- Underpayments occurring before the previous calendar period must be adjusted on Form M-941-AM, *Amended Return of Income Taxes Withheld*, along with payment for the additional amount.

- Refunds of overpayment of taxes withheld must be requested by submitting an *Application of Abatement* (Form CA-6) along with a copy of the return substantiating the overpayment.

Recordkeeping

Employers must keep the following on file:

- The name, address, Social Security number, and occupation of each employee.

- The amount and date of all wage payments, the periods of service covered by these payments, and the amount of tax withheld.

- Employees' statements of tips received.

- Employees' withholding exemption certificates (Form W-4 and Form M-4).

- Employer's copies of employees' *Wage and Tax Statements,* Form W-2.

- Copies of all withholding returns filed with the DOR.

Employers must retain these records for at least three years after the date the return was filed or the date it was required to be filed, whichever is later. There is no limitation on the period for which DOR may request records in cases where an employer failed to file a return or filed a false return.

Chapter 21
Healthcare Plans and COBRA

Introduction

Healthcare plans provide employees and their families coverage for essential and emergency medical needs. These programs are one of the most important benefits an employer can provide. This chapter provides an overview of employee group healthcare plans in general and details employee health benefits under COBRA, the Consolidated Omnibus Budget Reconciliation Act. The state laws regarding group health insurance follow the COBRA discussion.

Healthcare Plans

General Characteristics

Healthcare plans are subject to a number of rules regarding enrollment rights and the benefits that must be provided to plan participants and their beneficiaries. This section provides an overview of the rules on enrollment in group healthcare plans and on the benefits of these plans. Since many of the restrictions do not apply to dental and vision plans, the terms *healthcare plans* and *medical plans* as used in this section do not refer to dental and vision plans.

Medical plans are prohibited from denying enrollment or continuing enrollment in the plans because of factors relating to the health status of applicants or participants. Employers are also prohibited from requiring employees to pay increased contributions because of factors relating to health status. Factors relating to health status include the following:

- Actual health status.
- Medical conditions, including physical and mental illness.
- Claims experience.
- Receipt of healthcare.
- Medical history.
- Genetic information.
- Evidence of insurability.
- Disability.

Medical plans are limited in their ability to restrict coverage due to pre-existing conditions. A *pre-existing condition* is any condition for which medical care was recommended or received within six months prior to date of healthcare plan enrollment (including any waiting periods). In general, medical conditions may not be imposed if an employee or beneficiary enrolls in the plan in a timely fashion and had other healthcare coverage for at least 12 months before enrollment without an intervening "significant break in coverage." A significant break in coverage is a period of more than 63 consecutive days during which an individual does not have other healthcare coverage. Other healthcare coverage would include any other group health plan, individual coverage, Medicare, Medicaid, and various other types of plans and government programs. Certain exceptions may apply. When employees and beneficiaries are no longer covered by employers' plans, employers must issue certificates to the employees indicating the length of their coverage under the plan before the coverage ended.

Medical plans must permit immediate enrollment in certain circumstances notwithstanding any open-enrollment policies of the plan. Immediate enrollment must be offered under the following circumstances:

- The employee previously had COBRA coverage under another plan that is exhausted.
- The employee had other coverage that he or she has ceased to be eligible for other than for reason of the employee's nonpayment of premiums.
- The employee had other coverage for which the sponsoring employer has ceased to pay.

Immediate enrollment also must be offered to employees, spouses, and dependent children if an employee acquires a spouse or dependent child through marriage, birth, adoption, or placement for adoption. The length of the special enrollment period may be limited (not less than 30 days) and advance notice of these special enrollment rights must be provided.

Other Required Benefits and Features

Group health plans must permit and pay for a minimum-length hospital stay in connection with childbirth; 48 hours for vaginal births and 96 hours for caesarian deliveries.

In group health plans with dollar limits on plan benefits, the costs for mental health benefits must be grouped with the medical plan costs so that they are subject to the same dollar limits. Separate dollar limits for mental health benefits can be established as long as they are not less than the dollar limits for medical benefits. Benefits for alcohol and substance abuse are not considered mental health benefits and may have lower dollar caps.

A group health plan may be required to cover a child or dependent even if the child would not meet the usual dependency standards in the plan if a court issues a qualified medical child-support order requiring it to do so. Coverage for dependent children who are adopted or placed for adoption must be provided under the same terms and conditions as apply to natural children and without regard to pre-existing conditions.

State Law Regulations

State laws may also apply to group health plans. For example, if the plan is insured, the insurer's policy may have to include a number of benefits or other features as required by state insurance law. In addition, while insurance companies are generally required to follow the regulations outlined above relating to pre-existing conditions and open enrollment, states are permitted to adopt more generous insurance laws relating to these aspects of health plans.

If an employer obtains its healthcare coverage from an arrangement consisting of two or more employers, where there is not sufficient common controlling ownership, that arrangement may be considered a *multiple employer welfare arrangement* (MEWA). A MEWA may also be required to comply with various state insurance laws.

COBRA Healthcare Continuation Coverage

Background

Before 1985, group healthcare coverage for employees, spouses, and dependent children was discontinued when an employee was terminated, reduced in work hours, divorced, or when the company went out of business. These conditions changed in 1985 with the passage of the Consolidated Omnibus Budget Reconciliation Act (COBRA). COBRA amends the Employee Retirement Income Security Act, the Internal Revenue Code, and the Public Health Service Act to provide continuation of healthcare coverage that might otherwise be terminated. COBRA rules define *group health plan* as any health coverage that provides medical, dental, vision, or prescription drug coverage for employees and their dependents. Life insurance is not covered under COBRA. Medical benefits under COBRA may include:

- Inpatient and outpatient hospital care.
- Physician care.
- Surgery and other major medical benefits.
- Prescription drugs.
- Any other medical benefits such as dental and vision care.

With COBRA's health benefit provisions, the probability of continuing group healthcare coverage benefits is dramatically improved for employees and their families during specified times. The employees may, however, be required to pay more for COBRA coverage than active employees pay for health coverage. Employers are permitted to charge up to 102 percent of the plan's cost, but the cost is usually less than that of individual health coverage.

Covered Employers

The COBRA law generally applies to group health plans maintained by public and private employers with 20 or more employees. It applies to plans sponsored by local and state governments but not to plans sponsored by the federal government. Certain church-related organizations such as the following are also excluded:

- Private hospitals owned or operated by religious organizations.
- Private schools or orphanages owned or operated by religious organizations.
- Commercial establishments of religious organizations engaged in producing or selling products such as alcoholic beverages, bakery goods, or religious goods.

Small employers—usually those with fewer than 20 employees on at least 50 percent of their workdays during the previous year—do not have to comply with COBRA continuation coverage requirements. All employers who are members of the same affiliated "controlled group" for tax purposes are treated as a single employer.

Counting Employees

The final COBRA regulations make several changes in the rules for counting employees that should allow more employers to qualify for the "small-employer" exception. Under the new rules, only common law employees have to be counted. Self-employed individuals (for example, owners of unincorporated businesses), independent contractors, and directors do not have to be counted even if they are covered by the same plan as common law employees.

Part-time employees must be counted under the final regulations, but an employer may choose to count them as less than a full employee. Each part-time employee may be counted as a fraction of an employee equal to the number of hours he or she works divided by the number of hours he or she would have to work to be considered a full-time employee based on the employer's employment practices, up to a maximum of eight hours a day, 40 hours a week.

In addition, the final regulations allow employers to count employees by pay periods rather than on a day-to-day basis. The number of employees for the pay period can be applied to each typical business day in that pay period, as long as the same method is used for all employees for the entire year.

Note: A plan that was not a small-employer plan for a given period remains liable for COBRA coverage that was triggered during that period, even if the plan later becomes a small-employer plan.

Covered Plans

Other than the small-employee exception noted above, COBRA applies to any group health plan maintained by an employer. A healthcare plan includes any plan that provides medical coverage, dental coverage, prescription-drug coverage and/or vision care. A plan is considered a group health plan when an employer provides healthcare directly or though an insurance or reimbursement arrangement, such as a flexible-spending arrangement.

Exceptions

An arrangement to provide medical services on your company's business premises will generally be treated as a group health plan. However, an on-site facility that primarily provides first aid to current employees at no charge during working hours is not covered by COBRA requirements. Additionally, the COBRA rules do not apply to facilities and programs such as spas, swimming pools, or fitness centers that simply further general good health.

COBRA requirements also do not apply to employer-sponsored plans providing long-term care services, nor do COBRA requirements apply to amounts contributed by an employer to a medical savings account. COBRA does, however, cover high-deductible health insurance that an employer provides in connection with a medical savings account.

In the case of a cafeteria plan or flexible spending arrangement (FSA), the COBRA coverage requirements apply only to healthcare benefits an employee has actually chosen to receive. The regulations make it clear that health FSAs are generally subject to COBRA.

Covered Employees and Beneficiaries

A covered employee under COBRA includes anyone who is covered under a group health plan by virtue of an employment relationship with the employer. For example, retirees or former employees might be covered by the plan because of their former employment with the employer. Although self-employed individuals, independent contractors, and directors do not have to be counted as employees under the small-business category described above, they are eligible for COBRA if their relationship to the employer makes them eligible to be covered by the employer's health insurance plan.

Employees who are eligible for the plan are not, however, covered employees if they are not actually enrolled in the plan.

Under COBRA, a *qualified beneficiary* is an employee, spouse of an employee, or dependent child of an employee who is covered under the employer's healthcare plan on the day before certain triggering events occur and who would lose coverage under the plan because of the event.

Note: As with covered employees, qualified dependents—other than children born to or adopted by covered employees during a period of COBRA coverage—must be actually covered by the employer's plan on the day before the event that triggers termination of insurance coverage.

Loss of Coverage and Qualifying Events

Under COBRA, companies must continue to offer group healthcare to qualified beneficiaries if certain events occur that cause the qualified beneficiary to lose coverage under the plan before the end of the maximum COBRA coverage period. These specific events which cause a loss of coverage are called *qualifying events* and include the following:

- The covered employee's employment is terminated for any reason.
- The covered employee's work hours are reduced.
- The covered employee dies.
- The covered employee is divorced or legally separated.
- The covered employee becomes entitled to Medicare benefits.
- A dependent child of a covered employee ceases to be a dependent under the terms of the plan.

For purposes of COBRA rules, *loss of coverage* means that the employee or dependent is no longer covered under the same terms and conditions in effect immediately before the qualifying event. This would mean, for example, that an increase in premiums or contributions that the employee or a dependent must pay is considered a loss of coverage if the increase is caused by the qualifying event.

Example: Betty Finley retires after 30 years with Beta Corp. As a retiree, Finley is offered continued coverage, but is required to pay a higher premium for the same group health coverage she had before retirement. Finley's retirement is a qualifying event—termination of her employment. What is more, she has lost coverage because of the higher premium requirement, even if the premium requirement is less than the full cost of COBRA coverage. Therefore, Beta Corp must offer Finley COBRA continuation coverage.

This rule may seem somewhat paradoxical. Your company can charge an employee for COBRA coverage and may, as we will see, cut off COBRA coverage after a period of time. Thus, retirees may get a better deal as far as price and time, if they stick with regular coverage. However, to protect the right of an employee to decline coverage, but elect later to retroactively reinstate coverage during the COBRA election period, your company must satisfy the COBRA requirements and offer the COBRA coverage.

Loss of Coverage Before a Qualifying Event

If the reduction or elimination of coverage was made in anticipation of the event, COBRA coverage is required when the event occurs. For example, COBRA coverage is required if an employer eliminates an employee's health coverage in anticipation of termination of employment or if an employee drops coverage for a spouse in anticipation of a divorce. When determining COBRA coverage in these cases reduction in or elimination of coverage must be ignored.

Loss of Coverage After a Qualifying Event

A loss of coverage does not have to take place simultaneously with the qualifying event as long as the loss of coverage occurs before the end of the maximum COBRA coverage period for that event.

Example: Gamma Corp maintains a group health plan for active employees and retirees and their families. The coverage for employees and retirees is identical. Gamma does not require retirees to pay more for their coverage than do active employees. As a result, Gamma is not required to make COBRA coverage available when an employee retires because there is no loss of coverage on termination of employment.

However, Gamma decides to amend its plan to eliminate retiree coverage. At the time the amendment takes effect several retirees and their spouses have been covered for less than the maximum COBRA coverage period since they terminated employment. These retirees for whom the maximum COBRA period has not expired are eligible for COBRA. Beginning with the date of their retirement Gamma must make COBRA coverage available to those retirees and their spouses for the remainder of the maximum coverage. COBRA coverage is not required if the maximum coverage period has expired when a deferred loss of coverage takes place.

Coverage for Employees Terminated for Cause

The reasons for the termination of an employee's employment are irrelevant. It does not matter whether the employee quit voluntarily or was discharged; the employee is still eligible for COBRA coverage.

COBRA coverage does not need to be made available to employees discharged for gross misconduct. Courts generally narrowly define gross misconduct for this purpose and employers should exercise caution when attempting to apply this exception.

Reduction in Hours

As long as no immediate termination takes place, a reduction in hours occurs when there is a decrease in the number of hours a covered employee is required to work or actually works. Thus, a switch from full time to part-time would thus trigger COBRA coverage if the employee loses health benefits because of the change. An absence because of a disability or a temporary layoff is also a reduction in hours, even though the employee's hours are reduced to zero.

If a plan measures eligibility for coverage by the number of hours worked in a given period, such as the preceding month or quarter, an employee who fails to work the required hours has experienced a reduction in hours resulting in a loss of coverage.

Nature of COBRA Coverage

COBRA continuation coverage must be the same coverage as that provided to similarly situated non-COBRA employees and their dependents not covered by COBRA. This includes the same open-enrollment rights. Any change in benefits applies equally to COBRA and non-COBRA beneficiaries. However, an employer cannot cut off coverage for COBRA beneficiaries if it maintains any health plans. If an employer eliminates a plan, any COBRA beneficiaries enrolled in that plan must be offered the option of enrolling in another plan, **even if active employees are not offered that option.**

Generally a qualified beneficiary must continue the coverage he or she had immediately before the qualifying event. However, the same enrollment period rights must be given to the COBRA beneficiary if the employer has an open enrollment for employees to switch plans or benefit packages or to add or eliminate family members.

The following examples illustrate this concept:

- ♦ Omega Corp has several group health plans for its employees. Employees can choose the plan they want but all family members must be covered by the same plan. Joan Edmund, her spouse, and her two children are covered by Omega's Plan A. When Edmunds terminates her employment with Omega each member of her family must be offered COBRA coverage under Plan A. Omega does not have to allow any family member to switch to another plan.

- ♦ All members of the Edmunds family elect COBRA coverage under Omega's Plan A. Three months later, Omega has an open-enrollment period during which active employees can switch plans or add or eliminate coverage for family members. During this open-enrollment period each member of the Edmunds family must be offered the chance to switch to another plan. In this example, each family member is treated as a separate qualified beneficiary with independent rights. Thus, each member could choose to be covered under a different plan, even though family members of active employees must all be under the same plan as the employee. Omega could, however, charge family members separately for their coverage based on the applicable premium for individual coverage.

Under the Health Insurance Portability and Accountability Act (HIPAA), if your employee declined coverage for a spouse or dependent because he or she was covered under another plan, the spouse or dependent must be given the right to enroll in your plan if the other coverage is lost. You may, however, limit special enrollment rights to employees who declare in writing that they are declining coverage for a spouse or dependent because of other coverage. Under HIPAA your plan must also allow special enrollment rights if an employee has a new dependent because of birth, marriage, adoption, or placement for adoption.

These special enrollment rights apply to COBRA beneficiaries except in the case of a spouse or dependent who is added during the COBRA coverage period. The COBRA regulations provide that a spouse or dependent who is added to the plan during a COBRA coverage period is **not** a qualified beneficiary.

Employee Moves

A COBRA beneficiary who moves outside the area served by an employer's region-specific plan (an HMO, for example) must be provided an opportunity under special rules to elect alternative coverage available to any other active employee of the employer that can be extended to the place of relocation. There is no requirement to offer coverage where all coverages are region-specific and can't be extended to the place of relocation.

Length of COBRA Coverage

COBRA coverage generally lasts for 18 months if the qualifying event was termination of employment or a reduction in hours. For other qualifying events—death, divorce or legal separation, Medicare entitlement, or loss of dependent status—coverage lasts 36 months.

Disability Extensions

The initial 18-month COBRA coverage period can be extended to 29 months if a qualified beneficiary is determined by the Social Security Administration to be disabled at any time during the first 60 days of COBRA coverage. Individuals who become disabled before the COBRA coverage period began will qualify for the extension if they remain disabled on the date COBRA coverage begins. The 29-month coverage extension applies to each qualified beneficiary entitled to COBRA coverage because of the qualifying event, not merely to the disabled beneficiary.

To qualify for an extension, the affected qualified beneficiary must notify the plan administrator of the disability determination within 60 days after the date of the determination and before the end of the 18-month COBRA period.

If a final determination finds that the qualified beneficiary is no longer disabled, COBRA coverage for the disabled beneficiary and all qualified beneficiaries can be terminated within 30 days. It cannot, however, be cut off before the end of the 18-month period.

The initial 18-month coverage or the 29-month extension period will be extended to 36 months if a second qualifying event occurs during the COBRA period. The event must be one that would trigger 36 months of coverage; not, for example, a termination of employment following a reduction in hours, which are 18-month qualifying events. Death, divorce, legal separation, Medicare entitlement, or loss of dependent status would result in 36-month coverage. If an employee terminates employment and elects COBRA coverage, the coverage would be for 18 months. If, however, the employee dies during that period, the employee's spouse and dependents are entitled to 36 months of COBRA coverage from the first qualifying event; that is, the termination of employment.

Note: COBRA coverage is not extended if the employer provides non-COBRA coverage for a time after the qualifying event. The end of the COBRA coverage period is measured from the date of the qualifying event.

Conversion Plans

The right to enroll in a conversion plan at the end of the COBRA period must be offered to a qualified beneficiary only if the right is available to similarly situated non-COBRA employees under the plan. If a conversion option is not generally available, it need not be offered to a qualified beneficiary.

Termination of COBRA Coverage

Once COBRA coverage has been elected, it can be terminated before the end of the maximum coverage period for a number of reasons:

- The failure of the qualified beneficiary to pay the required premium. There is a minimum 30-day grace period for payment of premiums.

- The beneficiary becomes entitled to benefits under Medicare (either part A or Part B) after the date COBRA coverage is elected.

- The beneficiary becomes covered by another group health plan but only if:
  - The beneficiary becomes covered under the other group health plan after COBRA coverage is elected.
  - The other plan does not contain any exclusion or limitation with respect to a pre-existing condition of the qualified beneficiary (or the exclusion is waived under the HIPAA creditable service rules).
  - The employer stops offering any group health plan to any employee.

An employer can terminate a beneficiary's coverage for cause on the same basis that it would terminate the coverage of a non-COBRA beneficiary. For example, if a plan terminates the coverage of active employees who submit fraudulent claims, a qualified beneficiary's coverage can also be terminated for submission of a fraudulent claim.

If an individual who is not a qualified beneficiary has coverage only because of his or her relationship to a qualified beneficiary, that individual's coverage can be terminated whenever the qualified beneficiary's coverage ceases.

Notices of COBRA Rights

In cases of divorce or legal separation or of a dependent child ceasing to be a dependent under the terms of the plan, the law requires that the qualified beneficiary notify the plan administrator within 60 days after the event occurs. Once notice is provided, the employer's notice obligations described below must also be followed.

The employer or plan administrator must send an initial notice of COBRA rights to the covered employee, the spouse of the covered employee, and dependent children who do not reside with the spouse at the time they have been covered under the group health plan. The initial notice should include a statement that no COBRA coverage will be provided in the case of a divorce, legal separation, or child's ceasing to be a dependent, unless a qualified beneficiary notifies the plan administrator of that event within 60 days after the event.

The employer is required to notify the plan administrator within 30 days of a termination of employment, reduction in hours, death, or entitlement to Medicare. Once the plan administrator is advised of a COBRA event, he or she must provide an election notice to the qualified beneficiaries within 14 days. The Department of Labor has stated that when the employer is also the plan administer, the election notice must be provided to qualified beneficiaries within 44 days.

Electing COBRA Coverage

The Election Period

COBRA coverage is not automatic. The beneficiary must elect and pay for COBRA coverage within certain required periods. Once a qualified beneficiary has received a notice of his or her COBRA rights as a result of a qualifying event, he or she has at least 60 days from the date coverage would otherwise be lost to elect COBRA coverage. Once COBRA coverage is timely elected, a qualified beneficiary has at least 45 days after the date of election to pay premiums that are due for the period of coverage prior to the election.

Note: The employer or plan administrator—not the employee—is usually responsible for determining if a qualifying event has occurred and reporting the event to the plan. The two exceptions to this are those noted above, under **Notices of COBRA Rights:** The employee must notify the plan administrator when a covered employee divorces or separates, and when a child ceases to be eligible for coverage.

Coverage During the Election Period

During the election period, coverage must be provided from the date it would otherwise be lost in the following ways depending on the type of coverage. In the case of an insured plan or reimbursement arrangement the employer can:

- Continue the coverage during the election period and cancel it retroactively if payment is not timely made, or
- If the plan allows for retroactive reinstatement of coverage the plan can terminate the coverage of a qualified beneficiary and reinstate it when the election is made.

Note: Claims incurred during the election period do not have to be paid before the election is made. In the case of an HMO, PPO, or similar arrangement, the rules apply as described below under the section titled **Paying for COBRA: Payment During the Election Period.** Note, also, that healthcare providers (doctors, hospitals, pharmacies) who inquire about a beneficiary's coverage during the election period must be informed regarding COBRA rights. The plan administrator must, for example, inform the healthcare provider that the beneficiary is currently covered but that coverage may be terminated retroactively.

Employee Revocation/Reinstatement

Sometimes employees waive COBRA coverage before the end of the election period, then change their minds. Under COBRA rules, an employee may revoke a waiver at any time before the end of the election period. In this case, the beneficiary does not have to be given coverage from the date employer-provided coverage was lost until the date of the revocation.

An employer cannot withhold money or other benefits to get an employee to waive COBRA coverage. A waiver obtained by withholding other benefits is invalid.

Multiple Beneficiaries and Separate Election

Each beneficiary including a newborn or adopted child must be offered the opportunity to make an independent election to receive COBRA coverage. However, if a covered employee or spouse of a covered employee makes a COBRA election that does not specify whether the election is for self-only coverage, the election covers all beneficiaries who lost coverage because of the same qualifying event. A beneficiary cannot decline coverage on behalf of another beneficiary.

Paying for COBRA

Payment During the Election Period

Some plans, such as health maintenance organizations or walk-in clinics, provide health services directly. A beneficiary who seeks services before he or she elects COBRA may either pay for COBRA coverage or pay the reasonable and customary charge for the services. If the beneficiary pays for the services, he or she must be reimbursed within 30 days after the COBRA election is made and full payment for coverage is received. Alternatively, with notice to the beneficiary, the plan can, with notice to the beneficiary, treat the use of the services as a constructive (implicit) COBRA election. In that case, the beneficiary must pay the COBRA premium for the coverage.

Regular Payment for COBRA Coverage

The beneficiary, not the employer, pays for COBRA coverage. Employers may charge up to 102 percent of the applicable premium for COBRA coverage. The applicable premium is essentially the amount the plan pays to an insurer for the same coverage that is being provided to similarly situated active employees. If the plan is self-insured, an actuarial calculation of expected costs must be made. The payment for COBRA coverage may be raised to 150 percent of the applicable premium but only for the 18–29 month disability extension period.

The COBRA premium must be determined in advance and can be based on any 12-month period selected by the plan, but the same period must be used from year to year. The plan may charge the employee retroactively for the period of coverage after the qualifying event and before the COBRA election. The plan may require the first payment to apply first to the retroactive period of coverage.

Premium Increases

The plan may increase a beneficiary's premium during a 12-month COBRA coverage period in three situations only:

1. The plan initially charged less than the maximum amount permitted by COBRA rules. In this case it can raise the premium to the maximum.

2. The increase is made during the disability extension and the increased premium is not more than 150 percent of the applicable premium.
3. The qualified beneficiary makes permitted changes in the coverage.

Payment Dates

The plan must allow payment for COBRA coverage to be made in monthly installments. The plan can also allow payments at other intervals—weekly, quarterly, etc.

Non-payment or Late Payment

A plan may cancel coverage for failure to pay on time. However, the regulations state that a payment is timely if it is made within 30 days of the payment due date, and a longer grace period may be allowed, depending on the plan terms that apply to similarly situated non-COBRA beneficiaries.

Partial Payment

Payment for coverage must be made on time and in full. However, payments not significantly less than the required amount will be considered payment-in-full unless the plan notifies the beneficiary of the shortfall and grants a reasonable time, usually 30 days, for payment of the deficit. Final regulations provide that an underpayment is not significant if the shortfall amount does not exceed $50 or 10 percent of the amount due, whichever is lesser.

COBRA and Other Laws

A number of federal laws give employees and their beneficiaries special rights when it comes to healthcare. Each of these laws interacts with COBRA. For example, the final regulations point out that if an employer withholds healthcare coverage from a disabled employee in violation of the Americans with Disabilities Act, the employee is entitled to the coverage that was denied. The employer will also be required to offer continuation of that coverage under COBRA if the employee experiences a qualifying event.

Health Insurance Portability and Accountability Act

The Health Insurance Portability and Accountability Act (HIPAA) requires group health plans to offer special enrollment rights to employees and their dependents.

Under HIPAA, if an employee declined coverage for a spouse or dependent because he or she was covered under another plan, the employee spouse or dependent has the right to enroll in your plan if he or she loses the other coverage. You may, however, limit special enrollment rights to employees who declare in writing that they are declining coverage for themselves, a spouse, or dependent because of other coverage. The plan must notify the employee at the time of enrollment of the need for the declaration and the consequences of failing to provide the declaration. Under HIPAA, your plan must also allow special enrollment rights if an employee has a new dependent because of marriage, birth, adoption, or placement for adoption. The next chapter discusses HIPAA requirements in more detail.

Special enrollment rights continue to apply during the employee's COBRA coverage period. For example an employee who marries during a period of COBRA coverage may enroll his or her new spouse. The new spouse, in this case, is not a COBRA qualified beneficiary because the new spouse was not covered under the plan at the time of the employee's qualifying event.

Family and Medical Leave Act

The Family and Medical Leave Act (FMLA) requires companies to offer unpaid leave for family or medical emergencies. A company is required to maintain an employee's health coverage while the employee is on leave, although the employee may be required to pay for the coverage. Under the new COBRA regulations, taking FMLA leave is not a qualifying event. COBRA and FMLA interact under the following special rules:

- For an employee, who is covered under the plan immediately before or at any time during FMLA leave, a qualifying event occurs when the employee fails to return to work at the end of FMLA leave and coverage is then lost. FMLA leave ends as determined in accordance with separate Department of Labor regulations.

- Spouses and dependents covered under the plan immediately before or at any time during FMLA leave will also have a COBRA qualifying event at the end of the employee's FMLA leave if they lose coverage due to the employee's failure to return to work.

COBRA coverage cannot be conditional on the employee's reimbursement of any premiums paid by your company to retain the employee's coverage during the FMLA leave. COBRA coverage must be provided even if the employee's health coverage lapsed during the leave because the employee failed to pay required premiums.

Note: If you have eliminated health coverage prior to the end of the employee's FMLA leave for the class of employees to which the employee who was on leave belonged, your company does not have to provide that employee with COBRA coverage.

The Federal Government and COBRA Enforcement

Continuation coverage laws are administered by several agencies. The U.S. Public Health Service administers the continuation coverage law as it affects public-sector health plans. The Department of Labor and the Department of Treasury have jurisdiction over private health plans. The Labor Department's interpretative and regulatory responsibility is limited to the disclosure and notification requirements. Employees who need further information on election or notification of rights with a private-sector plan should contact the nearest office of the Pension and Welfare Benefits Administration. The Internal Revenue Service is responsible for publishing regulations on COBRA provisions relating to eligibility and premiums. The Labor and Treasury Departments share jurisdiction for enforcement.

Responsibility for COBRA Coverage
When a Business Is Sold

Generally, final IRS regulations (effective in 2002) provide that in the case of stock sales and sales of substantial assets, such as a division or a plant, the seller retains the obligation to provide COBRA continuation coverage to existing qualified beneficiaries, at the time of the sale, including those who lose coverage in connection with the sale. Only qualified beneficiaries whose qualifying event is associated with the sold company or assets are covered by this rule. In a stock sale, current employees who continue employment with the same company after the sale do not have a qualifying event and have no COBRA rights with respect to the seller's plan because there has been no qualifying event (for example, termination of employment). However, in the case of an asset sale, current employees continuing employment with the buyer after the sale may or may not have a qualifying event depending on the amount of assets sold and other factors even if they continue to receive health plan coverage under the buyer's plans. However, if the seller ceases to provide any group health plan to any employee in connection with the sale, the buyer must provide COBRA coverage to existing qualified beneficiaries associated with the sold company or assets.

On the other hand, the regulations provide that the buyer and seller are free to allocate the responsibility for providing COBRA coverage by contract, even if the provider is a different party. As long as the party to whom the contract allocates the responsibility follows through, the original provider will have no responsibility for providing COBRA coverage. If, however, the party responsible under the contract does not perform, the party responsible under the COBRA regulations will be held accountable.

Massachusetts Regulations

Massachusetts Annotated Laws provides extensive supplements to the federal healthcare laws. For a simplified overview, this section summarizes the state law under two major categories—Health Coverage and Continuing Coverage. The discussion on continuing coverage is expanded at the end of this section in a summary of the Massachusetts laws applying to small-business continuation insurance—that is, continuing insurance for employees of companies with fewer than 20 employees and thus not under COBRA regulations. Under Health Coverage we include, as subcategories, medical health, mental health, and a separate category for birth, infants, and children, since much of the Massachusetts law focuses on this area. In Massachusetts, most of the medical health regulations focus on health coverage for specific diseases, such as cancer.

For most of this section all Massachusetts' laws summarized are prefaced with the statement that each law holds true for any blanket or general policy of insurance that is promulgated or renewed to any person or persons in the commonwealth. In other words, the regulations summarized in this section have very broad coverage within the commonwealth.

Note: Massachusetts provides three very similar sets of laws:

- **Group Insurance Policies**—these laws apply to insurance companies insuring employees of corporations.
- **Hospital Service Contracts**—these apply to non-profit hospital service corporations insuring individuals or groups by contract.
- **Medical Service Agreements**—laws in this category apply to medical service corporations insuring individuals or groups under medical service agreements.

Massachusetts also provides a few regulations on Health Maintenance Organizations, summarized in this section.

Group Insurance Policies
Medical Health Coverage

The following regulations are in effect:

- Group insurance policies issued in Massachusetts must include coverage for nonprescription enteral formulas for which a physician has issued a written order. These are the medications used to treat various intestinal diseases—Chron's disease, ulcerative colitis, gastroesophageal reflux, etc.

- Under Massachusetts law no group policy in effect in the state can exclude coverage for drugs used to treat cancer, if the drug in question has been recognized in the medical literature. The drug need not have been approved by the United States Food and Drug Administration.

- Massachusetts requires that expenses for scalp hair prostheses to cover hair loss resulting from treatment of any form of cancer be covered if such prosthetic scalp hair is considered medically necessary and if the policy covers any other prosthesis. There is a $350-per-year limit on this coverage, however.

- Massachusetts requires that group policies in effect in the state cover the services of certified registered nurse anesthetists and nurse practitioners if similar services rendered by other healthcare providers are covered.

- Massachusetts requires that the services of certified chiropractors be covered as long as these services are within the lawful scope of the practice of a chiropractor.

Mental Health Coverage

Under Massachusetts law all group insurance policies issued in the state must provide benefits for expenses arising from mental or nervous conditions recognized by the American Psychiatric Association. This care must include coverage for at least 60 days in any year for confinement in a mental hospital. Any maximum monetary limit imposed on this care cannot be lower than that put upon healthcare for conditions other than mental or nervous conditions. Massachusetts is adamant that the benefits available to those with mental or nervous conditions not be different from those available to those with other conditions.

Infant Health Coverage

Massachusetts law requires that group insurance policies in effect in the commonwealth provide for the services of certified nurse midwifes if such services would be paid for if done by any other duly licensed practitioner.

Group insurance policies in effect in the commonwealth must provide for the expenses of prenatal care, childbirth, and postpartum care to the same extent as for medical conditions not related to pregnancy. Massachusetts allows for 48 hours of in-patient care following a vaginal delivery and 96 hours of care following a cesarean delivery.

Any group insurance policy issued in Massachusetts must include, as insured members under the blanket general policy, newborn infants of policyholders and newborn infants of dependents of policyholders living in Massachusetts. This coverage begins at the moment of birth. The coverage also applies to adoptive children of policyholders from the date of filing the petition to adopt or from the date of placement in the home.

Coverage of newly born and adoptive children must consist of coverage for injury and sickness, including care and treatment of congenital birth defects and abnormalities as well as premature birth.

Coverage for infants must include any special medical formulas prescribed by a physician to treat a variety of infant diseases. Note that under this requirement Massachusetts states that the insured must notify the insurer of the birth or adoption and must pay any required additional premium.

Newborn health coverage will also include testing for lead-poisoning and hearing screening tests.

Continuation Coverage

Massachusetts law requires that if a person covered by any group policy issued since 1968 leaves the insured group, the person shall remain insured for up to 31 days after leaving unless the person obtains similar coverage before then.

All group insurance policies in Massachusetts must include coverage so that if a person leaves an insured group because of a plant closing the person remains insured under the policy for 90 days or until similar coverage is obtained.

If an insured becomes ineligible for continued participation in any group insurance plan in effect in Massachusetts because of involuntary layoff or death, the coverage for the member and his or her spouse and dependents must continue for 39 weeks from the date of ineligibility or until similar group coverage is obtained. In this case, however, the member, spouse or dependents is responsible for the entire premium of the policy, including anything the employer normally contributes.

In cases of divorce, Massachusetts requires that the spouse of the insured individual remain eligible for insurance benefits under the group plan the insured individual belongs to, without additional premiums. This coverage will remain in effect until either party remarries or until the insured leaves the plan. This protection does not remain, however, if the divorce judgment specifically excludes it.

Hospital Service Contracts
Medical Health Coverage

As with companies providing group insurance for employees of corporations, non-profit health service corporations offering individual or group health service contracts in Massachusetts must provide coverage for nonprescription medicines for treatment of Chrohn's disease, ulcerative colitis, and other intestinal diseases.

Hospital service contracts in Massachusetts must provide for prescription drugs to treat cancer.

Massachusetts requires that hospital service contracts cover bone-marrow transplants and transplants for people with metastasized breast cancer.

Hospital service contracts under Massachusetts law must provide coverage for blood-glucose monitoring strips used to treat insulin-dependent diabetes.

Any individual or group health service agreement in effect in Massachusetts must provide for treatment for alcoholism, including treatment in a facility for detoxification or rehabilitation.

Mental Health Coverage

In any hospital service contract in effect in Massachusetts benefits will be paid for expenses arising from mental or nervous conditions, just as for medical conditions. Massachusetts specifies minimum length of in-patient and outpatient treatment for mental disorders.

Infant Health Coverage

Individuals or groups insured by non-profit hospital service corporations must be covered for all prenatal, childbirth, and postpartum care under any hospital service contract in effect in Massachusetts to the extent that benefits are provided for medical conditions not related to pregnancy.

In any hospital service contract in effect in Massachusetts newborn infants of insured members and their dependents are insured from the moment of their birth. This coverage also applies to adoptive children from the moment of placement for adoption.

Hospital service contracts must provide for special medical formulas for infants as prescribed by physicians.

All hospital service contracts in effect in Massachusetts must provide for health examinations for all covered children up to the age of six. This includes various immunizations and tests as appropriate.

Medically necessary early-intervention services including speech therapy and psychological counseling must also be covered in hospital service contracts.

Continuation Coverage

Massachusetts provides no supplemental regulations for non-profit hospital service corporations regarding continuation of coverage.

Medical Service Agreements

Medical Health Coverage

Under Massachusetts law medical service corporations with subscriptions in the state must cover expenses of subscribers relating to treatment for alcoholism as inpatients or outpatients.

As with group insurance contracts and hospital service contracts, subscriptions with medical service corporations must cover nonprescription enteral drugs intended to combat various intestinal disorders (ulcerative colitis, chronic intestinal pseudo-obstruction, etc).

Medical service agreements are required to cover chiropractic services.

Medical service agreements must cover bone-marrow transplants for certain breast cancer patients.

In the Commonwealth, medical service agreements must provide coverage for licensed hospice services to terminally ill patients with a life expectancy of six months or less.

Mental Health Coverage

Massachusetts has no separate requirements for coverage of mental health services by medical service corporations.

Infant Health Coverage

Massachusetts requires that any individual or group medical service agreement through subscription include as insured members newborn infants of the insured and of dependents of the insured for the day of their birth. Coverage is also required for adoptive children.

Medical service agreements in Massachusetts must provide benefits for expenses arising from illness of or injury to children, congenital malformations, or premature births.

Special infant formulas must be covered by medical service agreements in effect in the Commonwealth.

All preventative and primary care services for children must be covered under Massachusetts regulations for medical service agreements.

Medically necessary early-intervention services, including physical and speech therapy and psychological counseling, must be covered under subscriptions with medical service corporations operating in Massachusetts.

Expenses for the services of certified nurse midwives must be covered under subscriptions with medical service corporations.

As under group contracts with insurance companies and individual or group contracts with hospital service corporations, medical service corporation subscriptions must cover prenatal and postpartum care and the expenses arising from childbirth. Under this clause the state defines the term *attending physician* to include the attending obstetrician, pediatrician, or certified nurse midwife.

Continuation Coverage

There are no separate requirements for continuation coverage under the Massachusetts law covering hospital service corporations.

Health Maintenance Organizations

Under Massachusetts law there is a requirement that HMO's operating in Massachusetts cover costs of scalp hair prostheses for hair loss resulting from cancer or leukemia if the treatment is medically necessary and if the HMO covers other kinds of prostheses.

Massachusetts law also stipulates that HMO policies may not exclude any eligible employee or dependent on the basis of age, occupation, actual or expected health conditions, claims experience, duration of coverage, or medical condition. Waiting periods for coverage of pre-existing conditions may not exceed six months.

Small Business Healthcare Continuation

In a separate chapter of the law Massachusetts expands its continuation coverage requirements for small businesses, companies with fewer than 20 employees. COBRA regulations do not normally apply to these companies. In Ch. 176J, Small Group Health Insurance, Massachusetts requires every carrier of health benefit plans operating in the state to offer continuation coverage to any qualified beneficiary who would lose coverage under that health benefit plan as a result of a qualifying event and who makes a written election for continued coverage under the health plan within the election period.

Stipulations on the nature of this continuation coverage and the obligations imposed on the insurer and the insured are much the same as those set down under COBRA regulations:

- The continuation coverage must be identical to the coverage provided under the health benefit plan to similarly situated beneficiaries to whom a qualifying event has not occurred.
- Any modification of coverage under the health benefit plan must apply as well to beneficiaries under the required continuation coverage.
- Continuation coverage must generally extend from the date of the qualifying event for at least 18 months and up to 36 months in some cases. For example, coverage can be extended to 36 months for the spouse or dependents of a deceased employee or up to 29 months for employees deemed, under the Social Security Act, to have been disabled at the time of the qualifying event.
- Coverage under the continuation plan can cease if timely payments (that is payments within 30 days of the due date) are not received by the insurer.
- Coverage can cease if the covered employee becomes covered by another health benefit plan.
- The insurer may require payment of a premium of not more than 102 percent of the applicable premium either through the former employer or an intermediary.
- Continuation coverage may not be contingent upon proof of insurability.
- Qualified beneficiaries whose continuation coverage period has ended must be give the option to enroll under a conversion nongroup health plan generally available through the carrier to similarly situated employees.

- Any election of continuation coverage by a qualified beneficiary will be on behalf of any other qualified beneficiary, that is a spouse or other dependent who would lose coverage as a result of the qualifying event. Each qualified beneficiary may, however, make a separate selection among types of coverage available, if any.

- Eligible employees or qualified beneficiaries are required to notify the carrier of the occurrence of any qualifying event.

Under this chapter the definitions of the terms *qualified beneficiary, qualifying event,* etc., are the same as they were under the COBRA regulations.

Chapter 22
HIPAA

Introduction

The Health Insurance Portability and Accountability Act (HIPAA), signed into law by President Clinton on August 21, 1996, amended the Employee Retirement Income Security Act (ERISA) to provide new rights and protections for participants in group health plans. HIPAA offers new protections and rights for millions of American workers and beneficiaries by improving portability and continuity of health insurance coverage. Subsequent amendments to HIPAA add provisions for mental health parity and minimum hospital stays for mothers and newborn babies. HIPAA significantly changes federal law with the primary purpose of making healthcare coverage more widely available.

Employers and employees making decisions about future health coverage need to understand HIPAA. The rules for HIPAA contain protections for health insurance coverage offered by group health plans, church plans, and employer partnerships.

A group health plan must have two or more participants to be covered by HIPAA. Only nonfederal government employer plans that elect out of the requirement are not included. Eligibility for enrollment in a group health plan is determined according to the terms of the plan, not the employee's or dependent's health status. HIPAA does not require an employer to carry a group health plan and certain benefits such as dental, vision, or long-term care benefits generally do not apply.

HIPAA Requirements

The following summarizes HIPAA requirements:

- A group health plan may impose a pre-existing condition exclusion on employees and their dependents for up to 12 months (18 months in the case of late enrollees).

- A group health plan or insurer must give an employee who leaves his or her employer a certificate of creditable coverage. This certificate can be used to reduce or eliminate the application of a pre-existing condition exclusion of another employer's group health plan.

- A group health plan cannot discriminate against an employee or the employee's dependents by creating barriers to eligibility or continued eligibility on the basis of health status.

- A group health plan must provide special enrollment periods for employees and dependents who lost or exhausted other coverage due to no fault of their own, or when the employee has added a spouse or dependent.

- Additional disclosures must be made to participants in group health plan summary plan descriptions (SPDs), including an updated statement of ERISA rights, the identification of an

- insurer and/or service provider, and a disclosure of minimum newborn and maternity stays if such coverage is provided by the plan.

- According to the Mental Health Parity Act, a group health plan that offers mental health coverage must set the same annual or lifetime dollar limits for mental health as they set for medical or surgical benefits.

- For the protection of the health of newborns and mothers, the plan usually cannot restrict a hospital stay for childbirth to less than 48 hours for vaginal birth and 96 hours for a caesarian section.

This chapter will discuss the above requirements in detail and will also include two model forms for the employer to use to design certificates of group health plan coverage.

Pre-existing Condition Exclusion

On the date the group health plan or issuer becomes subject to HIPAA provisions the plan or issuer may not exclude coverage for any pre-existing condition for more than 12 months (18 months for a late enrollee). This restriction exists regardless of whether this date occurred before the HIPAA effective date of the plan. Thus, this period may have already passed. If this period has not passed, the plan or issuer is required to count the time employees have already served under the plan toward satisfaction of the pre-existing condition exclusion period. Also, in determining pre-existing conditions no more than the previous six months can be used. Under HIPAA, pregnancy cannot be excluded from coverage as a pre-existing condition. Pre-existing exclusions cannot apply to newborns or adopted children (under 18) who are covered under a group health plan within 30 days of birth or adoption.

Example 1: Mary has been working for ABC Corporation and has been covered under the corporation's plan since August 1, 1996. Before HIPAA requirements the corporation's plan did not cover any pre-existing condition. ABC's plan year begins on January 1, 1998. As of that date ABC may no longer exclude coverage for Mary's pre-existing condition because she has already satisfied more than the maximum 12-month pre-existing exclusion period.

Example 2: John worked for ABC Corporation and was covered under its plan from July 1, 1997, to October 1, 1997 (3 months). He then changed jobs and was covered by XYZ Corporation's plan on November 1, 1997. Before being required to meet HIPAA's requirements, XYZ Corporation's plan did not cover any pre-existing condition. XYZ's plan year begins on January 1, 1998. As of this date, XYZ's plan must use John's three months of creditable coverage from ABC Corporation and the two months (November and December 1997) he has already been subject to the pre-existing condition exclusion to reduce John's remaining pre-existing condition exclusion period. John's remaining pre-existing condition exclusion period is seven months.

Portability under HIPAA does not mean those employees and their dependents are given the opportunity to take the same group health plan coverage with them from employer to employer. Rather, a new employer's group health plan must offset (month for month) each month of a new employee's and the employee's dependents' prior creditable coverage against the new employer's plan's pre-existing-condition coverage exclusion. The concept of *portability* means that an individual receives credit for maintaining health coverage, although it may be under different health plans or policies.

Creditable Coverage

The term *creditable coverage* includes a variety of healthcare coverage arrangements that count toward reducing the pre-existing condition exclusion under a new employer's group health plan. These include prior coverage under a group health plan (including governmental or church plan), health insurance coverage (either group or individual), Medicare, Medicaid, an HMO, a military-sponsored healthcare program such as CHAMPUS, a program of the Indian Health Service, and other various public health plans.

Creditable coverage can be lost if there is a break of 63 days or more in individual coverage. For example, a new employee who has no creditable coverage for 72 days prior to starting with a new employer is subject to the pre-existing condition exclusion of the new employer's health plan.

Example: John had coverage for two years followed by a break in coverage for 70 days, and then resumed coverage for eight months. He would receive credit against any pre-existing condition exclusion only for eight months of coverage; no credit would have to be given for the break of 63 days or more. COBRA coverage is not used toward calculating the break of coverage under a prior employer's group health plan or the waiting period under a new employer's group health plan.

Certification of Prior Plan Coverage

A certificate signed by the representative of the group health plan verifying the employee's coverage is needed to offset any pre-existing condition exclusion of the new group health plan. Any employer that is self-insured or the issuer offering health coverage must provide an employee with the certificate of healthcare coverage. The following three conditions require certification:

- When an employee ceases to be covered under a group health plan or becomes covered under COBRA.
- When the employee ceases to be covered by COBRA.
- When the employee requests it within 24 months of the termination of coverage.

HIPAA does not specify the form for the certificate; however, sample forms are given at the end of this chapter.

If an employee cannot get a certificate of creditable coverage from his or her employer, other types of information are acceptable. These items include the following:

- An explanation of benefit claims.
- Pay stubs showing payroll deductions.
- A health-insurance identification card.
- A telephone call from a representative of the plan to a third party verifying coverage.

It is important to remind employees to keep good records of important documents verifying employment and benefits.

Example: Mary worked for ABC Corporation, which offers its employees a choice of three plans—a health maintenance organization (HMO), a fee-for-service indemnity plan, and a preferred provider plan (PPO). During the open season Mary switched from the HMO to the PPO. Six months later she left the corporation and the issuer of the PPO provided a certificate for the six months it had covered her. If Mary wants to demonstrate that she had 12 months of creditable coverage she needs to ask the ABC Corporation to give her a certificate for the entire time she was covered under the plan. (The plan should already have made arrangements that assured this result). This certificate would reflect all periods of creditable coverage that ended within 24 months of Mary's request.

No pre-existing condition exclusion can be imposed unless a plan or insurer has notified the employee in writing of the exclusion and the right of the employee to provide evidence of creditable coverage. Within a reasonable period of time following the receipt of evidence of creditable coverage, a plan or insurer must notify the employee of its determination to impose a pre-existing condition exclusion. The employee must be given an opportunity to appeal the determination and present additional evidence. These rules apply regardless of whether the plan is insured or self-insured.

The certificate must also include information about the creditable coverage of dependents. This requirement may present difficulty because employer plans may not track data necessary to prepare certificates unless a claim is filed for the dependent. The following rules concerning dependent coverage will help employer plans prepare certifications for dependents:

- Use reasonable efforts to determine any information regarding dependents. Unless the issuer of the plan is informed of a dependent cancellation, no certificate is issued.
- Ask all employees to provide updated dependent information yearly, including dates when any new dependents are added or removed.
- Allow the employee to verify dependent status if a certificate does not include the dependent's name.

Health Status

A group health plan cannot exclude an employee or dependents from coverage, extend the applicable waiting period, deny benefits, or charge a higher contribution based on the following factors:

- Health status.
- Medical condition (physical or mental illness).
- Claims experience.
- Receipt of healthcare.
- Medical history.
- Genetic information.
- Evidence of insurability (including conditions arising out of acts of domestic violence).
- Disability.

Special Enrollment Periods

HIPAA defines two other times (other than immediately after the plan's waiting period) when employees and their dependents may enroll in a group health plan. These enrollment times include the following situations:

- Loss of coverage.
- Special dependent enrollment.

When each of the following conditions is met employees or their dependents may enroll in a group health plan, eliminating the usual required wait time or open-enrollment period.

Loss of Coverage

Under HIPAA, employees or dependents who lose other coverage are permitted to enroll under the terms of the plan if the following conditions are met:

- The employee or dependent had other coverage when the plan coverage was offered.

- The employee stated that the coverage was the reason for declining enrollment. (The plan can require a written waiver of coverage if it notifies the employee in writing of the consequences of failing to sing a waiver).
- The other coverage was either:
  - COBRA continuation coverage that was exhausted.
  - Coverage that was terminated as a result of loss of eligibility including legal separation, divorce, death, termination or reduction of work hours, or termination of employer contributions.

The employee must request special enrollment 30 days after the date of exhaustion or termination of the coverage to meet these requirements.

Dependent Special Enrollment Period

A special enrollment period also applies if the following two conditions are met:

- An employee is enrolled in a group health plan.
- The employee marries, has a child, adopts, or places a child for adoption.

If the employee marries, the employee and his or her new spouse may enroll in the plan if they have not done so. If the employee has or adopts a child, the employee, spouse, and child may enroll in the plan if they have not done so.

The dependent special enrollment period must not be less than 30 days beginning on either the date dependent coverage is made available or the date of the marriage, birth, or adoption, whichever is later. The effective dates for coverage are no later than the first day of the first month after the date the completed request for enrollment is received (for marriage), the date of the dependent's birth, or the date of the adoption or placement for adoption.

Disclosure to Participants

Summary plan descriptions (SPD) have new requirements under HIPAA, such as the changes in information that must be disclosed to participants and beneficiaries no later than 60 days after the first day of the new plan year.

The following information is required in summary plan descriptions beginning July 2, 1997:

- Identification of insurer or service provider. If an insurance company, insurance service, or insurance organization (including HMO) is responsible for the financing or administration of a group health plan, the SPD for the plan must include:
  - The name and address of the entity.
  - Whether and to what extent benefits under the plan are guaranteed under a contract or policy of insurance.
  - The nature of the administrative services (claims payment) provided.
  - Statement of ERISA rights. The statement of ERISA rights must be updated with this statement:

    "If you have any questions about this statement or about your rights under ERISA, you should contact the nearest office of the Pension and Welfare Benefits Administration, U.S. Department of Labor, 200 Constitution Avenue, N.W., Washington, D.C. 20210."

The following must be included in summary plan descriptions beginning January 1, 1998:

- Newborns' and Mothers' Health Protection Act. Summary plan descriptions of group health plans that offer maternity benefits must include a statement notifying participants of the protections under HIPAA. Group health plans and health insurance issuers generally may not, under federal law, restrict benefits for any hospital length of stay concerning childbirth for the mother or newborn child to less than 48 hours following a cesarean section. However, federal law generally does not prohibit discharging the mother or newborn earlier than 48 hours (or 96 hours as applicable). In any case, plans and issuers may not require that a provider obtain authorization from the plan for prescribing a length of stay not more than 48 hours (or 96 hours).

- When a material reduction in covered services or benefits has occurred, each participant and beneficiary under a group health plan must be notified by a summary of those changes in the SPD. This must be no later than 60 days from the date of change. The only exception is when the plan provides participants and beneficiaries with a summary of changes at least every 90 days. Material reduction includes the elimination or reduction of benefits payable, an increase in deductibles, co-payments, or other amounts, the reduction in the service area covered by an HMO, and starting new conditions or requirements for obtaining services or benefits.

A new rule regarding distribution of SPDs through electronic media has been in effect since June 1, 1997. The new rule is a safe harbor rule and the following conditions must be met:

- The plan administrator must ensure that the document is actually received by the participants and beneficiaries.

- The form of the document must be comparable with other forms of disclosure.

- All participants must be notified electronically and have the ability to receive the document at their work sites.

- Notifications must include the following information:
  - That the disclosure documents are being furnished electronically.
  - The significance of the documents.
  - The participant's right to request and receive a paper copy of the document (free of charge).

The Mental Health Parity Act

The Mental Health Parity Act (MHPA), signed into law on September 26, 1996, requires that annual or lifetime limits on mental-health benefits cannot be lower than the dollar limits for medical and surgical benefits offered by a group health plan. MHPA applies to group health plans for plan years beginning on or after January 1, 1998, and does not apply to benefits received on or after September 30, 2001.

The law generally requires parity of mental-health benefits with medical/surgical benefits with respect to the application of total lifetime and annual dollar limits under a group health plan. The law provides that employers retain discretion regarding the extent and scope of mental health benefits offered to workers and their families (including cost sharing, limits on numbers of visits or days of coverage, and requirements relating to medical necessity). The law, however, does not apply to benefits for substance abuse or chemical dependency.

The law also contains the following two exemptions—small-employer and increased-cost exemption. MHPA does not apply to any plan or coverage of any employer who employed an average of between two and 50 employees on business days during the preceding calendar year, and who employs at least two employees on the first day of the plan year. MHPA does not apply to a group health plan or group health insurance coverage if the application of the parity provisions results in an increase in the cost under the plan or coverage of at least one percent.

Newborns' and Mothers' Health Protection

A group health plan generally cannot restrict benefits for any hospital length of stay concerning childbirth for the mother or newborn child to less than 48 hours (the usual length of stay following a normal vaginal delivery), or less than 96 hours (following a cesarean section).

Enforcement Provisions

States have the primary enforcement responsibility for group and individual requirements imposed on health insurance issuers, using sanctions available under state law. If the Secretary of Health and Human Services makes the determination that a state failed to "substantially enforce" the law, federal authority may impose sanctions on insurers as specified in the statute, including civil monetary penalties.

The Secretary of Labor enforces requirements on employment-based group health plans, including self-insured arrangements, under ERISA. In addition, individual employees can sue to enforce their rights under ERISA. Subject to certain limits, the Secretary of Treasury can impose a $100 a day tax penalty on employers or plans for periods of non-compliance with HIPAA. This liability may arise when the employer or plan new or should have known of the non-compliance.

Example: ABC Corporation maintains a group health plan that requires eligible employees to enroll within 30 days of starting their new job and provides for open enrollment on January 1 of each plan year. ABC's group health plan has a 12-month pre-existing condition exclusion that does not extend the exclusion to 18 months for late enrollees.

John became a manager of ABC Corporation on January 1 but he declines coverage under ABC's group health plan because he and his wife, Mary, have coverage under her employer's group health plan for 16 months. Later that year Mary becomes pregnant with an expected delivery date of November 1. Mary is hospitalized on November 1 and delivers that day. On November 3 John wants to enroll Mary, himself, and their baby in ABC's group health plan.

- **Q. Can John do this?**
- A. Yes. John can add Mary, their newborn, and himself based on HIPAA's special enrollment provisions for new dependents. In this example their coverage under ABC's group health plan will be secondary to the group health plan coverage provided by Mary's employer.

- **Q. What is the effective date of coverage?**
- A. Coverage for John, Mary, and the newborn begins on November 1 (the date of the newborn's birth).

- **Q. Are the newborn's and Mary's expenses covered?**
- A. Both of these expenses are covered. Under HIPAA, pregnancy cannot be treated as a pre-existing condition.

- **Q. Can the pre-existing condition exclusion under ABC's group health plan apply to John, Mary, and/or their newborn?**
- A. No. The newborn cannot be subject to pre-existing condition exclusions because the newborn was enrolled within 30 days of birth. Neither Mary nor John can be subject to the pre-existing

condition exclusion because they each had at least 12 months of prior continuous coverage under the group health plan provided by Mary's employer.

Q. If John and Mary have other children must they be enrolled as well?

A. Maybe. Currently, HIPAA does not specifically address this issue. Future regulations may clarify this point.

Q. Using the example above, except that on September 30 Mary drops her health coverage under her employer's group health plan because she decides it is too expensive. Is she entitled to enroll in ABC's group health plan?

A. No. Mary did not lose coverage under her employer's group health plan because of loss of eligibility, termination of employment, etc. Except for open enrollment she can only enroll if she loses her coverage for one of the reasons entitling her to special enrollment and not simply because she voluntarily drops her coverage.

Conclusion

This chapter summarized the provisions of HIPAA (applicable to nearly every group health plan) regarding new federal law requirements along with underlying principles of those requirements. Enforcement provision was also discussed and specific questions regarding the effect of HIPAA upon employee health plans was addressed.

The major points of HIPAA are summarized below:

- A group health plan may impose a pre-existing condition exclusion on employees and their dependents for up to 12 months (18 months in the case of late enrollees).

- The group health plan or insurer must give an employee who leaves his or her employer a certificate of creditable coverage. This certificate can be used to reduce or eliminate the application of a pre-existing condition exclusion of another employer's group health plan.

- A group health plan cannot discriminate against an employee or the employee's dependents by creating barriers to eligibility or continued eligibility on the basis of health status.

- A group health plan must provide special enrollment periods for employees and dependents who lost or exhausted other coverage due to no fault of their own, or when the employee has added a spouse or dependent.

- Additional disclosures must be made to participants in group health plan SPDs, including an updated statement of ERISA rights, the identification of an insurer and/or service provider, and a disclosure of minimum newborn and maternity stays if such coverage is provided by the plan.

- A group health plan that offers mental health coverage must set the same annual or lifetime dollar limits for mental health as they set for medical or surgical benefits.

- For the protection of the health of newborns and mothers, the plan usually cannot restrict a hospital stay for childbirth to less than 48 hours for vaginal birth and 96 hours for a caesarian section.

- Two model forms are included at the end of this chapter to help employers comply with HIPAA requirements concerning certification of coverage.

HIPAA Questions and Answers

Q. What is a pre-existing condition?

A. A *pre-existing condition* is a condition present before an employee's enrollment date in any new group health plan. Under HIPAA the only pre-existing conditions that may be excluded are those for which medical advice, diagnosis, care, or treatment was recommended or received within the six-month period before the enrollment date. The enrollment date is the first day of coverage or—if there is a waiting period to get into the plan—the first day of the waiting period.

If an employee had a medical condition in the past but had not received any medical advice, diagnosis, care, or treatment within the six months before his or her enrollment date in the plan, the condition is not a pre-existing condition to which the exclusion can be applied. Pre-existing condition exclusions cannot be applied to pregnancy regardless of whether the woman had previous health coverage.

A pre-existing condition exclusion cannot be applied to a newborn, adopted child under the age of 18, or child placed for adoption under age 18, if the child is enrolled for health coverage within 30 days of the birth, adoption, or placement for adoption. This exception does not apply to a subsequent group health plan if the child thereafter incurs a 63-day break in coverage.

Q. An employee has a pre-existing condition that may be excluded under HIPAA. How does the new plan determine the length of the pre-existing condition exclusion period?

A. The maximum length of a pre-existing condition exclusion period is 12 months after the enrollment date, 18 months in the case of a late enrollee. (A late enrollee is an employee who enrolls in a plan other than on the earliest date on which coverage can become effective and other than on a special enrollment date.)

A plan must reduce an employee's pre-existing condition exclusion period by the number of days of an employee's creditable coverage. Most health coverage, such as coverage under a group health plan (including COBRA continuation coverage), HMO, individual insurance policy, Medicaid, or Medicare is creditable coverage. However, a plan is not required to take into account any days of creditable coverage that precede a significant break in coverage (generally, a break in coverage of 63 days or more). A plan may receive information about an employee's creditable coverage when a certificate is furnished by the prior plan or health insurance issuer (for example, an insurance company or HMO). A certificate of creditable coverage is issued automatically when a loss of coverage exists under the old plan, when an employee is entitled to COBRA continuation coverage, when COBRA continuation coverage ceases, or when an employee requests one within 24 months of cessation of coverage.

Q. An employee receives a certificate from his or her former plan. What is the employee required to do?

A. The employee should ensure that the information is accurate (contact the plan administrator of the former plan if any information is wrong); retain the certificate (for enrollment in a new group health plan with a pre-existing condition exclusion period or for an individual policy from an insurance company).

Q. The employee is having difficulty getting the certificate from the former employer's group health plan? What is the employer required to do?

A. Under HIPAA, group health plans and health insurance issuers are required to provide documentation that certifies the creditable coverage the employee earned. Plans and issuers that fail or refuse to provide such certificates are subject to penalties under HIPAA.

Alternatively, the new group health plan is required to accept other evidence of creditable coverage if an employee cannot obtain certification from past insurers or plans. It is important for employees to keep accurate records (for example, pay stubs, copies of premium payments, or other evidence of healthcare coverage) that can be used to establish periods of creditable coverage in the event a certification cannot be obtained.

Q. When an employee enrolls in a new group health plan that contains a pre-existing condition exclusion period, how does crediting for prior coverage work under HIPAA?

A. Most plans will use what is known as the standard method of crediting coverage. Under this method, an employee receives credit for previous coverage that occurred without a break of 63 days or more. However, if health coverage is offered through an HMO or an insurance policy issued by an insurance company, the employee should check with the State Insurance Commissioner's office to determine the specific terms in this particular state. For example, suppose an individual had health insurance coverage for two years followed by a break in coverage of 70 days and then resumed coverage for eight months. Under the standard method, that individual would only receive credit for eight months of coverage. No credit would be given for the two years of coverage before the break of 70 days.

HIPAA also permits an alternative method for crediting coverage for employees. Under the alternative method of calculating creditable coverage, the plan or issuer separately determines the amount of an individual's creditable coverage. The categories used for coverage are mental health, substance abuse treatment, prescription drugs, dental care, and vision care. The new plan must notify the employee if it is using the alternative method for any of these benefits.

Q. What special enrollment opportunities does the new group health plan present?

A. A group health plan is required to allow special enrollment for employees before the next regular enrollment season. A special enrollment opportunity occurs if an employee with other health insurance loses that coverage or if a person has (or becomes) a new dependent through marriage, birth, adoption, or placement for adoption. However, the employee must notify the plan about the special enrollment within 30 days after loss of other coverage or addition of a new dependent.

Special enrollees may not be treated as late enrollees for the pre-existing condition exclusion period. Thus, the maximum pre-existing condition exclusion period that may be applied is 12 months, reduced by creditable coverage.

Q. Can employees be denied coverage or charged more for coverage by their new group health plan based on health status?

A. No. Group health plans and health insurance issuers may not establish rules for eligibility (including continued eligibility) based on any of the following factors:

- Health status.
- Medical condition (physical or mental).
- Claims experience.
- Receipt of healthcare.
- Medical history.
- Genetic information.
- Evidence of insurability and disability.

However, plans may establish limits or restrictions on benefits or coverage for all similarly situated individuals. In addition, plans generally may not require an individual to pay a premium or contribution that is greater than that for a similarly situated individual based on a health status-related factor.

Q. What if an employee is unable to obtain new group health plan coverage?

A. The employee may be able to purchase an individual insurance policy. HIPAA guarantees access to individual policies for eligible individuals. Eligible individuals are those who:

- Have had coverage for at least 18 months where the most recent period of coverage was under a group health plan.
- Did not have their group coverage terminated because of fraud or nonpayment of premiums.
- Are ineligible for COBRA continuation coverage or have exhausted COBRA benefits (or coverage under a similar state provision).
- Are ineligible for coverage under another group health plan (Medicare or Medicaid).

The opportunity to buy an individual policy is the same whether an employee is laid off, fired, or quits his or her job. However, the type of coverage that is guaranteed may differ between states. Individuals interested in obtaining individual health insurance coverage should check with the State Insurance Commissioner's Office. Additionally, individuals in a family whose income is temporarily reduced (for example, due to loss of a job) may be eligible for low-cost or no-cost health insurance through public programs. In many instances, children will be eligible for low-cost coverage. Eligibility for these programs varies by state and sometimes within a state. Employees can contact state government officials to find out if they are eligible.

Q. Can I receive credit for previous COBRA coverage?

A. Yes. Under HIPAA, any period of time that an employee receives COBRA continuation coverage is counted as previous continuous health coverage as long as the coverage occurred without a break in coverage of 63 days or more. For example, if an employee was covered for five months by a previous health plan and then received seven months of COBRA continuation coverage, he or she would be entitled to receive credit for 12 months by the new group health plan.

Q. If employees change jobs, are they guaranteed the same benefits that they had under their current plan?

A. No. When employees transfer from one plan to another the benefits they receive will be those provided under the new plan, which could be less or more coverage.

Q. Will coverage be immediate under the new employer's plan?

A. Not necessarily, because employers and insurance companies may set a waiting period before enrollees become eligible for benefits under the plan. HMOs may have an affiliation period during which an enrollee does not receive benefits and is not charged premiums. Affiliation periods may not last for more than two months and are only allowed for HMOs that do not use pre-existing condition exclusions.

Q. Does HIPAA require employers to offer health coverage or to provide specific benefits?

A. No. The provision of health coverage by an employer is voluntary. HIPAA does not require specific benefits nor does it prohibit a plan from restricting the amount or nature of benefits for similarly situated individuals.

Q. How does HIPAA affect COBRA continuation coverage?

A. HIPAA is different from COBRA although there are places where small employers may coordinate responsibilities for COBRA and HIPAA laws. For example, HIPAA makes three changes to COBRA's continuation coverage, as described below. These changes were effective on January 1, 1997, regardless of when the event occurs that entitles the individual to continuation coverage:

- A disabled individual (as determined under the Social Security Act) is entitled to 29 months of COBRA continuation coverage. Under prior law, the individual had to be disabled at the time of termination of employment or reduction in hours. Under HIPAA an individual is entitled to 29 months of COBRA coverage if he or she becomes disabled at any time during the first 60 days of COBRA coverage. The extension of continuation coverage to 29 months is also available to any non-disabled family members of the disabled individual who are entitled to COBRA continuation coverage.

- COBRA continuation coverage generally can be terminated when an individual becomes covered under another group health plan. COBRA cannot be terminated because of other coverage where the plan limits or excludes coverage for any pre-existing condition of the individual. HIPAA limits the circumstances under which a plan may impose a pre-existing condition exclusion period on individuals. If a plan is precluded under HIPAA from imposing an exclusion period on an individual it must cover the individual's pre-existing condition. COBRA continuation coverage may be terminated.

- COBRA rules are also modified so that children who are born, adopted, or placed for adoption with the covered employee during the continuation coverage period are treated as "qualified beneficiaries." (Under prior law, a "qualified beneficiary" must have been covered under a group health plan on the day before the COBRA qualifying event.)

Certificate of Group Health Plan Coverage
Explanation of Model Form #1

An employer plan completes Model Form #1 for an employee who lost coverage. This form is a general certification model that may be used to provide basic information about an employee's group health plan coverage. The determination of the amount of creditable coverage is made without regard to the specific categories of benefits included in the coverage. Use of this model form includes the required information for certifying group health plan coverage under the standard method. If the certificate shows 18 months of creditable coverage not interrupted by a 63-day break, the employer plans do not have to report the starting date of coverage and waiting period information.

Model Form #1: Certificate of Group Health Plan Coverage

This certificate provides evidence of your prior health coverage. You may need to furnish this certificate if you become eligible under a group health plan that excludes coverage for medical conditions that you have before you enroll. This certificate may need to be provided if medical advice, diagnosis, care, or treatment was recommended or received for the condition within the six-month period prior to your enrollment in the new plan. If you become covered under another group health plan, check with the plan administrator to see if you need to provide this certificate. You may also need this certificate to buy, for yourself or your family, an insurance policy that does not exclude coverage for medical conditions that are present before you enroll.

1. Date of this certificate.
2. Name of group health plan.

3. Name of participant.
4. Identification number of participant.
5. Name of any dependents to which this certificate applies.
6. Name, address, and telephone number of plan administrator or issuer responsible for providing this certificate.
7. Phone number to call for further information.
8. If the individual(s) identified in line 3 and line 5 has at least 18 months of creditable coverage (disregarding periods of coverage before a 63-day break), check here __ and skip lines 9 and 10.
9. Date waiting period or affiliation period (if any) began.
10. Date coverage began.
11. Date coverage ended (or check if coverage is continuing as of the date of this certificate).

Note: Separate certificates will be furnished if information is not identical for the participant and each beneficiary.

Explanation of Model Form #2

After receiving a certificate of prior coverage (for example Model #1), a group health plan that uses an alternative method of counting creditable coverage may request additional information from the plan that issued the certificate. Model Form #2 may be sent by the new plan to the prior plan to request coverage information based on specific categories of benefits. A plan that uses the alternative method will separately determine the amount of creditable coverage for any of five identified categories of benefits. These categories are coverage for mental health, substance abuse treatment, prescription drugs, dental care, and vision care. The new plan may ask for a copy of the summary plan description that applied to the employee's coverage or may ask for information that is more specific.

Even if the prior plan does not use this information for its own pre-existing condition exclusion, it is required to certify its coverage benefit by benefit to the new plan that does. The prior plan may charge the new plan for the reasonable cost of disclosing information.

Model Form #2: Information on Categories of Benefits

1. Date of original certificate.
2. Name of group health plan providing the coverage.
3. Name of participant.
4. Identification number of participant.
5. Name of individual(s) to whom this information applies.
6. The following information applies to the coverage in the certificate that was provided to the individual(s) identified above:
    - Mental health.
    - Substance-abuse treatment.
    - Prescription drugs.
    - Dental care.
    - Vision care.

For each category above, enter "N/A" if the individual had no coverage within the category and either (i) enter both the date that the individual's coverage within the category began and the date that the individual's coverage within the category ended (or indicate if continuing), or (ii) enter "same" on the line if the beginning and ending dates for coverage within the category are the same as the beginning and ending dates of coverage in the certificate.

Chapter 23
ERISA

Introduction

Many of the most common types of employee benefit plans are subject to the regulatory scheme introduced by the Employee Retirement Income Security Act of 1974, commonly known as ERISA. Plans that are subject to ERISA are generally not subject to state laws that relate to those plans, except for those laws that regulate insurance, banking, or securities and generally applicable criminal laws. In addition, many employee benefit plans also must comply with various requirements of federal tax laws and rules in order to obtain favorable tax treatment.

This chapter reviews the requirements that apply to employee benefit plans that are covered by ERISA and some of the federal tax laws and rules. State law is not discussed in this chapter.

Scope of ERISA's Coverage

ERISA does not obligate an employer to establish any type of plan. It is up to an employer to decide whether it will have employee benefit plans. But once an employer does decide to have a plan the employer must establish, maintain and terminate it consistent with ERISA's requirements. Those requirements relate to:

- Reporting certain plan information to federal agencies.
- Disclosure of certain information to eligible employees and plan participants.
- Plan participation.
- Vesting in plan benefits.
- Plan funding.
- Fiduciary responsibility.
- Plan administration.
- Enforcement of ERISA.
- Pension plan termination insurance, termination procedures, and termination liabilities.
- Multi-employer plans (typically established in connection with the collective bargaining process).

ERISA-covered Plans

Plans covered by ERISA are divided into two categories: pension plans and welfare plans. Any employee benefit plan that satisfies the definition of a pension plan or a welfare plan is covered by ERISA unless the plan is specifically excluded from ERISA's coverage.

Certain plans are excluded based on the character of the employer. Thus, plans offered by the following types of employers are generally excluded from ERISA's coverage:

- The federal government and federal agencies.
- State and local governments and agencies.
- Churches and certain church-related organizations.

Other plans are excluded from ERISA's coverage when an employer maintains the plans solely to comply with workers' compensation, unemployment compensation, or disability insurance laws. Certain other plans that are excluded from ERISA's coverage are described below in the discussion of what types of plans are considered pension plans or welfare plans under ERISA.

Pension Plans Subject to ERISA

Under ERISA, pension plans are any types of plans or arrangements which are designed to, or which as the result of surrounding circumstances, provide retirement income or defer income until termination of employment or beyond. Thus, under ERISA, pension plan refers to a traditional pension plan that pays a monthly benefit upon retirement, as well as to other types of plans including those designed to provide savings for retirement. Since the term pension plan encompasses a broad array of retirement plans in addition to the traditional company pension plan, this chapter will often refer to those plans using the more generic term retirement plans. ERISA applies to funded and unfunded retirement plans.

Thus, company profit-sharing or bonus arrangements generally are not ERISA pension plans because they usually provide for payments during employment. For the same reason, stock option plans or arrangements generally are not ERISA pension plans.

Retirement plans that are designed to be qualified under federal tax laws are almost always subject to ERISA because they are designed to provide retirement income or savings. Those types of tax-qualified plans include pension plans, profit-sharing plans, 401(k) plans, certain types of stock bonus plans or employee stock ownership plans (ESOPs), as well as simplified employee pension plans (SEPs), simple retirement accounts, and other arrangements that have an employer making contributions to an employee's IRA.

Schools and charitable organizations that are tax-exempt under Internal Revenue Code Section 501(c)(3) are permitted to make tax-deferred contributions to annuity contracts or custodial accounts that are qualified under Internal Revenue Code Section 403(b). Certain 403(b) plans are excluded from ERISA's coverage. Generally, the exclusion applies if employees contribute voluntarily to the plan, the employer does not contribute to the plan, and employer involvement is limited to deducting the employee contributions under the plan.

Welfare Plans Subject to ERISA

The list of welfare plans that may be subject to ERISA is very broad. However, by regulation the Department of Labor (DOL) has provided that many types of plans or payroll practices are not subject to ERISA. Some of the exceptions apply only if the plan is unfunded. Generally, this means that the employer pays for plan benefits out of its general assets, and the exception will not apply if there is insurance for the plan or there is a fund maintained to provide the benefits.

Plans designed to provide benefits for any type of healthcare, including plans that provide medical, dental, vision, or prescription drug benefits are subject to ERISA without regard to the funding arrangement for the plan. Thus, healthcare plans are subject to ERISA whether they are insured or fully or partially self-insured.

Death benefit plans also are subject to ERISA without regard to the funding arrangement for the plan. Thus, a death benefit plan is subject to ERISA whether it is paid for directly by the employer or whether it provides whole, universal, or group term-life insurance, or accidental death and dismemberment insurance.

Disability plans are subject to ERISA, except for arrangements designed solely to provide state-mandated short-term disability benefits. Thus, long- and short-term disability plans that are insured are ERISA welfare plans.

Leave and paid or unpaid time off arrangements generally are not included in the ERISA definition of a welfare plan. These include unfunded payroll practices that provide sick leave, vacations, holidays, military leave, jury duty, training, sabbatical, or educational leave.

Unemployment benefit plans (unless solely designed to comply with state unemployment laws) are ERISA welfare plans.

Severance plans that do not pay benefits that exceed twice an employee's annual compensation, do not extend payments more than two years following the employee's termination, and which do not otherwise satisfy the definition of an ERISA pension plan generally are subject to ERISA as welfare plans.

The following types of arrangements are not covered by ERISA:

- On-premises dining halls.
- Recreation facilities.
- First-aid facilities.
- Holiday gifts.
- Sales to employees.
- Hiring halls.
- Remembrance funds.
- Unfunded scholarship programs or tuition or educational expense reimbursement programs.

Finally, ERISA does not apply to a group insurance arrangement if it is fully employee-paid and offered by an insurer. The arrangement must meet **all** of the following requirements:

- The plan must be fully paid for by employee contributions.
- Participation in the plan must be completely voluntary.
- The only involvement of the employer is to permit the insurer to publicize its product and to deduct employee contributions.
- The employer must not receive any compensation in connection with the plan.

Reporting and Disclosure

The reporting and disclosure requirements of ERISA apply to both retirement and welfare benefit plans.

Annual Reports (IRS Form 5500)

All plans are required to file an annual report, unless an exception applies. One of the most widely used exceptions is for a welfare plan that involves the following:

- Fewer than 100 participants.
- Is unfunded, fully insured, or a combination of the two.

If required, the annual report is filed with the Department of Labor on Form 5500 and associated schedules. Annual reports may have to include a financial statement prepared by a qualified independent public accountant and a copy of the plan's annual statement of assets and liabilities for the plan's fiscal year.

Each participant in a plan must receive a copy of a summary of the annual report within nine months after the close of the plan year.

Summary Plan Descriptions

Each participant in a plan must be issued a summary plan description of the plan. Summary plan descriptions no longer have to be filed routinely with the Department of Labor (DOL); however, they must be provided to the DOL upon request.

The summary plan description must be provided to each participant within 120 days after the effective date of the plan. New participants in an existing plan must receive a summary within 90 days after the individual becomes a participant.

Participants also must receive a summary of any material modifications made to the plan. In general, the summary must be provided within 210 days after the end of the year in which the modification is made. However, there are significant exceptions to this general rule. For example, if the modification is a material reduction in covered services or benefits provided under a group health plan, the summary must be provided within 60 days of the adoption of the change.

In general, summary plan descriptions must be updated every five years.

Summary plan descriptions are supposed to be written in terms an average employee can understand. A summary plan description should include:

- The name and type of administration of the plan.
- For a group health plan, whether an insurance company or similar organization is responsible for financing and administration of the plan (including payment of claims) and, if so, the name and address of that organization.
- Name and address of the plan administrator.
- Names, addresses, and titles of any plan trustees.
- A description of the features of the plan, such as:
    - The types of benefits available.

- Participation and vesting requirements.
- How benefits are calculated.
- When benefits can be distributed.
- When benefits can be forfeited.

♦ The source of financing for the plan.

♦ A description of any relevant provisions of a collective bargaining agreement.

♦ The plan year dates and how plan records are kept.

♦ A statement of participants' rights and protections under ERISA.

♦ A statement of participants' right to examine all plan documents.

♦ A statement of participants' right to receive a summary of the plan's annual financial report.

♦ An explanation of the responsibilities of fiduciaries of the plan.

♦ A statement of the claims procedure under the plan and the participants' right to appeal the denial of benefits.

♦ For a group health plan, the address of the office of the Department of Labor to seek assistance regarding certain ERISA rights relating to healthcare plans.

Other Disclosure Requirements

Upon the request of a participant, the plan administrator must provide copies of the plan terms, summary plan descriptions, annual reports, and summary annual reports. Participants are also entitled to request information about their benefits accrued and vesting status under a retirement plan, but no more frequently than once during any 12-month period.

Participants must be notified if an employer maintaining a defined-benefit pension plan or money purchase pension plan fails to make a required contribution to the plan within 60 days of its due date.

Plan Administration

All plans are required to have a person or entity designated as the plan administrator. An employer may designate itself as plan administrator. However, if it does so, the employer also must specify which officers or employees are authorized to act on behalf of the employer. Many employers designate a committee of officers and employees to perform plan administrator duties.

The plan administrator is generally responsible for all aspects of plan administration, including claims processing. Plan documents should specifically authorize the plan administrator to interpret the terms of the plan.

Plan Asset and Investment Requirements

In general, ERISA requires that all assets of employee benefit plans be held in a trust. Certain types of insurance contracts or custodial accounts may be used instead of a trust. In any funding vehicle, the assets must be used for the exclusive purpose of paying benefits to plan participants and beneficiaries and paying plan expenses.

Trustees of plans are generally responsible for investing plan assets. However, an employer may reserve the right to direct the investment of plan assets, may appoint one or more investment managers, or in an individual account plan such as a 401(k) plan, may allow participants to direct the investment of certain portions of their plan accounts. Investment managers must be registered investment advisors or certain types of banks or insurance companies.

ERISA requires that any person who handles plan assets be covered by a fidelity bond. The required amount of the bond depends on the amount of plan assets.

Fiduciary Requirements

All persons who manage investment of plan assets are *fiduciaries*. In addition, persons who exercise discretion over the management and administration of the plan are fiduciaries. ERISA establishes high standards of conduct for fiduciaries. Fiduciaries are prohibited from using the plan to engage in transactions that benefit themselves, the employer, or other interested parties.

The Department of Labor and plan participants can bring lawsuits against fiduciaries for violation of their fiduciary duties. Thus, many employers buy fiduciary liability insurance to protect their officers and employees from liability arising under such lawsuits.

Conclusion

Employers must comply with the requirements of the federal law known as ERISA that governs employee benefit plans. This chapter covered such issues as the scope of ERISA, including plans that are excluded from its coverage, pension plans, and welfare plans; reporting and disclosure, including annual reports, summary plan descriptions, and other disclosure requirements; and plan administration, including holding and investing plan assets, and fiduciary requirements.

Chapter 24
Employee Leave

Introduction

This chapter reviews the federal law on family and medical leave, as specified by the Family and Medical Leave Act of 1993. Related laws that may affect employee leave, such as the Pregnancy Discrimination Act, are treated briefly, and any state law relating to employee leave is reviewed.

Family and Medical Leave Act of 1993

The Family and Medical Leave Act of 1993 (FMLA) requires that covered employers in the public and private sectors provide unpaid leave to their employees, both male and female, for the following:

- To care for a newborn child or for a newly adopted or foster child.
- To care for a family member with a serious health condition.
- For the employee's own serious health conditions under certain circumstances.

Covered Employers

An employer is subject to the FMLA's requirements if it employs 50 or more employees during each working day for a 20-week period in the current or preceding calendar year. An employer who has at least 50 employees working in separate worksites within a 75-mile radius is also covered by the act. FMLA also considers all public agencies and private schools as employers regardless of their size.

Full time Instructional Employees

There are special provisions governing FMLA leave and restoration of employment of full time instructional employees. Instructional employees include workers employed principally in an instructional capacity by an educational agency or school. This includes coaches, driving instructors, and special education assistants. It does not include teachers' assistants or aides whose principal function is not teaching or instructing, nor does it include counselors, psychologists, curriculum specialists, cafeteria workers, maintenance workers, or bus drivers.

Eligible Employees

To be eligible for leave under FMLA an employee must fulfill the following criteria:

- Work for a covered employer.
- Have been employed by his or her employer (or predecessor company) for at least 12 months.
- Have at least 1,250 hours of service with the employer during the 12-month period prior to leave.

Employers do not have to count hours paid, but not worked, nor unpaid leave in determining the 1,250 hours of service.

FMLA Requirements

Under FMLA, an employee who fulfills the criteria above is entitled to a leave without pay for up to 12 weeks in any 12-month period for any of the following reasons:

- The birth of a child of the employee. Eligibility for this leave expires 12 months after the birth and applies equally to men and women.
- The placement with the employee of a child for adoption or foster care. Eligibility for this leave expires 12 months after the child is placed with the employee.
- The care of a child, spouse, or parent of the employee with a serious health problem.
- A serious health condition that renders the employee unable to perform any one of the essential functions of his or her position.

Definitions

12-month Period

For purposes of the FMLA, the 12-month period during which an employee may take leave can be defined in several ways. Employers can use the calendar year, a fixed 12-month leave year, or a rolling period. Employers must designate their method for calculating the 12-month period or employees are allowed to calculate leave under whichever method is most beneficial to them. The rolling method would exclude the possibility of an employee's taking 12 weeks of leave at the end of one 12-month period and 12 weeks at the beginning of the next 12-month period.

Serious Health Condition

For purposes of the act, a serious health condition must require inpatient care or continuing treatment.

Inpatient care is an overnight stay in a hospital, hospice, or residential medical-care facility and any resulting period of incapacity and treatment.

Continuing treatment is defined as one or more of the following:

- A period of incapacity involving two or more treatments by a healthcare provider or treatment by a healthcare provider on one occasion resulting in a continuing regimen of treatment.
- Pregnancy or prenatal care.
- A period of incapacity because of a chronic serious health condition requiring periodic visits for treatment, continuing for an extended period, and which may cause episodic rather than continuing incapacity.

Medical Certification

Employers may require employees' healthcare providers to provide medical certification of employees' serious health conditions. An employer may only request information contained in the Department of Labor's Medical Certification form (such as name, category of serious health condition, medical support for certification, date of condition's beginning and probable duration, additional treatments required, etc.).

An example of an acceptable medical certification statement might be the following: "The employee is having surgery that requires at least a three-day inpatient hospital stay followed by two weeks' recuperation at home."

If the leave is based on the care of a covered family member, acceptable medical certification would be a statement from the healthcare provider that the employee is needed to provide the care (including, psychological comfort), along with an estimate of how long the need to provide care will last. If the leave is based on the employee's own health condition, proper medical certification would be a statement that the employee is unable to perform an essential function of the job. For intermittent or reduced-schedule leave, the certification statement would have to indicate the dates of the expected treatment and the duration of the treatment.

The employer cannot request additional information, but may, with the employee's permission, contact the healthcare provider for purposes of authentication of the medical certification.

If the employer requires employees to substitute paid sick, vacation, or personal leave for FMLA leave and the medical certification requirements for these leaves are less stringent than requirements for FMLA leave, the employer only may enforce the lesser leave-certification requirements.

Employers should request the medical certification within two business days of the employee's request for leave or within two business days of the start of the leave if the leave was an unforeseen one. If the leave is foreseeable and at least 30 days' notice has been given, the employee should provide the certification before the leave begins. In any event, the employee must provide the requested certification within 15 calendar days after the employer's request.

Second Opinion

If the employer has reason to doubt the validity of the serious health condition, the employer may require the employee to obtain a second opinion at the employer's expense. The second healthcare provider must be unrelated to the employer; that is, not the company doctor or nurse. If the second opinion conflicts with the certification from the employee's healthcare provider, the employer may require the employee to obtain certification from a third, jointly selected healthcare provider at the employer's expense. This third opinion is final and binding.

Recertification

Employers may require employees to provide certification of their continuing need for leave. An employer may not request such certification more often than every 30 days, unless special circumstances exist.

Fitness-for-Duty Reports

Employers may require fitness-for-duty reports (medical certificates) from employees who have taken FMLA leave for their own serious health condition, as long as they notify the employees of the certificate requirement before the leave starts and require such certificates from other similarly situated employees. The certificates may be sought only for the condition that caused the FMLA leave. The certification only needs to be a simple statement of an employee's ability to return to work.

Notification Requirements

Requirements for Employees

Employees do not have to mention FMLA expressly when notifying their employers of the need for leave. Employees merely must provide their employers with enough information to reasonably inform the employer that the request for leave is for an FMLA-qualifying reason. The notice can be oral or written.

Several restrictions do, however, apply:

- Employees must give the reason for the absence before being entitled to FMLA leave.

- Employees must generally provide at least 30 days' notice before taking an FMLA leave if the need for leave is foreseeable. If 30 days' notice cannot be given, notice must be given as soon as possible. This usually means that employees must provide notice within one or two working days of learning of the need for leave.

- Employees who are taking intermittent or reduced-schedule leave for planned medical treatment must consult with the employer and make reasonable effort to schedule the leave in such a way as to avoid undue interruption of their employers' operations. Such scheduling would, of course, be subject to the approval of the healthcare provider.

Requirements for Employers

When placing employees on FMLA leave, employers must provide written notice of the following:

- That the leave will be counted as FMLA leave.

- Whether medical certification is required and the consequences of failing to provide such certification.

- That the employee may elect to substitute available paid leave for any portion of unpaid FMLA leave.

- Whether and to what extent the employer requires substitution of paid leave.

- Whether the employee must make premium payments and the arrangements for making such payments.

- Whether a fitness-for-duty certificate is required to return to work.

- Whether the employee is a key employee.

- That the employee will be restored to the same or an equivalent position.

- That the employee is potentially liable for health-insurance premiums paid by the employer during FMLA leave if he or she fails to return to work for reasons other than the reason for leave or because of a serious health condition.

A unique requirement of the FMLA is that employers who have employee handbooks that discuss employee benefits or leave rights must include FMLA policies in those handbooks. Employers must also post a notice of the FMLA's requirements on their premises. This notice, which explains the FMLA provisions, is available from the Department of Labor.

If an employee takes leave for reasons that would otherwise qualify for FMLA leave, the employer may designate the leave as FMLA leave and count it against the employee's total FMLA leave. An employer must designate leave as FMLA leave within two business days of discovering that the reason for the leave is an FMLA-qualifying reason. If the employer does not designate FMLA-qualifying leave as actual FMLA leave, according to the Department of Labor, the leave taken may not reduce the 12 weeks of leave allowed under FMLA.

Maintenance of Health Benefits

While FMLA leave is unpaid leave, the employer is required to maintain health benefits during leave at the same level the employee would have if he or she were working.

For purposes of changes to benefit plans, employees on unpaid FMLA leave are treated as if they are still working. They are entitled to changes in benefit plans except for those that may be dependent upon seniority or accrual during the leave period. For example, if the benefit plan is conditioned on a pre-established number of hours worked each year and the employee does not have sufficient hours as a result of taking unpaid FMLA leave, the benefit is lost.

Employers need not pay any portion of the premium normally paid by the employee but may require the employee to continue paying this portion. Coverage may be terminated if the employee's premium payment is more than 30 days late as long as the employer provides 15 days' notice that the premium is late and the insurance may be terminated.

Restoration to the Same or Equivalent Position

At the end of FMLA leave, employees, except for certain key employees, are entitled to return to the same position or to an equivalent one. An equivalent position is one that is virtually identical to the employee's former position in terms of pay, benefits, and working conditions, including privileges and status.

"Key" Employees

Certain highly compensated employees, defined as those among the highest paid 10 percent of all employees, are excepted from the rule that an employee must be restored to the same or equivalent position upon returning from FMLA leave. Employers need not reinstate these individuals if doing so would result in "substantial and grievous economic injury" to the employer. An employer must, however, notify an employee in this situation **at the time the leave is requested** of its intent to deny reinstatement. The employer must then give the employee a chance to change his or her mind about taking the requested leave.

Employees are not entitled to accrue seniority during unpaid FMLA leave although employers may allow them to. FMLA cannot be counted against employees for qualification for attendance incentive plans or awards. Leave under FMLA cannot be counted against employees under no-fault attendance policies.

Intermittent or Reduced-schedule Leave

Employees may take intermittent leave or leave on a reduced schedule for medical reasons. For instance, an employee might need intermittent leave for cancer treatments.

Intermittent leave may be taken when medically necessary for medical treatment or when an employee is incapacitated and unable to perform the essential functions of the job because of a chronic serious health condition. A few conditions/requirements are imposed on this reduced-schedule leave:

- Employees must make reasonable arrangements in advance—subject to the approval of the healthcare provider—with their employer for leave time for treatments so as to avoid needless disruption of the employer's operations.

- Employers may deduct from employees' salaries for time taken for intermittent or reduced-schedule FMLA leave. Such deductions do not affect an employee's exempt status under the Fair Labor Standards Act.

- Employers may assign employees taking intermittent or reduced-schedule leave to an alternative position with equivalent pay and benefits that better accommodates the employee's intermittent leave or reduced schedule situation.

Recordkeeping Requirements

Employers are required to keep and preserve records regarding compliance with the FMLA for at least three years. Medical certifications or other medical information related to an employee's FMLA leave must be maintained in confidential files separate from the usual personnel records. In implementing the act it is important that employers keep proper attendance and wage records. Employers also must post notices containing information about the act that informs employees how to file a charge for alleged violations of the act.

Penalties and Enforcement

FMLA complaints may be investigated by the U.S. Department of Labor (DOL). The Secretary of Labor may bring a court action against an employer to recover damages on behalf of an employee or group of employees. An employee also may bring a private suit against the employer. Unlike some other employment laws, the filing of an administrative charge with the DOL is not a prerequisite to bringing a civil FMLA suit. Civil lawsuits must be brought within two years of the date of the suspected violation, or within three years if the violation was considered intentional or willful.

Damages awarded in successful actions may include the following:

- Wages, benefits, or any actual monetary losses by the employee.
- Interest on these wages and benefits.
- Liquidated damages equal to the total recovery plus interest.
- Attorneys and experts fees incurred by the employee.

Other relief such as reinstatement of employment or promotion also may be recovered if appropriate. Separate civil penalties may be assessed against employers for failure to provide notices required under FMLA. The penalties may not exceed $100 per offense.

FMLA Summary

FMLA leave provisions apply to both male and female employees. Employers, however, may limit the **combined** leave of a husband and wife employed by the same employer to a total of 12 weeks if the leave is for the birth, adoption, or for the care of or placement of a child, or to care for a parent with a serious health condition.

FMLA requires employers to allow a period of leave for qualifying reasons—caring for a newborn or newly adopted child; caring for a spouse, parent, or child with a serious medical condition; or the employee's own serious health condition. Employers can require employees to use available paid vacation, sick leave, or personal leave to substitute for all of the 12-week FMLA leave. Employees can choose to make the same substitutions. Employers must continue to pay health benefits during any FMLA leave on the same basis as if the employee was working.

For serious health conditions, employees may take their FMLA leave intermittently or by working a reduced schedule. Such employees may be transferred to positions better fitting their reduced schedules and their salaries may be reduced during this time.

When leave is foreseeable, employees must give 30 days notice. If the leave is not foreseen, notice must be given as soon as possible. Verbal notice is adequate. Employers may require medical certification of the need for FMLA leave because of a serious health condition.

Employees on family or medical leaves are disqualified from receiving unemployment compensation during the leave period even if the leave is unpaid.

Unpaid FMLA leave is not considered a "qualifying event" under COBRA. If, however, an employee who has healthcare coverage at the beginning of FMLA leave does not return to work at the end of the FMLA leave and would, therefore, lose healthcare coverage, the employee is covered by COBRA.

FMLA leave cannot be counted against an employee's attendance in situations where attendance is rewarded.

Pregnancy Discrimination Act

The Pregnancy Discrimination Act requires employers to provide leave for pregnant employees to the same extent that leave is available to other employees for disability or illness.

Other Leave Requirements Under Federal Law

The Americans with Disabilities Act and the Federal Rehabilitation Act—plus state anti-discrimination laws—may require employers to grant unpaid sick leave to employees with disabilities as reasonable accommodations of the disabilities, unless doing so creates an undue hardship on an employer.

Massachusetts Law

Under several chapters, the Massachusetts General Laws Annotated provides additional laws regarding maternity leave, school and family leave, leave for jury duty, leave to vote, and leave for holidays to supplement federal regulations.

Maternity Leave

Massachusetts law requires that a female employee be granted up to eight weeks leave for childbirth or adoption. Whether this leave is paid or unpaid is left to the discretion of the employer. Upon completion of maternity leave, the employee must be restored to her previous position or to a similar position with the same pay, status, seniority, etc. as her former position if the following stipulations have been met:

- The employee must have completed her probationary employment period if one exists, or have been employed full time by the employer for at least three consecutive months.
- The employee gives at least two weeks' notice to her employer of her intended leave and of her intention to return.

The employer is not required to restore the employee to her original position if during her maternity leave other employees of equal length of service and status in the same or similar positions have been laid off because of economic conditions or other changes in operating conditions affecting employment.

The provided maternity leave does not affect the employee's vacation time, sick leave, bonuses, advancement, seniority, length-of-service credit, benefits, plans or programs, or any other advantages or rights of her employment. Time taken for maternity leave does not, however, have to be included in computing these benefits. Additionally, employers do not have to provide for the costs of these benefits during the maternity leave unless they do so for all employee leaves of absence. Any bargaining agreements which provide employees with greater benefits than those provided by the Massachusetts law on maternity leave, are not affected by the Massachusetts law.

Massachusetts requires that employers post notices of this maternity-leave provision in every establishment where females are employed.

School and Family Leave

Massachusetts provides a short-term leave law to supplement the federal FMLA. Under this law, an eligible employee is entitled to a total of 24 hours of leave during any 12-month period in addition to leave available under the federal act for the following:

- To participate in school activities directly related to the educational advancement of a son or daughter of the employee. This would include parent-teacher conferences, interviewing for new schools, etc. Massachusetts here defines the term *school* as a public or private elementary or secondary school, a Head Start program, or a children's daycare facility.

- To accompany a son or daughter of the employee to routine medical or dental appointments such as check-ups or vaccinations.

- To accompany an elderly relative to routine medical or dental appointments or appointments for other professional services related to the elder's care, such as interviewing at nursing or group homes. Massachusetts here defines the term *elderly relative* as an individual at least 60 years old who is related by blood or marriage to the employee.

If this kind of leave is foreseeable, employees are required to notify their employers at least seven days before the leave is taken. If the leave is not foreseeable, notice should be given as soon as possible. Employers may require certification for the need to take such leave. Employees may elect to use accrued vacation/sick/personal time.

As with the federal act, under this leave law employers may require the employees to substitute accrued vacation leave, personal leave, or medical or sick leave for this short-term leave. Employers are not required to provide paid leave in these short-term situations if they would not normally provide paid leave in similar situations.

The attorney general is required to enforce this law. There is also a private right of action after 90 days.

Leave for Jury Duty

Massachusetts law provides that no employee—whether full-time, part-time or temporary—may be discharged from or deprived of employment because of attendance or service as a grand or traverse (that is, petit) juror in any court. The employer must pay regular wages for the first three days of jury service.

Employers that violate this law will be considered in contempt of the court upon which the employee has been in attendance and the employers may be prosecuted and punished for such contempt.

Voting Leave

Under Massachusetts law, employees who apply for voting leave must be given the two hours after the opening of the polls in the voting precinct, ward, or town as time to vote.

Legal Holidays

Massachusetts designates the following days as legal holidays:

- January 1st (New Year's Day).
- July 4th.

Employee Leave

- November 11th (Veteran's Day).
- December 25th (Christmas Day).
- The Monday following any of the above when they fall on a Sunday.
- The third Monday in January (Martin Luther King Day).
- The third Monday in February (President's Day).
- The third Monday in April (Patriot's Day).
- The last Monday in May (Memorial Day).
- The first Monday in September (Labor Day).
- The second Monday in October (Columbus Day).
- Thanksgiving Day.

The following are legal holidays for Suffolk County only:

- March 17th (Evacuation Day).
- June 17th (Bunker Hill Day).
- The Monday following if these fall on a Sunday.

Employee Leave

Chapter 25
Retirement Plans

Introduction

Federal regulation of retirement plans in part depends on the type of plan. There are two basic categories of retirement plans—defined-benefit plans and defined-contribution plans. This chapter distinguishes between those two categories of plans, describes other categories of retirement plans, describes retirement plan requirements under ERISA, and considers retirement plan requirements under federal tax law.

Descriptions of Common Types of Retirement Plans

Defined Benefit Plans

A *defined-benefit plan* is designed to pay a monthly pension upon retirement. The employer determines the formula to be used in calculating the amount of the monthly pension. For example, a defined-benefit plan formula could provide a monthly pension equal to 1 percent of the participant's pay, multiplied by his or her years of service. In other words, with a defined-benefit plan, the employer defines the benefits employees may be entitled to receive in the future and undertakes the obligation to fund the plan sufficiently to pay those benefits when they become due.

ERISA requires that all defined-benefit plans be funded based upon actuarial computations. The employer must make minimum contributions each year. Under federal tax law, there are maximum contribution limits and excise taxes imposed upon employers that do not make their required minimum contributions. Employers that do not make required contributions may have to provide notices to participants and also may have to notify a federal agency called the Pension Benefit Guaranty Corporation (PBGC).

ERISA provides for a termination insurance program, run by the PBGC, for defined-benefit pension plans. The termination insurance program is designed to provide benefits to participants if a defined-benefit pension plan is terminated and does not have enough assets to pay the pensions accrued by plan participants. Funding for the termination insurance program comes from premium payments that defined-benefit plan sponsors must pay to the PBGC. Employers who wish to terminate a defined-benefit pension plan must fully fund the plan and follow an extensive PBGC approval process. Further, the PBGC has authority to involuntarily terminate a plan if the PBGC believes that the circumstances warrant such action.

Defined Contribution Plans

A defined-contribution plan provides an individual account for each participant. An employer makes contributions to the plan and those contributions are allocated to participants' accounts. In other words, with a defined-contribution plan, the employer defines the contributions that will be made and how those contributions will be allocated among plan participants but has no obligation to provide any particular level or amount of future benefit.

In most plans, employer contributions are made in cash and then invested for the benefit of the participants. Thus, the ultimate benefit for the participant in part depends upon the investment performance of the plan. In some plans, employer stock is allocated to participants' accounts, either as the primary feature of the plan or as an additional benefit for participants. For example, employee stock ownership plans (ESOPs) are designed to primarily invest in employer stock. On the other hand, many plans also have employer stock contributed to the plan as an additional benefit for employees. Defined-contribution plans are not covered by PBGC termination insurance.

Hybrid Plans

In recent years, many employers have established *hybrid plans*, so called because they contain features of both defined-benefit and defined-contribution plans. A cash-balance plan is an example of a hybrid plan.

A cash-balance plan is a form of defined-benefit pension plan under which a participant's benefit is described as an account balance, like in a defined-contribution plan, rather than as a monthly pension as in the typical defined-benefit plan. The account balance may be credited with a certain number of dollars for each year of service and, usually, interest. The dollars to be credited for each year of service are determined under a formula designed by the employer. Often the amount to be credited is a percentage of pay. However, some plans are designed to provide credits based on pay, age, and/or years of service. A cash-balance plan pays a monthly pension to the participant, the amount of which is based on the amount of the participant's cash balance in the plan.

Money-purchase Plans

Money-purchase pension plans are defined-contribution plans that have mandatory employer contributions. For example, a money-purchase pension plan might require that the employer contribute to the plan 5 percent of each participant's pay. However, many plans have contribution formulas based on a participant's compensation, age, and/or years of service. Since employer contributions to a money-purchase pension plan are mandatory, employers that do not contribute to the plan may be required to notify employees and may be subject to certain excise tax penalties.

Profit Sharing Plans

A profit-sharing plan is a type of defined-contribution plan. In profit-sharing plans, employer contributions to the plan may be made at the discretion of the employer. Some plans provide for contributions determined by a specific formula, such as a percentage of the employer's profits. In any case, a profit-sharing plan must have a method for allocating the employer contribution to the individual accounts of participants. Many plans allocate the contribution in pro-rata amounts based on participants' compensation. Plans also may use allocation formulas based on a combination of the participant's compensation, age, and/or years of service.

401(k) Plans

A 401(k) plan is a profit-sharing plan that has special features. This plan received its name because it is designed to meet certain requirements of Section 401(k) of the Internal Revenue Code. Under a 401(k) plan, a participant may elect to make pre-tax salary reduction contributions to the plan. For example, a participant might elect to contribute 3 percent of his or her pay to the plan. The employer deducts that amount from the payroll and contributes it to the participant's account under the plan. The amount contributed is not subject to federal and most state income taxes (but does remain subject to Social Security taxes). Employers often design a 401(k) plan to also provide for employer matching contributions. Matching contributions are employer contributions based on the amount of a participant's salary reduction contributions. For example, a typical employer matching contribution might be 50 percent of the first 6 percent of pay contributed by a participant. Employers may design their 401(k) plan to allow the employer to make employer profit-sharing contributions to the plan.

403(b) Plans

A 403(b) plan of schools and charitable organizations have many similarities to a 401(k) plan. Employees may be permitted to make pre-tax salary reduction contributions to the plan. Employers may make matching contributions or other types of contributions based on compensation, age, and/or years of service. If the plan has employee salary reduction contributions, the salary reduction feature of the plan must be made available to all employees, with certain exceptions including student employees and employees who normally work fewer than 20 hours per week.

Stock Bonus Plans and ESOPs

Stock bonus plans and ESOPs are defined-contribution plans that permit the employer to contribute employer stock or securities directly into the plan. The amounts contributed are allocated to individual participant accounts. Like a profit-sharing plan, the allocation formula is usually based on the compensation of the participants, but can be based on a number of other factors, such as age and years of service.

Retirement Plan Requirements

Participation

An employer may establish age and service requirements that must be satisfied before eligible employees will be entitled to participate in the employer's retirement plan. However, the employer's age and service requirements must be consistent with the "minimum age and service" requirements contained in ERISA and the Internal Revenue Code (IRC). The maximum age an employer can require its employees to attain before allowing them to participate in the plan is 21. In general, the maximum service the employer can require its employees to accrue before allowing them to participate is one year. However, the service requirement may be increased to two years if the plan provides for immediate 100 percent vesting. Older employees cannot be excluded from plan participation on the basis of age.

Vesting

Employers are permitted to require employees to work a number of years before they become entitled to their benefits accrued under the plan. This is called a *vesting requirement*.

ERISA and the IRC provide two optional vesting schedules that are based on an employee's years of service. The first schedule provides that an employee need not have any vested rights to his or her accrued benefits under the plan until completing five years of service, but must then be 100 percent vested. The second schedule requires 20 percent vesting after three years of service, with an additional 20 percent after each of the four following years. Thus, under the second schedule a plan participant will be 100 percent vested after seven years of service. An employer may design an alternative vesting schedule, as long as the alternative schedule provides for vesting at least as fast as one of the two specified schedules.

ERISA and the IRC also require that retirement plans specify a normal retirement age and that all participants be vested if they are employed when they attain their normal retirement age. Normal retirement age is usually 65 but need not be, so long as it is not later than age 65 or, if later, the fifth anniversary of an employee's plan participation date.

Accrual of Benefits

ERISA and the IRC have benefit-accrual rules for defined-benefit pension plans. Among the provisions of the accrual rules is the requirement that the benefit under the plan must accrue ratably over an employee's career. Thus, an employer cannot design a defined-benefit pension plan so that little or no benefit accruals occur until an employee reaches retirement age.

Spousal Protections

ERISA and the IRC contain certain requirements designed to protect the interests of spouses of plan participants. In general, pension plans are required to pay pension benefits to married participants in the form of a qualified joint and survivor annuity (QJSA) unless the spouse of the participant consents to a different form of payment. Under a QJSA, if the participant dies before the spouse, the spouse must receive a survivor pension that is at least 50 percent of what the participant was being paid. Pension plans also are required to provide a similar qualified pre-retirement survivor annuity (QPSA) to the surviving spouse of a participant who is vested and dies before beginning payments under a plan.

Certain types of individual account plans can be exempt from the QJSA and QPSA requirements of ERISA and the IRC. Most profit-sharing plans, 401(k) plans, stock bonus plans, and ESOPs can be exempt from those requirements if the plan does not provide for an annuity distribution option and it provides that the spouse of the participant is automatically the beneficiary of the participant, unless the spouse consents to another beneficiary.

Any spousal consent to another form of payment or beneficiary must be made in writing and witnessed by a notary public or a representative of the plan. Consent to the payment of a pension in a form other than a QJSA must generally be made within 90 days of the pension starting date.

Other Retirement Plan Rules

ERISA and the IRC generally prohibit retirement plan benefits from being assigned or alienated. For example, this means that a participant cannot use his or her retirement benefits as collateral for a loan. Nor can the creditors of a participant attach, garnish, or otherwise obtain retirement plan benefits. However, the law does permit an employee's benefits to be assigned or paid over to a spouse, children, or other dependents pursuant to a qualified domestic relations order (QDRO). A *qualified domestic relations order* is a court order relating to alimony, marital property rights, or child support.

ERISA and the IRC prohibit the accrued retirement benefits of plan participants from being reduced because of plan amendments, plan terminations, mergers, or consolidation of plans. Plans may not be amended, merged, or consolidated in any way that would eliminate early retirement benefits, retirement type subsidies, or protected optional forms of payment for previously accrued benefits.

If an employer sponsors a defined-benefit pension plan or money purchase pension plan, the employer must notify participants 15 days in advance of any amendment to the plan that would significantly reduce the rate of future benefit accrual under the plan.

Employers are required to maintain records that are sufficient to administer the terms of a plan.

Exemption for "Top-hat" Plans

A top-hat plan of an employer is not subject to any of the foregoing requirements under ERISA or the IRC. A *top-hat plan* is a plan that is unfunded and maintained primarily for the purpose of providing deferred compensation to a select group of management or highly compensated employees.

Tax-qualification Rules for Retirement Plans

Benefits of Tax-qualification

Retirement plans can receive special tax benefits if they are designed to meet a variety of requirements specified in the Internal Revenue Code. If so, they are often referred to as *tax-qualified plans*. The vast majority of employer retirement plans are designed to be tax-qualified.

Tax-qualification generally assures that:

- Employers will be able to immediately deduct their contributions to the plan.
- Employees are not taxed on their benefits until they receive payments from the plan.
- All of the investment earnings in the plan are exempt from tax.

In addition, except for employee salary reduction contributions to the plan, all employer contributions to the plan and all payments from the plan are exempt from federal Social Security taxes.

Tax-qualified plans must follow all of the retirement plan requirements outlined above. Beyond those requirements, the general theme of the tax-qualification rules is that the retirement plan cannot be designed or operated in a way that discriminates in favor of *highly compensated employees* (HCEs). For this purpose, an employee will generally be considered to be an HCE if that employee earned in excess of a certain dollar amount ($85,000 for calendar year 2001) in the prior plan year or is a 5 percent owner of the employer.

To prevent employers from discriminating in favor of HCEs by creating separate legal entities, complex rules require subsidiaries and other affiliates of an employer to be considered as a single employer for purposes of determining whether a retirement plan is discriminatory. For example, an employer cannot avoid the nondiscrimination rules by setting up a separate company to be the employer of the HCEs.

Some of the more important remaining tax-qualification requirements are discussed below.

Coverage Requirements

A tax-qualified plan that provides benefits to HCEs must also provide benefits to a certain percentage of non-highly compensated employees (NHCEs). This requirement is often referred to as a *coverage requirement*.

In general, this requirement will be satisfied if the plan covers at least 70 percent of the NHCEs. If NHCE coverage is less than 70 percent, there may be alternative ways to satisfy the coverage requirement.

Note: Not all NHCEs have to be covered by a plan in order for it to be tax-qualified. However, an employer is not permitted to exclude employees from a plan simply because they are classified as part-time, seasonal, or temporary employees. Other types of business criteria are permissible distinctions. For example, an employer might elect to exclude all sales personnel from a plan.

Nondiscrimination in Benefits

The benefits provided under the plan cannot be designed in favor of HCEs. For example, defined-contribution plan benefits are not discriminatory if they are allocated based on an equal percentage of compensation for all plan participants (provided that "compensation" is defined in a nondiscriminatory manner). In addition, a plan is not permitted to base benefits on an employee's compensation that exceeds a specified limit ($170,000 for calendar year 2001). Finally, any optional forms of payment or other features of the plan may not be designed or operated in favor of HCEs.

401(k) plans have special tests to determine whether the plan is discriminatory. Under the 401(k) plan rules, the average of the salary reduction contributions of HCEs is limited to an amount based on the average of the NHCEs. A similar test must be satisfied for any matching contributions and after-tax employee contributions to the plan.

Chapter 26
Unemployment Compensation

Introduction

The unemployment compensation system—also referred to as unemployment insurance—is designed to pay workers who lose their jobs through no fault of their own. Most developed nations have created this sort of social insurance and all such systems are compulsory since each government enforces the coverage and uses taxes to pay for the insurance.

In addition to compensating employees during periods of unemployment brought about by periods of involuntary termination or periods of economic decline, unemployment insurance is intended to help employers by preventing the dispersal of a skilled labor force from a part of the country where jobs are scarce to parts where jobs are plentiful.

The U.S. system of unemployment compensation (UC) is a combination federal–state system, growing out of the Social Security Act of 1935, which levied a federal unemployment tax on employers. The act did, however, offer employers credit against federal taxes if they paid taxes to states with unemployment laws that met federal requirements. The Social Security Act also provided states with the autonomy to determine the tangible components of their own unemployment compensation. As a result, the varying state programs are often quite different with differing impacts on employer profits.

This chapter reviews federal unemployment insurance requirements along with related general state regulations and concerns and then summarizes specific state UC regulations, which are often complex and lengthy.

General Considerations: Federal and State Law

The Federal Unemployment Tax Act (FUTA) imposes a payroll tax on employers based on the wages they pay to their employees. The tax is paid by the employers and not withheld from the employees' wages.

Who Must Pay?

Employers must pay FUTA tax if during the current or preceding calendar year they met either of the following tests:

- Paid wages totaling at least $1,500 in any calendar quarter.

- Had at least one employee on any day in each of 20 calendar weeks. The weeks need not be consecutive and the one employee need not be the same individual. For this requirement, a *calendar week* is a period of seven successive days beginning with Sunday and ending at the end of the following Saturday. Short weeks at the beginning or end of a calendar year are, however, counted as calendar weeks.

Employers who meet either test are liable for the FUTA tax for the entire calendar year and for the next calendar year. If, for example, an employer meets the one-employee-in-each-of-20-weeks test in December of a certain year, that employer is responsible for paying taxes on all wages paid during that year, not only on wages paid after meeting the test requirement. Even if the employer fails to meet the requirement the next year, the employer is still responsible for FUTA taxes.

Computing the Tax

The FUTA tax is imposed on a single flat rate on the first $7,000 of wages paid each employee. Once an employee's wages for the calendar year exceed $7,000 the employer has no further liability for that employee for that year.

The FUTA tax rate is a flat 6.2 percent of the total wages paid by the employer during the calendar year. However, employers can generally claim credits against their gross FUTA tax based on the amount of state unemployment tax they paid, up to 5.4 percent of the federally taxable wages for employers who paid all state employment taxes on time and before the due date of the FUTA taxes. Under these circumstances, an employer's federal tax would be 0.8 percent. Even if the state tax rate is far below the 5.4 percent, employers will get the benefit of the full credit, fixing their tax rate at 0.8 percent.

Employers who are unable to pay their state taxes by the federal return date can preserve their right to the maximum allowable credit by requesting a filing extension for the federal return. If the extension is granted, the employers will get the full credit if they pay their state taxes before the federal due date.

State Tax Accounts and Experience Ratings

Federal and state laws define which employers are liable for unemployment taxes and which employees have unemployment compensation protection. Generally speaking, any employing unit, as defined by state law, must make quarterly tax payments (contributions) based on the taxable wages they report to the state unemployment agency. These monies are deposited into an Employer Trust Fund with the U.S. Treasury, designated solely for unemployment compensation and readily available to the state where the wages were reported.

All employers must establish an unemployment tax account in each state in which they do business. The state agency develops an unemployment experience for each tax account by compiling records of taxable wages reported quarterly, tax contributions, and unemployment claims experience. *Experience ratings calculations* are the state's method for measuring each employer's unemployment experience. Each year, employers are assigned a specific tax rate based on their overall experience in comparison to other tax-paying employers in the state and the health of that state's Employer Trust Fund.

The critical component in determining any employer's experience is the amount of unemployment benefits that employer has paid to its former workers. Usually, tax rates are calculated by using employers' unemployment claims experience in comparison to reported wages. Actual state tax rates are assigned according to these ratios and the prevailing tax schedule for the state. Employers should regularly review the state law requirements regarding these matters.

A state unemployment account is like an employer having a checking account, and employers should reconcile each assigned tax rate annually. Employers must balance their own records with the state-calculated tax rate to protect themselves from an improperly assigned rate, a frequent occurrence. Discrepancies should be protested in writing to the issuing authority **by the prescribed deadline.**

Problems with UC Taxes

Individuals often abuse unemployment compensation and it can be poorly administered by a state bureaucracy. In some states, unemployment compensation is so attractive (up to 70 percent of an individual's income) that it may deter some from accepting employment. Often, claimants awarded benefits spend much less time looking for a new job than those denied benefits. They remain unemployed an average of 14 weeks, compared to two weeks for those denied unemployment compensation.

A further problem is that nationally the average for overpayment is nearly 10 percent and in some states an employer's tax can be twice as much as claims benefits actually awarded. With all of these potential problems, it is essential that employers make every effort to control their unemployment compensation costs to keep these costs from eroding profits.

Controlling Unemployment Costs

To successfully control unemployment taxes, employers must understand all facets of the tax calculations and must know and comply with the administrative processes for each state. Employers must, therefore, assign the responsibility for managing their unemployment compensation control to individuals with power to take necessary action. Unemployment cost control must be a deliberate effort, based upon internal methods of investigation and response, and consistent with prevailing state laws and regulations.

Eliminating Employee Separations

The ideal way to control unemployment compensation costs is to keep your employees working. Employers can minimize employee separations by using good and consistent personnel practices including the following:

- **Providing well-written detailed job descriptions.** Clear and well-detailed job descriptions will minimize confusion about the scope of the job and inform a prospective employee of an employer's expectations. A good job description will also help the employer identify the qualifications needed to fill a particular position.

- **Require a completed application form.** Employers should require all candidates to affirm, through their signatures, that the information they provide is true and accurate. Whenever possible, each applicant's qualifications, experience, and references should be verified.

- **Test applicants when appropriate.** If specific skills are required for certain jobs (telephone skills, word-processing skills, etc.) employers should apply uniform testing of each applicant for such positions. Employers must keep records of tests as documentation of the hiring process.

- **Offer an information orientation session.** New hires should receive a standard orientation session, uniformly applied to all new hires. The goal of such an orientation is to help a new employee become a productive member of the company as quickly as possible. Employers should keep a record of those who attend the orientation sessions, verified by the employee's signature, including the dates and times they attended. This documentation will establish, at a later date, that employees were informed of the employer's expectations, policies, and rules from the beginning of their employment.

- **Provide workplace rules and employee handbooks.** Employers should establish and communicate specific workplace rules and personnel policies. Such policies are one of the best ways to protect an employer's state unemployment experience from unnecessary benefit charges. In a disputed unemployment case, where the claimant was discharged for violating a rule, policy, or procedure, the employer usually must prove the employee was adequately informed of the employer's expectations.

    The best way to be certain employees are aware of the rules, policies, and procedures is by issuing each new employee an employee handbook. Employees should be required to verify in writing that they have received the handbook and understand the company's policies. Changes or updates to the handbook should be distributed in writing to each employee, and employees must be required to acknowledge, again in writing, that they have received and understood any change in rules, policy, or procedure.

    Employers must also implement methods for uniformly enforcing rules, procedures, and policies. Violations of the rules should be properly documented and noted in the employee's personnel file. Failure to uniformly enforce rules across the company may eventually hurt an employer's unemployment experience. Unemployment claimants terminated for violating rules, procedures, or policies that were not uniformly enforced may be eligible for benefits.

- **Implement new employee performance appraisals.** Employers must determine whether a new employee meets the standards and expectations of the job during the employee's initial period of employment. If the employee does not, he or she should be counseled regarding specific deficiencies, how to correct those deficiencies, how long he or she has to improve, and what the consequences will be if there is no improvement. If an employer determines that a new employee cannot become an asset to the company, the employer may consider terminating the employee immediately to avoid increasing future potential unemployment liability. However, the employer also should consider if other potentially greater liability exits for immediately terminating the employee (for example, discrimination claim, breach of contract). These laws counsel that the employer should be able to demonstrate that it has given the employee a reasonable opportunity (including information and training) to perform the job before terminating.

- **Provide constructive counseling.** Employees should be given the benefit of a counseling session whenever their performance, conduct, and/or actions fall below standards. Verbal and written warnings should be used to verify the seriousness of the situation. The goals of counseling should be to improve an employee's chance of continued employment by making him or her more productive.

- **Apply progressive discipline.** Employers should adopt a standard process of progressive discipline for employees who fail to adhere to workplace rules or reasonable standards of behavior. Supervisors should use progressive discipline to address recurring infractions and workplace problems before actually discharging an employee. Note, of course, that such serious problems as fighting, theft, or posing a threat to the safety of others do not need progressive discipline but are rather a cause for immediate dismissal. Progressive discipline would take the following course:
    - When a work problem occurs, the supervisor should determine if the employee received proper job orientation and direction. Did the employee know exactly what was expected of him or her?

- If it is determined that the employee was aware of the employer's expectations and was properly directed, a verbal warning should be issued. The employee must be informed that he or she has violated a rule or acted in an unacceptable manner and that continued problems will result in additional disciplinary action. The employee should also be told exactly how to correct the problem.
- If the problem persists after a verbal warning has been issued, employers should issue a formal written warning. This warning should make it clear to the employee that further violations will result in additional disciplinary action, including possible discharge.
- If the employee fails to heed a written warning and the violation continues, the employer should immediately discharge the offending employee.

♦ **Use suspension, rather than firing, whenever possible.** In most cases employers should avoid firing employees on the spot and without careful consideration. Temporary suspensions may be used when more time is needed to investigate an apparent infraction or when a volatile situation needs to be defused. When a full investigation has been made and all legal liabilities considered, an employee can be reinstated or discharged.

♦ **Use exit interviews.** Exit interviews are effective ways to reduce unemployment benefit charges by identifying employment-related problems which cause employee turnover and hence unemployment liability. They also function as a useful way to determine the actual reasons for resignations and provide opportunities to obtain statements from separating employees. Note that employees who voluntarily quit without good cause are usually ineligible for state unemployment benefits.

Independent Contractors and Unemployment Compensation

Employers may engage independent contractors to provide services to their clients and/or themselves. These self-employed individuals normally provide these same services to other individuals or organizations and are free from the direction and control of the employer to whom they have contracted. True independent contractors cannot file a claim for unemployment benefits since no employer reports the payments made for these services as covered wages under state or federal unemployment laws.

Each state has its own regulations and guidelines to determine whether any specific contract worker qualifies as an independent contractor. Employers must be careful to comply with this distinct interpretation in the states where they use such workers. Employers can contact the appropriate state agency and request a copy of their interpretation of independent contractor status.

Refusal of Suitable Employment

As businesses grow and change, employment needs also change. At times, employers may choose to reassign workers from one job to another or change scheduled work hours and/or location of employment. If an employer offers an employee a reasonable (similar hours, pay, a practical location, etc.) employment alternative and the employee refuses the job offer, the employer should promptly inform the state agency of the specifics of the refusal. Refusal of suitable employment by claimants for unemployment benefits is a serious matter. The penalty in most states for refusing a job is an indefinite disqualification for unemployment compensation.

Employment Separations

An *employment separation* is when an individual's employment ends for any reason—lack of work, voluntary quitting, termination, or discharge. Depending on the issue, the state unemployment agency will assign the "moving party," usually the employer in lack of work and discharge situations, the burden of proving that the separation was for a good cause. In voluntary quitting situations, the employee who quit would be the moving party.

Recording Separations

Employers must record the precise reasons for a separation by detailing events leading up to it. This form of documentation (a separation notice) provides a useful record for the employer in several ways:

- Separating employees should be told exactly why their employment ended. Employers in most circumstances should provide a copy of the separation notice to the separating employee and request acknowledgment of receipt in writing.

- Supervisors can be made aware that their performance is partially reflected in the separation notice.

- An accurate separation notice will enhance the employer's position if a dispute develops regarding a claim for unemployment benefits. A copy of the notice should be placed in the employee's personnel file.

At the minimum, separation notices must contain the employee's name, Social Security number, date of actual last day on the job, and the precise reason for the separation, including specifics of the final incident causing the separation.

Separation Terminology

Separation notices must be clear and accurate. If the reader cannot visualize the final separation incident, the facts have not been accurately recorded. Subjective terminology should be avoided. Former employees should not be characterized as having a bad attitude or as being unable to do something. The reason for this is that the law makes a distinction between nonperformance stemming from an employee's inability to perform a job and nonperformance based on willful misconduct. In the former case, the employee will generally not be penalized, as the employer erred in determining the person could do the job. In addition, employees should not be called "unreliable," "careless," "undependable," "unsatisfactory," "unprofessional" and the like. Phrases such as "guilty of insubordination," "poor performance," and "not suited to the job" should be avoided. The separation notice should be specific, concrete, objective, and accurate.

Documentation

For employers to successfully protest unwarranted unemployment claims, supervisory personnel must record all relevant facts of every worker's employment history. Since unemployment claims can be filed against an employer's tax account as much as 18 months from the date of separation, written documentation is essential to recall the facts surrounding a separation. Documentation must be honest and fair, a reasonable portrayal of the situation. It must also be objective, representing the facts without assumptions or conjecture.

Good documentation helps control unemployment costs since it enhances the employer's position when a former employee files a claim. To prevail in a disputed unemployment case, employers generally must present evidence that is more convincing than that of the claimant, and accurate documentation that proves the truth of an employer's sworn statements will go a long way toward winning a case. Additionally, such documentation helps employers determine whether an employee has been warned or disciplined for previous employment infractions.

Documentation of any progressive discipline is an essential part of effective documentation. Most ex-employees discharged for work-rule infractions will be denied some or all benefits if it can be proven, through documentation, that the employer has reasonable rules, that employees are aware of these rules, that the employer enforces the rules uniformly, and that the employee was given sufficient warning before being discharged.

Employers should even document informal verbal discussions of personnel issues with employees. Supervisors need to record any incidents to help remember them.

Any written warnings should include the following:

- A description of the problem or behavior that needs to be corrected.
- A description of the employer's expectations regarding the employee's future behavior.
- An explanation of how the employer wants the problem resolved.
- An explanation of future disciplinary action that may be taken if the problem is not resolved.

Employers should have the employee receiving a written warning sign an original to indicate receipt of the warning. Employees must be able to express their disagreement with the warning and their response should be kept with the warning. Any witnesses should also sign documentation pertaining to what occurred.

Contents of Documentation

Good documentation in unemployment compensation cases should include at least the following:

- Names and titles of individuals involved in the incident.
- Indications of the time, date, and place of the incident.
- A description of the event and its results.
- Observations about the possible consequences to the employer.
- Signature of the preparer and any witness.

As with the actual Notice of Separation, documentation supporting separation decisions must use objective language and avoid making conclusions. Supervisors preparing separation documentation language should use objective language, as in the right-hand column below, rather than subjective language, as in the left:

Subjective Statements (Avoid)	Objective Statements (Use)
The employee is often late.	The employee was more than 10 minutes late on 2/17, 2/18, 2/25, 3/1, etc.
The employee was insubordinate.	The employee refused to clean up a broken shampoo bottle from Aisle 6. He shouted, "I'm tired of doing all the dirty work." When told this was part of his job, he stomped away.
The employee was intoxicated.	On 4/2/99, the employee returned from lunch 15 minutes late. His speech was slurred and he smelled of alcohol. He walked unsteadily and fell twice against a filing cabinet.

Documentation of this type will help employers defend themselves against unwarranted claims for unemployment compensation.

Massachusetts Law

Unemployment insurance in Massachusetts provides cash benefits to workers who have been employed in covered employment but who have become unemployed through no fault of their own. The benefits are financed through taxes or contributions paid in varying amounts by employers subject to the law. Some employers may choose to reimburse the commonwealth for the benefit payments for which they are responsible, in lieu of paying taxes.

Covered Employers

Employers who either pay at least $1,500 in wages in any calendar quarter or employ at least one individual for some portion of a day in each of 13 weeks are subject to the Massachusetts Employment and Training Law. Employers who are subject to the Federal Unemployment Tax Act are also subject to the Massachusetts law if they have a payroll of more than $200 per calendar quarter. Employers may become subject to the law by acquiring the business or assets of a subject employer.

Various duties, such as filing reports, devolve upon employers subject to the law, and penalties are provided for failure to comply.

Covered Employees

Under Massachusetts law any service performed for wages is subject to the law, whether or not the common-law relationship between master and servant exists. However, an individual is not considered a covered employee under the Law if the following can be shown:

The individual is free from control or direction over the performance of service under the contract of hire and in fact.

The service is performed outside the usual course of the employer's business or outside all the places of business of the employer.

The individual is engaged in an independently established trade, occupation, or business similar to that of the employer.

Some employment or employees are specifically exempt, including the following:

- Service by immediate relatives.
- Service by the employer's minor children.
- Insurance agents, real estate brokers, and salespersons on commission.
- Newspaper carriers.
- Students employed by the institutions at which they study.

Most services for the commonwealth and for tax-exempt nonprofit organizations must now be covered. Some services or workers, such as the following, remain exempt:

- Religious services.
- Sheltered workshop-type services.
- Services in certain work-relief or work-training programs.
- Certain services for hospitals.

- Services performed for the commonwealth as elected officials.
- Members of a legislative body or the judiciary.
- Members of the National Guard.
- Temporary emergency employees.
- Employees in nontenured policymaking or advisory positions.

Employee Wages

Employers' taxes are computed on the basis of the amount of taxable wages they pay. For purposes of this law, *wages* includes all remuneration, whether paid directly or indirectly, including salaries, commissions, bonuses, and the cash value of remuneration paid in a medium other than cash.

The most important limitation on the term wages is the taxable wage base. Remuneration with respect to employment of more than $10,800 paid in a calendar year to any individual is not considered wages and is thus not taxable. The Massachusetts law provides that wages paid by an employer's predecessor and wages paid for covered employment in another state may be included in determining the $10,800 limitation.

The following are not considered wages under Massachusetts' law:

- Certain cash tips of under $20.
- Sickness or accident disability payments under a workers' compensation plan.
- Sickness or accident disability payments made over six months after separation.
- Payments from, to, or under a trust or annuity plan exempt from federal income tax.
- Remuneration paid in a medium other than cash for services not in the course of the employer's trade or business.
- Stand-by pay to employees over 65.

Taxes or Contributions

Most employers pay taxes, called *contributions,* under the experience-rating provisions of the law. *Experience rating* is a means of varying individual employer tax rates on the basis of each employer's experience with employment, wages, and unemployment. A separate account is maintained for each employer and the employer's contributions are credited to that account. Only employers whose accounts have been charged with benefits throughout the 12 immediately preceding months is eligible to have their contribution rate established under the experience-rating provisions of the law. New employers pay a set rate, based on the rate schedule in effect, until they are entitled to an experience rate.

The relationship of the fund balance as of the computation date of each year (September 30) to the total taxable wages for the preceding calendar year determines the rates that will apply during the following calendar year. Employers' individual rates are determined by each employer's reserve percentage, which is the net balance in the employer's account as of the computation date, divided by the employer's total taxable payroll for the 12 months just before the computation date.

The Massachusetts law contains eight rate schedules. The maximum rate of any schedule is 9.3 percent, the minimum rate is 0.6 percent. Schedules are assigned for a calendar year on the basis of the amount available for the payment of benefits on the computation date and the total taxable wages in the preceding year. Employer rates are adjusted by an amount reflecting the solvency factor.

There is no provision for voluntary contributions under the Massachusetts law. Some employers are allowed to elect, or may be required to use, the reimbursement financing method for paying benefits.

Returns and Reports

Each Massachusetts employer is required to submit quarterly contribution reports on or before the last day of the month following the end of the calendar quarter covered by the report.

Benefits and Eligibility

The benefit amount for an individual is based on earnings prior to filing a claim. The basis for this computation is the *base period*, defined as the first four of the last five completed calendar quarters immediately preceding the benefit year. The *benefit year* is the 52 weeks beginning on the Sunday before the filing of the claim. To be eligible for benefits a claimant must have base-period wages equal to at least $2,400, must be able to and be available for work, and must wait for at least one week.

Under the Massachusetts law a claimant whose average weekly wage in the base period is $66 or less will receive benefits ranging from $14 to $34, depending on the wages in the high quarter of the base period. A claimant whose average weekly wage in the base period is over $66 will receive a weekly benefit equal to 50 percent of his or her average weekly wage in the base period, but not over 57 ½ percent of the average weekly wage of all employees covered by the law. The law also provides a weekly dependency benefit of $25 for each dependent child, not to exceed 50 percent of the individual's regular weekly benefit amount.

The total amount of benefits payable to an individual in a benefit year is the lesser of 36 percent of his or her base period wages or 30 times the weekly benefit rate, plus dependency allowances. However, benefits may be extended by the lesser of 50 percent of the total of regular benefits payable, including dependent allowances, or 13 times the individual's weekly benefit amount, including dependent allowances, during periods of high unemployment.

Disqualification from Benefits

Massachusetts' Employment and Training Law identifies a number of specific disqualifications from benefits:

- Leaving voluntarily without good cause.
- Refusing suitable work without good cause.
- Being discharged for misconduct.
- Being suspended for disciplinary reasons.
- Being unemployed because of a labor dispute.
- Receiving unemployment benefits under another state or federal law.
- Receiving certain types of income while employed.

In some cases the disqualification may be lifted by waiting out a certain number of weeks. In others, the claimant must have returned to work.

Chapter 27
Workers' Compensation and Massachusetts Law

Introduction

Workers' Compensation is an employer-financed, no-fault insurance program that compensates employees who have been disabled because of a work-related injury or accident. Every state has enacted some form of workers' compensation law to protect employees against loss of income and burdensome medical payments resulting from a work-related injury, illness, or disease.

Employers Affected

Most states have made workers' compensation coverage mandatory, although in Texas and New Jersey it is voluntary. Most states require employers with at least one employee to carry workers' compensation coverage, but some states exempt very small employers—although there is not total agreement about what constitutes a small employer. Some states exempt employers with fewer than five employees, some with fewer than four, some with fewer than three. Exempt employers may participate in the state workers' compensation program if they wish.

Massachusetts Requirements

Massachusetts requires all employers, including small employers whose only employees are family members, to comply with the law. For public employers--counties, cities, towns, districts having tax power, country tuberculosis hospital districts, and school districts—coverage is elective. Police and fire departments are not included. Contractors working on public buildings and public works must provide coverage during the full term of the contract. Coverage is also elective for employers of seasonal, causal, or part-time domestic employees working 16 hours or less a week (Massachusetts General Laws, 34A, 25B, 69, 74).

Employers are cautioned to check with their attorneys before setting up a workers' compensation program.

Employees Affected

Not all employees are covered by the workers' compensation laws of all states. Business owners, independent contractors, real estate salespersons working solely on commission, professional athletes, domestic employees in private homes, farm workers, maritime workers, railroad employees, unpaid volunteers, operators of leased taxicabs, and some others are frequently excluded.

Massachusetts Requirements

Massachusetts stipulates that laborers, mechanics, nurses, managers of municipal utility plants, and others working for public employers may be covered if the public employer elects coverage. Massachusetts Workers' Compensation law requires workers employed by employee leasing companies to be insured under the Act if the leasing company is responsible for obtaining such coverage for itself and all of its leased employees. Leasing companies must maintain separate policies for each client company, and premiums paid by leasing companies must be commensurate with exposure and anticipated claims experience. Leasing companies that fail to insure are subject to the same penalties as direct employers.

Massachusetts stipulates that minors must be covered by the Act and that they are entitled to double compensation if employed illegally, with the additional compensation being paid by the employer. The minor's future earning capacity is considered when benefits are awarded.

Under Massachusetts law certain employees are specifically exempted from coverage:

- Masters and seafarers on vessels engaged in interstate or foreign commerce.
- Professional athletes if their contracts provide for payment of wages while are unable to play.
- Taxi drivers.
- Real estate salespeople paid by commission.
- Direct sales persons.
- Persons employed in interstate and foreign commerce who are covered for liability for injury or death by the laws of the United States.
- Individuals who work outside the usual business or profession of the employer.

Massachusetts workers' compensation law stipulates that injured employees over 65 who have been out of the labor market at least two years and who are entitled to Social Security of employer-paid pension benefits are ineligible for wage-replacement benefits unless they can show they would be active in the labor market were it not for the injury.

Characteristics of Workers' Compensation Coverage

Employer-Financed Aspect

Obviously the characteristics of workers' compensation coverage of greatest concern to employers is the employer-financed aspect. Workers cannot be required to pay for any of the workers' compensation premium. Employers also cannot require employees to sign statements that they will not seek workers' compensation benefits if they are injured or become ill on the job. Any such agreements are invalid and unenforceable. Most states will mandate how much coverage an employer must purchase and what percentage of an employee's salary the employer must pay if the employee is hurt or becomes ill as part of the job.

Massachusetts Requirements

Massachusetts law states that all workers' compensation policies must include optional deductibles of $500, $1,000, $2,000, $2,500, and an aggregate deductible of $10,000 that will apply to each claim. A

$5,000-per-claim deductible may be allowed if the employer provided adequate collateral. The insurer will pay the deductible amount and then collect from the employer. The commissioner of Insurance will determine the premium reduction for the deductible amount chosen by the employer.

Purchasing Coverage

Most employers purchase an insurance policy to obtain protection from paying workers' compensation benefits. They may pay one lump sum annually or make regular payments throughout the year to obtain this coverage either from an insurance company or through a voluntary association of insurance companies formed to handle high-risk companies. In most states workers' compensation coverage is purchased from a workers' compensation insurance company. However, North Dakota, Ohio, Washington, West Virginia, and Wyoming require employers to buy the coverage through a state agency, although these states require employers to purchase employer liability insurance separately through commercial insurers.

State Fund

Massachusetts has no state fund.

In many states large insurance companies such as Liberty Mutual, CNA, Fireman's Fund, The Hartford, and Travelers handle most workers' compensation coverage. Employers who purchase their workers' compensation coverage from a commercial insurance company should be careful to select a commercial insurance agent capable of representing the company in dealings with the insurer. Even with careful selection of the agent, however, the employer should maintain involvement in the decision of which workers' compensation coverage to purchase since this decision can ultimately affect the employer's liability. Ideally, the workers' compensation agent should be familiar with the specific industry of the employer and thus be able to determine the most appropriate insurer. The agent must also know what discounts are available and how to negotiate the best discounts from the insurer. Employers with a multistate workforce should make certain the agent they select can write out-of-state policies.

Companies in high-risk categories—that is, companies with a poor safety record and above-average number of complaints—may have to purchase their workers' compensation insurance through state insurance pools, similar to high-risk health or automobile insurance pools. Of course, this sort of coverage would be more expensive.

Massachusetts provides a list of service carriers selected by the commissioner to provide insurance for employers unable to secure workers' compensation insurance through private companies.

Providing Your Own Insurance

About 20 percent of U.S. workers' compensation premiums were paid by self-insuring companies in 1998. These companies have chosen to take on the actual costs of paying benefits to injured employees, rather than to pay an up-front fee to an insurer for the insurer to take over the risk of providing benefits to injured employees. Except for the District of Columbia, Montana, North Dakota, and Wyoming, self-insurance is a viable alternative in all states for companies of a certain size. Smaller companies, not allowed to self-insure in many states, have the option of joining a pool of other small employers, usually as part of a trade association, to form a unit large enough to provide self-insurance under state requirements.

Views of the viability of self-insuring differ. Since the employer pays all costs for employee benefits and for administering the insurance program, a major accident or a large number of claims could result in serious financial problems. However, employers can purchase excess insurance, which provides insurance for claims over a specified amount. On the other hand, some say, companies that insure themselves have more control over their own workers' compensation program in such things as being able to say when an injury qualifies for workers' compensation. Many see self-insurance as considerably cheaper than insurance purchased from a commercial insurer. Self-insurance is seen by some as particularly good for manufacturing, construction, trucking, and similar industries where the premiums per employee are usually very high.

Massachusetts Restrictions on Self-Insurers

Massachusetts places the following restrictions on employers who wish to self-insure:

- They must have been in business at least five years.
- They must have 300 or more employees.
- They must have an unmodified annual premium of at least $750,000 (this may be waived).
- They must provide a financial study and cash-flow analysis or have a S&P or Moody's rating of AA, A1 or Aa, aa or have a Dun & Bradstreet rating of 5A1.
- The must provide an actuarial study and risk-management study if their experience-modification factor is 1.25 of higher.
- They must have a three-year history of profitability or, if a non-profit organization, a three-year history of revenues exceeding operating expenses.
- They must not have been declared insolvent or been discharged from federal bankruptcy proceedings within the past five years.

Special rules apply to companies formed by mergers, acquisitions, or reorganizations. (Massachusetts General Laws, 25A)

Massachusetts permits five or more employers engaged in the same or similar type of business who are members of a bona fide industry, trade, or professional association that has been in existence for at least two years to form a self-insurance group. At least 70 percent of the members must be experience rated and no group may have less than $250,000 annual gross premium or a combined net worth of less than $1,000,000. Such groups must be certified by the commissioner.

No-fault Aspect

There is no liability in workers' compensation. Benefits are paid regardless of who is to blame for the injury or job-related illness—with certain restrictions as detailed below. When benefits are paid the employer is not admitting liability for the injury or illness, and the employee is paid without resorting to a lawsuit. For purposes of workers' compensation payment, *injury* is any harmful change in the body as a result of work activities. This could be a direct trauma or a gradual wearing down of a body part through repetitive movement or minor traumas. Work-related illness can be caused by exposure to toxic substances, by exposure to unhealthful working conditions, or by exposure to the elements. It does not matter if the injury or illness was the result of the employee's own negligence, merely that the injury or illness was work related.

Covered Injuries and Illnesses

The legal language concerning workers' compensation is that the injury or illness "must arise out of and be in the course and scope of employment." That is, it must occur not only within the time and place of employment but also must arise out of activity that is an inherent part of the employment and which directly or indirectly furthers the employer's interests. Injuries occurring while employees are at lunch in a company-sponsored cafeteria may be covered and injuries sustained by telecommuting employees in the course of their duties are also covered. Injuries sustained by an employee while merely entering an employer's premises would be covered, as would injuries sustained by an employee while changing clothes or washing up before or after work in an employer's locker room or similar facility.

Occupational diseases—that is, any ailment or disease caused by the nature or circumstances of the employment—are covered if they are presumed to arise out of the employment or if the nature of the employment is such that a hazard of contracting such a disease is inherent in the employment.

Injuries and job-related illnesses not covered under workers' compensation include:

- Accidents resulting from "horseplay" or willful misconduct.
- Injuries occurring while traveling to or from work unless the employee was on an errand for the employer. Employees who are required to travel in the performance of their work (such as salespeople) are covered while traveling. Injuries that occur in the company parking lot or while using company-provided transportation are also covered by workers' compensation.
- Injuries resulting from the influence of drugs or alcohol.
- Injuries or illnesses resulting from violation of known safety rules.
- Injuries resulting from voluntary participation or attendance, as athletic events during work time. However, injuries sustained during required recreational or social activities or during acknowledged or permitted physical activities on company premises may be covered.
- Injuries occurring at parties, picnics, and similar functions.
- Intentional self-injury.
- Psychological injuries arising out of any personnel action (including demotion or termination) are not considered personal injuries and are thus not covered—unless the personnel action was intended to inflict emotional harm. If it can be proved that the predominant contributing cause of the mental or emotional disability was an event or events occurring as part of the employment, the disability may be covered.

Note: Employees who unjustifiably refuse to accept recommended medical treatment may be denied compensation or have their compensation suspended.

Coverage Provided

Workers' compensation insurance packages tend to be standardized. Basic coverage includes all necessary medical treatment including diagnostic procedures and medical supplies and equipment, rehabilitation costs, and replacement of lost wages, usually up to two-thirds of the employee's salary, for personal injuries caused by accidents "arising out of and in the course of employment." If an employee's disability is classified as permanent, additional benefits are provided as are death benefits if the accident results in death. Most policies also provide liability insurance in case a worker's family sues for damages resulting from a workers' compensation claim. Coverage is also usually provided for certain occupational diseases as specified in the state laws.

Injured workers are typically referred to a doctor or health plan of the employer's choosing. Employees who indicate they do not like the doctor provided by the employer or the insurance company may have the right to see another doctor. If the injury is serious, the employee usually has the right to a second opinion. In some states, after an injured employee has been treated by the insurance company's doctor for a certain period, usually 90 days, he or she may have the right to transfer treatment to the employee's own doctor or health plan, with the cost paid for by the workers' compensation insurance company

Massachusetts Benefits

Massachusetts workers' compensation law requires injured employees to be furnished with adequate medical and hospital services plus medicines, artificial eyes and limbs and mechanical devices considered necessary to restore the worker to productivity. The state's Rate Setting Commission determines the rate of payment for medical services but higher rates may be paid if agreed upon by the employee, the employer, the insurer, and the healthcare provider.

The state requires employees to submit to examinations as required by the insurer but provides an impartial medical examiner to decide medical disputes. Employees receiving benefits from the Workers' Compensation Trust Fund may be required to choose a physician from an HMO selected by the Fund. Employees may be required to choose physicians as prescribed by a Preferred Provider Arrangement entered into by the employer or insurer. The preferred provider must be approved by the commissioner and each injured worker must receive a list of preferred providers. A list of all current preferred providers must also be posted at each worksite. Injured employees who use the preferred providers may not be charged copayments or deductibles.

Utilization Review. Massachusetts workers' compensation law stipulates that insurers must contract with utilization review agents to develop utilization review programs (that is, systems for reviewing the necessity of healthcare services to determine whether such services should be covered. Utilization review agents must be approved by the department which will provide a list of approved agents annually.

Rehabilitation. Massachusetts provides a Rehabilitation Board to establish a list of physicians qualified to provide rehabilitation services for seriously injured workers. Insurers may ask the employee to be evaluated by vocational rehabilitation specialists but not more than once every six months. A vocational rehabilitation program lasting up to 104 weeks may be offered to eligible workers.

Compensation. Massachusetts requires that compensation payments begin within 14 days after the insurer receives the employer's first injury report, unless benefits have been denied. Compensation is not payable for the first five days following disability unless the disability lasts 21 or more days. If incapacity lasts more than five days but fewer than 21, compensation begins on the sixth day of incapacity.

Massachusetts law states that compensation is based on an employee's average weekly wage, but if the employee's wages would be expected to increase over the time compensation is paid this will be taken into consideration in determining benefits. Under Massachusetts law, temporary total disability is payable at 60 percent of regular wages up to a maximum of 100 percent of the average weekly state wage ($749.69 through September 30, 2000) for a maximum of 156 weeks. Permanent total disability is payable at 66 ☐ percent of regular wages, with the same maximum, after temporary benefits are exhausted. Partial disability payments under Massachusetts law equal 60 percent of the difference between pre-disability and post-disability wages, with the same maximum as for total disability. Massachusetts provides for an additional $6.00 weekly for each person dependent on the worker.

Massachusetts workers' compensation law provides for cost-of-living increases for workers who have been on permanent total disability for 24 months and sometimes for workers with permanent partial disabilities.

Second-Injury Fund. Under Massachusetts law, a second injury which results in a substantially greater disability or in death when added to a previous physical impairment is covered by the employer or insurer at the time of its occurrence through a special second-injury fund. Benefits must be paid in full for the first 104 weeks. After that, the second-injury fund will reimburse up to 75 percent of benefits paid. To qualify for this reimbursement, the employer must have known of the pre-existing condition and must request reimbursement within two years of the date of the benefit payment.

Survivor Benefits. Massachusetts provides for an unmarried widow or widower to receive 66 ⅔ percent of the deceased workers' average weekly wage, with the same maximum as above, plus $6 a week for each child. If there is no surviving spouse, the children divide the amount payable. Benefits to total dependents will continue for up to 250 weeks but will continue beyond this for dependent children under age 18.

Penalties under Massachusetts Law

Massachusetts law provides for the following penalties for violations of aspects of the workers' compensation laws:

- Failure to report losses as required for special assessment purposes is punishable by a fine of $1,000 a month.

- Failure to pay assessment is punishable by a fine of 5 percent of uncollected amounts every 30 days.

- An employer's failure to insure is punishable by criminal penalties including a fine of $1,500, one year's imprisonment, or both, plus a possible civil penalty of up to $250 a day. Uninsured employers are also subject to stop-work orders.

- Violations of preferred provider arrangements are punishable by a fine of up to $10,000 per violation.

- A late filing fee of $100 per day may be imposed for failing to meet deadlines.

- Employers or insurers who attempt to secure a release from an injured worker in return for a lump-sum payment may be fined $10,000.

- Illegal or fraudulent conduct in a dispute resolution is punishable by a penalty six times the state average weekly wage payable to the aggrieved employee or insurer.

- Employees who fail to report earnings to an insurer may be liable for civil or criminal penalties plus suspension of benefits.

- Required payments not made within 60 days of an employee's claim are subject to interest of 10 percent a year.

- Insurers who fail to pay compensation or to notify parties of denial of compensation within 14 days of receiving the injury report must pay the employee a $200 penalty.

Advantages and Disadvantages of Workers' Compensation

The workers' compensation system is designed to protect employees, and the advantages of the system for them are evident. There are some advantages for employers who participate in the system as well:

- Employer liabilities under the workers' compensation system are limited. In exchange for the benefits guaranteed by the workers' compensation laws, employees give up the right to sue employers for covered injuries. Employees still may be able to sue if the injury was caused by someone other than the employer (such as an independent contractor) or by a defective product.

- The laws specify the types of benefits employers must pay employees.

- Planning is easier because costs are predictable.

There are, of course, disadvantages for the employer:

- Employers' premiums may be high if they have a record of frequent accidents.
- Filing requirements may increase administrative burdens.
- Spurious workers' compensation claims may take up much time.

Note: The exclusive-remedy provisions in workers' compensation that protect employers from liability in case of occupational illness or accidents do not bar employees from pursuing ADA claims. Applying a state workers' compensation law's exclusivity provision to bar an individual's ADA claim would violate the Supremacy Clause of the U.S. Constitution and seriously diminish the civil rights protection Congress granted to persons with disabilities. The last part of this chapter details the interactions of the ADA and workers' compensation laws.

Procedures in Benefit Claims

Employees' Responsibilities

When a worker is injured or contracts a work-related illness, he or she must report the event to the employer. Most states require the employee to report the work-related sickness or injury within two to 20 days after its occurrence or as soon as the injury or illness is discovered in situations where the illness or injury occurs over time (as with breathing problems or carpal-tunnel syndrome).

Following the reporting of the problem employees should seek the medical treatment they need. They next must file a claim with the employer's insurance company or with the self-insuring employer, using forms that employers must provide. The required written report of the accident should contain the employee's name and address; the time, place, nature, and cause of the injury; and should be signed by the employee or a representative.

Employees also have certain rights under some state laws, including the right to a workers' compensation lawyer if their medical claims are rejected.

Massachusetts Administrative Procedures

Massachusetts workers' compensation law (Ch. 152) provides the following procedures for filing claims:

- Injured employees must file a claim within four years of the injury. Claims must be filed within one year of a death. The claim must be filed on an approved form and must state what benefits are due and unpaid and must be accompanied by an insurer's notice of denial.

- Injured employees must notify the employer in writing as soon as practicable. Notice is considered given if an employee is found dead at the worksite.

- If an insurer contests or stops or reduces payment the employee may file Form 110, *Employee Claim Form*, with the department. An informal conciliation proceeding will then be held. If the conciliation fails to settle the dispute a conference will be scheduled with an administrative judge who may issue a temporary order.

- If either side contests the judge's order, a full hearing will be held before the same judge. The judge's decision may be appealed to the Reviewing Board.

- If the Reviewing Board fails to bring the parties to a resolution either party may appeal to the Massachusetts Court of Appeals and then to the State's Supreme Judicial Court. No jury trial is available.

Employers' Responsibilities

In addition to ensuring they have the best types of workers' compensation coverage available to them, employers have specific responsibilities when employees notify them of work-related accidents or illnesses:

- **Take every accident report seriously.** Even if you suspect that an illness or injury report is spurious, you should still act as if you took the report seriously, since you could be sued if you fail to respond properly to a legitimate report.

- **Respond to the employee's needs.** Employers should ensure that the ill or hurt employee gets the needed medical help and they should accompany the employee to the medical provider if necessary.

- **Provide information on available insurance.** Employers should inform the injured or sick employee that insurance is available to cover the situation.

- **Document the incident.** Employers must detail exactly what happened within 24 hours of the incident.

- **File an accident report.** Employers are ultimately responsible for filing the accident report with the insurance company providing workers' compensation coverage, so they must follow up with the employee to ensure the report is filed within the time limit. Whenever possible, the report should be completed in the employee's own handwriting and should include the statement, "This is a true, correct, and complete statement," above the employee's signature. The supervisor should also sign and date the completed form. When an employee will not cooperate with the employer's procedures for filing the accident report, the lack of cooperation should be noted on the report: "Employee was requested to complete and sign this report as a true and complete statement of this alleged incident, but refused to do so on this date."

  Accident reports must contain the following:
  - Accident date and time.
  - Specific place of accident.
  - Details of how the accident happened.
  - Job activity, machines, products involved.
  - Precise description of the injury.
  - Names of any witnesses.
  - Supervisor's name.
  - Date and time incident was reported, to whom (name, title, etc.).

- **Designate an employee-contact person.** Someone should be designated to keep in touch with the injured or ill employee and this individual should be identified on the report. This person should be able to explain the benefits available to the employee and should follow up with the employee's medical provider to monitor the employee's status.

- **Investigate the accident.** Employers must investigate the accident or illness to determine how it happened and to ensure there is no recurrence. Someone should gather material evidence, take pictures, talk to witnesses, etc. Employers must determine whether the accident was indeed work-related, the ideal situation since workers' compensation laws thus protect employers from liability. Some injuries may not clearly be work-related and employers must ensure they gather any possible information to convince an insurer that indeed they are. Employers are also responsible for gathering any information relevant to a possible claim that a negligent third party or piece of defective equipment contributed to the accident.

- **Monitor the accuracy of claims reporting to the National Council on Compensation Insurance.** Since inaccurate claims reports affect an employer's premiums, employers should ensure that they or their agent monitors claims reporting. They should also monitor any insurers' audits of company payroll to ensure that workers are properly classified, thus further controlling premium costs.

Developing a Workers' Compensation Policy

When developing a workers' compensation policy, employers must consider the workers' compensation laws of the state in which they operate, although, as we have seen, there is much that is standard in all workers' compensation laws—the no-fault aspect, the fact that workers' compensation is the only remedy for workers injured on the job, the fact that the cost is borne entirely by the employer (although ultimately by the consumer), etc. Employers should formalize the procedures listed above along the lines of the two types of policies outlined below.

Standard Policy

A standard policy will spell out the responsibilities of employees and supervisors in cases of on-the-job injuries or work-related illnesses. Additionally, a standard workers' compensation policy will provide other guidelines for employees and employers:

- Employees will be informed that they are not permitted to use group health plans for injuries or illnesses covered under the Workers' Compensation Act.
- Employees are not allowed to use personal accrued leave time at the same time as they are receiving workers' compensation benefits.
- Employees filing fraudulent claims for workers' compensation will be subject to prosecution by the employer.
- Employers must investigate all workers' compensation claims.
- Employees with questions about their coverage or seeking information about the workers' compensation program must contact the Human Resources Department.

Detailed Policy

A more detailed workers' compensation policy would spell out the responsibilities of employees and supervisors in more detail, indicating the time limits for reporting injuries and illnesses. A detailed policy would also specify a workers' compensation manager and the responsibilities of this individual.

The detailed policy would also indicate the exact sorts of medical coverage available to the employee, the waiting period mandated by the state for wage replacement, and the relation between workers' compensation leave and payments and such things as the Family and Medical Leave Act, sick leave, and paid leave. A detailed policy would also spell out the penalty for fraudulent claims, including the possibility of disciplinary action including termination as well as imprisonment and fines.

Reducing Workers' Compensation Costs

Employers can do some things to help keep their workers' compensation premiums reasonable.

Provide Education and Safety Programs

The safer your workplace, the fewer the injuries and illnesses that will occur. The fewer injuries and illnesses, the lower your workers' compensation premiums. The better employees are trained, the better they will perform their jobs. As we discuss in **Chapter 35, Safety in the Workplace**, extensive safety programs—characterized by top-down management commitment—and the development of a safety culture in the workplace can go far towards creating an accident- and injury-free environment. Indeed, the existence of a strong safety program may be essential in persuading an insurer to provide coverage.

When injuries do happened, however, supervisors should know how to help workers fill out the necessary workers' compensation forms. They should also be prepared to follow the employees through the steps leading up to returning to work. Additional help and information will calm employees down, increase their sense of job security, and help them want to return to work rather than to try to "beat the system." At the very least supervisors must be trained in the proper way to report accidents and injuries. They must be cautioned not to authorize medical care without management's approval.

Investigate Claims Thoroughly

Employers must ensure that all claims are thoroughly investigated and they should follow up on all claims submitted. To guard against spurious claims for workers' compensation, employers need to pay attention to signs of possible fraud:

- Monday morning accidents.
- Unwitnessed accidents.
- Accidents occurring to new employees or employees about to retire.
- Injuries following discipline, demotion, or transfer.
- Claims from employees with private disability insurance.
- Claims from employees with histories of on-the-job injuries.
- Claims from employees with high-risk hobbies (skiing, snowmobiling).
- Delays in reporting accidents.
- Several versions of an accident.
- Claims from employees with financial or domestic problems.
- Claims for injuries not received on the job.
- Discrepancies between reported injuries and medical evaluations.

Monitor Each Case

A fundamental way to control costs is to keep in touch with the injured or ill employee after the claim is filed and benefits begin. Often the injured or ill employee is ignored and his or her only reminder of the job is the weekly compensation check. The lack of regular communication with representatives of the company may weaken an employee's resolve to return to work. Hospital visits, calls to employees' homes, and handwritten notes are all good examples of useful follow-up. All provide the personal touch and reassure the employee that the company cares and is concerned with his or her well being. Such contact also gives employers the chances to ensure that indeed the worker is at home recuperating and not participating in activities that might inhibit recovery or working elsewhere.

Employers should ensure that injured or ill employees have the best medical care available. An employer should know which medical facilities and doctors are available in the area and should choose the best available. The medical facilities and doctors should be told the nature of your company's work, the job descriptions of your employees, and whether light duty is an option. Selecting the best medical care and properly communicating with the medical care providers may get the employee back to work sooner; reduce the degree of permanent disability; and save money on extended, improper, or unnecessary care.

The injured or ill employee should be required to have his or her physician provide reports dealing with diagnosis, prognosis, and course of care before you approve paying medical bills or for lost time. Employees should be required to see an employer-selected doctor as soon as possible if they have been treated by their own doctor. Payment for ongoing medical care and lost time should be based on the opinions of physicians.

Develop a Return-to-Work Program

The employer's most important involvement in the workers' compensation system may begin when the treating physician releases the injured employee to return to work in some type of modified form. The employer can make a difference in the system by developing an aggressive rehiring program, especially in the areas of light work. Such a program can result in significant savings.

A job offered to an employee recovering from an occupational illness or injury need not be the same job the employee was performing at the time he or she left work. It can be lighter work or at different hours. It does, however, need to fit the physical limitations imposed by the doctor and be within the worker's abilities. If the job is initially refused it should be re-offered regularly. The employee cannot collect benefits if he or she continues to refuse, unless a judge rules that the refusal is justified.

Once an employee returns to work, employers must document the return and subsequent duty status. Throughout the entire series of events--from the initial incident and the reporting of the incident through the medical care and regular reporting by physicians, up to the return to work and after--employers should strive to maintain the best possible relationship with their employees. Employers should treat all claims alike, legitimate or not, and follow them through to their conclusion. Employees should be shown that the company cares about them, their families, and their return to productive employment, and they will respond with a sense of loyalty and responsibility.

Coordinate Workers' Compensation Benefits and Other Benefits

In some instances it may be possible to reduce workers' compensation premiums by offsetting workers' compensation benefits with benefits from other sources. Some possibilities are listed below.

Retirement Plans

If an employee is receiving workers' compensation benefits and retires, it may be possible for an employer to offset the workers' compensation benefits with the retirement benefits rather than paying both—as long as the retirement plan does not prohibit this.

Medical Plans

If an employer's medical plan pays benefits for some of the same workplace-related medical expenses as workers' compensation, the two insurance carriers should work out a coordination of benefits that would preclude overlapping coverage.

Social Security

Employees who are entitled to workers' compensation benefits should be instructed to see what Social Security benefits they are entitled to, since sometimes Social Security will pay for disability benefits and many states do not allow double payment to an employee.

Workers' Compensation and the Americans with Disabilities Act

General Interactions

An employee injured or made ill on the job may become subject to the Americans with Disabilities Act if the accident or illness creates a mental or physical impairment substantially limiting a major life function. In this case the employer would have to make reasonable accommodation in finding the employee a suitable job, including a light-duty job. The employee cannot simply be fired. Additionally, reasonable accommodation may have to include extending the leave period.

Some questions that may arise out of the simultaneous application of the ADA and the Workers' Compensation Act include the following:

- **Does everyone with an occupational injury have a disability within the meaning of the ADA?** The answer to this is "No," since the ADA defines *disability* as a physical or mental impairment that substantially limits a major life activity, along with a record of having such an impairment or as being regarded as having such an impairment. Impairments resulting from occupational injury may not be severe enough to substantially limit a major life activity or they may be only temporary, with little or no long-term effect.

- **Does every person who has filed a workers' compensation claim have a disability under the "record of" portion of the ADA definition?** This is another "No" answer since a person has a disability under the "record of" portion of the ADA definition only if he or she has a history of or has been regarded as having a life-activity-limiting disability.

- **Could a person with an occupational injury have a disability under the "regarded as" portion of the ADA definition of disability?** This might be a "Yes" answer. A person with an occupational injury would be considered to fall under the "regarded as" portion of the ADA definition of disability in the following instances:

    - If he or she were treated by the employer as if the injury were substantially limiting even if, in fact, the injury does not substantially limit a major life activity. If, for example, an employer refuses to return an employee who had a temporary back injury to the employee's former job because the job requires some lifting, that employee has a disability under the ADA.

    - If the attitude of others toward the impairment substantially limits a major life activity for the individual. For example, if an occupational accident results in an employee's facial disfigurement and the employer refuses to return the employee to his or her former position of dealing with customers because of a fear of negative reactions, that employee would have a disability under the ADA.

    - If an employee with no impairment is treated as having a substantial limiting impairment. For example, an employee with a temporary back injury is fired from a position requiring heavy labor because of the employer's fear of the worker's re-injuring his or her back. The employer regards the employee as having an impairment that disqualifies him or her from a class of jobs and thus as having a major limitation on the life activity of working—that employee has a disability under the ADA.

The ADA interacts with workers' compensation in other ways, specifically in such employment decisions as hiring, allowing injured employees to return to work, and providing reasonable accommodation.

Interviewing and Hiring

Several questions can illustrate the relationship between the ADA and workers' compensation in the interviewing and hiring process:

- **May an employer ask questions about an applicant's prior occupational injuries or workers' compensation claims?** This gets a limited "Yes" answer in that such questions may be asked only after the employer has made a conditional offer of employment and only if these questions are asked of all entering employees in the job category.

- **May an employer require a medical examination of an applicant to obtain information about the existence or nature of prior occupational injuries?** This is another qualified "Yes," since such an examination could be required but only after a conditional offer of employment has been made and only if all entering employees in the same job category are required to undergo a medical examination. Follow-up examinations based exclusively on findings from initial medical information may be required of specific employees.

- **May an employer obtain information about an applicant's prior occupational injuries or workers' compensation claims from a third party?** At no time may an employer request information about an applicant from a third party (for example a previous employer) that it could not lawfully get from the applicant.

- **May an employer refuse to hire a person with a disability simply because of the assumption that the applicant poses some increased risk of occupational injury and subsequently of increased workers' compensation costs?** Unless the employer can show that such an individual poses a direct threat, such a refusal would violate the intent of the ADA to eliminate stereotyping because of disability. A potential health or safety risk is not enough to justify failure to hire here. There must actually be a direct-threat level of risk involved, that is, a significant risk to the health or safety of the individual or others that cannot be eliminated or reduced by reasonable accommodation. Even if state laws might permit or require exclusion of such an individual, the ADA supercedes such laws.

- **May an employer refuse to hire a person with a disability simply because the person sustained a prior occupational injury?** The mere fact that a disabled individual has sustained a previous occupational injury does not in itself establish that his or her current employment in the position in question poses a direct threat. In some cases, however, evidence of a previous occupational injury may be relevant to the direct-threat question in the following ways:

  - The relationship between the previous occupational injury and the person's disability. If employees without disabilities had similar injuries, the injury may not be related to the disability.

  - The circumstances surrounding the previous occupational injury. The injury may have been caused by the actions of others or by the lack of appropriate safety devices or procedures. For example, a person with insulin-dependent diabetes was seriously injured while operating a saw for a lumber mill. The injury was caused by the failure of a safety device and was unrelated to the individual's diabetes. The individual applies for a similar position with another lumber mill but, after making a conditional job offer, the employer learns of the previous injury and assuming it was related to the diabetes refuses to hire the individual. The employer in this case is violating the ADA since the previous injury does not constitute evidence that the applicant poses a direct threat in the saw operator's position.

- The similarity between the position in question and the position in which the injury occurred. The previous position may have involved hazards not present in the position under consideration.

- The relationship between the person's present condition and his or her condition at the time of the previous injury. If the person's condition has improved, the prior injury may have little significance. For example, if a person with a previous back injury suffered on the job is now completely recovered, an employer could not refuse to hire him or her because of fear that the individual would re-injure his or her back doing heavy labor and thus increase workers' compensation premiums.

- The number and frequency of previous occupational injuries. If, for example, an employer discovers that an applicant for a position requiring heavy lifting has had several previous shoulder injuries in similar positions over the past few years, and that further such employment could render the shoulder useless, refusal to hire would not violate the ADA since the position poses a direct threat to the individual. Here, of course, the employer would also have to consider whether some reasonable accommodation could be made that would allow the employee to perform the job without causing possible injury to him or herself.

- The nature and severity of the prior injury. If the injury was minor it may have little significance.

- The amount of time the person has worked in the same or similar position since the previous injury without subsequent injury.

- Whether the risk can be lowered or eliminated by a reasonable accommodation.

Continuing Employment/Return to Work

The ADA and workers' compensation considerations also interact in some decisions relating to continuing employment as the questions below illustrate:

♦ **May an employer ask disability-related questions or require medical examinations of an employee when the employee experiences an occupational injury or when the employee seeks to return to work after such an injury?** Provided that the questions and examination are job related and consistent with business necessity, the answer to both the possibility of asking disability-related questions and to requiring a medical examination is "Yes." The questions and the exam must grow out of an employer's legitimate belief that the occupational injury will impair the employee's ability to perform essential job functions or that the injury could pose a direct threat to the employee or the employee's coworkers. The questions and the examination must not exceed the scope of the specific injury and its impact on the employee's ability to do the job.

♦ **May an employer ask disability-related questions or require a medical examination of an employee with an occupational injury to ascertain the extent of the workers' compensation liability?** The ADA does not prohibit this but the questions and the examination must be consistent with the state law's intended purpose of determining an employee's eligibility for workers' compensation payments. The questions and examination must be limited to the specific occupational injury and may not be required more often than is necessary to determine the employee's initial or continued need for workers' compensation benefits. Excessive questioning or requiring of medical examinations may constitute disability-based harassment, prohibited by the ADA.

- **If an employee with a disability-related occupational injury requests a reasonable accommodation may the employer ask for documentation of the disability?** If the need for reasonable accommodation is not obvious, the employer may require documentation of the employee's entitlement to such accommodation. This does not, however, allow an employer access to unrelated medical records.

- **May an employer require that an employee with a disability-related occupational injury be able to return to full duty before allowing the employee to return to work?** An employer cannot require that an employee with a disability-related occupational injury who can perform essential job functions but who may not be able to perform marginal functions or who may require an accommodation to return to full duty. Here the employer may try to define full duty to include the performance of essential and marginal duties of a position without accommodation, but the employer may not make this designation.

- **May an employer refuse to allow an employee with a disability-related occupational injury to return to work because the employer fears that the employee poses some increased risk of re-injury and thus of increasing workers' compensation costs?** A refusal such as this would constitute discrimination on the basis of disability unless the employer can show that the return of the employee to the position would pose a direct threat. The existence of the disability-related occupational injury does not in itself constitute proof that the employee is unable to perform his or her job or that returning him or her to work constitutes a direct threat.

    Example: A clerk typist who has broken her wrist moving office furniture has been certified by her physician as completely healed and ready to return to work. Because of fear the employee will re-injure her wrist performing her duties, the employer refuses to allow her to return to work. The employer is in violation of the ADA for the following reasons:

    - The injury was not caused by normal office duties.
    - The wrist has completely healed.
    - There is little risk the employee will injure her wrist through repetitive motion.

    On the other hand, if an employee returns to work after an occupational injury and is unable to carry out duties as before—as in the case of a supervisor whose fractured ankles have only partially healed and who no longer can do the extensive walking the position requires—an employer is justified in refusing to allow the employee to return to work if there is evidence that doing so would likely cause the employee serious harm. In such a situation, however, the employer would be expected to try to reassign the employee.

- **May an employer refuse to let an employee return to work simply because of a workers' compensation determination that the worker has a permanent disability or is totally disabled?** Since workers' compensation laws are different from the ADA and may use different standards for evaluating whether an individual has a disability or is capable of working, employers cannot make their re-employment decisions on workers' compensation determinations. For example, under a workers' compensation statute a person who loses vision in both eyes or who loses the use of either arm or of both legs may have a permanent total disability although he or she may be able to work. The workers' compensation determination may be helpful in deciding whether an employee can perform the essential functions of a certain job or whether the employee may pose a threat upon returning to work—but it is not relevant regarding the individual's ability to return to work in general.

- **Under the ADA, is a rehabilitation counselor, physician, or other specialist responsible for deciding whether an employee with a disability-related occupational injury is ready to return to work?** It is the employer's responsibility to decide if an employee can perform the essential functions of the job, with or without accommodation, and can perform them without posing a direct threat. Employers may find it helpful to get information from specialists regarding the specific functional limitations and abilities of disabled employees and appropriate reasonable accommodations. If, for example, an employer provides a rehabilitation counselor with details of the employee's position and the nature of the work to be performed, plus the nature of the work environment including possible hazards, the counselor could contribute information helpful to the employer in making the return-to-work decision.

Reasonable Accommodation and Workers' Compensation

The ADA requires employers to make reasonable accommodation to the known physical or mental limitations of an otherwise qualified individual with a disability. The questions below explain some problems associated with providing ADA-mandated reasonable accommodation in the context of workers' compensation:

- **Does the ADA require an employer to make reasonable accommodation for an employee with an occupational injury who does not have a disability as defined by the ADA?** In cases where an employee has received workers' compensation for an occupational injury not considered a disability under the ADA, employers are under no obligation to make reasonable accommodation.

- **May an employer discharge an employee who is temporarily unable to work because of a disability-related occupational injury?** In a situation such as this, if leave is a reasonable accommodation and would not impose an undue hardship on the employer the employee may not be discharged.

- **What are the reinstatement rights of an employee with a disability-related occupational injury?** Unless an employer can demonstrate that holding the position open would impose an undue hardship, the employee is entitled to return to the same position. If the employee needs more leave than can be given without imposing an undue hardship on the employer, the employer must look for a vacant equivalent position to which the employee can be assigned for his or her continuing leave. If no vacant equivalent position is available, the employer must try to find a vacant position at a lower level. If this is impossible, continued leave is not required as a reasonable accommodation.

    Note: Employers may provide reasonable accommodation other than leave, even when an injured employee has requested leave as a reasonable accommodation, unless the employee requests leave which is available to all employees, such as accrued paid leave or unpaid leave.

- **Must employers reallocate job duties of an employee with a disability-related occupational injury as part of reasonable accommodation?** If the duties to be reallocated are marginal ones that the employee cannot perform because of the disability, they must be reallocated. Employers do not, however, need to reallocate essential functions of the position.

- **May employers reassign employees with disability-related occupational injuries to different positions instead of trying to accommodate the employees in their original positions?** Employers must first determine if the employees could perform the essential functions of their original job with or without reasonable accommodation such as job restructuring, modification of equipment, or a part-time work schedule. If accommodation is impossible, reassignment may be considered.

- **Must employers reassign employees who can no longer perform the essential functions of their former jobs with or without reasonable accommodation?** If employees with disability-related occupational injuries are no longer able to perform the essential functions of their former job with or without reasonable accommodation, they must be reassigned to an equivalent vacant position if one is available or to a lower graded position for which they are qualified, unless such reassignment imposes an undue hardship on an employer. Note here that the ADA does not require employers to create a new position or to bump current employees from their positions to create vacancies for disabled workers.

- **May employers substitute vocational rehabilitation services for a reasonable accommodation for employees with disability-related occupational injuries?** Since an employee's rights under the ADA are separate from workers' compensation entitlements, employers cannot substitute vocational rehabilitation for reasonable accommodation. Employers must accommodate employees in their current positions unless this imposes undue hardship on the employer.

- **May employers make workplace modifications that are not required forms of reasonable accommodation under the ADA to offset workers' compensation costs?** Nothing in the ADA prohibits employers from making workplace modifications to accommodate employees with occupational injuries. An employer may, for example, lower production standards for an occupationally injured employee as a way of returning the employee to work more quickly.

- **Does the ADA prohibit employers from creating light duty positions for employees injured on the job?** Employers may recognize a special obligation to create a light duty position for an employee injured on the job as long as this is done on a non-discriminatory basis. Employers need not create light duty positions for non-occupationally injured disabled individuals, since the ADA does not require employers to create positions as a form of reasonable accommodation. Employers must, however, make other reasonable accommodations for disabled individuals, including redistributing marginal functions of a job, providing modified scheduling, or reassigning an individual.

The term *light duty* can mean a variety of things. Generally, light duty refers to temporary or permanent work that is physically or mentally less demanding than normal job duties. Some employers use the term to mean simply excusing an employee from performing the job functions he or she is unable to perform because of an impairment. Light duty may also identify certain positions with less-demanding duties created specifically to provide alternative work for employees unable to perform some or all of their normal duties. Employers may also refer to any positions that are sedentary or less demanding as light duty.

It may be that in some cases the only reasonable accommodation for an individual with a disability not the result of an on-the-job injury may be similar to—or indeed equivalent to—a light duty position. Employers may not refuse to provide this sort of accommodation because such positions are reserved for employees injured on the job. The ADA would require reassigning a disabled individual to a light duty position unless this could be proven to impose an undue hardship on the employer. If, for example, an assembly-line worker with multiple sclerosis requests reassignment to a vacant light duty position and is refused the reassignment because the position is reserved for employees injured on the job even though the reassignment would impose no hardship on the employer, the employer has violated the ADA.

- **If an employer has only temporary light duty positions must it still provide a permanent light duty position for an employee with a disability-related occupational injury?** The ADA does not require employers to change the content, nature, or functions of their positions. Employers are free to determine if light duty positions are temporary or permanent. If an employer decides that light duty positions are only temporary the employer is under no obligation of offer permanent light duty positions for employees with disability-related occupational injuries.

Workers' Compensation and Other Federal Laws

Employers must also be aware of employees' Family and Medical Leave Act rights and of their COBRA rights when employees are on extended disability leave under workers' compensation laws. If, for example, an employee with an occupational injury requests leave as a reasonable accommodation and qualifies for leave under the FMLA, an employer may not require the employee to remain on the job with modification of duties or some other accommodation in lieu of taking the leave of absence.

Chapter 28
The NLRA and Labor Relations

Introduction

The National Labor Relations Act (NLRA) regulates private-sector employers, employees, and unions. The NLRA is administered and enforced primarily by the National Labor Relations Board (NLRB), which gets its authority from Congress. This chapter looks at the functions of the NLRB, clarifies the relationship between collective bargaining and the NLRA, and reviews some unfair labor practices the NLRB is designed to prevent.

The National Labor Relations Act is intended to define and protect the rights of employees and employers and unions, to encourage collective bargaining, and to eliminate certain practices on the parts of labor and management that are considered to interfere with interstate commerce. In its enforcement of the act, the NLRB excludes certain types of employment and industries. For these types of employment and industries, state labor law, the Federal Railway Labor Act, or other state and federal laws may apply. Additionally, public-sector employers are generally exempt from the NLRA and are instead governed by state public employment laws.

Federal Law: The National Labor Relations Act

NLRB Functions

The NLRB has two main functions:

- To conduct representation elections and certify the results.
- To prevent employers and unions from engaging in unfair labor practices.

Jurisdictional Limits

The NLRB could enforce the NLRA in all cases involving enterprises whose operations affect interstate commerce. It has, however, chosen to limit itself to cases involving enterprises whose effect on commerce is substantial, as determined by a minimum yearly total dollar value of business. These limits are detailed below.

Non-retail Enterprises

The NLRB will assert jurisdiction over a non-retail employer with $50,000 or more of direct or indirect outflow of goods or services across state lines or that has at least $50,000 of direct or indirect inflow of goods or services from suppliers in other states.

Retail Enterprises

The NLRB will assert jurisdiction over a retail enterprise with at least $500,000 in total annual business.

Other Enterprises

The NLRB has also established annual revenue-based standards for other businesses:

- **Office Buildings.** Total annual revenue of $100,000, of which $25,000 or more is derived from organizations that meet any of the standards established for non-retail enterprises except the indirect standard.
- **Hotels, Motels, and Residential Apartment Houses.** Total annual volume of business of at least $500,000.
- **Private Universities and Colleges.** At least $1,000,000 in gross annual revenue from all sources (excluding contributions not available for operating expenses because of limitations imposed by the grantor).
- **Privately Operated Healthcare Institutions.**
    - Hospitals: Gross annual revenues of at least $250,000.
    - Nursing homes, visiting nurses associations, and related facilities: total annual volume of business of at least $100,000.
- **Public Utilities.** At least $250,000 total annual volume of business, or $50,000 direct or indirect outflow or inflow.
- **Newspapers.** At least $200,000 total annual volume of business.
- **Radio, Telegraph, Television, and Telephone Enterprises.** At least $100,000 total annual volume of business.
- **Social Services Providers.** At least $250,000 gross annual revenues except for those for whom the NLRB had already set a specific standard; for homemaker services and visiting nurse associations, that amount was set at $100,000.

In addition to the standards listed above, the NLRB applies separate revenue based standards for other businesses:

- Transportation enterprises, links and channels of interstate commerce.
- Transit systems.
- Taxicab companies.
- Associations.
- Symphony orchestras.
- Law firms and legal-assistance programs.
- National defense.

- Legally operated gambling casinos.
- Enterprises in the Territories and the District of Columbia.

Areas Not Covered by the NLRA

The NLRB has decided not to exercise jurisdiction over racetracks; owners, breeders, and trainers of racehorses; and real-estate brokers. Additionally, the NLRA specifically excludes the following employees:

- Agricultural laborers.
- Domestic servants.
- Individuals employed by their parents or spouses.
- Independent contractors.
- Supervisors and managers.
- Individuals employed by employers, such as airlines and railroads, subject to the Railway Labor Act.
- Government employees, including those employed by the U.S. Government, any government corporation except the U.S. Postal Service and the Federal Reserve Bank, or any state or political subdivision such as a city, town, or school district.

Collective Bargaining under the NLRA
Selecting Bargaining Representatives

The NLRA requires employers to bargain with the representatives selected by employees. The most common way for employees to select bargaining representatives is by a secret ballot election conducted by the NLRB pursuant to a petition filed by an employee, group of employees, or any individual or labor organization acting on behalf of employees.

When a petition is filed, the NLRB must investigate it, hold a hearing if necessary, and direct the election if it finds that a question of representation exists. The investigation is intended to determine, among other things, the following:

- Whether the NLRB has jurisdiction to conduct an election.
- Whether there is sufficient employee interest to justify an election.
- Whether a question of representation exists.
- Whether the election is sought in an appropriate unit of employees.
- Whether the representative named in the petition is qualified.
- Whether there are any barriers to an election in the form of contracts or prior elections.

Determining what is an appropriate unit of employees is often the most critical determination the NLRB makes. A *unit of employees* is a group of two or more employees who share a community of interests and may therefore reasonably be grouped together for purposes of collective bargaining. In general, those employees who have the same or substantially the same interests concerning wages, hours, and working conditions are placed in a bargaining unit.

Types of Elections

Petitions for several types of elections can be filed under the NLRA:

- A *certification election*, an election to determine if nonunion employees want to be represented by a union.

- A *decertification election*, an election to determine if employees wish to retain or vote out (decertify) the individual or labor organization currently acting as their bargaining representative.

- A *union-security deauthorization election*, an election to determine, by secret ballot, whether employees covered by a union-security agreement wish to withdraw their representative's authority to continue the agreement. This type of election can be brought by the filing of a petition signed by at least 30 percent of the employees covered by the agreement.

Additionally, elections can be conducted in the following situations:

- When one union attempts to replace another as the bargaining agent, a practice known as *raiding*.

- When an employer requests an election to determine if an incumbent union has the continuing support of a majority of the employees. This request can only be made on the basis of an employer's reasonable, good faith doubt that such support exists.

The Representation Election

The NLRB makes its determination regarding employee representation by a secret-ballot election. In a representation election, employees are given a choice between one or more bargaining representatives or no representative at all.

If the employer and the individual or labor organization claiming to represent the employees agree to voluntarily resolve the details of the election, either of two types of consent-election agreements may be used:

- *Agreement for Consent Election (pure consent agreement).* This provides for the NLRB Regional Director to resolve any dispute arising from the proceedings.

- *Stipulation for Certification on Consent Election (stip agreement).* This provides for the NLRB to determine any subsequent dispute.

In either agreement, the parties state the time and place agreed upon, the choices to be included on the ballot, and a method to determine who is eligible to vote. They also authorize the NLRB Regional Director to conduct the election.

If the parties are unable to reach an agreement, the NLRA authorizes the NLRB to order an election after a hearing. The act also authorizes the NLRB to delegate to its regional directors the determination of matters concerning elections. Such matters as who may vote, when the election will be held, and what standards of conduct will be imposed upon the parties are decided in accordance with the NLRB's rules and its decisions.

Conducting Elections

NLRB elections must be conducted in accordance with strict standards designed to give the voting employees an opportunity to freely indicate whether they wish to be represented for purposes of collective bargaining. Election details include the following:

- Date, time, and place of the election.

- Voter eligibility determined by the appropriate payroll period. In the case of either type of consent election agreement, the appropriate payroll period is usually the one, which precedes the approval of the agreement. In the case of an election directed after hearing, the appropriate payroll period is usually the one immediately preceding the direction of election.

- Notice of election. Although the NLRB does not specify a particular time for posting the notice before the election, it has set aside elections because of late posting of notices. The NLRB has an affirmative-action duty to present election notices in languages employees will understand.

- Determination of the respective parties' election observers and their duties (a pre-election conference of the parties and the board agent is usually held).

- Number of polling places.

- Voter release schedule, if required. Typically, voting times will be selected to give all eligible employees a chance to vote. In elections held in multishift, multiplant, or multi-employer situations, a schedule of voters and relief workers is established in which employees are released to vote as relief workers fill in. This schedule is determined before the election.

- Mail ballots. In appropriate circumstances, to be determined by the regional director, voting may be conducted by mail ballots.

The Excelsior List

Before an election, the employer must prepare a voter-eligibility list and file it with the NLRB regional director. This list, known as the Excelsior List, which contains the voters' names and addresses, must be filed with the director within seven days of an election's being directed or approval of a consent-election agreement. The regional director makes the list available to the parties as a way to facilitate communication and avoid the need for a challenge to the election. Deviations from the Excelsior requirements (failure to properly list eligible voters or failure to meet time requirements) may cause an election to be set aside.

Election Challenges

Any party to an election who believes the NLRB's election standards were not met may file objections to the election with the NLRB regional director under whose supervision the election was held. This must be done within seven days after the election results are furnished. If objections to the election are filed within this time, the regional director will not certify the election until the matter has been resolved. In most cases, the regional director's ruling on the objections may be appealed to the NLRB.

Objections to the conduct of an election may be based on any of the following:

- A situation where eligible voters have been deprived of the opportunity to vote, either because they were prevented from reaching the polls or because of departures from the scheduled election time.

- Interference because of conduct in and around the polling areas; for example:
  - Prolonged conversations between parties and voters waiting to vote.
  - Employer's officials being present near the voting area.
  - Extended consumption of alcohol at the election site.

- Interference with the integrity of the ballot and the ballot box.

- Conduct of NLRB agents that violates the election standards and affects the neutrality of the NLRB's procedures, such as an agent's trying to influence an employee to vote for the union.

Upon timely receipt of objections, and the furnishing by the party filing the objection of *prima facie* evidence to support the objections, the NLRB regional director must conduct an investigation. If the NLRB sustains the objections to the election, the election will be set aside and a new election conducted. If the objection is overruled, a certification of the results of the election will be issued. Where appropriate, a certification of representation will also be issued.

Prohibited Pre-election Conduct on the Part of Employers

In election proceedings, the NLRB's function is generally to assure that "laboratory conditions" exist—conditions nearly as ideal as possible so that the employee vote takes place in an atmosphere allowing free choice. Employers are prohibited from interfering with this free choice. The following are examples of employer conduct that the NLRB might consider wrongful interference with an employee's free choice:

- Prohibiting solicitation of employees during "nonworking" time such as, breaks, lunches, and before and after work.

- Prohibiting employees from wearing union emblems except in cases where such emblems would interfere with production, discipline, or safety.

- Giving a "captive audience" speech to affected employees within 24 hours of a manual ballot election.

- Unnecessarily prohibiting access to the employees such as by refusing off-duty employees access to exterior areas of the facility or by prohibiting any activity on private property open to the public.

In all of these situations, the NLRB will examine the employer's conduct to determine if a new election should be held.

More serious pre-election employer conduct may be seen by the NLRB as constituting unfair labor practices and may result in the NLRB's setting aside the election and ordering a new election. Or, in rare cases, issuing a bargaining order recognizing a union without an election.

Unfair Labor Practices

The second primary function of the NLRB is to prevent employers and unions from engaging in unfair labor practices. The NLRB, therefore, protects the statutory rights of employees from improper interference or other prohibited conduct by employers or unions.

Unfair Labor Practices by Employers

Section 7 of the NLRA, "Rights of Employees," is the focal point of the NLRA and pertains to employee right to organize and bargain collectively: "Employees shall have the right to self-organization, to form, join or assist labor organizations, to bargain collectively through representatives of their own choosing, and to engage in other concerted activities for the purpose of collective bargaining or other mutual aid or protection, and shall also have the right to refrain from any or all such activities."

Employers are forbidden to engage in five core unfair labor practices:

1. **Employers may not interfere with, restrain, or coerce employees in the exercise of the rights guaranteed in Section 7 of the NLRA.**

    Examples of employer conduct that violates this restriction include the following:

    - **Threats of reprisal and withdrawal of benefits.** Employers may not make expressed or implied threats that an employee's exercise of union activity will lead to withdrawals of benefits, including such benefits as coffee breaks, discount privileges, and employee stock plans. An employer may not threaten to close a plant or to discharge employees who vote for or promote the election of a union.

- **Promises and granting of benefits**. The employer may not promise to grant or actually grant benefits to employees to coerce them not to support or to vote against a union.

- **Interrogation and polling**. An employer may not interrogate an employee about his or her union sympathies or the sympathy of another employee if the circumstances of the interrogation demonstrate coercive conduct. Examples of coercive conduct might be interrogation near the time of an election or interrogation by the employee's supervisor requiring the employee to admit to a preference for or against a union in front of the supervisor.

- **Surveillance and photographing**. An employer may not conduct surveillance of union activities, whether conducted by supervisors, other employees acting as employer agents, or third parties such as detective agencies. An employer also may not create the impression that surveillance is being conducted. Although this prohibition does not stop employers from observing employee activities where it is conducted openly, it will in most circumstances prohibit their photographing union activity.

2. **Employers may not dominate or interfere with the formation or administration of any labor organization or contribute financial or other support to it.**

This provision outlaws company unions dominated by an employer and forbids an employer from contributing money to a union it favors or giving one union improper advantages denied to rival unions. An employer can violate this section by any of the following:

- Taking an active part in organizing a union or an employee committee to represent employees.

- Bringing pressure on employees to financially support a union, except in the enforcement of a lawful union-security agreement.

- Allowing one of several unions competing to represent employees to solicit on company premises while denying other unions the same privilege.

- Soliciting and obtaining applications for union membership and signed authorizations for deducting union dues from employees and applicants for employment during the hiring process.

The NLRB has recently extended this prohibition to prohibit employer domination of employee participation committees, where the committees are structured so that they fall within the NLRA's definition of a labor organization. These committees have become increasingly prevalent and could include quality circles, worker-improvement networks and Total Quality Control (TQM) committees.

Under recent NLRB decisions, an employee participation committee may constitute a labor organization if all of the following are true:

- Non-supervisory employees participate in the committee.

- The committee exists, at least in part, for the purpose of dealing with the employer.

- The committee deals with the employer about subjects that include grievances, labor disputes, wages, rates of pay, hours of employment, or conditions of work.

If an employee participation committee meets the statutory definition of a labor organization, the employer may not dominate or interfere with the committee. In this context, domination, interference or support may be demonstrated by the fact that the employer created the committee and defined its mission, pays employees for their time spent attending committee meetings and provides facilities and supplies for conducting the meetings.

Because of complex rules governing which types of employee participation committees might constitute labor organizations under the NLRA, employers might seek legal advice when establishing employee committees.

3. **Employers may not discriminate against employees in regard to hiring or tenure of employment or any term or condition of employment for the purpose of encouraging or discouraging membership in a labor organization.**

    In general, the NLRA makes it illegal for an employer to discriminate in employment because of an employee's union activity. Under the NLRA, discrimination is taken to include such actions as refusing to hire, discharging, demoting, assigning to a less-desirable shift or job, or withholding benefits.

    Examples of illegal discrimination under this section include the following:

    ♦ Discharging employees because they urged other employees to join a union.

    ♦ Refusing to reinstate employees when jobs they are qualified for are open because they took part in a lawful strike.

    ♦ Granting of super-seniority to those hired to replace employees engaged in a lawful strike.

    ♦ Demoting employees because they circulated a union petition.

    ♦ Discontinuing an operation at one plant where employees had joined a union and discharging the employees, followed by opening the same operation at another plant with new employees who are not in the union. This is sometimes called the runaway shop.

    ♦ Refusing to hire qualified applicants for jobs because they belong to a union.

The NLRB has adopted the following test to determine whether wrongful discrimination has occurred. The NLRB's general counsel must establish the existence of the following:

   ♦ Union activity by the employee.

   ♦ Knowledge of that activity by the employee.

   ♦ Anti-union animus on the part of the employer.

An employer who cannot disprove the fact of an employee's union activity and of having knowledge of that activity must prove that anti-union animus was not behind the employment decisions made regarding that employee. An employer must prove that the challenged action would have taken place regardless of the employee's union activity. For example, an employer may show that other employees who committed the same offense were similarly disciplined, that the employee's performance was inadequate, or that there was an economic need for the employment action such as in a plant layoff or plant closing situation.

4. **Employers may not discharge or otherwise discriminate against an employee because he or she has filed charges, given testimony under the NLRA, or engaged in other protected activity.**

    This provision guards the right of employees to seek the protection of the NLRA by using the processes of the NLRB. Employers may not discharge, lay off, or engage in other forms of discrimination in working conditions against employees who have filed charges with the NLRB, given affidavits to the NLRB, or testified at an NLRB hearing.

5. **Employers may not refuse to bargain in good faith about wages, hours of employment, or other conditions of employment with the representative selected by a majority of the employees in a unit appropriate for collective bargaining.**

    Examples of violations of this section include the following:

    ♦ Refusing to meet with the employees' representative because the employees are out on strike.

- Announcing a wage increase without consulting the employees' representative.
- Refusing to supply the employees' representative with cost and other data concerning a group-insurance plan covering the employees.
- Failing to bargain about the decision to relocate, or subcontract work or the effects of a decision to close one of the employer's plants. This type of violation is discussed further in the following section.

Duty to Bargain Over Plant Closings, Relocating, and Subcontracting

Perhaps the most difficult questions concerning an employer's duty arise with respect to major operational changes, such as sales and mergers, partial closings, relocation of unit work, and subcontracting. In general, employers do not have to bargain over decisions that are motivated by core entrepreneurial concerns. This includes such decisions as whether to shut down part of a company's business or close a plant or a subsidiary. The NLRB and the courts have not formulated consistent rules regarding an employer's duty to bargain over such issues.

Relocation Decisions

Employers are obligated to bargain over a decision to relocate a plant if the NLRB's general counsel can establish that the decision involved a relocation of unit work unaccompanied by a basic change in the nature of the employer's operation. The employer may avoid bargaining over the relocation decision, however, if one of the following can be established:

- The work performed at the new location varies significantly from the work performed at the former plant.
- The work performed at the former plant is to be discontinued entirely and not moved to the new location.
- The relocation decision involves a change in the scope and direction of the enterprise.
- Direct and/or indirect labor costs were not a factor in the relocation decision.
- If labor costs were a factor in the decision, the union could not have offered labor-cost concessions that could have changed the employer's decision to relocate.

Subcontracting

If the employer subcontracts by replacing employees in an existing bargaining unit with those of an independent contractor to perform the same work under similar employment conditions, the subcontracting decision will most likely be subject to mandatory bargaining. However, there may not be a duty to bargain over subcontracting when some of the following conditions are met:

- The subcontracting decision fundamentally alters the company's basic operation.
- The work is no longer performed at the same plant.
- The subcontracting decision is accompanied by capital investment.
- The company does not merely replace existing employees with those of an independent contractor to do the same work under similar employment conditions.
- The decision to subcontract is not motivated by factors within the collective bargaining framework, such as labor costs.

The NLRB nevertheless, is extremely reluctant to excuse bargaining in a subcontracting situation. The prudent course is to engage in decision bargaining.

Unfair Labor Practices by Unions

In addition to its restrictions on unfair labor practices by employers, the NLRA also limits certain union activities, including the following:

- Unions may not interfere with, restrain, or coerce employees in the exercise of rights guaranteed in Section 7.

- Unions may not cause or attempt to cause an employer to discriminate against an employee in violation of the anti-discrimination provision relating to union membership, or to discriminate against an employee whose membership in a labor organization has been denied or terminated on some ground other than failure to tender the dues and initiation fee uniformly required as a condition of acquiring or retaining membership.

    Under this provision of the NLRA, unions who under certain circumstances force employers to discriminate against employees are guilty of unfair labor practices. The following are some examples of unfair union labor practices in this area:

    - Insisting upon an illegal contract, such as a contract that provides that any change in the employees' choice of union would cause a termination of the employees' benefits.
    - Picketing to coerce an employer to discharge nonunion employees.
    - Applying union rules that cause an employer to discriminate against union members over nonmembers.
    - Causing an employer to force employees to become union members under threat of reprisal.

- To refuse to bargain collectively with an employer when the labor organization is the representative of the employees for the purposes of collective bargaining may constitute an unfair labor practice. Activities that may constitute an unlawful refusal to bargain include the following:

    - Insisting that an employer agree to include contract provisions that are not mandatory subjects of bargaining as a condition to the union's signing the agreement.
    - Refusing to answer an employer's request for a collective bargaining conference.
    - Refusing to bargain with the employer's chosen representatives.
    - Threatening to strike to force agreement on a non-mandatory subject of bargaining.

- To require excessive or discriminatory payments as a prerequisite to membership of the labor organization may constitute an unfair labor practice. In determining whether such payments are excessive, the NLRB will consider such factors as the practices and customs of labor organizations in the particular industry and the wages currently paid to the affected employees.

- To cause or attempt to cause an employer to pay or agree to pay for services not performed is an unfair labor practice.

- To picket or cause an employer to be picketed where the object of the picketing is to force the employer to recognize or bargain with a labor organization, unless the labor organization is currently certified as the representative of the employer's workforce may be unfair labor practice under circumstances described below:

    - An unrecognized union cannot picket when the employer has lawfully recognized another union rather than the union engaged in picketing and there is no lawful question of representation.

- An unrecognized union cannot picket to be recognized or to organize when a valid election has been held within the preceding 12 months.

Additionally, where picketing is otherwise permissible because it is not barred by either situation above, picketing may be limited to not more than 30 days if a representation petition has not been filed with the NLRB. If a petition has been filed in a timely fashion, the 30-day limitation is removed and picketing may continue pending the processing of the petition. However, picketing may be lawful if its purpose is to inform the public that the employer does not employ members of or have a contract with a labor organization. It is not lawful, however, if the picketing persuades employees of other employers not to perform services such as making pickups or deliveries. If the object of picketing is only to make an employer conform its employment standards to those prevailing in the area, so that area standards will not be undermined, the picketing may be lawful as well.

The NLRA provisions concerning the unfair labor practices of unions, particularly in cases involving the use of pickets and boycotts, are complex. Employers are strongly advised to contact a knowledgeable attorney if questions or concerns regarding these subjects arise.

Procedure in Unfair Labor Practice Cases

Filing of a Charge

The first step in an unfair labor practice case is the filing of a charge alleging a violation of the NLRA. This charge may be filed by an employee, an employer, a labor organization, or any other person within six months of the alleged violation. Charge forms, available at the NLRB regional office and on the NLRB's website, must be signed, sworn to or affirmed under oath, and filed with the regional office in the area where the alleged unfair labor practice was committed.

Investigation and Disposition of Charge

Upon receiving the charge, the NLRB regional office will investigate to determine if there is reasonable cause to believe an unfair labor practice occurred. If the regional office's investigation finds that the charge lacks merit, the charge will be dismissed. This dismissal may be appealed to the general counsel in Washington. If the general counsel agrees with the dismissal of the charge, no further appeal is available.

If the regional office's investigation indicates that there is reasonable course to believe unfair labor practice has occurred, it will issue a complaint stating the charges and notifying the charged party that a hearing concerning the charges will be held before an administrative law judge.

Pre-hearing Procedures

Settlements

Many agreements to settle unfair labor practices are informal, although sometimes formal settlements are sought where ongoing or violations of the NLRA have occurred. Settlement can occur before or after a complaint has been issued. Under an informal settlement arrangement, the withdrawal of the complaint if issued is usually provided for when the party that has been charged has taken appropriate corrective action and when notice of the settlement terms has been passed by the employer. The settlement must be approved by a regional director (or if a complaint has been issued and a hearing commenced, by an administrative law judge).

Grievance Arbitration Procedure

In certain limited circumstances, when an employer and union have an agreed-upon grievance-arbitration procedure that will resolve the dispute, the NLRB will defer processing an unfair labor practice charge and await resolution of the issues through that grievance-arbitration process. If this process meets the NLRB's standards, the NLRB may accept the final resolution achieved. If the procedure fails to meet all the NLRB's standards for deferral, however, the NLRB may resume processing the unfair labor practice charge.

Injunction Proceedings

The regional director may determine during his or her preliminary investigation that there is reasonable cause to believe that the alleged unfair labor practice is true and that a complaint should be issued. In such cases, the NLRA permits the regional director to petition the district court to grant an injunction against an employer or a union (an order by the court that a party perform or desist from a particular act) pending final determination of the unfair labor practice complaint. In some cases involving allegedly unlawful "secondary boycotts and related activity by a union," NLRB approval is not needed before the regional director seeks injunctive relief.

Hearing

If a case in which reasonable cause exists is not settled, the regional director will issue a formal complaint. The unfair labor practice complaint contains a statement of the jurisdictional facts, a brief description of the alleged unlawful conduct, and notice of the time and place of hearing.

The party against whom a complaint has been filed is required to file an answer to the complaint within 14 days after the complaint is served. Unless the respondent is without knowledge of the situation, the answer must specifically admit or deny each of the points alleged in the complaint. The complaint may be deemed admitted if the respondent files in a timely fashion. The answer may be amended before or, with permission, during a hearing.

An unfair labor practice hearing is conducted before an administrative law judge in accordance with the applicable rules of evidence, and where practicable, with the rules of evidence applicable in the U.S. district courts. Based on the hearing record the administrative law judge makes findings and recommendations to the NLRB. All parties to the hearing may appeal the judge's decision to the NLRB. If the NLRB determines that the party named in the complaint has engaged in or is engaging in the unfair labor practice charged, the NLRB is authorized to issue an order requiring that party to cease and desist from such practices and to take appropriate affirmative action.

The NLRB has considerable discretion to determine the remedy in a particular case. Ordinarily, its order in regard to any particular unfair labor practice will be designed to remedy the unfair labor practice. Typical affirmative-action orders of the NLRB may require employers found to have engaged in unfair labor practices to do the following:

- Disestablish an employer-dominated union.
- Offer certain individuals immediate and full reinstatement to their former positions with backpay including interest.
- On request, bargain collectively with a certain union as the exclusive representative of the employees in a certain described unit and sign a written agreement if an understanding is reached.

The NLRB's order usually includes a directive requiring the employer to post notices in the plant informing employees that the employer will cease the unfair labor practices and take affirmative action to remedy the violation.

Enforcement

An order of the NLRB is not self-enforcing. If an employer or union fails to comply with a NLRB order, the NLRA empowers the NLRB to petition the U.S. court of appeals for a court judgment enforcing the order of the NLRB. The NLRA provides that any person aggrieved by a final order of the NLRB granting or denying in whole or in part the relief sought may obtain a review of such order in any appropriate circuit court of appeals.

When the court of appeals hears a petition concerning a NLRB order it may enforce the order, remand it to the NLRB for reconsideration, change it, or set it aside entirely. If a court of appeals issues a judgment enforcing the NLRB order, failure to comply may be punishable by fine or imprisonment for contempt of court.

In some cases, the U.S. Supreme Court may be asked to review the decision of a court of appeals, particularly when there are conflicting court decisions on the same issue.

Public Employees Excluded From the NLRA

In general, public employees are exempt from the NLRA. As such, states are free to regulate labor relations among public sector employers and their employees.

Chapter 29
Alternative Dispute Resolution

Introduction

Managers and employees working under collective bargaining agreements have long recognized the value of settling contract disputes before actually going to court. This chapter reviews some of the ways to avoid expensive and time-consuming court proceedings through what is generally known as *alternative dispute resolution* (ADR).

Traditionally, collective bargaining agreements include formal multi-step grievance procedures culminating in binding arbitration to resolve contract disputes. Arbitration is only one of many alternatives to which employers are turning to avoid traditional federal or state court proceedings. Encouraged by Congress and the courts to solve their own problems, employers now have available many avenues short of full blown litigation through which to resolve conflicts with employees.

Types of ADR Solutions

Many employers are unaware that they already practice alternative dispute resolution. The simple principle underlying ADR is that disputes are best settled quickly, before they worsen. A model ADR program tries to bring disputes to the attention of key decision-makers as soon as they arise. Principle ADR solutions include open-door policies, internal mediation, and arbitration.

Open-door Policies

One way to resolve disputes quickly is to encourage employees to bring grievances to their immediate supervisors. An open-door policy requires a commitment by managers to listen and react to employees. Managers must be trained to identify particular problems that may need special investigation. For example, allegations of sexual harassment or safety concerns should be referred immediately to senior management for appropriate investigation and resolution.

Successful open-door policies allow employees to take their grievances to different levels in the organization when the immediate supervisor is the cause of the problem or lacks authority to resolve the problem.

Open-door policies may prevent litigation by correcting problems before employees become upset enough to get a lawyer or before someone is injured. Also, records from a good-faith open-door policy may show that an employer was trying to accommodate employees. Of course, a disgruntled employee can still pursue litigation after exhausting options under an open-door policy, and employers should be careful in dealing with chronic troublemakers who may use open-door meetings as bases for court complaints.

Internal Mediation

A more formal way to resolve complaints is to designate an individual to whom employees can take complaints. Sometimes called an ombudsman, the mediator functions as a go-between, trying to work out the dispute. The intervention of a mediator may be more successful than an open-door policy when a personality conflict exists between the employee and a manager or when an employee is embarrassed to make the complaint. A good mediator can help both sides see issues objectively and help those involved in the dispute reach a mutually satisfactory solution.

A system of internal mediation will rise or fall on the skill and credibility of the mediator, so careful selection of the individual who will fill this important role is crucial. Employees must trust the individual to keep their confidences and they must feel that the mediator has enough influence with management to effect change. Key decision-makers must publicly support the mediation process so that supervisors will respect the process and the mediator.

From management's view, mediation conserves resources better than an open-door policy since only one individual is working on the disputes. It is also easier to find one individual with good listening and problem-solving skills than to teach those skills to all managers. A mediator may be likely to investigate complaints more promptly and thoroughly, since he or she should have fewer operational responsibilities than line supervisors.

At worst, if mediation fails, the employer has had a chance to clarify the employee's complaint and assess the merit of its own position. If the employee chooses to go to court, the employer will already have much of the information necessary to defend itself.

Ombudsman

An *ombudsman* is a person who is authorized by an employer to receive complaints or questions confidentially about alleged acts, omissions, improprieties, and broader, systemic problems within the ombudsman's defined jurisdiction, and to address, investigate, or otherwise examine these issues independently and impartially. It is essential that the ombudsman operate by fair procedures to aid in the just resolution of the matter.

An ombudsman may make formal or informal reports regarding the results of a review or investigation. The ombudsman may also make recommendations regarding how disputes should be resolved. An ombudsman may initiate litigation only to enforce or protect the authority of his or her office, based on an agreement with the employer.

Peer Review

An employer may opt to utilize a peer review panel to review and resolve employee disputes, at least as to disciplinary action or discharge. The panel consists of a mix of employees and managers (some employers use peer review panels consisting exclusively of employees) who hear and evaluate employee appeals from employer disciplinary or other actions. While these peer review panel decisions are not final and binding and do not legally preclude employment litigation, as a practical matter, they unquestionably reduce the risk of employment litigation. The reduced risk is based upon the employees' perception that the employer has treated the employee fairly, the fact that employees have had some form of "due process" in reviewing the disciplinary action, and that plaintiffs' attorneys recognize that a decision by the employees' peers reduces the sympathy factor in an employment lawsuit.

Although peer review primarily is used for handling employee disciplinary complaints, with properly trained panelists, it may also be designed to cover other workplace issues. However, matters such as compensation, performance reviews, benefits, layoffs, and company policy, would normally be excluded from their consideration.

Groups acting in a true peer review capacity generally are excluded from the National Labor Relations Act's proscription on dominated labor organizations, which may affect the legitimacy of employee committees. Peer review panels do not deal with the employer within the contemplation of the ban by making proposals to management, which the employer accepts or rejects, but rather act in a decision-making capacity. (The availability of further review by top management does not alter the fundamental nature of their role.)

Arbitration

Final binding arbitration is the most formal ADR method. In an arbitration agreement employees and employers agree to submit their dispute to a neutral third party and to abide by the arbitrator's decision. While arbitration hearings are not as formal as court proceedings, they usually involve the presentation of witnesses, evidence, and arguments.

Employers may also use non-binding arbitration. This option is the same as binding arbitration except that the parties may reject the arbitrator's decision. Except in unusual cases, non-binding arbitration offers few advantages over binding arbitration.

Advantages of Arbitration

Arbitration has several advantages over traditional litigation:

- The parties have more influence over the selection of the arbitrator than they would over the selection of a judge.
- Arbitrators are less likely to award excessive actual or punitive damages than are judges.
- Arbitrators tend to be less influenced by passion or prejudice than are juries.
- The discovery process in arbitration is generally more streamlined so the administrative cost and inconvenience of preparing for a case is less than in state or federal court.
- Arbitration generally takes less time than a traditional court action.

Disadvantages of Arbitration

Of course, arbitration does have some disadvantages:

- Unlike a trial court decision that can be appealed to a higher court, arbitration decisions cannot generally be appealed on their merits.
- Many employment cases are dismissed by judges based on pretrial motions to dismiss or for summary judgment. Arbitrators traditionally reserve judgment until after a hearing so some cases may proceed further in arbitration than they would in court.
- Because many employers are taking advantage of this form of ADR, some arbitrators may be unfamiliar with the exact legal standard to be applied in each employment action.
- Arbitrators are traditionally more lax in admitting evidence than courts, so damaging evidence may come to light in an arbitration that would be excluded from a court procedure.
- Some arbitrators try to satisfy both sides by issuing split decisions reinstating employees without awarding them damages.

Arbitration to Avoid Civil Litigation

The U.S. Supreme Court has ruled that binding mandatory arbitration is lawful and enforceable as a substitute for civil litigation based on fair employment practice laws. Employers are including arbitration clauses in employment agreements, requiring the employer and employee to submit any disputes arising from the employment relationship to binding arbitration; for example, wrongful discharge disputes, infliction of emotional distress, discrimination, harassment. The U.S. Supreme Court is currently considering the enforceability of such agreements under the Federal Arbitration Act.

The federal appellate courts are divided over the interpretation of this law. Employers may wish to consult with counsel when drafting an arbitration clause to make sure the clause is consistent with the latest decisions.

Terms of Arbitration Clauses

An arbitration agreement should explicitly set forth certain terms:

- The kinds of claims that must be submitted to arbitration.

- The rules to govern the arbitration. Various organizations such as the American Arbitration Association and the Federal Mediation and Conciliation Service publish standard rules for arbitration, including the availability of pre-hearing discovery. These organizations can be used to supply lists of arbitrators and procedures for selecting the arbitrator.

- The types of remedies the arbitrator can award. For purposes of avoiding parallel litigation, the awards should be defined broadly enough to include the kinds of legal and equitable remedies available in a court. Remedies should include such things as actual damages, including front pay and backpay, as well as punitive damages, attorneys' fees, and arbitration costs.

- The responsibility for the payment of the costs of arbitration. Employees cannot be expected to bear substantial administrative or arbitrator fees.

In a recent decision, the Supreme Court re-emphasized the rule that arbitration clauses must be particularly clear. Accordingly, when drafting such a clause, employers should be as explicit as possible.

Chapter 30
Independent Contractors

Introduction

Many employers hire independent contractors to decrease employment costs. *Independent contractors* are workers who have contractual agreements to complete jobs and who have complete control over how they perform the job. State and federal agencies often question the status of independent contractors to increase their tax revenues. This chapter considers some of the advantages to using independent contractors, outlines ways to distinguish between employees and independent contractors, and looks at some legal issues that may be concerns for employers using independent contractors.

Benefits of Independent Contractors

Retaining independent contractors rather than hiring additional employees may have a variety of advantages for employers. By using independent contractors, employers can do the following:

- Avoid paying FICA and FUTA taxes, contributions to employee pension plans, payments of premiums for employee health-insurance programs, and workers' compensation insurance costs.

- Obtain qualified and experienced personnel with specialized skills without the cost of training, developing, and maintaining those specialized skills among their own employees.

- Reduce human resource, payroll, and bookkeeping expenses associated with employees.

- Reduce the overall number of employees in the workforce, which could eliminate an employer's need to comply with certain statutes that apply to employers with more employees.

- Be free of the obligation to comply with a variety of employment-related statutes and regulations applying only to actual employees.

Legal Issues

Courts and agencies have increasingly declared independent contractors to be employees because of federal income tax, state unemployment taxes, and workers' compensation laws, thus exposing the employers to unexpected liabilities and penalties.

Because many employment statutes and regulations apply only to actual employees and not independent contractors, the proper determination and classification of independent contractor status is critical. The following is a partial list of state and federal employment-related statutes that may apply only to employees and not to independent contractors:

- State wage laws and the federal Fair Labor Standards Act.
- Federal and state income tax.
- Unemployment tax.
- State and federal discrimination statutes.
- State safety regulations.
- The Family and Medical Leave Act.

Workers' compensation laws and various protective statutes may also apply to employees and not independent contractors. Workers injured on the job may challenge their status as independent contractors to receive benefits under workers' compensation laws. The first step in determining whether an individual is an employee or an independent contractor under state workers' compensation law is to classify the individual's occupation, including the criteria for that occupation.

In some states, statutory employee provisions cover workers who are classified as non-employees. Likewise, employee protection statutes such as the Fair Labor Standards Act, Title VII of the Civil Rights Act of 1964, the Americans with Disabilities Act, and the Age Discrimination in Employment Act may review the validity of the independent contractor relationship.

The courts and administrative agencies charged with administering and enforcing these employment statutes use a variety of tests to determine whether an individual is an employee or an independent contractor. Employers should not reach their own conclusions about whether an individual is an employee or an independent contractor without first reviewing applicable statutes, accompanying regulations, and any interpretative case law.

Ways to Determine Employee/ Independent Contractor Status

State law may consider several factors in deciding whether an individual is working as an employee or an independent contractor. Whether the employer or the individual has the right to control the means and manner of performance is often a significant consideration. The employee/independent contractor distinction is basically between a person who is subject to orders as to **how** he or she does the work and one who agrees only to do the work, in whatever way he or she prefers.

National Labor Relations Act: "Common Law Agency Test"

The National Labor Relations Act (NLRA) excludes independent contractors from its employee definition. However, labeling a worker an independent contractor does not necessarily mean that the worker is an independent contractor. The National Labor Relations Board uses common law agency principles to decide whether a worker is an employee or an independent contractor within the meaning of the NLRA. Under the common law agency test, several factors determine whether an employee or independent contractor relationship exist.

Among the significant factors that indicate the existence of an employee relationship include the following:

- Employer controls the details of work performance.
- Employer provides work supplies and a place to work.
- The work performed requires more time.
- The work is a part of the employer's regular business.

Significant factors that indicate the existence of an independent contractor relationship include the following, among others:

- Workers are engaged in a separate business or occupation, particularly if they are professionals.
- A specialist does the job without supervision at the place of work.
- Skill required to do the job is greater.
- The employer pays the worker for each job completed.
- The worker has a business.

The National Labor Relations Board warns that these factors do not apply to every situation. The facts of each relationship must be reviewed using the appropriate common law principles.

The Fair Labor Standards Act: "Economic Realities Test"

The federal Fair Labor Standards Act (FLSA) and state wage laws may apply only to workers designated employees and not to independent contractors. Thus, the proper classification of workers is critical to determine the application of these laws.

State courts often use the same test to determine an individual's employment status under state law, as federal courts have developed to determine whether an individual is an employee or an independent contractor under the FLSA. Under this test, the courts examine factors focusing on the "economic realities" of the relationship. An *employee* is one, who as a matter of economic reality, is dependent upon the business to which he or she renders service.

Significant factors under the "economic realities" test include the following:

- An employee status is more likely if the services performed are an important part of the employer's business.
- Longer-term relationships reflect employee status.
- An independent contractor status is more likely if the worker has an investment in the facilities and equipment.
- An independent contractor status is more likely if the worker has a greater chance for profit or loss.
- An independent contractor status is more likely if the worker has an independent business.
- An independent contractor status is more likely if the employer only controls the result to be obtained.

Unemployment Compensation Coverage: The "ABC Test"

To decide whether a worker is an employee or independent contractor, some state unemployment insurance statutes use the "ABC Test." If the worker is an employee, the worker's employer must pay unemployment compensation on wages paid to the worker.

Under the ABC Test, work performed for payment will be treated as wages and taxed by the state and federal government unless the following factors exist:

A. The employer does not and will not control or direct the worker's performance, under contract of service and in fact.

B. Work is performed off the premises of the employer, or the work is done outside the usual course of the employer's business.

C. The individual works in an independently established trade, occupation, profession, or business of the same type in which the work is performed.

Liability

An employer is responsible for injuries caused by employees but is not usually responsible for injuries caused by independent contractors. However, a third party that is injured by an independent contractor may contest the status of the independent contractor in order to sue the company.

Federal and State Income Tax

As in determining employment status under the Workers' Compensation Act, the first step in determining independent contractor status for state or federal income tax purposes is to examine the criteria of the particular individual's occupation. State tax withholding obligations are usually consistent with the federal tax withholding obligations.

The status of an individual as an independent contractor or an employee for purposes of the federal tax laws is determined, with few exceptions, under the common law tests for determining whether an employment relationship exists.

The Internal Revenue Code provides that individuals who perform work in the following categories will not be treated as employees for federal employment tax purposes (FICA taxes, FUTA taxes, and income tax withholding): qualified real estate agents and direct sellers.

The code provides that certain individuals who are otherwise classified as independent contractors will be treated as employees solely for FICA tax purposes (but not for income tax withholding): certain agent-drivers or commission drivers; full time life insurance salesmen; home workers; and traveling or city salesmen. These workers are referred to as *statutory employees*.

Common law Employee Status

The Federal Employment Tax Regulations (FICA taxes, FUTA taxes, and income tax withholding) provide that an individual generally is an employee if, under the usual common law tests, the relationship between the individual and the person for whom he performs services is the legal relationship of employer and employee. Such a relationship generally exists if the person for whom the services are performed "has the right to control and direct the individual who performs the services, not only as to the result to be accomplished by the work but also as to the details and means by which that result is accomplished. That is, an employee is subject to the will and control of the employer not only as to what shall be done but [also] how it shall be done."

The regulations state that the determination is to be based upon the particular facts in each case and warn that the designation or description of the relationship by the parties will not be determinative where the facts prove otherwise.

IRS Common law Factors

Over the years, the IRS developed a list of 20 common law factors to be used as guidance in assessing whether sufficient control exists to establish an employer-employee relationship. According to the IRS, the presence of the following factors tend to indicate that an individual is an employee:

1. **Instructions.** Workers are more likely employees if they must follow your instructions as to when, where, and how they work.
2. **Training.** The more training you give your workers, the more likely it is that they are employees. The reason of this guideline is that independent contractors should know how to do their work, and therefore, should not need training from employers.
3. **Integration.** The more significance placed on your workers' services as regards to your business success or longevity, the more likely it is that they are employees.
4. **Services rendered personally.** Workers are more likely employees if you require them to personally perform the services for which you are paying them. Independent contractors, on the other hand, generally have the right to substitute other people's services for their own in fulfilling their contracts.
5. **Hiring assistants.** Workers are more likely employees if they are not in charge of hiring, supervising, and paying their own assistants.
6. **Continuing relationship.** Workers are more likely employees if they perform work for you for long periods of time or at recurring intervals.
7. **Set hours of work.** Workers are more likely employees if you assign them set hours of work. Independent contractors, however, can usually determine their own work hours.
8. **Full time required.** Workers are more likely employees if you require them to work or be available full time. In contrast, independent contractors can choose when and for whom to work.
9. **Work done on premises.** Workers are more likely employees if they must work at your premises or at a place you designate. Independent contractors, on the other hand, usually work at their own place of business.
10. **Order or sequence set.** Workers are more likely employees if you set the order or sequence in which they perform their services.
11. **Reports.** Workers are more likely employees if they must submit regular reports to you.
12. **Payment method.** Workers are more likely employees if you pay them by the hour, week, or month. In contrast, independent contractors are generally paid by the job.
13. **Expenses.** Workers are more likely employees if you pay their business and travel expenses. Independent contractors, on the other hand, generally pay their own overhead expenses.
14. **Tools and materials.** Workers are more likely employees if you supply them with tools, materials, and other equipment.
15. **Investment.** The more the workers invest in the facilities and equipment they use in performing their services, the more likely it is that they are independent contractors.

Independent Contractors

16. **Profit or loss.** Workers are more likely independent contractors if they have a greater chance of either making a profit or suffering a loss in performing their services.

17. **Works for more than one person at a time.** The greater number of businesses that your workers render services to at the same time, the more likely it is that they are independent contractors.

18. **Services available to general public.** Workers are more likely independent contractors if they offer their services out to the general public through promotional items such as business cards and advertisements.

19. **Right to fire.** Workers are more likely employees if you can fire them at any time. Your right to terminate an independent contractor, on the other hand, is usually limited to the terms specified in the contract.

20. **Right to quit.** Workers are more likely employees if they can quit at any time without having liability to you. In contrast, if independent contractors do not finish a service, they can be held financially accountable.

The IRS guidance states, however, that some of the common law factors do not apply to certain occupations and that the degree of importance to be given to any factor may vary in a particular case. The IRS guidance also states that any single fact or small group of facts will not necessarily establish conclusive evidence of employee or independent contractor status.

As a result, the application of these factors is extremely subjective and the IRS itself has acknowledged that "in many cases, applying the common law test in employment tax issues does not yield clear, consistent, or satisfactory answers, and reasonable persons may differ as to the correct classification." In sum, even the IRS apparently acknowledges that the factors do not provide reliable practical guidance in assessing the status of the workers for employment tax purposes.

IRS Training Materials on Worker Classifications

Because of the difficulty in applying the 20-factor test and because business trends have changed over the years, the IRS recently has begun using a new approach with respect to worker classification. See *Internal Revenue Service Training Materials on Worker Classifications for Tax Purposes as Independent Contractors or Employees* (issued 3/4/1997). Rather than listing items of evidence under the 20 factors, the approach now is to group the items of evidence into the following three main categories: behavioral control, financial control, and the relationship of the parties.

- **Behavioral Control**

    Evidence in this category includes facts regarding whether the business has the right to direct and control how the worker performs the specific tasks for which the worker is hired. Facts that show behavioral control include the type and degree of instructions given to the worker and the training the business gives the worker.

- **Financial Control**

    Evidence under this category includes facts regarding whether there is a right to direct and control how the business aspects of the worker's activities are conducted. Facts that show financial control include whether the worker has a significant investment or incurs significant expenses in the business and whether the worker provides services to the relevant market.

- **Relationship of the Parties**

    Evidence under this category includes facts that illustrate how the parties perceive their relationship. Relevant facts include those which show the intent of the parties with respect to their relationship and whether the parties were free to terminate their relationship at will. The permanency of the relationship between the worker and the business is also relevant in assessing the relationship.

Employers can request an IRS determination by filing Form SS-8, *Determination of Employee Work Status for Purposes of Federal Employment Taxes and Income Tax Withholding*. This form is supplemented with additional information about the employment relationship between the employer and the worker(s), for example, a description of the nature of the supervision and method of payment.

Federal Tax Penalties for Misclassification

Income Tax Withholding

The Internal Revenue Code generally limits an employer's liability for federal employment taxes when an IRS audit has found an individual to have been misclassified as an independent contractor. The liability is as follows:

Tax Category	Employer Liability
Income Tax Withholding	1.5% of wages per year
Social Security Tax—Employer plus Employee Portion	7.44% of wages (up to maximum Social Security wage base) per year *plus* 1.74% of wages (no maximum wage base) per year
FUTA Taxes	$434 per worker per year

In addition, the IRS has established several audit settlement programs under which the IRS, depending on the circumstances, may reduce or eliminate an employer's liability for the employment taxes for misclassified workers.

Exceptions

To add to the problem of distinguishing employees from independent contractors are the following considerations:

- Some independent contractors who perform certain types of duties are taxable as employees.
- Some individuals may be statutorily exempted from federal employment withholding taxes.
- The employer may be exempt under the "safe haven rule" from withholding taxes for individuals who normally would be classified as employees.
- Employed family members are exempt from certain taxes as employees.

Taxable Independent Contractors: Statutory Employees

Employers will be required to withhold FICA taxes in certain circumstances for independent contractors who are considered statutory employees. These are individuals performing the following services:

- Deliver specified products as agent drivers or commission drivers. This includes individuals who operate their own trucks or trucks of the persons for whom they perform services, serve customers designated by their employer as well as customers they solicit on their own, make wholesale or retail sales, and are paid commissions on their sales for the products or services they sell or earn the difference between what they charge their customers and what they pay their principals for the products or services. This includes drivers who distribute beverages, meat, vegetables, fruit, or bakery products, and drivers who pick up and deliver laundry or dry cleaning. It does not include drivers who distribute milk.

- Work full time for an employer as traveling salespersons. This includes individuals who remit orders for items that will be resold or used as supplies in their businesses from customers who are retailers, wholesalers, contractors, or operators of hotels, restaurants, or other furnishers of food and lodging.

- Perform work at home on a contract or piecemeal basis. This would include individuals hired as word processors who do their work on their home computers.

- Work full time selling life insurance primarily for one insurance company.

Ordinarily, these individuals are considered independent contractors and employers would not have to withhold income taxes from their pay. However, if the following conditions exist, employers must withhold and pay FICA taxes:

- The contract requires the individual to perform most of the work personally (in other words, he or she is not free to hire someone to do the job).

- The individual has invested little in equipment and property other than the necessary vehicle.

- The services are performed on a continuing basis.

Employers must withhold FICA taxes on all wages they pay individuals working at home if the individuals are paid more than $100 in a year. Additionally, if the conditions above exist in the cases of drivers and salespeople, employers must pay federal and state unemployment taxes as well.

Untaxed Employees

Employers may be relieved of all taxes for two types of employee salespersons—real estate agents and direct sellers (that is, individuals who sell consumer products to consumers or to buyers for resale at a place that is not a permanent retail establishment)—if the following are true:

- Substantially all of the compensation these individuals receive is directly related to sales or other output, rather than to the hours they work.

- The salespeople are subject to written contracts indicating that they will not be treated as employees for federal income tax purposes.

Statutory Safe Harbor Relief From IRS Reclassification (Safe Haven Rule)

The Safe Haven Rule under Section 530 of the Revenue Act of 1978 protects an employer from liability for federal employment taxes.

- **Requirements for Safe Haven Rule**

    The employer must have a reasonable basis for not treating the individual as an employee. The Safe Haven Rule provides that a reasonable basis exists where an employer relies on anyone or more of the following safe havens:

    - Judicial precedent or published rulings whether or not relating to the employer, or IRS technical advice or letter ruling issued with respect to the employer.

- Past IRS audit of the employer in which there was no assessment of employment taxes attributable to the treatment of workers holding positions substantially similar to the position held by the individual in question. (The audit need not have been conducted for employment tax purposes.)
- Long-standing recognized practice of a significant segment of the industry.
- An employer who fails to meet any of the three safe havens may still be entitled to the Safe Haven Rule if it can demonstrate, in some other manner, a reasonable basis for not treating the individual as an employee.

The employer must consistently treat the individual, and any other individual holding a substantially similar position, as an independent contractor at all times. For this purpose, consistency is determined by whether:

- The employer has timely filed Form 1099s for all tax periods.
- The employer has not withheld federal income taxes or FICA taxes for any tax periods, and filed federal employment tax returns for any tax periods.

♦ **Burden of Proof**

The IRS has the burden of proving that a taxpayer is not entitled to relief under the Safe Haven Rule with respect to an individual, if:

- The taxpayer establishes a prima facie case that it was reasonable not to treat the individual as an employee.
- The taxpayer has fully cooperated with reasonable requests from IRS.

♦ **Effect of the Safe Haven Rule**

The Safe Haven Rule terminates an employer's liability for federal employment taxes attributable to the erroneous classification of an individual as an independent contractor.

- The Safe Haven Rule prevents retroactive employment tax assessments against the employer.
- As long as the requirements of the Safe Haven Rule are met, the IRS is prevented from making future employment tax assessments against the employer with respect to such individuals.
- The Safe Haven Rule applies solely for federal employment tax purposes.
- It does not prevent an individual's classification as an employee for all other purposes under the code; for example, an individual may be treated as an employee for purposes of the tax qualification requirements applying to retirement plans and various other employee benefit nondiscrimination requirements under the code.
- The Safe Haven Rule also does not apply for purposes of other federal or state statutes.

Important Forms
IRS Form SS-8

The IRS has created Form SS-8, *Information for Use in Determining Whether a Worker is an Employee for Federal Employment Taxes and Income Tax Withholding.* It asks detailed information about every aspect of the employer's relationship with the worker to assess the proper classification of workers characterized as independent contractors.

A worker may also complete and submit the SS-8 form to obtain a definite determination on his or her employment status. If the IRS finds that the worker is an employee rather than an independent contractor, the IRS may start an audit and then may apply the SS-8 determination to all others performing similar services for the company. Thus, a review of a single worker by the IRS, with an adverse ruling that the worker is an employee rather than an independent contractor, can prevent the employer from treating the entire class of workers as independent contractors. This poses a significant risk because in completing the form, the worker is unlikely to be aware of the significance of many of the questions and most likely will not consult with an accountant or attorney regarding his or her responses.

Form 1099

If a worker is an independent contractor who is not incorporated, the employer must annually report payments to the worker of $600 or more on a Form 1099-MISC, available from the local IRS office. If all four of the following conditions are met, a payment is generally reportable as non-employee compensation:

- The payment was made to a non-employee.
- The payment was for services rendered in the course of your trade or business, including government agencies and nonprofit organizations.
- The payment was made to someone other than a corporation or partnership.
- Payments totaled at least $600 during a year.

As with W-2 forms, Form 1099 must be distributed to recipients by January 31 of the following year and a transmittal form, Form 1096, must be filed with the IRS no later than February 28 of that year.

Independent Contractors and Discrimination and Safety Standards

Employers using independent contractors must be aware of the various laws concerning discrimination in employment and safety in the workplace, just as with regular employees.

Federal Discrimination Statutes

The federal discrimination statutes, including Title VII of the Civil Rights Act of 1964, the Americans with Disabilities Act, and the Age Discrimination in Employment Act define employee and employer in similar ways. Under the test used by federal courts, the term employee is construed in light of general common law concepts. The most critical factor is again the issue of control. Factors examined include the factors set forth in the sections on determination of independent contractor status under common law principles as well as the 20 common law factors examined by the IRS.

State Human Rights Act

State anti-discrimination laws often define employees in much the same way as the federal discrimination statutes. Thus, most state courts will apply the common law test as outlined above for the federal discrimination statutes to determine an individual's employment status under the state law.

Drug and Alcohol Testing in the Workplace

State drug testing laws may define employee to include independent contractors and persons working for the independent contractor. Therefore, any worker, including independent contractors and their employees, who is tested for drugs and alcohol must be provided the rights set out in state law.

Occupational Safety and Health Laws

Many states have recently altered the standards applied to independent contractors in the context of occupational health and safety. Until a few years ago independent contractors may have enjoyed a number of exemptions under state laws but now the trend among state legislatures is to restrict such exemptions, and many independent contractors must comply with state safety and health laws. For example, independent contractors doing building construction or improvements in the public or private sector may now be required to comply with the state's OSHA standards for employers and employees.

Contingent Workers

Many employers rely on contingent workers to meet workforce needs. *Contingent workers* refer to independent contractors, subcontractors, and workers from temporary agencies and leasing companies. Contingent workers not receiving benefits—for example, health and retirement benefits—from other sources may seek coverage from the contingent employer. To ensure that your company does not have to provide such coverage, you should do the following:

- Review all benefit plans for definitions of employee, eligible employee, creditable hours, and classes of employees that can be included or excluded. Make sure these definitions are consistent within plans, contracts, and policies so they are interpreted in the same way.

- Make sure all benefit documents give discretion to the plan administrator to interpret plan provisions.

- Have clear contracts with independent contractors, temporary agencies, leasing companies, and subcontractors. Include indemnification provisions in case an employee of one of these firms (or an independent contractor) makes a claim for benefits.

- Include language in benefit plan documents excluding independent contractors, leased employees, and temporary workers from coverage to the extent permitted by the Internal Revenue Code and regulations.

- If a contingent worker makes a claim for benefits, analyze and document the plan administrator's decision about benefits eligibility. Do not automatically refuse to give the worker the requested documents. Even a non-participant may be entitled to plan information.

- Before entering into contingent work arrangements, seek competent advice, conduct a thorough analysis of benefit plans and policies, and make changes to reflect the intended status of the workers.

Conclusion

Properly classifying workers as employees or independent contractors is critical. An adverse determination that an employer has incorrectly classified a worker as an independent contractor can have serious consequences, including liability for back taxes, interest, penalties, and workers' compensation premiums. Thus, employers should consult an attorney to ensure proper classification and to draft independent contractor agreements when appropriate.

Chapter 31
Contingent Employment

Introduction

What is the Contingent Workforce?

The term "contingent employment" was coined almost a decade ago by labor economist Audrey Freedman to describe the range of employment relationships which had developed to meet employers' perceived need for flexible work arrangements to control labor costs in a global economy. Although the definition of the contingent workforce is still evolving, the following list defines the most common types that fall within the ranks.

Part-time Workers

Part-time workers are employees scheduled to work less than a 40-hour workweek. They may be hired directly by the company or may be provided by a staffing firm. Part-time employees represent the largest segment of contingent workers, accounting for about 20 percent of the entire U.S. workforce, and are most common in the clerical, sales and service industries.

Temporary Workers

Temporary workers are hired, trained and paid by a staffing firm and assigned by the firm to work for a particular company, normally to supplement the company's own workforce (usually on a task/assignment basis or for a specific time period). About 50 percent of temporary workers are clerical, 25 percent are industrial, and 25 percent are professional.

Contract Workers

Another segment of the contingent workforce is contract workers; they may be employed by a primary employer but provide services to a secondary employer on a contract basis. Some industries that most often utilize contract workers include construction, janitorial services and garment manufacturing. However, contract workers can be found throughout all segments of the economy.

Outsourced Employees

In an outsourcing relationship, a firm undertakes the full responsibility for managing a particular function for a company, including personnel and operations. Companies primarily outsource functions that are not considered essential to their operations (for example, cafeteria, cleaning and security services).

Independent Contractors

These workers are self-employed and are engaged to provide specialized services on a contract basis. This type of employee, as opposed to an independent contractor, is complex, and can involve as many as 20 criterions in an unweighted appraisal of a job situation. Also included within the independent contractor category are the day laborers that gather to find work each day in labor pools that have proliferated around the country. Often, these workers are paid by the day.

Leased Employees

Leased employees are initially hired by a company and transferred to the payroll of a professional employer organization (PEO). The PEO then leases the workers back to the company, but the PEO continues to perform human resources functions for the workers, such as administering the payroll and benefits and handling personnel matters.

Regardless of the form of the contingent work arrangement or the designation given to a particular worker, the critical question, from the employer's perspective, is whether the contingent worker will be considered their "employee" for purposes of various employment laws. Determining a contingent worker's status is never a simple matter. In making a determination about who actually employs a particular worker courts consider and evaluate a number of factors including:

- Which party exercises the right of control.
- Which party pays employee wages.
- Whether the parties consider the worker an employee or an independent contractor.
- Which party has the power to modify employment conditions.

In those instances when a contingent worker exercises primary control over his or her work and satisfies certain other criteria, the worker is considered an independent contractor and no other party shall be considered his or her employer. Conversely, when another party controls the contingent employee's work, the question of who is the appropriate "employer" remains. Depending on the facts, a contingent worker may be considered either the employee of the company receiving the benefit of the employee's services ("the recipient employer") or the employee of the temporary, leasing or placement agency ("the employment agency") that hires and contracts out contingent workers.

Temporary Employees and Employment Laws

Discrimination

It is essential that employers recognize the broad reach of Title VII, the Americans with Disabilities Act (ADA) and the Age Discrimination in Employment Act (ADEA). All applicants for employment and contingent workers, with the exception of independent contractors, are entitled to all of the same protections against discrimination as permanent employees. Both Title VII and the ADEA expressly cover most employment agencies.

Employers specifically covered by statute are not the only parties subject to potential liability. Any contingent worker, with the exception of independent contractors who operate without the assistance of any employment agency, may pursue a cause of action against both the employer and the employment agency if both companies had joint control over the employee. In order to be held liable, the recipient employer must exercise sufficient and meaningful control over the terms and conditions of the contingent worker's employment–beyond the mere fact the employee is performing work for the employer's benefit. Whenever there is a true joint employer situation, each employer can be held responsible for the other employer's independent actions.

The EEOC Enforcement Guidance on Contingent Workers addresses the application of the federal employment discrimination statutes -Title VII, the ADEA, the ADA, and the Equal Pay Act (EPA) to individuals placed in job assignments by employment agencies. The Guidance provides that an employment agency or the recipient employer can be liable for discriminating against a temporary worker even if it does not qualify as the worker's employer. Moreover, the Guidance requires that an employment agency must take immediate and appropriate corrective action if it learns that its client has discriminated against one of its workers.

In light of the potentially broad liability, recipient employers should thoroughly investigate any employment agency before entering into a contract. Employers are advised to include an indemnification clause in contracts with an employment agency in order to avoid liability for discriminatory actions, like referrals, over which the employer has no control. Employers are also advised to include a clause in the contract clearly identifying which party is ultimately responsible for the contingent employees.

Employers should also be aware that an employment agency is not a vehicle for circumventing the law. The ADA, for example, specifically prohibits an employer from participating in a contractual or other relationship that has the effect of subjecting a covered employer's qualified applicant or employee with a disability to discrimination. Under the ADA, it would be illegal for an employer to reject a particular contingent worker on the basis of his or her disability. Similarly, to the extent the employment agency is also covered by the law, it would be unlawful for that agency to comply with a recipient employer's request for only nondisabled workers. It is unclear whether a recipient employer will have a duty to accommodate a contingent employee who is disabled.

Workers Adjustment and Retraining Notification (WARN)

The use of contingent workers raises a number of questions under WARN, some of which do not yet have clear answers. WARN applies only to business enterprises with "100 or more employees, excluding part-time employees." For purposes of determining the coverage of the act, it is essential to know how contingent workers will be counted.

It is clear that WARN does not cover independent contractors or consultants who are self-employed or who have an exclusive relationship with another employer. Similarly, temporary workers, hired to perform discrete tasks for a short period of time, are also excluded.

It is less clear, however, how the use of leased employees will affect the determination of whether WARN notification and other WARN requirements have been triggered. Under the act, employers are required to give notice whenever plant closings or mass layoffs cause a loss of employment for a specified number of employees. Arguably, there is no employment loss where a contingent worker is released from a recipient employer, but remains on the payroll of the employment agency and is relocated to another employer within a six month period. If, however, there is a true joint employer arrangement, notice may still be necessary since the regulations require notice be given to workers who lose their jobs with a particular employer, regardless of whether other employers may hire those workers.

Family and Medical Leave

The FMLA regulations specifically cover joint employer situations. For purposes of determining employer coverage and employee eligibility under the FMLA, all employees, including those shared with a joint employer, must be counted by both employers. This is true even when the employee is only on one employer's payroll.

Notwithstanding these similarities, the responsibilities of the joint employers differ. For example, only the primary employer (the employment agency) must provide the required FMLA notice, provide the required leave, and maintain the employee's health benefits during the leave. The primary employer is also responsible for job restoration after the employee returns from FMLA leave.

Although the primary employer carries more responsibility for a contingent worker exercising his or her rights under the FMLA, the secondary or recipient employer is not without legal restriction. A secondary employer may not retaliate or discriminate against a contingent worker who is eligible for and elects to take FMLA leave. Neither may the secondary employer interfere with or attempt to restrain efforts of the primary employer to restore an employee returning from FMLA leave to his or her previous position with the secondary employer so long as the primary employer is still providing the same services to the secondary employer.

Immigration Reform and Control Act (IRCA)

Federal law requires that "any person or entity that hires or recruits or refers for a fee an individual for employment" must verify the employment eligibility of each individual.

Although employers are responsible for verifying the employment status of independent contractors, under IRCA a recipient employer is typically not required to verify the employment status of contingent workers provided by an employment agency. Under IRCA it is the responsibility of the primary employer (the employment agency) to verify the status of contingent workers and to complete the necessary paperwork.

Not surprisingly, the law in this area is not fully developed and, in the event a recipient employer is determined to be a joint employer with the employment agency, the government could argue that joint liability is appropriate. Therefore, as in other areas, it is advisable for recipient employers to include in their contracts with employment agencies a provision allocating the parties' responsibilities and liabilities under the act.

The Fair Labor Standards Act (FLSA)

Like the anti-discrimination statutes, the FLSA has broad definitions of employer, employee and employment. Under the FLSA, all individuals whose work is controlled by an employer are considered to be employees and are entitled to the wage and hour protections of the statute. Although independent contractors are generally excluded because of the control they exercise over their own work, most other contingent workers are covered.

Under the FLSA, the primary employer (the employment agency) has principal responsibility for FLSA compliance with record keeping and payment of overtime requirements. However, where a secondary or recipient employer is considered a true joint employer, both will be liable for wage and overtime violations.

Because the issue of whether an employee will be considered jointly employed under the FLSA is difficult to predict, it is advisable for a recipient employer to include provisions in its contract with an employment or staffing agency that clearly indicate which entity shall be responsible for FLSA compliance. Recipient employers are also encouraged to include provisions in their contract for reimbursement from the staffing agency in the event they are held liable for FLSA violations as a joint employer.

National Labor Relations Act (NLRA)

Independent contractors are not covered by the NLRA and are therefore neither entitled to union representation, nor protected by the act.

As with other federal statutes, the treatment of contingent workers depends upon whether the employee works for the recipient employer, the employment agency, or both. If the recipient employer and the employment agency are joint employers, both controlling the daily activities of the employee, then both may be held liable for unfair labor practices committed by either party.

For purposes of collective bargaining, the National Labor Relations Board has consistently held it would be improper to place eligible contingent employees in a bargaining unit (a group of employees covered by a collective bargaining agreement) with the recipient employer's regular employees, unless the employer consents to such a unit. Absent such consent, it is generally improper to allow such contingent employees to vote in union elections.

By contrast, where contingent employees are able to demonstrate they have a sufficient "community of interest" with the recipient employer's regular or full-time employees, they may be allowed to join the regular employees' bargaining unit. It is also relevant in making the bargaining unit determination, whether the contingent employee has been given a specific date for his or her layoff.

Recipient employers who regularly hire new employees from the contingent workforce should be prepared to face the argument such workers have a sufficient community of interest and expectation of future employment such that they should be included in the regular employees' bargaining unit and should be able to vote in any representation election.

Alternatively, even where contingent workers are precluded from joining the regular employees' bargaining unit, contingent workers could organize their own separate unit. In that event, it is likely the union could force the recipient employer and the employment agency to bargain over the termination of any worker's assignment as well as other terms and conditions of employment. These are clearly mandatory subjects of bargaining.

Occupational Safety and Health Act (OSHA)

Under OSHA and the accompanying regulations, all employers have a general duty to maintain a safe workplace.

The allocation and determination of OSHA liability in situations involving two or more potential employers (for example, general contractor and subcontractor, recipient employer and employment agency) is the subject of ongoing litigation. Nevertheless, since the general rule of OSHA is that a party is liable for workers exposed to hazards the party created or controls, it is unlikely a contingent employment situation could be structured to avoid liability for contingent workers exposed to hazards in the workplace. Employers are advised to consider the risks of liability and to strive to create for all employees, regular and contingent, a workplace free from the hazards identified in OSHA standards.

Administrative and Financial Concerns

Income Tax Withholding

Employers are legally obligated to withhold taxes from the wages of employees. Therefore, the question of whether an individual is an independent contractor, an employee of the recipient employer, or an employee of the employment agency is an important one with respect to the Internal Revenue Service. Indeed, an employer's failure to withhold taxes may result in substantial financial penalties, unless the individual is an independent contractor. It is unnecessary to withhold taxes for independent contractors as they are legally exempt, but it is generally required that payments made to them by an employer be reported separately on a Form 1099.

The determination of whether a contingent worker is the employee of the recipient employer or the employment agency will depend on the facts and circumstances of each case. The Internal Revenue Service evaluates the following 20 factors, which are analogous to the traditional right to control test in reaching its conclusion:

1. Is the worker required to comply with instructions?
2. Is training required or provided for the worker?
3. Are the worker's services integrated into the business operations?
4. Does the worker have to personally render the services?
5. Can the worker hire, supervise, and/or pay assistants?
6. Is there a continuing relationship with the worker?
7. Does the worker have to perform his services during set hours of work?
8. Does the worker render, or have to render, full-time services? Is he free to offer his services elsewhere at the same time?
9. Where is the work conducted?
10. Does the work have to be performed according to a set order or sequence?
11. Does the worker have to submit regular oral or written reports?
12. Is payment made by the hour, week, month, etc. vs. payment by a lump sum or commission?
13. Is the worker responsible for payment of his expenses?
14. Does the worker furnish his own tools and materials?
15. Does the worker have an investment in any facilities that are used in rendering the services?
16. Can the worker realize a profit or a loss?
17. Does the worker render services to more than one firm, client, etc. at a time?
18. Does the worker make his services available to the general public on a regular and consistent basis?
19. Can the worker be fired or discharged at-will?
20. Does the worker have the right to terminate the relationship at-will?

Generally, the IRS will view the employment agency as the employer for payroll tax purposes if it has control of the payment of wages, provided the taxes are timely paid. However, some courts have held the recipient organization liable for payroll taxes. There is legislation pending in Congress that would make it clear that the staffing firm is the employer of individuals covered by staffing arrangements for purposes of employment tax liability. Until the question of who is an "employee" for IRS purposes is resolved, recipient employers are advised to address the issue in their contracts with the employment agency.

Conclusion

Although the issues raised by the contingent workforce are many and varied, at least one unifying theme rings true, That is, across the various areas of labor and employment law, the benefits, protection, and flexibility that once attracted employers to the contingent workforce are beginning to erode under the weight of increasingly burdensome federal and state laws. Employers interested in employing contingent workers should do so carefully and only after constructing contractual agreements that specifically address the multitude of attending risks and liabilities.

Chapter 32
AIDS/Communicable Diseases in the Workplace

Introduction

With an increase in the number of employees contracting AIDS and HIV, employers, assisted by federal law, must implement AIDS policies to ensure reasonable care is exercised toward employees in the workplace. This chapter addresses AIDS-related issues such as testing, employment, protection by law, health insurance, confidentiality, and other issues. A list of organizations that provide AIDS information is given at the end of the chapter.

AIDS and HIV in the Workplace

AIDS as a Disability

The principal laws applicable to AIDS in the workplace are those prohibiting handicap and disability discrimination, including state anti-discrimination laws. AIDS and the virus that causes AIDS, HIV, can be a disability under the American With Disabilities Act (ADA), the Rehabilitation Act, and state discrimination laws. Recently, the Supreme Court ruled that asymptomatic HIV is a disability because it substantially limits a major life activity. In addition, employers should be aware asymptomatic HIV could constitute a perceived disability.

Pre-employment Inquiries

Employers generally are not permitted to make pre-employment inquiries that are likely to elicit information about a disability, including AIDS or HIV. Employers may, however, inquire into a job applicant's ability to perform any and all specific job functions as long as these questions are not directed at a particular disability.

If an applicant voluntarily discloses that he or she has AIDS or HIV, an employer may ask whether the applicant needs reasonable accommodation and, if so, what type? An applicant is not required to disclose reasonable accommodations that may be needed in the distant future.

Medical Examinations

An employer may not test for AIDS or HIV before offering a job to an applicant. After a job offer, an employer may require a medical examination as long as all employees in the same job category are subjected to the examination and all medical information is kept confidential. After employment, begins, any medical examination, other than routine wellness checkups, must be job related and consistent with business necessity. Equal Employment Opportunity Commission (EEOC) regulations specify that employers may not require an HIV test just because an employee looks sick, misses work, or uses more sick leave than other employees.

Policy Statements on Risk of Transmission of AIDS or HIV

Current medical opinion is that there is no risk of contracting AIDS or the virus that causes AIDS through normal daily contact with infected persons in the workplace. For example, the Center for Disease Control (CDC) estimates that even between a surgeon and a patient the risk of transferring the HIV virus during surgery is between 1 to 41,600 and 1 to 416,000. Likewise, a recent study published in the *Annals of Internal Medicine* calculated the risk of transmission of the HIV virus during professional football games as less than 1 in 85 million. By comparison, airplane passengers risk death in 1 out of 1.6 million flights.

The CDC also has determined that AIDS or HIV is not a disease that can be transmitted through the handling of food. The CDC has issued guidelines that persons with AIDS or HIV cannot be barred or restricted from using office equipment, telephones, toilets, mowers, cafeterias, or water fountains.

Protection for Applicants and Employees With HIV or AIDS Under the ADA

With these statistics and policy statements in mind, employees or applicants for employment who have AIDS or HIV and are otherwise qualified for the position are protected from adverse employment action on the basis of their disability. An employee is otherwise qualified if he or she can perform the essential functions of the job with or without reasonable accommodation.

Under the ADA and the Rehabilitation Act, an employee is not otherwise qualified if he or she poses a direct threat to the health or safety of others that cannot be eliminated by a reasonable accommodation. The Supreme Court has defined *direct threat* to involve a significant risk of harm and has proposed several of the following factors to consider in assessing whether the employee poses a direct threat:

- The nature of the risk (how the disease is transmitted).
- The duration of the risk (how long is the carrier infectious).
- The severity of the risk (what is the potential harm to third parties).
- The probability the disease will be transmitted and cause varying degrees of harm.

Analysis of AIDS and HIV is unique and often difficult because the probability of transmission is slight but the nature of the risk, duration of the risk, and the severity of the risk are great. Even so, courts have allowed employers to consider AIDS or HIV in making employment decisions only in limited situations such as certain healthcare providers or public safety professionals whose job duties expose members of the public to greater risk of transmission.

Courts have not been receptive to broad rules excluding persons with AIDS or HIV from particular types or categories of jobs. Thus, employers must make a case-by-case determination whether a particular employee or applicant poses a significant risk of communicating AIDS or HIV to others. A mere diagnosis of AIDS or HIV infection is not sufficient for this purpose.

Reasonable Accommodation

If an employee with AIDS or HIV cannot perform the essential functions of the job or is not otherwise qualified for the job because of AIDS or HIV, the employer must consider whether any reasonable accommodation would enable the employee to perform the essential functions of the job. Reasonable accommodation does not require the employer to take on undue financial or administrative burdens. It also generally does not require an employer to significantly restructure the job to allow the employee to continue working.

Health Insurance Benefits

Health benefits are a significant concern under the ADA and are specifically addressed by the statute and its implementing regulations. Under EEOC regulations, an employer may have a bona fide benefit plan that is not a subterfuge for evading the requirements of the ADA.

The major focus of recent enforcement efforts by the EEOC has been the capping of healthcare benefits for individuals infected with AIDS. Several courts have held that AIDS-based distinctions in the level of such benefits do not violate ERISA; the federal statute that regulates health-benefit plans. Drastic cuts in health benefits have been held, however, to violate the Americans with Disabilities Act.

Employers also may not make employment decisions about persons with AIDS or HIV based on actual or perceived increases in healthcare costs or workers' compensation costs. Similarly, an employer cannot fire or refuse to hire an individual because the employer's current health plan does not cover AIDS or HIV.

Confidentiality

The release of information about employees with AIDS or HIV or those who are suspected of having AIDS and HIV can have serious social and financial repercussions. The ADA requires that records relating to disabilities and accommodations be confidential. Additionally, that medical information is kept in separate medical files, not the employee's regular personnel file. Medical information may not be released except for the following limited exceptions:

- Supervisors and managers may be told about necessary restrictions or accommodations.
- First aid and safety personnel may be told if the disability might require emergency treatment.
- Government officials investigating compliance with the ADA must be provided with requested information.
- State workers' compensation offices, state second injury funds, or workers' compensation insurance carriers in accordance with state workers' compensation laws may have access.
- Insurance purposes may require information.

Employers should establish a policy or statement regarding the confidential nature of the information and enforce disciplinary measures for the unauthorized release of such information.

AIDS- and HIV-infected individuals and those falsely suspected of infection have sought to recover damages under the ADA, state disability laws, and other common law for the unauthorized release of such information.

Occupational Safety and Health/Workplace Safety

Both federal and state health and safety statutes regulate bloodborne pathogens and infectious disease. Employers, even those with employees unaffected by AIDS or HIV, should take care to implement and administer the necessary policies to avoid liability. Employers should work with employees to ensure they understand the policies and the risks of improper handling of bodily fluids or contaminated materials.

Family and Medical Leave Act

Employees with AIDS or HIV may qualify for up to 12 weeks of unpaid leave annually under the Family and Medical Leave Act (FMLA) because of treatment, illness, or hospitalization. The employer must continue to provide existing health benefits during this period and restore the employee to his or her position upon return from leave. Any documents relating to FMLA leave or the need for FMLA leave must be treated as confidential.

Considerations for Employers When Drafting AIDS Policy

A 1994 study by the American Management Association indicated that more than 37 percent of American employers have dealt with employees who had or were perceived to have HIV or AIDS. With these increasing percentages, employers should consider adopting policies to address the treatment of persons with AIDS or HIV and to educate their workforce about AIDS and HIV. Employers should ensure they have effective and coordinated policies to address the Americans with Disabilities Act (ADA), the Family and Medical Leave Act (FMLA), and the Occupational Safety and Health Act (OSH Act).

In drafting these policies an employer should consider the following factors:

- Educating decision-makers about HIV and AIDS to ensure that decisions are based on medical facts.

- Centralizing the decision-making function to promote greater uniformity and consistency in implementation.

- Providing guidance and directives addressing the maintenance of health and benefits information.

- Issuing strict guidelines regarding the confidential nature of such information.

- Establishing methods for handling AIDS-related concerns in the workplace.

- Including referral sources or agencies for additional assistance or information.

Employers may wish to supplement these policies with educational programs, counseling, and outreach programs to encourage employees to be candid about their HIV status and to assist other employees in understanding and accommodating co-workers with HIV or AIDS.

Commonly Asked Questions and Answers

Q. Are employees with AIDS protected by laws prohibiting handicap and disability discrimination?

A. Yes. AIDS and the virus that causes AIDS, HIV, may qualify as disabilities under state law, the ADA, and the Federal Rehabilitation Act.

Q. Since employees with AIDS are protected by laws prohibiting discrimination, does that mean terminating an employee who has AIDS exposes an employer to liability?

A. Not exactly. An employer may not terminate an employee with AIDS on the basis of his or her disability, merely because he or she has AIDS. However, an employee with AIDS may be terminated for one of the following reasons:

- If he or she is unable to perform the essential functions of the job with or without a reasonable accommodation.
- If he or she poses a direct threat to the health or safety of others that cannot be eliminated by a reasonable accommodation.

Q. What is a reasonable accommodation?

A. The nature of the accommodation depends on the employee's condition and the work environment. Under the ADA, it is the employee's responsibility to request the accommodation, and then the employer must discuss possible accommodations with the employee. An employer has no obligation to provide an accommodation if to do so would cause undue financial or administrative burdens.

For Further Information

The following organizations provide information and resources to help employers address AIDS and HIV in the workplace:

Business and Labor Resource Service (formerly National AIDS Clearinghouse)

Provides information on national, state, and local resources related to AIDS/HIV.
(800) 458-5231
http://www.brta-lrta.org/

Centers for Disease Control

Provides an employer kit addressing the key elements of a workplace policy, training of managers, employee education, and community involvement.
(800) 342-2437
http://www.cdc.gov/

The American Red Cross
Conducts one- to three-hour presentations on basic facts about HIV and AIDS including role-play and videos.
(202) 737-8300
www.redcross.org/services/hss/hivaids/

Job Accommodation Network
(800) 526-7234
(800) 232-7675
http://www.jan.wvu.edu

Chapter 33
Smoking in the Workplace

Introduction

This chapter briefly reviews some federal laws relevant to smoking in the workplace, including the Occupational Safety and Health Administration (OSHA) proposed standards on indoor air quality. It also outlines some ways to prevent or minimize the problem of secondhand smoke in the workplace and provides a checklist of considerations for implementing a company smoking policy. The chapter also discusses state and local regulations on smoking in the workplace.

Smoking in the workplace has long been under attack from a variety of sources. The campaign against workplace smoking involves health, financial, and legal issues. The focus of the controversy is currently environmental tobacco smoke (ETS), or secondhand smoke.

Federal Laws

A U.S. Supreme Court decision noted that 37 percent of adult nonsmokers reported environmental smoke at work. In response to concerns about the effect of exposure to tobacco smoke in the workplace, President Clinton issued an executive order in August 1997, prohibiting the smoking of tobacco products in most interior spaces owned, rented, or leased by the executive branch of the federal government.

Workers' Compensation

Workers' compensation laws are generally not based upon fault. Thus, workers who can show that ETS caused an injury or disease in the workplace can receive compensation even if the employer can demonstrate lack of knowledge of the harmfulness of secondhand smoke. If the Environmental Protection Agency (EPA) report survives legal challenge, it will be easier to establish the required relationship between ETS and disease.

Americans with Disabilities Act

The Americans with Disabilities Act applies to employers with 15 or more employees. Under the ADA, an *individual with a disability* is anyone with "a physical or mental impairment that substantially limits one or more of such person's major life activities."

The act may affect employer smoking policies. If an employee has suffered impairment to the respiratory system (allergies, asthma, etc.), which precludes that employee from working in an environment with tobacco smoke, that individual may have a disability that requires a reasonable accommodation to allow that individual to perform the job's essential functions.

Employers may be required to provide a smoke-free environment for employees whose sensitivity to tobacco smoke is deemed a disability. Providing a smoke-free environment may require something as simple as moving the employee away from the source of the smoke, or it may require installation of special ventilation systems to reduce the amount of second-hand smoke.

Employers covered by the ADA as a place of public accommodation may also be required to reasonably accommodate patrons with allergies or sensitivity to smoke, if these allergies or sensitivities constitute disabilities. A court recently held that a total ban on smoking in fast-food restaurants would constitute a reasonable accommodation for three children with asthma and a woman with lupus. In contrast, other courts have held that a total ban would fundamentally alter the nature of the services provided and would not be a reasonable accommodation. Employers faced with this sort of dilemma should ensure that the economic realities of their businesses and of similar businesses support whatever decision will be made.

Rehabilitation Act of 1973

The federal Rehabilitation Act of 1973 also prohibits discrimination in employment against qualified individuals with disabilities or handicaps. Section 504 of the law applies to all employers receiving federal financial assistance. Employees have filed lawsuits under the Rehabilitation Act alleging that their employers' failure to prohibit or limit workplace smoking or accommodate their respiratory affliction was unlawful discrimination.

National Labor Relations Act

Smoking policies and rules are mandatory subjects of bargaining under the National Labor Relations Act. Employers must meet bargaining obligations with any union before implementing or changing any smoking policies for employees. Failure to do so may lead to grievance arbitration under collective bargaining agreements and/or unfair labor practice proceedings at the National Labor Relations Board.

The Occupational Safety and Health Act Standard

OSHA studied reports on ETS and indoor air quality and concluded that 20 to 35 percent of American workers have problems caused by poor indoor air quality and ETS. These problems result in absences, illness, lost productivity, and discomfort for the affected workers. In response to this problem, OSHA in 1994 proposed regulations on indoor air quality standards and solicited comments and conducted hearings on the proposed regulations. Based on issues raised in the comments, OSHA sponsored a scientific workshop to evaluate risk-assessment methodology to estimate risk due to exposure to environmental tobacco smoke in the workplace.

OSHA's proposed standard would require all industrial and non-industrial work environments subject to OSHA jurisdiction to do the following:

- Write and implement an indoor air quality compliance plan.
- Implement procedures for maintaining air quality during construction, renovations, and remodeling.
- Implement controls for special contaminants, including outdoor air, pesticides, and maintenance and cleaning contaminants.
- Maintain records of inspection and maintenance of ventilation systems, compliance with the indoor air quality plan, and complaints regarding indoor air quality.
- Train employees and maintenance personnel regarding indoor air quality and compliance with the indoor air quality plan.

If the proposed standard is implemented, OSHA has indicated that employers will have 14 months to comply.

Since findings suggest that at least 19 percent of employed smokers are exposed to secondhand smoke in the workplace and that ETS results in an increased risk of cancer, the proposed standard is designed to decrease or eliminate exposure of nonsmoking employees to ETS caused by other employees and customers. The standard requires that work environments and enclosed workplaces either ban smoking or limit smoking to designated areas. OSHA has indicated that this standard would include banning smoking by customers if employees would be exposed to secondhand smoke. The standard, if adopted, would ban smoking on work-related transportation where nonsmoking employees could be exposed to secondhand smoke.

Final action on the proposed standard has been delayed indefinitely. As of 1998, OSHA's administrator suggested that Congress should supersede the rulemaking by legislatively restricting smoking in the workplace and providing OSHA with enforcement authority.

State and Local Regulations

A number of states have adopted legislation regulating smoking in the workplace by requiring that nonsmoking areas be provided for members of the public and employees. Other governmental bodies within the state (for example, city governments) may have adopted restrictions on smoking in the workplace or in public buildings. Some state courts have imposed on employers a duty to provide a safe workplace for employees, and this may require the imposition of smoking restrictions.

Controlling ETS

Limiting or prohibiting smoking in the workplace and the resulting control of ETS may have the following practical and legal benefits for employers:

- Decreased injuries, illnesses, and deaths among smoking employees.
- Reduced health-insurance costs.
- Lower repair and maintenance bills for equipment and furnishings damaged by smoke.
- Reduced danger of fire and other safety hazards.
- Less irritation of nonsmoking employees and thus fewer claims resulting from second hand smoke.
- Increased worker productivity.

Smoking Bans

An employer may be able to totally or partially ban smoking in the workplace. Such bans have generally withstood legal challenges, except where imposed unilaterally by a unionized employer in derogation of its duty to bargain.

Total Bans

A total ban on smoking in the workplace has obvious problems. Certainly such a ban will be hard on employees who smoke and may lead to employee alienation, organized resistance, or clear and malicious violation of the rules. On balance, it may be welcomed by a majority of employees who do not smoke. Employers should carefully study the possible effects of a total smoking ban on employee morale.

Employers who do decide to implement a total ban on smoking should consider this two-step approach:

- The workforce—including management, the union, and the employees—should be familiarized with the dangers of ETS and the reasons for imposing a ban on smoking.

- The ban should be accompanied by a company-paid wellness program designed to help employees and their families quit smoking. Wellness programs designed to help people quit smoking are generally recognized as providing a good return on investment because of reduced health-insurance costs and improved productivity.

Partial Bans

Partial bans on smoking are generally more acceptable to the smoking employees. Under a partial smoking ban, employees can still smoke in specified areas and segregated lunchrooms, while work areas, hallways, restaurants, conference rooms, private offices and employee lounges, are usually designated as no smoking areas. A negative side effect of specifying nonworking areas as smoking areas is that smoking employees may take more frequent or longer breaks away from their work areas.

Engineering Controls

The most effective engineering control for ETS is to create separate smoking lounges with separate ventilation directly to the outside. Such areas should be under negative pressure so that smoke does not migrate to adjacent hallways and other areas of the building. A less effective control is to create separate smoking lounges on the same ventilation system as the nonsmoking areas but accompanying this setup with an air-filtration system.

The American Society of Heating, Refrigerating and Air-Conditioning Engineers recommends that up to 60 cubic feet of outdoor air per minute be provided to smoking lounges. Effective ventilation measures include ensuring that outdoor air supply dampers are open, removing partitions that might interfere with fresh-air flow, and locating outside air intakes away from potential sources of contaminants. Fans should be installed within the smoking areas to improve the dilution of pollutants. If necessary, the entire air distribution system should be redesigned or rebalanced to ensure proper replacement of air and the proper inflow and outflow of contaminated and replacement air.

Air can be treated for the removal of contaminants through the use of filtration, electronic air cleaners, or by chemical treatment with activated charcoal or other absorbents. Keeping the temperature under 76°F and the humidity between 20 and 60 percent will also help reduce airborne pollutants. Filters should be replaced regularly and regular maintenance should be performed on the air handling system.

Administrative Controls

Some reduction of ETS may be achieved through such administrative controls as designating separate times for smokers and nonsmokers to use a specific area, such as the cafeteria. Smoking should be allowed only during breaks and lunch, and not at the workplace.

Employees who are hypersensitive to ETS should be evaluated and their problem identified and corrected before they return to work. If their illness persists they should be considered for reassignment to another area.

Rewards such as lower health-insurance rates can be offered to employees as incentives for not smoking. Such nonsmoking incentives tie in well with employer-supported programs to stop smoking.

Workforce Screening

The U.S. Supreme Court refused to hear an appeal from a Florida woman who would not sign an affidavit stating that she had not used tobacco products for one year before applying for a job with the City of North Miami. Because the Supreme Court refused her appeal, it left intact a ruling by the Florida Supreme Court that the City of North Miami has a legitimate interest in reducing its healthcare costs due to smoking and the use of tobacco products. The Florida Supreme Court also ruled that it was not a violation of privacy rights to require an applicant to provide information regarding his or her use of tobacco products.

However, it would be unwise for employers to have a policy of employing only nonsmokers. Such a policy might bring the risk of a reverse handicap or disability discrimination lawsuit based upon perceived addiction to nicotine. There may also be adverse impact based on race, sex, or national origin that could lead to accusations of violating Title VII.

Considerations in Implementing a Smoking Policy

Employers should consider what they are attempting to accomplish by developing and implementing a smoking policy. Is the policy a response to complaints by nonsmokers? Is the goal an attempt to cut insurance costs? Specifying these goals in advance will help the policy meet its intended goals.

Employee concerns should also be addressed in developing a company smoking policy. If employees are already following their own informal rules, for example, the policy may simply require a formalization of these rules. Employees should be included in the process of developing any smoking policy to help gain the cooperation of employees who smoke.

Employers should also be sure they have defined the ways by which a smoking policy will be enforced. The policy must clearly state disciplinary procedures, which must be followed closely and administered uniformly.

Some issues which must be addressed in considering and designing a smoking policy are included in the following list:

- Will a smoking policy affect productivity?
- Will a smoking policy affect insurance costs?
- Will a smoking policy affect customer or client relations?
- Should the smoking policy include a total or a partial ban on smoking?
- In cases of partial bans on smoking, are designated smoking areas truly isolated or can smoke be transmitted through vent or air conditioning systems?
- Would confining smoking to certain areas protect those working near those areas?
- Should a smoking policy include all forms of tobacco use, such as cigars, pipes, and smokeless tobacco?
- Does the smoking policy apply during nonworking hours, weekends, or holidays?
- Should the smoking policy apply to all employees, including managers, supervisors, directors, administrators, etc.?
- Will the smoking policy apply to customers or clients?

- If smoking employees are given additional smoke breaks during the workday should nonsmoking employees also receive additional breaks?
- If a smoking policy is implemented should guidance services or workshops be offered to encourage employees to quit smoking?

Massachusetts' Smoking in the Workplace Law

Massachusetts' smoking-in-the-workplace law appears in the Massachusetts Statutes, Part IV, Title I, Ch. 270, Crimes Against Public Health.

Basic Provisions

Massachusetts law prohibits smoking in public elevators, supermarkets or retail food outlets, on any public mass transit conveyances or on indoor or enclosed outdoor platforms of public mass transit, and at any open meeting of a governmental body.

Additionally, Massachusetts prohibits smoking in courthouses, schools, colleges, universities, museums, libraries, trains, airplanes, airport waiting areas, healthcare facility waiting areas, group childcare centers, school-aged daycare centers, family daycare centers, or in any public building.

Massachusetts law further prohibits smoking in the state house and in any buildings owned by the commonwealth or in any space occupied by a state agency or department of the commonwealth. Furthermore, smoking is not permitted in any restaurant with a seating capacity of 75 or more. Finally, under Massachusetts law an individual admitted to a healthcare facility must, upon request, be assigned a no-smoking room for the entire stay in the facility.

Flea Market No-Smoking Prohibition. Under Section 23 of the Massachusetts law, smoking is prohibited in any building used for a flea market, except in specifically designated areas clearly indicated by signs. Smoking is not permitted in any snack bar portion of a flea market.

Exceptions

Under Massachusetts' smoking law, smoking may be allowed in public buildings in areas designated specifically as smoking areas. An area can be designated a "Smoking Area" only if nonsmoking areas of sufficient size are available to accommodate nonsmokers.

The provisions of this section do not apply to residents or patients of state hospitals, the Soldiers' Home in Massachusetts, the Soldiers' Home in Holyoke, and any substance-abuse treatment center under the jurisdiction of the commonwealth.

Restaurants that seat over 75 may designate smoking areas if nonsmoking areas of sufficient size are available for nonsmokers. Smoking and nonsmoking areas in restaurants do not have to be separated by walls, partitions, or other physical barriers as long as the nonsmoking areas have at least 200 square feet of floor space.

Nothing in the law prohibits smoking in a completely enclosed private office used by an individual within a facility, public building, vehicle, or place described above.

Regardless of any exceptions provided in this section, nothing can be construed to permit smoking in any area in which smoking is prohibited by law or ordinance because of fire, health, or safety regulations.

Employers' Requirements

Massachusetts requires owners, managers, or other persons in charge of any of the facilities, buildings, or vehicles listed above to post a notice at each entrance indicating that smoking is prohibited except in specifically designated areas. Smoking and no-smoking areas must be conspicuously indicated by signs.

In the case of snack bars in flea markets, owners, managers, or other persons in charge must post notices or signs in conspicuous places at each entrance of the snack bar indicating that smoking is only permitted in specifically designated areas. These individuals must make reasonable efforts to ensure that no one smokes in the no-smoking areas. This reasonable effort must include requesting that a person smoking in a no-smoking area either stop smoking or move to a designated smoking area.

Retaliation Prohibition. Massachusetts law prohibits employers from terminating or otherwise discriminating against employees, independent contractors, or other workers for refusing to work in a smoking area or for exercising rights under the law.

Penalties

Individuals aggrieved by the willful failure or refusal to comply with any of the provisions of this section may complain in writing to the local health officer in the case of a restaurant, supermarket or retail food outlet; to the head of the department or agency where the violation occurs in the case of any public building; or to the local building inspector in the case of all other facilities. Authorities appealed to must respond in writing within 15 days to the complainant, indicating that they have inspected the area described in the complaint and that the provisions of the law have been enforced. The authorities must file a copy of the original complaint and the response to the complaint with the Department of Public Health.

Individuals that violate the provisions of the Massachusetts no-smoking law by smoking in no-smoking areas may be subject to a civil fine of $25 for each day in which the violation occurs. Any person violating the law in any way other than by smoking in a no-smoking area shall be subject to a civil fine of $50. Fines assessed for this violation are payable to the city or town in which the violation occurs. Local boards of health or health departments will enforce the prohibition through noncriminal disposition. Cities or towns may establish funds for the disposition of revenues received from smoking fines, with the funds expended to educate the public on the hazards of secondhand smoke environmental tobacco smoke.

Chapter 34
Workplace Violence

Introduction

The violence so common in our society does not occur only outside the workplace. Many employees each year are victims or perpetrators of violent acts. In 1993, for example, homicide was the second leading cause of death in the workplace, with more than 1,000 people murdered. In the 1992–93 fiscal year, more than two million people were attacked at work. Studies done over the past few years have shown that violence in the workplace is rising. This chapter reviews the serious problem of workplace violence and potential employer liability for workplace violence. It also considers Occupational Safety and Health Administration (OSHA) requirements concerning workplace violence and ways employers may lessen the chances for violence in their companies.

The Problem of Workplace Violence

According to a report issued by the Department of Labor and the Department of Justice, there has been a dramatic increase in the number of homicides, violent acts, and associated traumas in the workplace:

- Approximately 20 employees a week are killed in work-related homicides.
- Homicide has become the leading cause of death at work among women and the second-leading cause among men.
- Nearly one million people a year are the victims of violent crimes while at work.
- Eight percent of all rapes and 15 percent of all violent criminal acts occur at work.
- There are more than 200 suicides at work a year.
- Approximately two million workdays are missed annually because of workplace violence.

Workplace violence is not limited to homicides and physical assaults. It also includes more subtle behaviors such as stalking, threatening words or conduct, harassment, and similarly menacing conduct. Together these forms of physical and nonphysical violence victimize more than 25 million people a year. This results in a major decline in employee morale, management efficiency, and productivity, as well as significant costs in lost wages, higher benefits payments, and greater use of sick leave.

Workplace violence can also affect non-employees unlucky enough to be in the workplace during a violent incident. Workplace violence can create a variety of liabilities for employers. Even a single violent incident can result not only in the death or injury of employees or bystanders, but also in huge economic costs in the form of medical and psychiatric care, liability lawsuits, lost business and productivity, repairs or cleanup of a damaged worksite, and higher insurance rates.

Workplace Violence and Federal Regulations

Workers' Compensation

Employees injured as a result of workplace violence might have claims for workers' compensation. To be eligible for workers' compensation an employee must have been injured in the course of or out of employment. For example, the courts have held that an employee who was raped and murdered in the company employee parking lot was covered by workers' compensation. Her death or injury arose out of her employment since she was in the parking lot because of her work and she had been working. In contrast, the murder of an employee by a co-worker was not covered by workers' compensation when the murder took place in the employee's driveway and not at the workplace.

Although employers may try to reduce their liability for workplace violence by claiming workers' compensation as the exclusive remedy or means of recovery for any injuries, employees will try to prove that the conduct does not meet the requirements for workers' compensation exclusive coverage. Workers' compensation will provide the exclusive means of recovery if the following are true:

- The injury arises out of employment.
- The injury arises in the course of employment.
- The injury is not caused by an act against the victim personally or for personal reasons. Rather, it is directed at the employee **as an employee** or because of the employment.

In some cases, employees injured on the job have avoided workers' compensation pre-emption. These employees successfully sued their employers' subsidiaries where the related companies exclusively or owned the facilities in which the employees were injured. They were successful even though normally they would be entitled only to workers' compensation benefits. Such cases are highly dependent upon state law.

Anti-discrimination Laws

Title VII, as well as most state anti-discrimination laws, prohibits harassment based on protected classes such as race, color, creed, religion, sex, national origin, age, or disability. Aggression or violence against co-workers based on one of these protected areas is considered a form of harassment. Such behavior can lead to liability for employers who fail to prevent or attempt to prevent harassment in the workplace. Recent studies indicate that sexual harassment is often a precursor to violence, so an employee's complaints of sexual harassment must be taken seriously. Employers should conduct a careful and confidential investigation, being careful to avoid potential liability relating to discrimination, workplace violence, and a possible slander/libel action by the accused harasser.

Catch 22: Restricting Employers' Access To Information

Federal Protection of Potentially Violent Applicants and Employees

Employers attempting to identify potentially violent employees and applicants must consider federal legislation that protects individuals. An employer that screens out a disproportionate number of minorities through the use of arrest records may be held liable for racial discrimination because of disparate impact. Thus, the employer making use of such records should have a clear and articulated justification for doing so, and should be careful to treat all persons with arrest records in a consistent manner. Exclusion of an applicant with an arrest record is justified only where it appears the applicant in fact engaged in the conduct for which he was arrested, and such conduct was job related, and was relatively recent. Because a person convicted of a crime has been found to have committed the wrongful act beyond a reasonable doubt, the employer need only consider whether the crime occurred recently and is related to the job duties.

Another federal protection is the Employee Polygraph Protection Act of 1988 (EPPA), which prevents most private employers from using polygraph to screen prospective employees, but an employer may request a current employee to take a polygraph test where it is administered in connection with an ongoing investigation involving economic loss or injury to the employer's business.

The use of medical or psychological examinations on employees or applicants is limited by the American with Disabilities Act (ADA), which covers individuals with a physical or mental impairment that substantially limits one or more major life activities, or who has a record of such impairment, or who is regarded as having such impairment.

Federal law also prohibits interception of wire or oral communications by employees except where the employee has consented to monitoring or pursuant to the business extension exception, which provides that monitoring done in the ordinary course of business is permissible. Where an employer has a reasonable suspicion that a particular employee poses a threat of violence and reasonably believes that monitoring calls could help prevent the problems contemplated, the employer has a strong argument that such monitoring is being done in the ordinary course of business and would therefore enjoy the protection of the business extension exception.

Additionally, employers who are party to certain government contracts may not disclose medical information about employees except in limited circumstances. Pursuant to the Rehabilitation Act of 1973 and the Vietnam Era Veterans' Readjustment Assistance Act of 1974 (VEVRAA), covered employees may disclose medical information only where supervisors have a need to know because of possible work restrictions or accommodations, where safety and first aid personnel would need such information for emergency treatment, or where government personnel administering the statute request such information. Where the employer has reasonable belief that an employee has violent propensities, supervisors most likely need to know such information.

State Law Issues

Employers attempting to identify potentially violent employees and applicants must also consider state law restrictions such as drug testing statutes, potential claims for defamation, and claims for invasion-of-privacy. For example, a number of states restrict employers' ability to refuse to hire former convicts who have completed their sentence of imprisonment and are seeking to become re-employed. States also have their own polygraph and similar restrictions, as well as their own fair employment acts covering individuals with disabilities. Many states have restrictions on when, where, and how an employer may test an applicant and/or an employee for drugs. These statutes must be reviewed in conjunction with an employer's hiring and recruitment activities.

Employees and applicants also have common law protections. To prove a claim for defamation, the employee must prove a public disclosure, by the employer, of a false statement of fact that the employer knows to be false or in reckless disregard of truth. A claim for invasion-of-privacy requires a public disclosure of private facts that would be objectionable to a reasonable person of ordinary sensibilities. Employers must consider the possibility of receiving such claims by employees and/or applicants and must limit the information regarding these individuals released to the public and within the company itself.

OSHA Requirements

On March 14, 1996, OSHA released its *Guidelines for Workplace Violence Prevention Programs for Health Care and Social Service Workers.* Also, on June 28, 1996, OSHA issued a draft version of its *Guidelines for Workplace Violence Prevention Programs for Night Retail Establishments.* OSHA is currently working on guidelines for general industry. However, since no specific federal job safety standard has been issued to address workplace violence, OSHA is utilizing a 1992 agency enforcement policy against employers who do not protect workers from criminal violence in the workplace. Pursuant to the "general duty" clause of OSH Act (section 5(a)(1) of the act), employers have a responsibility to provide a workplace free from recognized hazards that are causing or likely to cause serious physical harm or death to employees. OSHA has promised more aggressive agency enforcement actions.

The first step in the regulatory area for more aggressive enforcement is the Health Care and Social Services Guidelines for Workplace Violence. Proclaiming, "[v]iolence in the healthcare and social services industries is endemic," the agency identified psychiatric facilities, community mental health clinics, infirmaries in correction departments, pharmacies, and community care facilities as particularly troublesome sites of violence. OSHA also noted that about two-thirds of the workplace violence occurs in these two industries.

OSHA cited risk factors arising from the general environment, administrative and work practices. The first category includes the prevalence of handguns, including those carried by patients and their families, and the early release of acute and chronically ill patients from hospitals. Drug and alcohol use frequently characterize the assaulter, particularly younger males, seeking to rob pharmacies. Older patients are often involved in assaults of healthcare personnel in long-term facilities.

Administrative and work practice risk factors include inadequate staffing patterns, particularly during periods of increased activity such as meal times, visiting hours, and the transportation of patients. But they also include isolated work with patients or working alone in remote areas, long waits by patients to obtain services or the inability to obtain these services as perceived by patients, lack of control access to facilities by the public, and poorly lighted parking areas.

Home and community health and social service workers are additionally at risk because they work outside of any fixed worksite, in neighborhoods with which they may not be familiar, and in places "that even armed police don't like to visit."

To assist employers in assessing the risk factors for violence to which their employees might be exposed, OSHA has developed a checklist that it has appended to the guidelines. The guidelines describe the kind of program development OSHA expects employers to undertake. This includes top management committee and employee involvement.

The guidelines also call for a written program including a worksite analysis (a record review and observation and identification of security hazards), hazard prevention and control (including engineering controls, administrative and work practice controls, and proper maintenance of security systems), and post-incident response (including proper medical and trauma-crisis counseling). Specific program elements are also specified for different work settings. Training for management and staff should include, among other things, the causes and early recognition of escalating behavior or warning signs of assaults, and means of preventing or diffusing volatile situations.

Recordkeeping is also detailed. In addition to recording any injury, requiring more than first aid to the OSHA 200 form, records should be maintained on incidents of abuse; verbal attacks or aggressive behavior; with respect to patients, history of past violence, or other factors such as drug abuse and criminal behavior; and minutes of safety meetings and inspections, including corrective action, and records of training program contents. Finally, ongoing evaluations are also required to determine where improvements are needed.

While the present guidelines relate to social services, as well as healthcare establishments and programs, similar guidelines relating to other industries, including night retail facilities, are expected from OSHA. However, if the experience with ergonomics is any indication, OSHA may seek to apply the principles of these guidelines to other industries and circumstances on a case-by-case basis, despite the initial setback it has suffered at the hands of the Occupational Safety and Health Review Commission (OSHRC).

Under OSH Act, employers are required to furnish workplaces free from recognized hazards that are likely to cause death or serious physical harm to employees. Under the OSH Act general-duty clause, an employer may be held liable when an employee is subjected to violence in the workplace. OSHA has used the general-duty clause to cite employers in situations where customers or patients have assaulted employees. Courts have also held employers legally responsible for injuries resulting from workplace violence, even for actions not directly attributable to the employer.

OSHA has issued guidelines for preventing workplace violence in institutional and community healthcare settings to reduce healthcare and social service workers' risk of physical harm. While not mandatory, the advisory guidelines establish a program to deal with and prevent workplace violence. The program includes violence-prevention techniques, workplace analysis, hazard prevention and control, training and education, and recordkeeping and evaluation.

Preventive programs, such as compliance with OSHA guidelines, cannot only help ensure the safety of employees and others who frequent the workplace, but can also help eliminate the likelihood that an employer will be held liable for an incident of workplace violence. Employers that institute training and preventative programs and that maintain good safety records can often avoid liability, since these efforts show that the employer is working to meet OSHA standards.

OSHA's List of Potentially Dangerous Work Environments

OSHA has identified certain work environments as having heightened potential for injury and possibly death for employees from violent conduct. For example, the rate of nonfatal injuries to employees in nursing homes and residential care facilities is more than 10 times that in all private industries. Employment situations that might lead to employee injury or death include the following:

- Contact with the public.
- Delivery of goods and services.
- Exchanging money with the public.
- Working alone or in small numbers.
- Working late at night or early in the morning.
- Working in high-crime areas.
- Guarding valuable property.
- Working in community settings (taxi drivers, police officers).

Employer Obligations/Liabilities

Employers generally are legally responsible for the employment-related actions of their employees. Employers can incur liability through negligent hiring and retention and negligent supervision, discussed in **Chapter 17, Negligent Retention and Supervision.**

Negligent Hiring/Negligent Retention

For more than 100 years, various courts have recognized negligent hiring or negligent retention as an independent basis for a court action. Negligent hiring occurs when an employer knew or should have known of an employee's unfitness even before the employee was hired. In these cases the employer's liability is based primarily on the adequacy of the pre-employment investigation into the employee's background.

Negligent retention occurs when the employer becomes aware—or should have become aware—of an employee's unfitness during the course of employment, and the employer nevertheless fails to take further action, such as investigating, discharging, or reassigning.

A claim for negligent hiring and negligent retention can be made even if the violent act by an employee takes place outside the workplace and is not part of the employee's work duties. For example, one court held an employer liable when an employee was murdered by a fellow employee at her home several hours after her shift ended. Actions based on negligent hiring or negligent retention will not succeed, however, unless the individual bringing the claim has been physically injured or has been threatened with physical injury.

Negligent Supervision

Employers may be held liable for failure to more closely monitor an employee who erupts into violent behavior. This is particularly true when there is evidence that an employee has a tendency toward violent or aggressive behavior and works in a situation where there may be a chance for such violent behavior to occur.

Particular care should be taken in supervising employees whose jobs require frequent high-stress contact with the public, supervision and discipline of other employees, or demanding production quotas, especially if the work atmosphere among co-workers is competitive.

Anticipating Trouble

Certain characteristics of a troubled work environment and a troubled workforce can provide employers with warnings of potential workplace violence. By heeding these signs employers may be able to avoid liability for violent incidents in the workplace.

Signs of a Troubled Work Environment

Employers should be on the lookout for any of the following signs suggesting potential problems with the work environment:

- Chronic labor/management disputes.
- Extraordinary number of injury claims.
- Frequent employee grievances or complaints, particularly of harassment.
- Understaffing or excessive demands for overtime.
- High worker stress.
- Layoffs and a corresponding increased workload for remaining employees.
- Authoritarian management.

Identifying Potentially Problematic Employees Before and During the Employment Relationship

Through the interviewing process, employers can learn more about the individuals they hire. Moreover, by training supervisors to recognize potential problems and implementing policies to handle threats of violence, employers can increase the possibility of recognizing and containing situations that could lead to acts of violence.

As a reasonable employer, certain steps should be taken in order to spot dangerous individuals. A background check should be performed on every individual prior to hiring. The intensity of that investigation should be commensurate with the opportunity that a particular position will afford an individual to injure others. All background information should be carefully checked, paying close attention to gaps in employment and patterns of brief employment.

A criminal records search also should be considered. The level of investigation must correspond, however, with the amount of contact that an employee will have with the public. Of particular concern are employees that will enter the homes of customers. Remember that a job applicant wants a job. Ask applicants to sign a waiver consenting to a background check. As discussed later, he or she can waive certain rights to privacy.

If a position is particularly prone to stress, psychological screening may be in order. Keep in mind, however, that as a potential medical test, psychological screening may violate the Americans with Disabilities Act (ADA). Thus, such screening should only be done post-offer as a condition of employment. Remember also that such screening must be job related, and consistent with business necessity.

The correlation between drug abuse and erratic behavior is irrefutable. The U.S. Department of Transportation and its operating administrations require testing of its applicants and employees in transportation-related, safety-sensitive positions. States vary with regard to drug testing laws, some being more liberal than others. All states permit substance abuse testing of some kind, although certain states and locations impose conditions on the basis for or manner of testing. Some states, for example, have statutes that provide an employee may be asked to take a drug test if the employer has a reasonable suspicion of drug use. An employer should educate itself or seek assistance in researching applicable drug testing laws, and its applicability to its operations.

If possible, human resource representatives should consider periodic walk-throughs of the workplace and keep office hours for employees to stop in with concerns. Second- and third-shift employees pose special risks without the same resources and level of supervision as the daytime employees. If you have a second or third shift, consider making yourself available at least one night a month or early in the morning. Bi-weekly or monthly meetings may also be helpful to communicate workplace policies to second- and third-shift employees and give them a feeling of belonging to the organization. These same suggestions apply to the weekend crew.

Dealing With the Violent Individual

Standard strategies for coping with violent individuals include the following:

- Give the potentially violent person enough physical space.
- Avoid glaring or staring, which may be seen as a challenge.

- Speak softly.
- Listen carefully. Don't be judgmental.
- Observe the individual's body language.
- Avoid touching a potentially violent person.
- Try to have a colleague with you.
- Have a code or signal that informs others of potential violence.
- Mentally design a safety plan.

Ways to Avoid Incidents of Workplace Violence

Unfortunately, even employers sensitive to potential violence-related problems in their workplace or with their employees are limited by a variety of legal issues in their ability to maintain a safe workplace. Potential liability under federal and state statutes increases an employer's difficulty in securing the workplace. The following elements should be included in any employer's program to establish and maintain a safe working environment:

- An anti-violence policy.
- Pre-employment screening.
- Informed management.
- Fair treatment of employees.
- Education programs.
- Counseling.
- Security.
- Threat assessment team.
- Aftermath training.
- Substance-abuse policy.

Anti-violence Policy

Employers must begin by developing a strong policy statement—similar to an anti-harassment policy—confirming that aggression and violence will not be tolerated in the workplace. The policy must be crafted in accordance with federal and state laws. Employers must communicate this policy to their employees. The anti-violence policy statement should indicate that its purpose is intended to be protective and not punitive, and it should encourage employees to actively cooperate in making their workplace safe.

Note: Employers of unionized employees should plan to involve the union in developing any anti-violence program.

Pre-employment Screening

Inadequate pre-employment screening may lead not only to negligent-hiring problems, but also to a less-desirable applicant pool and workforce. Pre-employment screening should include drug testing, background checks, and careful interviews. Employers should use employment applications that include a release allowing them to verify information reported by applicants. Before extending an offer of employment employers should check references and inquire about any previous incidents of violence. Gaps in employment history should be scrutinized.

Questions such as the following could be used:

- Have you ever been disciplined for fighting, assaults, or related behavior?
- Have you ever been discharged or disciplined for violating safety rules?
- Have you ever been disciplined for harassing another employee?

Included in the application should be a statement that the information being provided is truthful and accurate and that omissions or false statements will result in termination of employment.

Informed Management

Management must be informed about the risks of workplace violence and be committed to working to reduce those risks. A good safety program begins with management committed to making the program work. Management should present the anti-violence policy as a positive preventive measure for the safety of employees and should be constantly on watch for signs of a troubled work environment that may indicate a need for intervention.

Fair Treatment of Employees

One of the greatest risks of workplace violence occurs with employees who feel they are not being treated fairly. Employers should treat employees as the employers themselves would like to be treated. They should develop a system of due process for employees who are being disciplined. Complaints about employees should be investigated promptly and the results of these investigations should be communicated to the appropriate parties.

An anti-violence policy should contain an employee dispute-resolution program that could help management identify and resolve workplace disputes before they become incidents of violence or dissension.

Education Programs

Education programs should be developed for management and employees. Managers and supervisors need to be able to recognize signs of potential workplace violence. Supervisors need to be trained to treat all employees fairly and consistently. Employees should be trained to deal with workplace diversity. Everyone should be trained to deal with emergency situations and to implement an emergency action plan. Security and conflict-resolution training can also be helpful.

Counseling

When problems arise, employees need to be dealt with quickly, before a crisis develops. Employers should consider establishing an Employee Assistance Program (EAP) if one does not exist. Employers should be open to the possibility of medical referrals for employees who may need medical evaluations or whose drug, alcohol, or behavior problems indicate the need for a reasonable accommodation in order to avoid violating the Americans with Disabilities Act.

Security

Employers should take the following steps to protect their employees:

- Make sure there is adequate security to protect employees from outside dangers. Provide locked areas, require security passes, limit access by outsiders, improve lighting, and install cameras and mirrors.

- Eliminate obstructions, for example, hedges, to views of the interior of night retail establishments so that police or passers-by may observe any criminal activity.

- Have escape routes for employees.

- Consider hiring security guards who are fully trained to respond to incidents of workplace violence.

- Specify in the anti-violence policy that locker or desk searches may be conducted in appropriate situations.

- Consider conducting safety audits. A safety audit should rate each area and identify those areas needing improvement. It should contain a realistic improvement plan for areas in need of improvement. Honest reporting and tracking of incidents, with proper follow-up, are essential.

- Provide telecommunication devices to summon assistance, where practicable.

Threat-assessment Team

A formal procedure should be developed for handling threats. A threat-assessment team is a group intended to deal with threats. Since a multidisciplinary approach is necessary to deal with the complexities of an actual situation, the team might include a health professional, an attorney, a risk manager, and security and human resources personnel. The team should draft procedures to follow in evaluating a threat and it should recommend a response to the appropriate officer. The team should recommend any potential discipline, counseling, or the adoption of special security measures when a threat occurs.

Aftermath Training

Plans should be put in place to handle the occurrence and aftermath of acts of workplace violence. A clear plan can go a long way toward restoring order in an employer's facility after a violent act has occurred. Employers should take advantage of community resources, such as the local police department, to formulate the company's after-crisis plan and to communicate that plan to employees.

Chapter 35
Safety in the Workplace

Introduction

State laws may impose obligations on employers to maintain a safe and healthy workplace. In addition, the federal Occupational Safety and Health Act (OSH Act) and approved state safety and health programs require virtually all private-sector employees to observe safety standards throughout the workplace.

This chapter covers the federal standards that govern safety and health in the workplace, including AIDS and the Bloodborne Pathogen Standard, the Clean Indoor Air Act, OSH Act, and workplace violence. The section on the Occupational Safety and Health Administration (OSHA) focuses special attention to on-site inspections and hazard communication standards. Contacts for further information on the subject of health and safety in the workplace are given at the end of the section on the federal government and safety and health.

A separate section, before review of any specific state law, presents basically a "Workplace Safety and Health Guidebook," detailing some ways organizations can reinforce the importance of safe and healthful practices in the workplace.

The Federal Government and Workplace Safety and Health

AIDS and the Bloodborne Pathogen Standard

All states have adopted the Federal Bloodborne Pathogen Standard and essentially follow the federal guidelines. OSHA determined that certain categories of employees face a significant health risk as a result of occupational exposure to blood and other potentially infectious materials that might contain bloodborne pathogens. The pathogens of most concern are Hepatitis B and HIV, which causes acquired immune-deficiency syndrome (AIDS). The standard requires employers to identify those tasks and procedures in which occupational exposure may occur and to identify employees who must perform such tasks. The standard requires employers to use universal precautions and work-practice controls to safeguard against exposure to bloodborne pathogens. Affected employees must be given the opportunity to receive, at no cost, Hepatitis B vaccinations but cannot be required to participate in a vaccination program.

If an employee is exposed to bloodborne pathogens, the employer must immediately make available confidential medical evaluation and follow-up and make all reasonable efforts to have the source individual tested to determine his or her infectious status. If the source individual refuses to undergo testing, an employer cannot require him or her to submit to testing.

Where employees are potentially occupationally exposed to blood and other infectious materials, a written bloodborne pathogen program must be developed. Affected employees must be appropriately trained, records of the training must be kept, and all medical records created under the program must be maintained in a confidential file.

Occupational Safety and Health Act

The federal Occupational Safety and Health Act of 1970 (OSH Act) became effective April 28, 1971. The stated purpose of the act is to provide "every working man and woman in the nation safe and healthful working conditions." The act places the primary burden of achieving this goal on employers by requiring each employer to do the following:

- Provide a workplace free from safety and health hazards.
- Comply with standards set by the Occupational Safety and Health Administration (OSHA).

The act extends to private sector employment in any of the 50 states, the District of Columbia, Puerto Rico, the Virgin Islands, and several other U.S. possessions. However, federal and state public employment is not subject to OSHA coverage under the act. Federal employment worksites were made subject to OSHA inspection by an executive order.

The OSH Act allows the states to assume responsibility for occupational safety and health by adopting their own state plans. Any state plan must be "at least as effective" as the federal plan before the Secretary of Labor will approve it. Such plans may cover public employees in addition to private sector employees, or may be restricted to public employees alone (in Connecticut, New York, and New Jersey). Twenty-four states plus the commonwealth of Puerto Rico and the territory of the Virgin Islands have approved plans.

Administration

The primary responsibility for carrying out the act rests with the Secretary of Labor and the Assistant Secretary of Labor for Occupational Safety and Health. The assistant secretary directs the day-to-day activities of the Occupational Safety and Health Administration (OSHA). OSHA's national headquarters are located in Washington, D.C., at the following address:

Headquarters Office
Occupational Safety and Health Administration
200 Constitution Avenue, N.W.
Washington, D.C. 20210
(202) 693-2000
OSHA 24-hour emergency hotline: 800-321-OSHA

In addition to the national office, the country is divided into 10 geographic regions, each headed by a regional administrator. Each region has a regional office and several area and district offices. The regional and area offices are responsible for conducting safety and health inspections. The employees who conduct these inspections are called *compliance officers*. Each regional director supervises and coordinates a staff of compliance officers.

The Occupational Safety and Health Act also created the National Institute for Occupational Safety and Health (NIOSH), which is part of the Department of Health and Human Services. NIOSH conducts research, develops occupational safety and health standards, and provides technical services to government, labor, and industry. NIOSH also tests and approves most personal protective devices such as breathing devices, and respirators. The primary function of NIOSH is research and testing. However, NIOSH has asked some employers to allow health inspections on their premises. The act allows NIOSH to conduct inspections and gives it authority to seek search warrants where necessary. Such NIOSH inspections will not result in a citation or penalty.

Enforcement

The Occupational Safety and Health Review Commission (OSHRC), composed of three commissioners, hears appeals of decisions of the agency's administrative law judges. The commission is designed to be independent of the Department of Labor. Administrative law judges hear all cases where an employer has questioned a citation or a proposed penalty. The full commission may then review the administrative law judge's decisions. If no review is directed, the judge's order becomes final 30 days after it is filed.

Consultation Services

OSHA, through federally funded state agencies, offers free consultation service to small businesses to help them comply with health and safety laws and regulations. Consultants will perform an on-site inspection of an employer's workplace and review specific health and safety programs to determine how well a company is complying with health and safety laws. An employer may request a consultant to visit the workplace and conduct a mock inspection. After the consultation, the consultant prepares a confidential written report containing the findings and recommendations and submits it to the employer. Although the employer must agree to correct any serious violations found during the inspection, no penalties are assessed and no referrals to OSHA enforcement are made. The consultants will help employers find acceptable solutions to workplace hazards noted during the mock inspection.

If a serious violation is not corrected or an imminent danger is discovered, the state consultation service will refer the violation to OSHA.

Employers should be prepared to correct the problems immediately or as soon as possible to avoid fines for violations that may be imposed for potentially dangerous situations.

Regulations and Standards

The Occupational Safety and Health Act has two basic components:

- Each employer is required to furnish each employee with a place to work "free from recognized hazards which are causing or are likely to cause death or serious physical harm." This provision is commonly referred to as the General Duty Clause. The section has been used as a catchall for unsafe conditions where there is no applicable safety or health standard. In recent years, the review commission and several courts have found that OSHA has overused this section and have tried to limit its application.

- The employer must comply with occupational safety and health standards. The Secretary of Labor has the authority to adopt safety and health standards—rules of conduct and minimum safeguards for the workplace.

Regulations are broken down into the following categories:

- **General industry standards.** General industry standards apply to all employers not engaged in construction or agriculture industries.

- **Construction standards.** A number of the general industry standards have been made applicable to the construction industry.

- **Agricultural standards.** Special standards apply to agricultural employers.

Inspections

The secretary of OSHA is authorized to inspect and investigate any covered place of employment. Some restrictions are placed on the time and manner of conducting an inspection, which may be viewed as creating certain rights for employers. Such restrictions are reviewed in the following sections.

Presentation of Credentials

The OSHA representative may only conduct an inspection "upon presenting appropriate credentials to the owner, operator, or agent in charge." Before allowing a compliance officer to enter the workplace and begin inspection, the employer may, and in fact should, insist on a presentation of credentials. In some situations, the employer may choose to contact the area OSHA director to confirm the identity of the compliance officer.

Reasonable Times

A second limitation placed upon compliance officers is that they may enter the workplace only at reasonable times; that is, during regular working hours and at other reasonable times. Employers should not hesitate to use this reasonable time requirement to ask for a postponement of an inspection if there is a good reason for doing so. For example, employers have successfully requested the postponement of an inspection when the company safety director was on vacation, when a critical order was nearing the end of production, and when major maintenance and repair work was being performed. However, if OSHA is concerned that the employer may use any delay to conceal evidence of a violation it may request prompt entry. In any event, OSHA instructions to staff permit an employer to request reasonable time (up to about an hour) in order that a responsible official may return to the premises to meet the inspector.

Reasonable Limits

OSHA also requires that inspections be made "within reasonable limits" and "in a reasonable manner." There is very little case law to explain these limitations, but employers should be aware of them. By administrative determination, OSHA has announced that it will not conduct inspections of home worksites of telecommuters.

Search Warrants

The Supreme Court has ruled that employers may force OSHA to obtain search warrants before OSHA inspectors are allowed into the workplace to conduct inspections. This is an important right that employers may wish to exercise in appropriate circumstances.

If an employer refuses entry to an OSHA compliance officer, OSHA may or may not try to get a search warrant. If no attempt is made, the compliance officer simply will not return. However, where serious hazards have been reported, OSHA generally will seek a warrant. If OSHA decides to pursue the matter it must apply to a federal district court for a warrant and present specific facts showing a belief that a violation existed or that the employer was selected on the basis of a neutral administrative plan. The warrant should describe with particularity the premises, or portions thereof, to be searched. It normally takes a minimum of two or three days to obtain a warrant. Employers who elect to demand a warrant should use this time to ensure compliance with all OSHA standards. An employer's refusal to honor a valid warrant may result in contempt of court sanctions.

Three Phases of OSHA Inspection

OSHA inspections have three main phases:

1. The opening conference.
2. The inspection or walk around.
3. The closing conference.

Employers have a right to participate in—and should participate in—all three phases of the inspection to effectively protect their interests.

Opening Conference

Once the employer is satisfied that the inspector's credentials are in order, the opening conference will begin. The employer should ask the inspector why OSHA has chosen its facility. For example, it is helpful to know whether the inspector is there as a result of an employee complaint, to investigate an accident, or under a general administrative plan. If the inspection is based on a complaint, the employer should request a copy of the complaint. (If an employee is the complainant, the complainant's name generally will be omitted.) This information is necessary for the employer to properly limit the scope of the inspection. The employer should take the opportunity during the opening conference to explain the company's safety program.

Walk Around

The next portion of the inspection is the walk around. The company representative has a right to and should stay with the inspector throughout the entire inspection. The company representative should keep detailed notes concerning the entire safety inspection and write a detailed report once the inspection is completed. The company might also consider having a maintenance employee on site to correct any minor violations the inspector points out during the inspection.

OSHA has encouraged its field offices to use photographs, videotape, and audiotape to document violations and otherwise gather information during the walk around. The OSHA representative must advise the employer that a video or audio record of the inspection will be made. Refusal to allow the recording will be treated as a refusal of entry. However, taping in security-clearance areas must be expressly authorized.

The OSHA inspector is not permitted to stage hazards or employee exposures or suggest that reenactments be videotaped. An employer should accompany the OSHA inspector throughout each phase of the walk around inspection, including photographs, video or audiotaping. In fact, the employer should consider making its own video or audiotape at the same time for documentation. (Side-by-side exposure monitoring for noise or toxic substances may also be used, where appropriate.)

Closing Conference

Following the completion of the inspection, the company official and OSHA inspector will hold a closing conference. In the closing conference, the inspector will discuss the alleged violation he or she observed during the inspection. At this time, the company official should inquire about the specifics of the violations but not make a verbal admission of violations. The OSHA inspector must show the existence of each violation and the appropriate correction for each violation. The company official should ensure that the OSHA representative provides a suggested abatement if a violation has been cited.

Citations and Penalties

If the compliance officer observes a violation of the safety and health standards, regulations, or the general duty clause, OSHA will issue a citation. The citation will advise the employer of the standard or regulation that has been violated, when correction must be completed, and the amount of any penalty the employer is expected to pay. Violations are classified as "non-serious," "serious," and "willful" or "repeated." No financial penalty is usually assessed for non-serious violations, although a penalty of up to $7,000 **may** be assessed for each such violation. Maximum penalties for serious violations, and failure to post warnings could be as much as $7,000 per violation. OSHA penalties for willful and repeated violations range from $5,000 to $70,000 per violation.

A serious violation is present if a substantial probability that death or serious physical harm could result from a condition that exists or from a practice that is adopted by the employer. However, a serious violation may be challenged if the employer did not know of and could not even with the exercise of reasonable diligence have known of the violation.

Appeals or "Contests"

An employer has the right to contest a citation and argue that it is improper before an OSHRC administrative law judge. The employer may contest any or all of the citations, the proposed penalties, or the proposed abatement dates. To contest a citation, the employer in most states must file a *Notice of Contest* within 15 working days of receiving the citation. Failure to file a timely *Notice of Contest* results in loss of the right. A *Notice of Contest* is filed with the area director who issued the citation.

OSHA and the employer will present their positions to an administrative law judge. The administrative law judge will issue a decision and either party may request a review by the review commission.

Recordkeeping Requirements

OSHA has two types of recordkeeping and reporting requirements. First, all employers are required to record and report employee accidents and illnesses. Second, some OSHA standards require specific recordkeeping.

The form used for recording work injuries and illnesses is OSHA Form 200—*Log and Summary*. Employers must prepare and maintain a separate form for each facility. Injuries and illnesses that must be recorded are those resulting in the following:

- Fatalities.
- Lost workdays.
- Transfer to another job, discharge, or medical treatment other than minor first aid.

Recordable injuries and accidents must be entered on the log as soon as possible, but no later than six working days after knowledge that a recordable injury has occurred.

In addition to the log, employers must also prepare an individual report for each recordable occupational injury or illness. OSHA Form 101 is designed for this purpose. This form must be completed within six working days from the time the employer became aware of the recordable injury or illness. At the end of the year, employers must prepare a summary of all recordable occupational injuries and illnesses for the calendar year and post it from February 1 to March 1 of each year.

In addition to the forms and reports described above, employers must report any accident that results in the death of an employee or the hospitalization of three or more employees. A verbal report must be submitted to OSHA's area director within eight hours of the incident. These reports can be made by telephone and will normally result in an on-site investigation.

Employers with no more than 10 employees at any time during the year are exempt from the requirements of maintaining OSHA Form 200 and OSHA Form 101, although these small employers are not exempt from the requirement of reporting accidents that result in fatalities or multiple hospitalizations. However, some small employers can anticipate being selected by the Bureau of Labor Statistics to participate in an annual survey. If so chosen, the small employer will not be exempt from recordkeeping requirements.

Under OSHA's new recordkeeping rule, these forms would change in 2002.

Refusals to Work

Under OSHA regulations, employees may refuse to perform unsafe work under certain conditions. If those conditions are present and an employee refuses to work, employers are prohibited from taking any action against the employee. Violation of this regulation can result in the reinstatement of discharged or suspended employees with an award of backpay.

Several circumstances must exist before an employee is protected under this regulation. Each of the following factors must be present:

- Good faith by the employee.
- Reasonable basis for believing conditions are unsafe.
- Risk of death or serious bodily injury.
- Opportunity given to employer to correct the unsafe conditions.
- Insufficient time for OSHA to act.

Employers should contact an attorney before taking any action against an employee who refuses to work because of unsafe conditions.

Employee Access to Exposure and Medical Records

An OSHA standard gives employees and their representatives the right to see and copy their exposure and medical records. The term *employee* includes current and former employees. Union representatives and designated representatives may also request exposure records, and persons with specific written authorization from the employee, may request his or her medical records. OSHA also may request such records; in the case of medical records, they may need a *Medical Records Access Order*. An employer has up to 15 days to comply with an employee's request for access. The standard does not create any new recordkeeping requirements; it simply requires that any exposure or medical records must be made available to employees who request access.

The OSHA Hazard Communication Standard

The Hazard Communication Standard establishes requirements for the evaluation of physical and health hazards of all chemicals produced, imported, or used within the U.S.

Coverage

The standard covers all employers within OSHA's jurisdiction if employees are exposed to hazardous chemicals.

Written Program

Covered employers must establish a comprehensive written hazard communication program that includes provisions for container labeling, Material Safety Data Sheets (MSDSs), and an employee training program. The program must contain a list of the hazardous chemicals in each work area and a method for informing employees of the hazards of various tasks. The written program need not be lengthy or complicated, but the written program must be available to employees, their designated representatives, the Assistant Secretary of OSHA, and the Director of the National Institute for Occupational Safety & Health (NIOSH).

Hazard Evaluation

Chemical manufacturers and importers are required to review the available scientific evidence concerning the hazards of chemicals they produce or import, and to report the information they find to their employees and to employers purchasing their products. Those employers may rely on the evaluation performed by the manufacturers or importers when establishing compliance programs for the hazardous chemicals purchased. Employers must conduct their own evaluations for hazardous chemicals created in their workplaces.

Each chemical is to be evaluated for its potential for adverse health effects and physical hazards. Certain chemicals are listed in the standard as hazardous in all cases. When evaluating chemicals, an employer must describe, in writing, the procedures used to determine the possible hazards. These written procedures must be made available upon request to employees, their designated representatives, OSHA, and NIOSH.

Labels and Other Forms of Writing

With a few exceptions, each appropriate container in the workplace must be identified as a hazardous chemical and include appropriate warnings. The term *container* includes stationary processing equipment in the workplace. Exceptions to the above labeling procedures are the following:

- Employers can post signs with information for a number of containers within a single work area that have similar hazards.

- Various types of written materials can be substituted for container labels on stationary equipment if they contain the same information as a label and are readily available to employees in the work area.

- Employers are not required to label portable containers, used by only one person on a single shift.

- Employers are not required to label pipes or piping systems.

Material Safety Data Sheets

Chemical manufacturers and importers must develop MSDSs for each hazardous chemical they produce or import. An MSDS is a technical bulletin intended to be the primary vehicle for transmitting information about a hazardous chemical to affected employers and employees. Each MSDS must be in English and include the following:

- The specific chemical identity and common names of the chemical.

- The physical and chemical characteristics of the material.

- The known health effects of the chemicals.

- Limits of exposure permitted under OSHA.

- Whether the chemical is considered to be a carcinogen.

- Safe handling procedures.

- Emergency and first-aid procedures.

- The identification of the organization responsible for preparing the MSDS.

Employers are responsible for obtaining or developing an MSDS for each hazardous chemical used in their workplaces. Copies must be readily available to employees and must be made available to an employee's designated representative and to OSHA inspectors.

Employee Information and Training

Employers must establish a training and information program for employees exposed to hazardous chemicals in their work areas at the time of initial assignment and whenever a new hazard is introduced into their work area. The program must include the following:

- The requirements of the standard.

- The employer's hazard communication program.

- The location of hazardous chemicals in an employee's work area.

- The location of evaluation procedures, list of hazardous chemicals, and required MSDSs.
- How to read and interpret information on labels and MSDSs.
- The physical and health hazards of the chemicals in the employee's work area.
- Protective measures for employees to take against hazards, including the use of protective equipment.
- Methods to be used to detect the presence of a hazardous chemical.

Employers should make their labeling system MSDSs known to contractors who come on site to do work, so they may instruct their employees as to the chemical hazards they may encounter. Likewise, the employer should ask the contractor for its MSDSs and labeling system so that the employer may protect its employees from chemical hazards brought on site.

Trade Secrets

A trade secret is a specific chemical formula, process, or make-up that gives an employer an advantage over competitors. Disclosure of trade secrets may, therefore, be limited to health professionals, employees, and their designated representatives under specified conditions of need and confidentiality. The extent to which employers must disclose trade secret information depends on whether a medical emergency exists or not.

Enforcement and Penalties

OSHA will enforce the Hazard Communication Standard through workplace inspections. Any covered employer violating the standard will be subject to a citation for each violation. Civil penalties may be up to $70,000 per violation.

OSHA Regulations on AIDS Virus and Other Bloodborne Viruses

This regulation sets a mandatory standard for limiting the risk of exposure to viruses carried in human blood, especially the AIDS virus and the Hepatitis B virus. The standard covers any worker in any industry with "occupational exposure" where it may reasonably be anticipated that the employee may contact human blood as the result of performing his or her duties. It does not cover employees who merely perform Good Samaritan acts, but does include employees whose duties at times may include providing first aid or medical assistance. The standard identifies 24 industry areas where workers are in contact with or handle blood, but the list is not intended to be exhaustive. OSHA estimates that 4.9 million healthcare workers and 1.2 million other workers will be protected by the standard.

The key provisions of the standard are summarized below:

- Each employer must prepare:
  - A list of job classifications in which all employees are exposed.
  - A list of job classifications in which only some employees are exposed and list the tasks and procedures involved.
- Each employer having one or more employees with occupational exposure must establish a written exposure control plan. Such plans must:
  - Establish a procedure for the evaluation of an incident involving the unprotected exposure of an employee to blood where transmission of a virus was possible.

Safety in the Workplace

- Be accessible in copy form to employees or their representatives.
- Be reviewed and updated at least annually.

♦ The standard establishes "universal precautions" to be observed to prevent contact with blood and other potentially infectious materials. Compliance with the precautions is to be monitored by the employer and included in employee discipline and performance evaluations. Special universal precautions apply to research laboratories and production facilities. Employers are also required to evaluate engineering controls and work practices to protect employees.

♦ Employers must require employees to use personal protective equipment when there is exposure. The equipment must be provided by the employer at no cost to the employee, must be readily accessible or issued to the employee, must be clean and in good repair, and must be appropriate to the exposure.

♦ Work sites must be maintained in a clean and sanitary condition. There must be an appropriate written schedule for cleaning and decontamination.

♦ Medical evaluations and procedures, including the Hepatitis B vaccination series, must be provided at no cost to employees with exposure. Post-exposure evaluation and follow-up must also be provided at no cost to all employees who have been exposed.

♦ Warning labels or red bags must be used as containers of regulated waste and infectious materials.

♦ Employers must provide a training program to employees who have "occupational exposure" at no cost to the employee and during working hours. The training must be appropriate to the educational level of the employees and conducted by someone knowledgeable. Training must be provided at the time of initial assignment and at least annually thereafter. Additional training must be provided whenever new tasks or procedures affect occupational exposure. The training must include the following:

- A copy of the standard with explanation.
- Information on viruses carried in blood and how they are transmitted.
- A description of the employer's exposure control plan.
- A description of universal precautions, engineering controls, and work practices that reduce the risk of such transmission, including the use of personal protective equipment.
- Information on the Hepatitis B vaccine.
- Information on exposure incidents.
- Information on labeling when appropriate.
- A question-and-answer session with the person conducting the training session.

♦ An accurate and confidential record of exposure incidents must be maintained for the duration of employment plus 30 years.

♦ A complete record of training sessions must be maintained for three years from the date of training.

As mandated by the Needlestick Safety and Prevention Act, OSHA has revised its bloodborne pathogen standard to clarify the need for employers to select safer needle devices as they become available and to involve employees in identifying and choosing the devices. The employer also has to record a log of injuries from contaminated sharps.

OSHA Personal Protective Equipment Standard

OSHA issued revised standards on the use of personal protective equipment in April, 1994, imposing strict requirements on all employers including those that do not currently require the use of personal protective equipment. The revised standards require employers to prepare and maintain written certifications that document the name of the person who has conducted assessments of the workplace. Employers that must require personal protective equipment must also provide specified training to affected employees and maintain certification that the training took place.

Employers are required to furnish appropriate eye and face protection during exposure to hazards from flying particles, fumes or gases, or light radiation. The revised standard requires the additional use of side protection and filter protection.

If there is a potential for head injury, the standard requires the employer to provide protective helmets, which must also include protection against electrical shock for employees near exposed electrical conductors. Protective footwear must be furnished if there is a danger of foot injuries from falling or rolling objects that might pierce the soles of the feet or if the feet are exposed to electrical hazards.

Employers must furnish hand protection if hands are exposed to harmful substances, cuts, chemical burns, or harmful temperatures. Appropriate hand protection must be selected based on evaluation of the conditions of the workplace, duration of use, and characteristics of the task to be performed.

The employer's workplace hazard assessment may not require the purchase of new equipment. However, if assessment is done as required by the standard and on a regular basis, the employer should inspect existing personal protective equipment for defects or improper fit, establishing compliance and further reasonable steps to ensure safety.

Workplace Violence

The violence rate in business throughout the country continues to be a grave concern. Employers could face possible OSHA citations for failure to protect employees from workplace violence. See **Chapter 34, Workplace Violence,** for more information.

OSHA currently requires employers to report all multiple hospitalizations and deaths that occur due to various on-the-job accidents, including workplace violence incidents, within eight hours of the accident. Failure to make such a report will subject the employer to fines and penalties. Employers can receive a free booklet from OSHA, titled *How to Prepare for Workplace Emergencies*, by writing to:

OSHA Publications
P.O. Box 37535
Washington, D.C. 20013-7535

The publication is No. 3088 and has been recently revised with the small-business owner in mind.

Whom to Contact

Federal Occupation Safety and Health Administration
www.osha.gov/
Federal Occupational Safety and Health Act
29 U.S.C §651 et. seq.

Guidelines for a Safe and Healthful Workplace—Developing a Program

Professionals in the safety and health industry are concerned with developing what they call a *safety culture* in the workplace. Basically, this is a pervasive feeling, shared by each employee of a company, that each employee is responsible for his or her own safety and health and for the safety and health of every other worker in the company. This feeling is grounded on each individual's conviction that he or she has a right to a safe and healthful workplace, a conviction reinforced by the company's placing an actual value on safety. Only with sincere commitment from management and serious involvement by employees can safety and health programs be successful.

The key term here is *value*, defined as a principle or standard or belief considered worthwhile and desirable. A safe and healthful workplace should be treated in a way that parallels more familiar values—free speech, right to assembly, even religion—in that safety and health are permanent parts of the organization's culture, not transitory things that are important at some times but not at others.

The Need for a Safety and Health Program

Every company needs some sort of a program to prevent injuries and illnesses on its premises. Even complete compliance with OSHA's guidelines will not eliminate all injuries and illness from the workplace because the workplace is filled with people and people make mistakes. However, physical safeguards, training, proper maintenance, and good management may help ensure the safety and health of most of a company's employees.

Benefits of a Safety and Health Program

Obviously, following OSHA guidelines should result in fewer injuries and illnesses in the workplace, but more rewards will result from a strong safety and health program. Workers' compensation costs may be lowered, employee morale and work efficiency may be improved, operating costs will be lowered and profits will be higher.

Accidents are expensive. They add to workers' compensation and medical costs, they make the company have to repair or replace equipment, they slow production, and they may require the company to hire and train new workers. These are just the material costs. The pain and suffering that accidents cause employees and their families can be even more damaging.

Requirements of a Safety and Health Program

Management Leadership

The National Institute for Occupational Safety and Health (NIOSH) identifies management commitment as the major controlling influence in creating a safe workplace. Managers must lead by using a variety of techniques to demonstrate their commitment to workplace safety and health. Managers may demonstrate their commitment in a variety of ways:

- Attending safety organization meetings.
- Participating in volunteer groups promoting various safety topics.
- Setting an example by following safety rules and regulations.

- Allowing employees free access to tools and equipment necessary to do a job safely.
- Offering employees training on specific safety issues.
- Attending training programs if appropriate to reinforce employee training.
- Participating in or leading safety and health committees.
- Making presentations on safety and health topics.
- Regularly emphasizing to the community the company's concern with safety and health.
- Conducting regular inspections.
- Rewarding the best safety and health suggestions.

Managers should regularly seek employees' opinions on safety and health issues and especially on how the employees view management's efforts to achieve a safe and healthful workplace. Managers should be available to hear employees' concerns about safety and health, and employees should feel free to express their views without fear of reprisal. Any suggestion that management is not totally committed to achieving a safe and healthful workplace will undermine any program in place and reduce an organization's chances of achieving stated safety and health goals. However, employers must be careful in dealing with employees and having employees acting in a committee actively involved in determining how safety problems and concerns are resolved. The National Labor Relations Board could consider such activity an unfair labor procedure.

Employee Involvement

Since rank-and-file employees are the ones most in contact with potential safety and health hazards in the workplace, it is essential that they be involved in any safety and health program a company sets up. Since these employees have a vested interest in achieving workplace safety—and have often been demonstrated to be valuable problem-solvers—their suggestions should be encouraged and taken seriously. The wider the field of experience brought to bear on solving safety problems, the better the solution. Additionally, employees are more likely to support a program they have helped develop.

Employees can be involved by allowing them an opportunity to participate in the process of establishing a safety and health program. Employees should have a way to make suggestions and, whenever possible, their suggestions should be implemented, or the employees should be told why their suggestions could not be implemented. When employees' ideas are implemented, their success should be communicated to other employees. In all instances, employees must be protected against harassment resulting from their involvement in a safety and health program.

Employees can be involved in developing safety and health programs in a number of specific ways beyond simply making suggestions for improvements:

- Employees can assist in conducting site surveys.
- Employees can assess routine hazards in each step of a job and help design safe practices to eliminate or reduce the hazards.
- They can participate in the development and revision of site safety and health rules.
- They can be involved in training new employees.
- The can give presentations at safety meetings.
- They can assist in conducting accident/incident investigations.
- Employees can participate on committees and other advisory or specific-purpose groups.

Individual Responsibility

Importance of Job Descriptions

Everyone in an organization is responsible for workplace safety and health, but specific responsibilities, authority, and accountability are essential if a safety and health program is going to work.

One excellent way to identify an individual's responsibilities in the safety and health program is through clearly detailed job descriptions. Obviously, job descriptions identify the particular duties and responsibilities of a position, and if these duties and responsibilities include those relating to the organization's safety and health program a good portion of assigning responsibility for safety and health issues will be accomplished.

Administrator Responsibility

The duties and responsibilities of administrators (presidents, site managers, even owners) should be written to include the ultimate responsibility for carrying out the stated company safety and health policy. These individuals should be required to set objectives for the safety and health program, support the program by providing equipment and training, assign clear responsibility for various aspects of the program, and require all employees and visitors—including vendors, subcontractors, customers, etc.—to follow the program.

Supervisor Responsibility

First-line supervisors must be held responsible for supervising and evaluating all safety- and health-related aspects of an employee's performance. They must encourage and support employee involvement in the safety and health program, and they must recognize and reward outstanding individual and group performance.

Additionally, first-line supervisors must maintain up-to-date knowledge of safety procedures and methods of detecting safety and health hazards. They must ensure that good housekeeping, including repair or replacement of equipment, is practiced in their area. They must discourage unsafe or unhealthful shortcuts. Finally, they must make certain that emergency procedures are in place and that everyone under their supervision knows what to do in an emergency.

Employee Responsibility

Employees must know the rules for ensuring safety and health in the workplace and they must observe these rules. Employees must review safety and health materials regularly, get instructions when necessary, and must be fully aware of their responsibilities in an emergency.

Safety and Health Director or Coordinator Responsibility

Safety and health directors must continue to develop their expertise in this area. They must keep informed of new laws and standards dealing with employee risk reduction and with injury and illness recordkeeping requirements. They must regularly evaluate the company's safety and health program and practices.

Company safety and health officers must conduct hazard analyses, develop plans for hazard prevention and control, and ensure that any required safety equipment or materials are available. They must help management enforce safety and health practices and help with inspections. Finally, health and safety officers should be responsible for handling investigations of employee reports of hazards and for responding to employee suggestions for improving safety and health.

Importance of Accountability

If a system of accountability is in place, the chances that everyone will fulfill his or her responsibilities will be enhanced. Individuals will be better able to understand and appreciate the importance of their performance if they are rewarded or punished for their successes or failures in safety and health practices. Accountability here must apply to administrators as well as employees if a company has any hope of its safety program being followed.

Job descriptions help with accountability as they do with responsibility. Job descriptions detail each individual's responsibilities in regards to safety and health, for example, "The employee must know how a respirator works and when it must be used." The individual's periodic evaluation can include assessment of his or her performance in matters of safety and health. The individual's safety and health performance must be evaluated in terms of stated safety and health objectives to determine if changes must be made in either the performance or the goals.

If an individual's safety and health performance is evaluated negatively, for example, a supervisor does not properly investigate an accident, some follow-up monitoring may be necessary to ensure the problem is corrected. Improvement or lack of improvement should be included in later performance evaluations. Whenever possible, positive reinforcement should be used to get cooperation on safety and health matters. Individuals should want to do well and be recognized verbally, in writing, through awards, incentives, etc. If, however, positive reinforcement fails, some consequences for poor safety and health performance must follow, ranging from counseling through written reprimand, suspension, demotion, or termination.

Ample Safety and Health Resources

Another essential aspect of any safety and health program is identifying—and subsequently providing—ample resources to ensure compliance with your company's safety and health program. If safety and health improvements are not made because of costs, an organization may be frustrating its safety and health program through shortsightedness. If only the least expensive measures to improve workplace safety and health are taken, for example, good equipment maintenance and housekeeping, benefits may be limited.

Resources for ensuring safety and health improvements include sufficient funding for improvements and new equipment as well as for training programs and, often, the cost of outside consultants. However, arguments can be made that safety and health improvements will save an organization money in medical and insurance expenses, workers' compensation costs, lost productivity, losses due to absenteeism and turnover, costs of equipment damage, and waste of materials, etc.

Existence of a Written Policy Statement

Any worthwhile safety and health program needs a policy statement, a written philosophy underlying the existence of the policy. The policy must be written in the clearest language possible, beginning with an introduction expressing the company's real concern for the safety and health of its employees and continuing with detailed descriptions of management and employee responsibilities. Since it is, in fact, the cornerstone of the company's safety and health program, the policy statement must have the support of management and employees.

By clarifying company safety and health policy, the statement will help ensure consistency and continuity in the application of the policy. It will also provide a checkpoint whenever safety and health concerns appear to conflict with production or other priorities and will support supervisors when they enforce safety and health rules and practices.

Contents of Policy Statement

Policy statements usually have the five parts explained below:

- **Introductory Statement.** This is simply a statement showing your concern for employee safety and health and should include a statement such as, "We consider the safety and health of our employees more important than any other aspect of company operations."

- **Purpose/Philosophy.** Your company's safety and health program should have a clear purpose or philosophy stated in the written policy so that management and employees are reminded of the program's intent and value: "Accidents and health hazards have no place in our company. We will involve management and employees in planning, developing, and implementing this safety and health program."

- **Management Responsibilities.** A company's safety and health policy statement should describe exactly who is responsible for ensuring that the program works and who has specific responsibilities, duties, and authority within the program. The policy should specify the responsible individuals and summarize their responsibilities, perhaps following a general statement such as, "Management representatives who have been assigned the safety and health responsibilities listed below will be held accountable for fulfilling those responsibilities."

- **Employee Responsibilities.** The contributions of employees to the company's safety and health program should be acknowledged and rewarded: "Employees must continue to work to prevent injuries and illnesses. The performance of each employee in this regard will be measured along with that employee's overall performance."

- **Closing Statement.** The written policy's closing statement should reaffirm the company's commitment to providing a safe and healthful workplace and should make a final appeal for management and employee cooperation.

Implementing a Safety and Health Program
Step 1: Clarifying Goals and Objectives

Underlying any written policy statement describing a company's health and safety program are, of course, the goals and objectives of the program. Goals can be either numerical—for example, a goal of zero hazards at any time—or descriptive—for example, a program that identifies and attempts to eliminate all potential hazards at a worksite.

To set goals and to identify the steps needed to attain these goals—the short-term objectives—management needs to answer several key questions:

- Where is the company currently with regard to safety and health?
- Where does it want to be?
- What must be done to get from where it is to where it wants to be?

Nature of Goals and Objectives

Successful goals and objectives have the following characteristics:

- They are realistic and attainable.
- They are readily understood by everyone seeking them.
- They provide maximum payoff for the time and resources expended to obtain them.
- They are consistent with available resources.
- They are consistent with basic organizational policies and practices.
- They relate directly to the roles of those accountable for attaining them.

Example: An objective such as this one is readily attainable, understandable, requires minimal time and resources, and should lead to the company's desired goal of eliminating workplace hazards: "Conduct weekly inspections with emphasis on good housekeeping, proper use of protective equipment, condition of critical parts of equipment, and preventive maintenance."

Communication of Goals and Objectives

To be effective, safety and health program goals and objectives must be communicated to everyone in the organization. This communication will reinforce the company's commitment to safety and health and help ensure that employees know their role in the safety and health program.

Review of Objectives

Management should review its objectives regularly to determine if supervisors and employees are working toward the ultimate goal of a safe and healthful workplace. If too many accidents or near accidents continue to occur, if too many days continue to be missed because of illness caused by workplace conditions, the objectives in place may need to be changed or supplemented.

Step 2: Providing Safety and Health Training

Once your organization has established and communicated its health and safety goals, training must be provided to ensure that managers, supervisors, and employees can attain these goals. Training can range from simple cautionary warnings given to new workers to elaborate formal training programs. Although training needs will vary from one organization to another, it is likely that all organizations will have to provide some training for new workers, instructing them on how to do a job and how to avoid the hazards associated with the job. Contract workers may need to be trained in the potential hazards of a particular workplace.

The installation of new equipment and changes in certain processes may create a need for training since hazards may be increased or new ones introduced. All employees may require regular refresher training to keep them prepared for potential emergencies. Finally, certain federal and state regulations require training; for example, hazard communication and lockout/tagout.

Training Design

The success of training depends on the commitment of managers, supervisors, and employees to an organization's safety and health program. To ensure that this commitment exists, employers must be sure of the following:

- The company's safety and health policy clearly addresses its commitment to training.
- Employees were involved in policy development or at least fully understand the policy.
- Management and employees were involved in developing the training program.
- The company shows its commitment to training by offering paid time for training.
- Ample resources are available to develop the training program.
- The training program will be conducted in such a way that employees will be able to understand it, including alternate languages if necessary.

Training programs need not be complex or lengthy. They may simply be based on your company's worksite analysis program. Accident and incident reports, including near misses, may be another indicator of training needs. A review of new work practices, new equipment, and new materials would provide a useful starting point for training programs.

Specialized Training Programs

Well-developed training programs focus on certain populations of workers:

- **New Employee Training.** New employees and temporary employees may need training in specific potential hazards of their job or the worksite. They also need to learn the company's attitude toward safety and health in the workplace. For these individuals, it is essential to communicate the purpose of each instruction in relation to their jobs and to provide them an opportunity to practice their newly learned skills. Errors must be pointed out immediately and successes rewarded. Training methods that use interesting and varied activities work best with this population. Regardless of the length or elaborateness of training, employees must receive instruction in emergency response before they start their jobs.

- **Safety and Health Training for Employees.** New and experienced employees need regular training on identifying workplace hazards and how to protect themselves and others from these hazards. A common approach here is a combination of classroom and on-the-job training. Often fellow employees can provide useful peer training.

All employees and their supervisors must be taught the proper selection, use, and maintenance of personal protection equipment. Employee training must include motivation to wear personal protective equipment in spite of its awkwardness and the discomfort it may cause.

Employees must be trained to respond to emergency situations. They must learn emergency telephone numbers, evacuation routes, emergency exits, etc. Trainers should conduct emergency evacuation drills to ensure that every employee is familiar with evacuation signals and procedures.

Note: Such drills should account for visitors, contract workers, and service employees who are frequently overlooked in emergencies.

Employees should also be given periodic training to refresh their memories about safety and health measures and to update them on new measures. Periodic safety meetings are frequently used to keep employees abreast of changing situations.

On-the-job training for employees frequently takes the form of supervisors observing employees at work and then meeting with them to evaluate their work practices, complimenting them on their safe work practices and suggesting changes or providing additional instruction when problems are noted.

To ensure that employee training is efficacious, instructors should follow the following guidelines:

- Prepare employees for training by putting them at ease.
- Recruit employees who show signs of being good trainers of their colleagues to conduct training sessions.
- Explain the job or training topic.
- Determine how much the employees already know.
- Boost employees' interest by explaining the benefits of training.
- Pace the instruction to the employees' learning speed.
- Present the material clearly and patiently.
- Present only as much in one session as the employees can master.
- Have the employees perform each step of specific operations.

Employees should be grouped into practice pairs to work on new skills. They should be closely monitored initially, less as they master the skills. They should be encouraged to build their new skills into their work gradually, ideally under supervision:

- **Safety and Health Training for Supervisors.** Since supervisors often do much on-the-job training, they need to be taught how to train employees and how to reinforce the training employees have received. They must also be trained to reward safe working practices and discipline unsafe ones fairly and consistently.

- **Safety and Health Training for Managers.** Training managers about their responsibilities regarding a safety and health program is essential to their understanding and support of the program and, indeed, to the program's survival.

  Training for managers should emphasize the importance of managers' visibly showing their support for the safety and health program. They must be taught how to communicate the program's goals and objectives to employees. They should also be taught the importance of their showing good example by scrupulously following all safety and health rules. Training for managers can be handled in a short time but should be repeated at least annually.

Evaluating Training Programs

Training programs should be evaluated regularly to see if they are actually improving employee safety and health. Programs can be evaluated by testing workers before and after they attend the programs to see if improved performance is evident. Interviews with employees who have attended the programs can show if the employees have understood and can explain appropriate safety and health practices. Based on the evaluation of the program, the employer can decide if it is meeting its goals, should be offered again, or needs to be improved.

Recordkeeping

Organizations should keep records of each employee's attendance at training sessions, including a brief evaluation of the individual's participation and success, if appropriate. These records will help ensure that everyone who needs training is receiving it and that refresher courses are provided regularly. They will also provide documentation, when needed, that the appropriate training was conducted.

Step 3: Identifying Hazards

Identifying workplace hazards is a necessary early step in implementing a safety and health program. Administrators who are not fully aware of existing and potential hazards in their facility must find a way to systematically identify the hazards, using approaches such as the following:

- Conducting regular site inspections.
- Performing periodic comprehensive safety, industrial hygiene, and health surveys.
- Analyzing potential hazards relating to changes such as new or planned facilities, equipment, materials, and processes.
- Performing routine hazard analysis of individual jobs, processes, production phases, etc.

Workplace Surveys

Surveys are not the same as inspections. Employees at the workplace may perform inspections. Surveys should be performed by people who can bring fresh vision and extensive knowledge of safety, health, and industrial hygiene to the workplace. Survey services may be provided by outside experts, although this is not required. Bringing in a person from outside can, however, add a fresh perspective and possibly the individual's experience other facilities will enhance the survey.

Periodic surveys allow an organization to take advantage of any new engineering or scientific knowledge of hazards and their prevention. They will also help identify new hazards that have evolved along with changing work processes and procedures.

Role of the Safety Professional

The safety professional, industrial hygienist, or occupational health professional will, among other things, look into the processes in use in a facility, watch each operation, talk with employees, check the chemical

Safety in the Workplace

inventory, inspect welding operations, evaluate smoking areas, review respirator maintenance, evaluate personnel training, conduct shift sampling for air contaminants, take noise measurements, conduct ergonomic assessments, and suggest improvements in the monitoring of health issues. Because of their important role in developing a workplace safety and health program, individuals selected to conduct these surveys must be well trained, have excellent references, and have relevant experience conducting such surveys.

Initiating a Survey

Surveys should start with the OSHA Form 200 Log, in which employers are required to record information about occupational deaths, injuries, and illnesses. The following questions should be asked at the beginning of a survey:

- Have any incidents occurred?
- Do any patterns exist?
- Are applicable written safety programs (for example, hazard communication, hearing conservation) in place?
- Are records of employee visits to clinics or first-aid stations available?
- Are training records maintained?
- Are safety programs communicated to employees?
- Are required posters, warning signs, and tags in use?

Analyzing Potential Hazards

It is usually less expensive to eliminate a problem before it occurs than to correct it after the fact, so individuals conducting surveys should be alert to some frequent causes of workplace problems:

- **Leased equipment or buildings.** The age and design of leased buildings—often designed for other purposes—can increase the potential for safety and health problems. Asbestos may be present. Hurried renovations may have omitted some basic considerations, such as repair to loose railings. Safety surveyors should review the facility and any available blueprints or renovation plans.

- **New equipment and materials.** Management cannot rely completely on manufacturers of equipment and materials to have analyzed all potential hazards of their products, since they cannot always know exactly how the products will be used at each facility. New materials and equipment can be hazardous and must be inspected carefully to identify potential hazards. Materials and equipment produced outside the U.S. must be checked for conformity with U.S. standards and laws.

- **New processes.** Since new processes require employees to perform new tasks they may cause new hazards, even if employees are using familiar equipment, materials, and facilities.

- **Changes in workers or staff.** The difference in skill and expertise whenever one employee is replaced by another can lead to greater risk to the new worker and to co-workers.

- **Changes in an individual worker.** Changes in an employee's health or attitude may affect the employee's ability to function on the job and can affect workplace safety and health. Organizations must provide orientation and training and reasonable adjustments or accommodations to remove such hazards.

Hazard analysis is usually broken down into routine hazard analysis, which consists of job hazard and process hazard analysis, and complex-process hazard analysis, which involves such areas as failure mode and effect analysis, fault tree analysis, and hazard operability studies. These include mechanical and chemical operations, low- and high-temperature operations, possible radiant energy, direct contamination of employees, etc., and are best left to outside experts.

Job Hazard Analysis

Job hazard analysis breaks down a job into its component steps, listing them in order, and determining if the job can be done without any hazards and what steps can be taken to eliminate existing hazards. Job hazard analysis should be done with the participation of the affected employee and any changes should be reviewed with the employee.

Process Hazard Analysis

Process hazard analysis analyzes any series of actions or operations that convert raw material into a product, from the entrance of the raw material into the factory, through intermediate stages, to the final product and any by-products and waste materials. This form of analysis includes analysis of the use, storage, manufacture, handling, or movement of any chemicals.

Process hazard analysis is usually performed by a team representing different disciplines, opinions, and perspectives, since a single person would usually not have the necessary background to understand all parts of the process. The process hazard analysis team can make use of flow charts to gain a visual and verbal understanding of each step in the process and how each step relates to the next. Additionally, the team can gain information by looking at each employee's actions and locations throughout the day. The team must consider the worker's potential exposure to hazards, the substances and equipment the worker uses, the safety implications of the worker's actions for others, etc. Measurements must be made of employee exposure to physical agents (for example, microwave radiation) and air contaminants. Results of a process hazard analysis may lead to recommendations for preventive measures and controls, including engineering controls, new work practices, and increased use of personal protective equipment.

Step 4: Preparing for Emergencies

Another step in implementing a workplace safety and health program is the anticipation of and preparation for the unexpected, a step even harder than identifying potential hazards. Those conducting surveys must analyze the hazards associated with unplanned events, not merely hazards associated with normal operations. Where in a company's operations could something go wrong? What problems would such aberrations cause? During emergencies hazards may appear that are not normally found in the workplace. These may be natural hazards—earthquakes, tornadoes, hurricanes, floods, ice storms, etc.—or they may be systems' hazards caused by failure of one or more hazard control systems.

Regular site inspections—conducted by supervisors and by employees inspecting other employees' worksites—will help identify some potential emergency situations, especially where dangerous chemicals or volatile explosives are involved, and an effective safety and health program should have procedures in place for handling the unexpected. Beyond inspecting the actual premises for possible emergencies, inspectors should consider hazards beyond the actual workplace. They should, for example, consider the chances for natural disasters likely to occur in the area. They should also consider the potential for human errors beyond the control of anyone in the plant. This might include possible problems from nearby airports or railroad tracks or from potentially dangerous sites in the area. Even political turmoil, such as terrorist activities, might be considered in designing emergency procedures.

As with all aspects of a safety and health program, employee involvement is essential. Employees have special knowledge gained from their close involvement with equipment, materials, and processes. Their involvement in hazard analysis will ensure their cooperation in identifying and correcting existing hazards and in anticipating potential ones. Employees must be trained to cope with emergencies and to contribute to resolving emergency situations by handling emergency equipment.

Once most of the possible emergency situations have been determined, a plan of action must be developed to reduce their potential impact. This would entail informing all employees of their roles in potential emergencies, arranging for training in fire prevention and hazardous waste disposal and other dangerous situations, planning for first aid and medical responses required for such emergencies, making plans with outside medical or emergency response providers, conducting regular drills to develop the necessary responses to emergencies, etc. Emergency communication systems must be installed and be in working order. Emergency supplies must be available. Fire exits, evacuation maps, and other emergency directions must be installed.

Step 5: Providing for Hazard Reporting

Another essential step in implementing a safety and health program is developing a hazard reporting system. Employees should be encouraged to report their concerns about safety and health conditions in their workplace, and the written policy detailing aspects of the safety and health program should include information on the procedures to report hazards. Stating in writing that the organization actively encourages employees to report what they see as hazards reaffirms management's commitment to the safety and health policy. It also reaffirms management's intention to protect employees from reprisal for reporting safety or health problems.

Employees should be told to report potentially hazardous conditions or practices in person to a supervisor or in writing through some specific channel. Oral reports should be combined with other methods of reporting hazards. Oral reports do not allow for easy tracking of corrections, do not enable the organization to identify trends and patterns, and are less likely to be followed up than are other forms of hazard reports. Suggestion programs, which allow employees to report hazards on cards reviewed by management, are frequently used means of increasing employee involvement. Such suggestions must be reviewed as soon as possible, however, to ensure timely action.

There should be a clear distinction between suggestions that are basically improvement ideas and suggestions—or rather hazard notices—indicating a real or perceived workplace hazard. Some companies use hazard cards, which employees fill out and submit to a safety department or similar authority to warn of workplace hazards. Additionally, existing maintenance work orders can log and track unsafe conditions. If the hazard is noted on a work order and a high-priority code is assigned to maintenance requests dealing with safety and health hazards, potential hazards can receive a timely response. Work orders can also be used to document the follow-up and correction of the hazard.

Some organizations have developed anonymous reporting of hazards. Responses to anonymous reports can be through posting of the response in conspicuous areas.

Prompt acknowledgment of receipt of the report and information on management's assessment of the situation should be given to the employee to eliminate his or her worries about the hazard. Employees should be told what steps, if any, are being taken to correct the identified hazard. If the situation is considered not to be a problem, the employee should be told of this also, but should still be thanked for the report.

Step 6: Correcting Hazards

Once hazards are identified through inspections, surveys or reports, they must be corrected; a key step in the safety and health program. If possible, the hazard should be eliminated immediately. If not, interim protection must be provided to temporarily eliminate or control a hazard until more permanent corrections can be made, say when ordered parts or materials are available or work can be completed. Temporary measures must be taken no matter how soon complete correction is anticipated, since there is no way to know when a hazard will cause serious harm. There is no justification for needlessly exposing employees to risk.

Step 7: Tracking Corrections

When hazards are identified either by inspection or report, they must be tracked until they are corrected, and tracking corrections becomes another essential step in the effective safety and health program. Tracking ensures that corrective action was implemented and completed, especially in situations where the correction cannot be made immediately. It also keeps reporting employees informed about the organization's response to the hazard report. Tracking also helps determine where a safety and health program might be improved if the same hazard occurs again.

Step 8: Investigating and Analyzing Accidents and Incidents

Accidents will occur with the best-designed safety and health program, perhaps because some hazards were not identified or because improvements were inadequate or have not had time to work. Accidents and incidents must be investigated and analyzed to identify their root causes and to prevent their recurring. Even simple mishaps or near misses, where no property was damaged and no injuries occurred, should be investigated if there was the potential for harm.

Selecting the Investigator

Investigators must have proper training and resources. Many companies use trained employees plus a safety supervisor. The trend is to use safety teams with special training.

Seeking Information

Since the purpose of an investigation is to determine the root causes of the accident or incident, assigning blame should be avoided. Fact-finding interviews should be conducted seeking answers to the following questions:

- What happened? This elicits a description of the accident or incident.
- When did it happen? This would include the date and time of day.
- Where did it happen? This includes the rooms, workstations, etc.
- Who was involved? This could include witnesses, if any.
- How did it happen? This would require a description of the work being done at the time, the condition of the work environment, etc.
- Why did the accident or incident occur? This searches for root causes and contributing factors.

Investigators should identify facts and opinions as such and be wary of statements laying the blame on others rather than on actual causes.

Identifying Patterns and Causes

If the same type of accident recurs, the hazard control system may need revision or replacement. Trends or patterns may also identify training needs. Trends may be found by reviewing the OSHA 200 Log, inspection records, employee reports, first-aid logs, and by interviewing employees and first-aid personnel. After discovering a pattern or root cause, investigators must document the cause and inform management and employees of needed corrections and the time required for completion.

Step 9: Continuing Hazard Control and Equipment Upkeep

Regular inspections and surveys, along with employee reports, allow organizations to keep hazard information current. With hazards continually identified, they can be controlled or prevented using standard methods:

- **Engineering controls.** The work environment and the job itself should be designed to eliminate or reduce employee exposure to hazards. This can be done by completely removing the hazard from facilities, equipment, or processes through design, an ideal solution. When hazards cannot be eliminated or replaced with less-hazardous alternatives, they may be enclosed. For example, moving parts of machinery or heat-producing processes may be enclosed with special materials. Finally, if hazards cannot be removed or enclosed, barriers can be put between employees and the hazards in the form of machine guards, ventilation hoods, or isolation of a process.

- **Safe work practices.** Implementation of special workplace rules may be necessary to continue to protect employees from hazards. Such special rules include specific procedures regarding the use of potentially hazardous equipment or materials, identification of safe acts or behaviors, lockout or tagout procedures, requirements for personal protective devices, and good housekeeping practices. Special safety and health rules are most effective when they are written, posted, and discussed with affected employees and when employees have a role in formulating the rules.

  Safe work practices are used in conjunction with engineering controls, not as a substitute for them. Such rules are generally derived from the job hazard analysis.

- **Training.** Employees must be taught to identify and avoid hazards. Such training can be achieved through positive reinforcement of employees' following safe work procedures. Note, however, that reward programs for hours without injury may lead to employees' not reporting injuries or illnesses and are disfavored by OSHA.

- **Enforcement.** Safe work practices must be made a condition of employment and violation of workplace safety and health rules must be linked to some sort of corrective action appropriate to the seriousness of the violation. Enforcement must be based on letting employees know what is expected of them regarding workplace safety and health and giving them a chance to correct their own behavior. It should not exist merely to punish employees.

- **Personal protective equipment.** Engineering controls and safe work practices may not completely eliminate hazards. Personal protective equipment—face shields, steel-toed boots, safety glasses, hardhats, etc.—may be required, and must be provided at no cost to the employees. Employees must be trained in the need for and proper use of such equipment and the limitations of this equipment must be made clear to the employees.

- **Administrative controls.** Administrative controls such as lengthened rest breaks, additional relief workers, exercise breaks to vary body motions, and rotation of workers through different jobs to reduce exposure to hazards may also be employed to help with the continuing control of hazards. Administrative controls should be used in conjunction with other controls that work to eliminate hazards and control exposure more directly.

- **Preventive maintenance.** Preventive maintenance is designed to eliminate possible equipment problems and may play a major role in ensuring that hazard controls continue to function effectively and that equipment malfunctions do not cause additional hazards.

  An organization should have at least one person who knows the equipment and can schedule the maintenance required to keep the equipment or process operating properly. A preventive maintenance program should include a workplace survey to identify all equipment or processes that may require routine maintenance. This information should be listed and reviewed periodically to ensure its accuracy.

Maintenance should be performed at least as often as the manufacturer recommends. It may be necessary to establish a maintenance timetable for performing maintenance of all equipment listed to ensure that all timetables are being met. Records of all maintenance performed must be maintained, either by a computerized system or simply by dating the posted work schedule. These records can help identify employees who have helped prevent costly repairs and accidents.

Step 10: Designing a Medical Program

Despite everyone's best planning, injuries and illnesses will occur, and you must be ready to provide emergency medical service at your worksite. OSHA requires this for worksites that are not within a five-minute response time of medical facilities. First aid and CPR assistance must be available on every shift.

For this discussion, a medical program is any program employers put in place to ensure adequate occupational health expertise within a safety and health program. Medical programs provide occupational healthcare onsite and nearby, making use of varied sources of occupational health expertise. The nature and extent of a medical program depends on the availability of medical expertise in the area, but the goals of all programs are basically the same—to reduce the impact and severity of injuries and illnesses caused by workplace hazards and accidents.

Program Management

The size and complexity of a medical program will depend on the size and complexity of your worksite, the worksite's location in relation to healthcare providers, and the types of hazards that exist at the worksite. Whichever medical program is put in place, it should use the services of a medical specialist with occupational health/medical training. Not every nurse or doctor is trained to recognize the relationships between the workplace and medical problems. Medical programs work best when they are run by occupational health professionals and especially when a network of occupational health professionals—physicians, nurses, paramedics, and physical therapists—is involved, since one individual usually cannot supply all the service and expertise necessary.

Program Services

Employers will have to decide, based on the special characteristics of their organization, exactly what services a medical program should provide. Factors such as the type of materials handled, the specific processes in which employees are engaged, the type of facilities, the number of employees, the location of the facility in relation to healthcare services, and the characteristics of the workforce must be considered. A company with few employees might find onsite health services impractical, whereas a company with many employees might find onsite services economical. Some employees might be covered under the Americans with Disabilities Act and be especially vulnerable to illness or injury. Certain materials or processes involved at the worksite might increase the importance of rapidly available health assistance.

Some companies may find they have employees who fall within the scope of the bloodborne pathogens standard, and the medical program must provide appropriate protections for occupational exposure to infectious diseases, even if there is no obvious risk of such exposure. These are just a few of the many factors employers must consider in designing a medical program.

Using the Program

Medical programs serve three basic functions:
1. To work as part of the larger safety and health program to prevent hazards that cause injuries and illnesses.

2. To recognize and treat work-related injuries and illnesses.
3. To limit the severity of work-related injuries and illnesses.

The occupational health professional who runs the medical program should be available to provide expertise to the safety and health committee members, and the medical program should be included as part of any annual review of the organization's safety and health program.

Occupational health professionals should help decide the basis on which existing or potential hazards are treated at a workplace. They should help determine when employees must be tested for evidence of exposure as required by OSHA standards and perform the testing needed for health surveillance. The occupational health professional should review any employee symptoms and diagnoses to see if patterns appear which indicate an occupational health problem.

Those in charge of the medical program are responsible for coordinating the emergency response duties of all employees and any emergency response organizations—fire departments, paramedics, etc.—off the worksite. Occupational health professionals in charge of organizations' medical programs should ensure that all healthcare is delivered in accordance with federal and state regulations.

The occupational health professional should be responsible for keeping confidential records of all accident and health matters involving employees, including visits to first-aid stations, clinics, and hospitals. The occupational health professional should also maintain contact with employees who are off work because of occupational illness or injury and with the physicians of these employees. A registered nurse or physician should advise employees off work for an extended time about workers' compensation rights and benefits. Finally, those in charge of the medical program are responsible for helping employees who have been off work because of occupational illness or injury return to work, under modified duty positions if necessary.

Program Evaluation

Once a safety and health program is in place and running, evaluate it by periodically asking the following questions—the more "Yes" answers, the better the program:

- Are the program's safety and health goals in writing and understandable by everyone in the workplace?
- Do the goals relate directly to the company's overall safety and health policy?
- Are the goals written in such a way as to reinforce the concept of a culture of safety in the organization?
- Does senior management support the goals?
- Have achievable objectives related to specific deficiencies been stated?
- Are the objectives clearly assigned to responsible individuals?
- Is there a measurement system to indicate progress toward fulfilling the objectives?
- Can the objectives be explained to everyone in the workplace?
- Does everyone in the workplace know how progress toward fulfilling objectives will be measured?
- Is everyone in the workforce an active participant in reaching your safety and health goals?

An organization should review all systems that contribute to the safety and health program—from the program's initial objectives through the training programs implemented and the emergency procedures set in place to the medical program developed. As a program review identifies weaknesses or needs, the basis for new safety and health objectives emerges. Regular review of the health program is essential to achieving a safe and healthful workplace. High-quality programs must continuously improve to keep up with the changing nature of the organization and to ensure that an organization's real commitment to the safety and health of its employees is fulfilled.

Chapter 36
Whistleblower Protection

Introduction

Whistleblowing is the revelation by an employee, usually to the authorities, of any dangerous, illegal or unethical activities or practices engaged in by an organization or one of its employees. Sometimes whistleblowing can be as simple as complaining to another employee or to the media about allegedly illegal or unsafe practices of an employer. It can involve raising concerns about misconduct within an organization or within an independent structure associated with the organization.

The underlying purpose of whistleblower protection laws is to allow employees to report and testify about employer actions that are illegal, unhealthy, or that violate specific public policies. However, the exact definition of protected whistleblower activity is a hotly contested issue with wide variation among states.

Federal Law

OSHA's Anti-discrimination Provisions

Section 11(c) of the Occupational Safety Health Act of 1970 protects employees from termination, or any other form of discriminatory or retaliatory treatment, based upon an employee's exercise of any right provided by the act. The agency's regulations broadly construe both the scope of protected conduct and the scope of prohibited retaliation. Therefore, Section 11(c), Protected Conduct, includes not only employee-filed OSHA complaints, but also employee complaints communicated to virtually any other governmental entity. Complaints made only to the employer are also protected. The only qualifier is that complaints must involve work-related safety or health concerns. Likewise, prohibited retaliation includes not only termination, but any other negative change in the conditions or privileges of employment, including wage reductions, reduced overtime opportunity, negative evaluation, job transfers, and the like. The employer is subject to liability if OSHA is able to demonstrate that the protected activity provided a *substantial reason* (that is, not necessarily the *only* reason) for the employer's action.

To invoke OSHA's jurisdiction in such matters, an employee who believes he or she has received retaliatory treatment as a result of exercising a protected right must file a discrimination complaint within 30 days of the alleged violation. OSHA ordinarily will conduct an investigation in response to the complaint and will provide notice of its determination to the complainant within 90 days. If the agency determines the complaint is well founded, it usually will attempt to resolve the matter by negotiating a settlement, which may include reinstatement and backpay. If the agency decides to pursue litigation, the courts are empowered to enjoin further violations by the employer and to order any other appropriate relief. The scope of appropriate relief encompasses a broad assortment of remedies, and certainly can include ordering the rehiring of a terminated employee or the reinstatement of a demoted employee, with backpay and interest. At least one federal appeals court has said that OSHA also may seek compensatory and punitive damages in an appropriate case. Such litigation involves no cost to the employee.

Another set of employee protections involves a collection of whistleblower provisions in several acts of Congress. These provisions protect employee reports of unsafe conditions associated with the regulatory goals of the individual acts. At present, the Secretary of Labor has delegated to OSHA the authority and responsibility for enforcement of whistleblower provisions in 11 acts. These are:

- The Surface Transportation Assistance Act.
- The Asbestos Hazard Emergency Response Act.
- The International Safe Container Act.
- The Energy Reorganization Act.
- The Clean Air Act.
- The Comprehensive Environmental Response, Compensation, and Liability Act.
- The Federal Water Pollution Control Act.
- The Safe Drinking Water Act.
- The Solid Waste Disposal Act.
- The Toxic Substances Control Act.
- The Wendell H. Ford Aviation Investment and Reform Act for the 21st Century.

As with section 11(c) complaints, if an OSHA investigation determines an employer acted against an employee because of conduct protected by these statutes, the agency will attempt to resolve the matter by negotiating with the employer to restore employment, recover lost wages and benefits, or to collect other damages. If OSHA is unable to accomplish its goals by negotiation, it may take the employer to court seeking such remedies by court order, and at no expense to the employee.

The U.S. Code contains a significant number of other federal whistleblower statutes, but most of them apply only to federal employees who face reprisals for reporting violations by government agencies or employees. Employees of civilian defense contractors are, however, afforded special whistleblower protection for reporting contract-related violations to the government.

Protected Employees

The federal defense contractor whistleblower statute protects against reprisal for whistleblowing any employee of a civilian contractor awarded a contract by one of the following agencies:

- The Department of Defense.
- The Department of the Army.
- The Department of the Navy.
- The Department of the Air Force.
- The Coast Guard.
- The National Aeronautics and Space Administration (NASA).

Employees Who Report Unlawful Activities

The first category of employees protected by whistleblower statute is those employees who report violations or suspected violations of federal or state statutes or regulations. To be entitled to whistleblower protection on this basis, an employee must show the following:

- The employee or a person acting on behalf of the employee reported a violation or suspected violation of a federal or state law or regulation.
- The employee or the employee's agent reported the violation or suspected violation to a governmental body, law enforcement official, or to the employer.
- The employee acted in good faith in reporting the violation or suspected violation.

Most states have made it clear that whistleblower statutes protect only employee reports of violations of a law designed to protect the public interest. Thus, in situations in which employees have reported violations of purely internal management policies and standards, the courts have repeatedly held that the whistleblower statute does not apply.

Employees Who Participate in an Investigation or Hearing

The second category of employees commonly protected by whistleblower statutes is those employees requested by a public body or office to participate in an investigation, hearing, or inquiry. Employers may not take any adverse employment action against such employees.

Employees Who Refuse to Follow an Unlawful Order

Whistleblower statutes protect employees who refuse to follow orders they believe to be unlawful. To be entitled to whistleblower protection on this basis, employees must show the following:

- The employer ordered the employee to perform the action.
- The employee believed the action to be prohibited by a law or regulation.
- The employee had an objective basis in fact to support that belief.
- The employee refused the order.
- The employee informed the employer that the refusal to obey the order was based on the belief that the order was unlawful.

Employees Who Report Healthcare Services Violations

Whistleblower statutes often protect employees who report a situation in which the quality of healthcare services provided by a healthcare facility, organization, or provider violates a federal or state law or a professionally recognized standard and places the public at risk. To be entitled to whistleblower protection on this basis, an employee must show the following:

- The employee reported a situation in which the quality of healthcare services provided by a healthcare facility, organization, or healthcare provider violated either a state or federal law or a professionally recognized national clinical or ethical standard.
- The employee acted in good faith in making the report.
- The employee in good faith believed the violation potentially placed the public at risk.

Protected Activities

Protected activity includes any disclosure by a covered employee of information relating to a substantial violation of law related to a contract. This includes the competition for or negotiation of a contract with one of the six covered agencies named above. To be protected under the whistleblower statute, a covered employee must disclose the information either to a member of Congress or to an authorized official of one of the listed agencies of the Justice Department.

Protection Provided

Federal Defense Contractor Whistleblower Statute

The federal defense contractor whistleblower statute prohibits the discharge or demotion of a protected employee and any other form of discrimination against the employee as reprisal for making a protected disclosure. The statute prohibits an employer from taking **any** adverse employment action against a protected employee if that action is motivated by the employee's protected conduct—that is, whistleblowing as defined above. In addition to not being able to discharge or demote an employee because the employee has reported illegal activity, employers may not discipline, threaten, penalize, or discriminate against the employee with regard to pay or terms, conditions, location, or privileges of employment.

Employees who believe they have been subjected to a prohibited reprisal may file a complaint with the Inspector General of one of the six covered agencies. The Inspector General is required to investigate all such complaints except those determined to be frivolous. The Inspector General must prepare a report of the findings of the investigation and must submit the report to the complaining employee, the contractor concerned, and the head of the agency.

The head of the agency is responsible for determining, based on the Inspector General's report, whether the contractor subjected the employee to a prohibited reprisal.

If the agency head determines that a prohibited reprisal occurred, the employer is notified of the violation determination and efforts are made to conciliate the situation. The employer may appeal a violation determination to an administrative law judge within five days of the determination. The administrative law judge's decision is referred to the Secretary of Labor for a final order. The secretary may accept or set aside the administrative law judge's decision.

In cases in which the secretary concludes that a violation has indeed occurred, he or she may order the contractor to do the following:

- Reinstate the employee with the compensation, backpay benefits, etc. to which the employee would have been entitled had the reprisal not occurred.

- Pay the employee all costs, expenses, and attorneys' fees reasonably incurred to bring the complaint of reprisal.

- Take other affirmative action to abate the reprisal.

Civil False Claims Act

The Civil False Claims Act represents another federal whistleblower statute designed to reward and protect persons who assist in the discovery and prosecution of fraud against the federal government and to improve the government's ability to deter and redress crime.

The act permits actions by *qui tam relators,* which means private persons who sue on behalf of themselves and the government seeking recovery for a wide range of fraudulent conduct against the government. In essence, the False Claims Act provides a private bounty, consisting of 15 to 30 percent of the recovery, to individuals who discover fraudulent conduct and other unfair practices toward the government and who file actions seeking to recover money damages on behalf of the government.

Any employee discharged or otherwise discriminated against in the terms and conditions of his or her employment because of lawful acts done under the act "shall be entitled to all relief necessary to make the employee whole." This "make whole" relief includes reinstatement with the same seniority status the employee would have had without the discrimination, two times the amount of backpay, and compensation for any special damages sustained as a result of the discrimination, including litigation costs and reasonable attorneys' fees.

Environmental Acts

Various environmental acts provide protection from discharge or other discriminatory actions by employers in retaliation for employees' good-faith complaints about safety and health hazards in the workplace. The following acts cover all private-sector employees:

- Clean Air Act.
- Comprehensive Environmental Response, Compensation and Liability Act.
- Energy Reorganization Act of 1974.
- Safe Drinking Water Act.
- Solid Waste Disposal Act.
- Toxic Substances Control Act.
- Federal Waste Water Pollution Control Act.

These acts prohibit employers from discharging or otherwise discriminating against employees in retaliation for their disclosure to the employer or to the appropriate federal agency of safety and health hazards. They also protect employees who participate in formal government proceedings in connection with health and safety hazards. Under these acts, employees have the right to refuse to work in hazardous or unsafe conditions.

The acts specifically exclude from protection the disclosure of hazards deliberately caused by the employee, and they do not protect frivolous complaints.

Employees who believe they have been discriminated against in violation of the protections offered by these acts may file a complaint with the Employment Standards Administration's Wage and Hour Division within 30 days of the alleged violation.

Proving a Violation of Whistleblower Laws

To prove a violation of whistleblower statutes, an employee must establish the following:

- He or she engaged in statutorily protected conduct, for example, that the employee was in one of the categories of protected employees.
- The employer took adverse employment action against the employee.
- The employer's action was a direct result of the employee's protected conduct.

If an employee successfully establishes that the above occurred, the employer must then articulate a legitimate nonretaliatory reason for taking the adverse employment action. If the employer does so, the employee must then show that the employer's reason is merely a pretext for its retaliation against the employee for whistleblowing conduct.

Minimizing Whistleblower Complaints

Employees may be the first to see or suspect misconduct, which may be innocent or which may turn out to be fraud, a public danger, or some other malpractice. Employers must involve their employees in detecting and eliminating potential causes for whistleblowing. Listen to the employees' views of what is right and wrong and clarify for the employees the meanings and effects of fraud and other forms of malpractice. Employers should make it clear that they are serious about tackling all forms of serious malpractice and abuse.

Employers should take the following precautions to minimize instances of whistleblowing and to protect themselves against whistleblower claims in instances in which whistleblowing does occur:

- Make it clear that your organization is committed to eliminating fraud and abuse, whether those responsible are inside or outside of the organization.

- Let employees know how seriously you intend to treat issues of fraud or other malpractice.

- Inform employees exactly what practices are unacceptable and encourage them to seek clarification of questionable issues.

- Inform employees of the seriousness of raising unfounded allegations maliciously.

- Take employee complaints about alleged illegal conduct seriously. Investigate such complaints and document the investigation. Report back to the concerned employee about the outcome of the investigation and on any proposed action.

- Listen and respect legitimate employee concerns about their own health or safety.

- Assure employees verbally and in employment documents such as employee handbooks that reports of alleged unlawful conduct will not result in retaliation. Do everything possible to respect employee confidentiality.

- Construct an ethics complaints procedure for employees by which an employee may make a complaint regarding alleged unlawful conduct to his or her supervisor or to someone else in a position of authority in cases in which the employee's supervisor may be the source of the alleged illegal conduct. The personnel or human relations coordinator may be an appropriate alternate for complaints.

- Train supervisors to treat potential whistleblowing situations—for example, when an employee alleges that an order is illegal—very carefully. Instruct the supervisors to refer the complaint to the ethics officer, to document the conversation(s) with the employee, and to assure the employee that he or she is safe from retaliation.

- Emphasize to management and staff that trying to deter employees from raising a legitimate concern about fraud or abuse is a serious offense.

- Think twice before taking an adverse employment action against a whistleblowing employee. Make absolutely certain that the action is being taken for reasons unrelated to the whistleblowing and document your proof of this.

- Contact an attorney before taking an adverse employment action against a whistleblowing employee.

Whistleblower claims are among the most dangerous employment claims. They may generate adverse publicity and/or spark government investigations in addition to creating employer liability to the employee. The precautions detailed above may make it easier to live with the whistleblower laws.

Massachusetts Laws

Massachusetts provides additional and explanatory material on whistleblower protection in Massachusetts General Laws Annotated, Ch. 149, Sec. 185.

Statute

The Massachusetts statute on whistleblower protection repeats the federal law. The following is in almost the original wording of the Massachusetts statute, with minor changes made for clarity:

An employer shall not take any retaliatory action against an employee because the employee does any of the following:

- Discloses or threatens to disclose to a supervisor or to a public body an activity, policy, or practice of the employer—or of another employer with whom the employee's employer has a business relationship—that the employee reasonably believes violates a law or a rule or regulation based on the law. Similar protection is afforded an employee who reports activities that the employee reasonably believes pose a risk to public health, safety, or the environment.

- Provides information to or testifies before any public body conducting an investigation, hearing, or inquiry into any violation of law or any activity or policy threatening public health, safety, or the environment of the employer or by another employer with which the employee's employer has a business relationship.

- Objects to or refuses to participate in any activities or policies which the employee reasonably believes violate a law or regulation or which the employee reasonably believes pose a risk to public health, safety, or the environment.

Definitions

Massachusetts provides the following definitions to clarify the statute:

- *Employee*—any individual who performs services for and under the control and direction of an employer for wages or other remuneration.

- *Employer*—the commonwealth and its agencies or political subdivisions, including but not limited to cities, towns, counties, and regional school districts, or any authority, commission, board, or instrumentality of these agencies or subdivision.

- *Public body*—includes:
  - The U.S. Congress.
  - Any state legislature including the general court.
  - Any popularly elected local government body, or any member or employee thereof.
  - Any federal, state, or local judiciary or any member thereof, or any grand or petit jury.
  - Any federal, state, or local regulatory, administrative, or public agency or authority or any instrumentality of such agencies or authorities.
  - Any federal, state, or local law-enforcement agency, prosecutorial office, or police or peace office.
  - Any division, board, bureau, office, committee, or commission of any of the public bodies described in the above paragraphs.

- *Supervisor*—any individual to whom an employer has given the authority to direct and control the work performance of the affected employee. This individual has authority to take corrective action regarding the violation of the law, rule, or regulation of which the employee complains. *Supervisor* also includes the individual who has been designated by the employer on the notice required under the statute, as explained under **Employer Obligations** below.
- *Retaliatory action*—the discharge, suspension, or demotion of an employee, or other adverse employment action in the terms or conditions of employment taken against an employee.

Exclusions

Massachusetts law has an exclusion to the whistleblower protection against retaliation. The protection is only afforded employees who notify their supervisors in writing of the problem and who give the employer a chance to correct the situation.

The protection against retaliatory action shall not apply to an employee who makes a disclosure to a public body unless the employee has first brought the activity, policy, or practice violating a law, or which the employee feels poses a health, safety, or environment risk, to the attention of a supervisor. This notification to the supervisor must be in writing and the employer must have been afforded a reasonable opportunity to correct the activity, policy, or practice.

There is, however, an exclusion to the exclusion in the Massachusetts statute. An employee is not required to notify the supervisor in writing if he or she:

- Is reasonably certain the activity, policy, or practice is known to one or more supervisors of the employer.
- Feels the situation is an emergency.
- Reasonably fears physical harm as a result of the disclosure.
- Makes the disclosure to a public body—here limited to any federal, state, or local judiciary or any grand or petit jury, or any federal, state, or local law-enforcement agency, prosecutorial office, or police or peace officer—for the purpose of providing evidence of what the employee reasonably believes is a crime.

Enforcement

Massachusetts enforcement guidelines for violations of whistleblower-protection laws provide that any employee or former employee aggrieved of a violation of this section may, within two years, institute a civil action in the superior court. Any party to said action may be entitled to a jury trial.

Under Massachusetts law, employees who win these cases are entitled to all remedies available in common law tort actions in addition to any legal or equitable relief provided in the law.

The court may do the following if the employee prevails in the case:

- Issue temporary restraining orders or preliminary or permanent injunctions to restrain continued violation of the statute.
- Reinstate the employee to the position held before the retaliation or to an equivalent position.
- Reinstate full fringe benefits and seniority rights to the employee.
- Compensate the employee for three times the lost wages, benefits, and other remuneration, and interest on these.
- Order the employer to pay reasonable costs and attorneys' fees.

If the court finds the action brought by an employee under the statute was without basis in law or in fact, the court may award reasonable attorneys' fees and court costs to the employer. Massachusetts law does provide an escape clause from this potential employee liability:

> An employee shall not be assessed attorneys' fees if, after exercising reasonable and diligent efforts after filing a suit, the employee determines that the employer would not be found liable for damages and, within a reasonable time after discovering this, moves to dismiss the action against the employer or files a notice agreeing to a voluntary dismissal.

Massachusetts law provides that nothing in the whistleblower-protection statute diminishes the rights, privileges, or remedies of the employee under any other federal or state law or regulation. The employee may also be entitled to certain rights under a collective bargaining agreement or employment contract unless he or she instituted a private action under as described above. Instituting a private civil action in superior court will, according to the Massachusetts statute, be deemed a waiver by the plaintiff of his or her rights and remedies, for the actions of the employer, under any contract, collective bargaining agreement, state law, rule, or under the common law.

Employer Obligation

Under the Massachusetts statute, employers must conspicuously display notices designed to tell employees of their protections and obligations under the whistleblowing laws. Employers must also use other means to keep their employees informed of their protections and obligations. Notices posted with this required information must include the name(s) of the person(s)—that is, the supervisors—the employer has designated to receive the written notice required in the exclusion described above.

The Massachusetts Healthcare Whistleblower Law

All licensed attorneys' fee providers have a right against retaliation if they report a violation of law or a professional practice that they believe poses a risk to public health. Specifically, the law states that a healthcare facility shall not retaliate against a healthcare provider who does the following:

- Reports to a manager or to a public body any activity, policy or practice that the healthcare provider reasonably believes violates the law or if the healthcare provider reasonably believes a violation of professional standards which poses a risk to public health is occurring.

- Provides information or testifies to a public body conducting an investigation.

- Objects to or refuses to participate in any activity which the healthcare provider reasonably believes is in violation of a law or professional standard of conduct which the healthcare provider reasonably believes poses a risk to public health.

- Participates in a committee or peer review process, files a complaint or report discussing allegations of unsafe, dangerous or potentially dangerous care.

Employees are first required to report any complaint to the attention of a manager in writing, to afford the employer a reasonable opportunity to investigate and address the activity, policy or practice. Employees do not need to follow this procedure if they:

- Are reasonably certain that the activity is known to one or more managers and the situation is emergency in nature.

- Reasonably fear physical harm as a result of disclosure.

- Make the disclosure to a public body for the purpose of providing evidence of what you reasonably believe to be a crime.

Chapter 37
Privacy in the Workplace

Introduction

This chapter reviews some of the methods employers may use—and some of the restrictions imposed on the use of these methods—to gather information in the workplace on job-related concerns. The contrast between employees' expectations of personal privacy and employers' understandable desire to collect and use employee information for efficient management of the workforce has increased the tension over workplace privacy issues.

Although public attention has been focused on drug and alcohol testing in the workplace, this testing is not the only privacy issue. Employers are using an increasing number of screening devices and investigative tools to ensure that potential and current employees are honest, loyal, and productive, and many of these devices and tools intrude on what employees consider their personal space.

Not all states have recognized a constitutional right to privacy. Most states have, however, recognized the right of a person to be left alone, to be free from unwarranted publicity, and to live without unwarranted interference by the public. However, the workplace is not generally considered to be a private place and reasonable investigations of suspected misconduct and other job-related concerns are not generally considered intrusions into employees' privacy.

Of course, some exceptions to employer intrusions into employee privacy do exist. In the employment context, invasion-of-privacy personal-injury claims are usually made for the following actions of employers:

- Publicizing the private affairs of an employee.

- Intruding into an employee's private activities in an outrageous way or in a way that causes mental suffering, shame, or humiliation to a person of ordinary sensibilities.

Investigative Methods

Searches

Public sector employees are protected by the Fourth Amendment to the U.S. Constitution. The Fourth Amendment's protections include the right to be secure "against unreasonable searches and seizures" by the government. Because the amendment only prohibits action by the government, it is not usually applicable to searches and seizures by private employers.

A key factor courts use to determine whether searches of employee desks and lockers and similar property were proper searches is whether the employee had a reasonable expectation of privacy concerning that property. Obviously, employees have a greater expectation of privacy with respect to searches of their persons and their personal belongings such as purses or briefcases than they do of searches of their desks and lockers.

Company policies and posted notices regarding searches may influence a court's determination of whether there was a reasonable expectation of privacy. Employers should inform their employees that lockers and desks are company property, and thus subject to searches. Information on the likelihood of desk and locker searches should be distributed as part of the company's policy manual and by notices posted throughout the workplace.

Common-sense guidelines for conducting workplace searches include the following:

- Do not search an employee without a reasonable reason for thinking the employee has engaged in wrongdoing.
- Do not conduct intrusive body or strip searches.
- Make certain that two agents of the management conduct searches, at least one of which is of the same gender as the employee being searched.
- Limit the search to necessary areas and persons.
- Treat similar situations similarly.

Surveillance

Employers should consult legal counsel before instituting any surveillance of employees. While today's employers have access to increasingly sophisticated ways to monitor employees, the law imposes certain limits on when and how these new monitoring techniques may be used. Employers should generally obtain employee consent for surveillance and treat acceptance of reasonable surveillance as a condition of employment.

Employers may conduct surveillance of employees to investigate or defend against a personal injury or workers' compensation claim. Employers in these situations would typically have another employee or a private security agency conduct surveillance of the employee making the claim as a way to investigate the validity of the claim. For the most part, the courts have held that reasonable and unobtrusive surveillance of an employee during a claims investigation does not constitute an invasion-of-privacy. This surveillance should, however, be done without audio.

Employers may also monitor aspects of employees' work performance. For example, an employer might monitor the number of keystrokes of a clerical employee or monitor when the employee logs on or off. Employers might also use an electronic security system to determine when an employee has been on company premises. Information obtained from such work-performance monitoring may generally be used in evaluating or discharging employees. To avoid potential claims, however, employers should obtain employee consent for such monitoring.

Monitoring Telephone Conversations

With few exceptions, state and federal wiretapping laws prohibit interceptions or recordings of phone or other oral communications without prior consent from at least one of the parties to the communication. The Omnibus Crime Control and Safe Streets Act of 1968, more commonly known as the Federal Wiretapping Act bans the interception of any wire, oral, or electronic communication without the express or implied consent of a party. An employee's knowledge of the employer's intention to monitor a phone conversation is not considered implied consent. Employers must obtain written consent from employees to monitor wire or phone communication. Criminal and civil penalties may be imposed for violating this requirement. In addition, many states allow employees and other individuals to sue for invasion-of-privacy for eavesdropping on phone conversations by unauthorized phone "taps."

Monitoring E-mail and Computer Use

In 1986, Congress amended the Wiretapping Act with the Electronic Communications Privacy Act to include electronic communications within its scope. Employers should also obtain written consent from employees to monitor electronic mail and other computer activities. Employers who have not obtained this consent may be subject to civil and criminal penalties for violating federal wiretapping laws or invading an employee's privacy. In certain circumstances, restricting e-mails or monitoring employee accessing of known websites may be asserted as a violation of the National Labor Relations Act.

Video Surveillance

Employers may conduct video surveillance of employees. However, unless an employer has obtained employee consent, the surveillance should be done without audio to prevent violating wiretapping laws. These laws prohibit interception of oral communication but do not apply to videotaping. Employees can sue for invasion-of-privacy based on videotaping so video surveillance should not be done in areas where employees can reasonably expect privacy, such as bathrooms. The National Labor Relations Board has determined that in dealings with unions, employers must bargain over video surveillance.

Drug and Alcohol Testing

Some states prohibit or restrict suspicionless drug and alcohol testing—such as random testing or "automatic" post-accident testing—unless the employee is in a " safety-sensitive" position, because of a right of privacy that is recognized in that jurisdiction, either by constitution, statute, or case law. Such states include California, Minnesota, Massachusetts, and New Jersey, among others.

In one case, for example, the New Jersey Supreme Court upheld random drug testing, **but only for employees in highly safety-sensitive positions.** Recognizing that employee privacy rights under the state's constitution or common law are affected by drug-testing programs, the New Jersey Supreme Court held that the reasonableness of a drug-testing program will be determined by balancing the employer's and employee's respective interests. In the case at issue, workplace safety was found to outweigh the employee's privacy interests where an "employee's duties are so fraught with hazard that his or her attempts to perform them while in a state of drug impairment would pose a threat to co-workers, to the workplace, or to the public at large…." As a lead pumper at an oil refinery (Coastal), the plaintiff employee supervised and instructed gaugers, whose duties included blending gasoline with additives and managing the flow of gasoline products through the refinery. The employee's job required him to make precise calculations, interpret orders and convey them to the gaugers, and to keep accurate records for the next shift's lead pumper. Errors in the lead pumper's judgment or calculations could result in product overflow, which in turn could cause a fire or explosion. In sum, New Jersey's highest court agreed with the intermediate court that "[b]ecause the safety-sensitive nature of Hennessey's employment raises the potential for enormous public injury, the public policy supporting safety outweighs any public policy supporting individual privacy rights."

The Court's decision, however, contained guidelines for employers conducting random testing to minimize the impact on privacy. These included:

- Using the least-intrusive testing measures necessary to determine drug use.
- Maintaining confidentiality of the results.
- Giving employees notice of the drug-testing program's implementation.
- Detailing employee selection methods.
- Warning employees of the lingering effect of drug use.

- Explaining how the sample will be analyzed.
- Notifying employees of the consequences of testing positive or refusing to submit to a drug test.

These issues can and should be addressed in a comprehensive substance abuse policy.

Polygraph Testing

The federal Employee Polygraph Protection Act of 1988 (EPPA) covers most private employers. The law does the following:

- Prohibits most private employers from using lie-detector tests to screen applicants.
- Prohibits most private employers from requiring or causing an employee to take a lie-detector test.
- Permits private security firms and drug companies to use polygraph tests with applicants and employees.
- Exempts federal, state, and local governments from the law and allows the federal government to test private consultants and experts.
- Authorizes civil suits by the Secretary of Labor, employees, and job applicants and gives federal courts power to prohibit further testing and to award relief such as employment, reinstatement, backpay, and fines up to $10,000.

The federal law does not pre-empt any state or local law or collective bargaining agreement that prohibits lie-detector tests or that is more restrictive than federal law.

Honesty Testing

The EPPA does not apply to paper and pencil tests. Unless prohibited by state laws, employers may use honesty tests to attempt to identify individuals likely to engage in dishonest behavior. Employee groups have questioned the reliability of these tests and have claimed the tests are an invasion-of-privacy.

To minimize legal challenges, employers giving honesty tests should adhere to the following guidelines:

- Use only professionally developed tests administered by qualified personnel.
- Use each test only for the purpose for which it was designed.
- Administer all tests under the same conditions and to all applicants for the specific position or job category.
- Do not disseminate test data.
- Avoid entering test scores into unsecured databases.
- Have applicants sign an informed-consent agreement before they take the honesty test.

Honesty tests are subject to the Americans with Disabilities Act as medical examinations and, therefore, may not be used to inquire into an individual's health or medical condition.

Consumer Credit and Character Reports

The Fair Credit Reporting Act of 1970 (FCRA) regulates the use of credit information and investigative consumer reports for employment purposes. Recent amendments to the act took effect in late 1997, so employers should ensure they are complying with the current law. Briefly, employers that use an outside third party to investigate an applicant or current employee's background, including criminal history and reference checking, must notify the individual and obtain his or her consent prior to obtaining the report. Before taking any adverse employment action, the individual must be notified of his or her rights under the FCRA and be given a copy of the report. After taking adverse action, the employer must notify the individual, provide the name, address, and telephone number of the consumer reporting agency, provide a statement that the consumer reporting agency did not make the decision to take adverse action and is unable to provide specific reasons why the actions was taken; provide the report and notify the individual of the right to obtain a copy of the report from the agency and information regarding how to dispute the accuracy of the report. Employers should review with legal counsel, the specific requirements of this law for conducting background checks through third parties. Some states, such as New York, have their own fair credit reporting acts, which also should be consulted, where applicable.

Recordkeeping

An efficient recordkeeping system can be an effective way to reduce vulnerability to claims by applicants and employees of invasion-of-privacy. Employers should take the following steps to ensure they have an efficient recordkeeping system:

- Limit the collection of applicant/employee information to that which is strictly relevant to the business decisions to be made (hiring, disciplining, terminating, etc.).
- Limit the number of sources through which employee information is collected and stored.
- Verify information through reliable sources before it is made part of an employee's record.
- Periodically review all employee records to remove inaccurate, outdated, or unnecessary materials.
- Maintain separate employee personnel files for the following:
  - Routine personnel information (job performance, discipline, etc.).
  - Medical information.
  - Restricted information; that is, information not available to the employee such as records of investigations or letters of reference.
- Limit access to personnel files only to those persons with a legitimate business need to know.
- Obtain applicant/employee consent, where feasible, before releasing any information concerning the applicant or employee.

A Note on Privacy and Employees' Private Behavior

Occasionally the private behavior of employees may become a concern for employers. Romantic relationships may develop between co-workers, for example, and this may concern employers, especially when the relationship is between a supervisor and a subordinate. An employee's off-duty conduct may be seen or reported as offensive, and this could become a concern for an employer.

The standard generally applied by courts is that an employer has a legitimate concern with an employee's private conduct only when the employer can establish a connection between the private conduct and the employer's business interests. Employers who discipline or terminate employees for their private conduct are required to apply the same standards to men and women, particularly in the area of sexual conduct.

Chapter 38
E-mail and Voicemail Systems

Introduction

Technological advances have had a great impact on communication and the distribution of information in today's business world. With internal voicemail systems, computer networks, and worldwide electronic mail, workplace communication is more extensive and faster than ever. As business moves toward the paperless office with the increased use of e-mail and voicemail, employers will confront unique and complex legal issues such as the following:

- Employee privacy.
- On-line defamation and trade disparagement.
- Electronic harassment.
- Confidentiality of trade secrets and proprietary information.
- Copyright infringement.
- The right of unions to solicit employees and distribute information via e-mail.
- The discovery of stored communications.
- The right of employees to access and monitor workplace communications.

This chapter reviews some of these legal issues in relation to existing federal laws and, if applicable, state laws. This is merely an introduction to what is a very complex area and one that is changing rapidly as the law changes to accommodate new issues.

General Issues and Federal Law

Privacy Rights

The widespread introduction of technology into the workplace is likely to intensify the conflict between employees' privacy rights and the competing right of employers to oversee the workplace. One source estimates that employers already monitor an estimated 400 million telephone calls a year, and employer monitoring of e-mail communication and computer files is also common. Such monitoring can be complicated since it involves the federal constitution's definition of an employee's right to privacy for public employees, some state constitutions' protections of the right to privacy, statutory and common law, and the employer's right to ensure that communications systems are properly used.

Fourth Amendment

The Fourth Amendment's guarantee of protection from unreasonable searches and seizures by the government provides public employees with the right to privacy in their workplace. Like the federal constitution, many state constitutions protect individuals, including government employees, from government searches and seizures as part of the individual's right to privacy. Monitoring of e-mail or voicemail by a public employer falls under this Fourth Amendment protection and, accordingly, must satisfy constitutional standards. A government employee's Fourth Amendment right to privacy has been infringed if the following are true:

- The employee has a reasonable expectation of privacy.

- The particular search or seizure by the government employer is unreasonable based on a balance between the nature of the intrusion and the importance of the government interest justifying the intrusion.

A court's determination of whether there is reasonable expectation of privacy in e-mail or voicemail communications will depend largely on the facts of each case. A public employee may have a reasonable expectation of privacy in e-mail and voicemail transmissions if the particular communications system limits access to users with personal passwords even though the employer owns the computer or equipment. Given the routine electronic storage of e-mail and voicemail communications, however, courts may conclude that employees have little real expectation of privacy in these messages. Most importantly, employees' expectations of privacy may be diminished or eliminated in cases where employees know the employer has access to their e-mail or voicemail systems. All public employers who intend to monitor e-mail and voicemail need to adopt a monitoring policy informing employees that it is the employer's policy to monitor e-mail and voicemail communications.

Federal Wiretapping Statutes

In addition to potential constitutional and common law constraints on an employer's ability to monitor e-mail and voicemail communications, the federal government has adopted legislation designed specifically to protect the privacy of electronic communications. Title III of the Omnibus Crime Control and Safe Streets Act of 1968, more commonly known as the Federal Wiretapping Act, as amended by the Electronic Communications Privacy Act of 1986 (ECPA), prohibits the interception, use, or disclosure of protected wire, oral, and electronic communications. Many state legislatures have adopted similar restrictions. Accordingly, state and federal wiretap legislation may severely limit an employer's ability to monitor its employees' e-mail and voicemail messages.

The ECPA defines an *electronic communication* as "any transfer of signs, signals, writing, images, sounds, data, or intelligence of any nature transmitted in whole or in part by a wire, radio, electromagnetic, photoelectronic, or photo-optical system that affects interstate or foreign commerce ...." In many cases, e-mail will constitute such an electronic communication. The ECPA further defines a *wire communication* as "any aural transfer made in whole or in part through the use of facilities for the transmission of communications by the aid of wire, cable, or other like connection furnished or operated by any person engaged in providing or operating such facilities for the transmission of interstate or foreign communications affecting interstate or foreign commerce and such term includes any electronic storage of such communication." Voicemail communication may fall within the coverage of the ECPA.

Many states have adopted wiretapping statutes, modeled after the federal ECPA, that prohibit the interception, use, or disclosure of any wire, oral, or electronic communications. Unlike federal law, the state law may apply regardless of whether the e-mail or voicemail communications affect interstate or foreign commerce, thus significantly expanding the number of employees covered.

ECPA Restrictions

In general, the ECPA prohibits the interception, use, and disclosure of electronic communications. Under the ECPA, persons whose communications are intercepted, disclosed, or used in violation of the Act may bring a civil action against the violator. When a party has been found in violation of the ECPA, the plaintiff may recover actual damages, any profits made by the defendant as a result of the violation, or statutory damages of $100 a day for each day of the violation or $10,000, whichever is greater. A plaintiff may also obtain injunctions, punitive damages in appropriate cases, and reasonable attorneys' fees and other litigation costs. The ECPA also provides for criminal liability. Damages under some state wiretapping statutes may exceed those provided by federal law.

Exceptions to ECPA Restrictions

Although the ECPA and state wiretapping statutes generally restrict an employer's ability to intercept e-mail and voicemail messages, these statutes provide several exceptions that may authorize employers to monitor electronic communication in their workplace:

- **Communications may be monitored with the employee's consent.** An "interception" is lawful when it is done with the prior consent of one party to the communication. Consent may be express or implied, but must include language or acts that tend to prove that a party knows of, or assents to, encroachments on their expectation that electronic communications are private. Due to the uncertainties and the possible narrowness of other expectations described below, the safest exception for employers in the context of Internet and e-mail monitoring is the consent exception. Many states that have wiretapping statutes require dual party consent, for example, Pennsylvania and Maryland. Therefore, employers must determine whether their state requires the consent of one or both parties when monitoring employee electronic communications. Employers that wish to monitor e-mail and voicemail communications should adopt a coherent monitoring policy, distribute this policy to employees, and obtain from employees a signed acknowledgement of the policy.

- **Readily accessible communication can be monitored.** Any person may intercept or access an electronic communication "made through an electronic communication system that is configured so that such electronic communication is readily accessible to the general public." Thus, an employer may access communications on a bulletin board system with wide user access.

- **Telephone extension exception may be allowed under certain conditions.** The ECPA contains a "telephone extension exception" which is derived from the statute's restrictive definitions of the terms intercept and device. Interceptions of communications are unlawful if accomplished through the use of any electronic, mechanical, or other device. Excluded, however, are "any telephone or telegraph instrument or facility, or any component thereof furnished to the subscriber or user by a provider of wire or electronic communication service in the ordinary course of its business and being used by the subscriber or user in the ordinary course of its business or furnished by such subscriber or user for connection to the facilities of such service and used in the ordinary course of its business ...."

    Courts have held that monitoring calls within the telephone extension exception only if it has a legitimate business purpose. The courts have suggested that the monitoring of employees falls within the exception in situations in which the monitoring program is designed to allow supervisors to train and instruct employees regarding their telephone technique and in which the employees were aware of the monitoring. Employers may also use an extension telephone to monitor employees' phone calls when the employer has a reasonable concern about the disclosure of confidential information.

In contrast to cases such as the above, most courts have held that a personal call may be intercepted in the ordinary course of business to determine its nature but never its content. Thus, even when the employer's monitoring is initially motivated by a business goal, the employer does not have an unlimited right to listen to employees' personal calls, and the employer must stop listening once recognizing that the call is personal in nature.

Courts have not resolved whether the telephone extension exception authorizes monitoring of e-mail or voicemail messages. The exception may not apply to e-mail monitoring unless telephone equipment or facilities are specifically involved, and it is unclear whether courts will consider a network manager's modem, computer, or software program to be telephone or telegraph equipment. Interception of voicemail messages may fit within the exception in cases where the employer's equipment is used in the ordinary course of business. However, courts have yet to expressly apply the exception to the interception of e-mail or voicemail communications and employers have been forced to justify their monitoring policy on some other exception.

- **Some business-use monitoring may be an exception to the ECPA.** The ECPA provides that "an operator of a switchboard, or an officer, employee, or agent of a provider of wire or electronic communication service" may intercept, use, or disclose communications "in the normal course of his employment while engaged in any activity which is a necessary incident to the rendition of his service or to the protection of the rights or property of the provider of that service …."

This exception has historically been interpreted to allow telephone companies to intercept and disclose calls as necessary to protect their equipment and rights. Thus, the exception has routinely been applied to excuse inadvertent interceptions by telephone company employees and switchboard operators. In at least some circumstances, courts have applied the exception to authorize intentional interceptions of telephone calls. For example, courts have permitted telephone companies to monitor calls to identify a corrupt employee abusing their long-distance system and to monitor calls by employees to ensure that designated telephone lines remain open for business calls.

Given the historical application of the business-use exception to telephone companies, it is unclear whether the exception covers employers who have established e-mail or voicemail systems. Application of the exception will depend on courts' interpretation of the phrase "provider of wire or electronic communication service." Unfortunately, courts have not yet interpreted the phrase in the context of electronic communications in the workplace, but presumably the phrase does include public e-mail networks (such as Prodigy and CompuServe). Companies with their own e-mail systems on their own wide-area (interstate) networks could also fall under this exception as electronic communication service providers. It is less clear if companies that maintain their own internal e-mail systems fall under the exception. Thus, there is considerable uncertainty surrounding the potential application of the business-use exception to employers who wish to monitor employees' e-mail or voicemail communication.

Access to Stored Communication

In addition to the ECPA's restrictions on the interception, use, and disclosure of electronic communications, the act prohibits unauthorized access to electronically stored wire and electronic communications. Although this restriction was directed towards protection of stored e-mail communications, voicemail may also be covered. *Electronic storage* includes "any temporary, immediate storage incidental to the electronic transmission" and permanent storage by the system provider "for purposes of backup protection."

A successful plaintiff may recover actual damages and any profits made by the defendant as a result of the violation, but in no case shall a person be entitled to receive less than the sum of $1,000. A plaintiff may also obtain injunctions and reasonable attorneys' fees and other litigation costs, although punitive damages are not available. The act also establishes criminal penalties.

The ECPA exempts conduct authorized by the agent or provider of a wire or electronic communication service from the restrictions against unauthorized access of stored communications. Depending on how broadly courts interpret the phrase "person or entity providing a wire or electronic communications service" a company that provides its employees with e-mail or voicemail service may have the right to access stored communication at its discretion. Given the federal law's distinctions between interception, disclosure, and use of transmissions on the one hand and access to stored communications on the other, an employer with no right to intercept electronic transmissions may avoid liability by accessing employee communications after they have been stored. Until this apparent inconsistency is resolved by the courts, however, an employer's safest course is to adopt a company policy authorizing it to monitor and access e-mail and voicemail communications.

Legislation Concerning Monitoring

At least one state, Connecticut, has passed a law regarding electronic monitoring by employers. Under the Connecticut statute, employers must post a notice concerning the types of electronic monitoring that the employer may engage in. Electronic monitoring under the statute is defined very broadly and would likely include activities ranging from review of telephone records to actual monitoring of phone calls. The statute provides limited exceptions for investigations of employee misconduct.

The California legislature passed bills regarding electronic monitoring based on the Connecticut statute. However, California's governor vetoed the bills. A number of bills have been introduced in state legislatures around the country regarding electronic monitoring and other states will likely introduce electronic monitoring restrictions.

Congress has also proposed legislation intended to limit electronic monitoring. The Privacy for Consumers and Workers Act was first introduced in both the House and Senate in 1993. Under the proposed legislation, employers would have to post a written notice informing employees and prospective employees that the employer engages in workplace monitoring. Employers also would be required to provide individual notice of monitoring to prospective employees at the time of the first personal interview. Since 1993, several other electronic monitoring bills have been introduced in Congress and the issue continues to be of interest to several members of the House and Senate.

"On-line" Defamation, Slander, and Trade Libel

The advent of electronic communication via e-mail and voicemail has increased the potential for defamation, slander, and trade libel or disparagement of co-workers, customers, vendors, and competitors. Electronic communications tend to be more casual, more subject to misinterpretation, and distributed to a much wider audience than other modes of communication. In addition, there is also often a stored record of the message, making it much easier to establish the existence of the statement.

In light of the inherent dangers associated with electronic communications, the potential for defamation liability arising out of such communication cannot be ignored. To succeed in a claim of defamation, a plaintiff must normally prove that the defendant made a false statement, published it to a third party, negligently failed to ascertain the truth of the statement, and caused injury to the plaintiff's reputation. An employer may be liable for defamatory statements made by its employees if the statements were made within the scope of employment. Given this broad standard, it is easy to imagine scenarios in which e-mail communications may give rise to defamation lawsuits.

Electronic communication may also expose an employer to potential liability for trade libel or disparagement, which is unlawful in most states. Trade libel or *product disparagement* has been defined as "an injurious falsehood that demeans the plaintiff's goods or the character of his business." The risk of liability for trade libel or product disparagement is especially great if employees transmit e-mail messages concerning customers, vendors, and competitors through public e-mail networks. If a poorly drafted message falls into the wrong hands, the employer may well face substantial liability for trade libel or product disparagement. Thus employers should strictly limit the use of e-mail and voicemail systems and train employees to recognize the risks associated with such forms of communication.

Harassment and Discrimination Through Electronic Communication

The use of e-mail, voicemail, instant messaging programs, electronic employee bulletin boards, and other forms of electronic communication in the workplace may encourage employees to make potentially offensive statements. Employees have a tendency to use e-mail to disseminate inappropriate jokes or to play pranks on co-workers, even though the jokes and pranks are intended in good fun. Such conduct has the potential to offend or to create a hostile work environment, leading to charges of harassment.

Hostile work environment sexual harassment exists when an employee is subjected to verbal or physical conduct of a sexual nature when such conduct has the purpose or effect of unreasonably interfering with an individual's work performance or creating an intimidating, hostile, or offensive work environment. Although the hostile work environment claim first arose in the context of sexual harassment, courts have also recognized claims of non-sexual harassment based on other protected characteristics such as age, race, and disability.

From an employer's perspective, the very nature of electronic communications can magnify the potential liability for e-mail or voicemail harassment in the workplace. Unlike personal communications, there will almost always be a record of e-mail and voicemail messages, stored either by the employee or by a backup system or both, thus leaving a trail of evidence confirming the existence of a hostile work environment. Given the ease of discovering and obtaining copies of such communications through litigation, the potential for discovery of a "smoking gun" is increased.

A number of sexual harassment or sex discrimination lawsuits have been caused, at least in part, from inappropriate e-mail or voicemail communications. Plaintiffs have also relied on electronic communications records to support race, age, retaliation, and other types of harassment and discrimination claims. Other employees have asserted related claims for negligent or intentional infliction of emotional distress and other common law damage claims based in part on conduct related to electronic communications.

To avoid such litigation, employers should train employees to use electronic communications appropriately, emphasizing the unique aspects of e-mail and voicemail systems that may heighten the risk of harassment and discrimination claims. In addition, employers should forbid all employees from making threatening, harassing, or offensive comments via e-mail or voicemail. Employers may also wish to initiate lawful monitoring procedures to determine if harassment has taken place by tracing the harassment through the electronic system.

Trade Secrets and Confidential Information

Another troublesome issue surrounding the widespread use of computers and electronic communication systems is the erosion of an employer's ability to protect trade secrets and other confidential information. It may be difficult, for instance, for an employer to prevent employees from using e-mail, voicemail, and computers to seize exclusive/private business information. Employees can easily download information onto a computer disk or disseminate the information outside of the company.

In addition to the damage caused by an employee's intentionally misappropriating or inadvertently disclosing confidential company information, employers that fail to guard against such misappropriation diminish their rights to protect the information. Most statutory protections of trade secrets require the employer to make reasonable effort to keep the information in question confidential. For example, the Uniform Trade Secrets Act, adopted in many states, defines a *trade secret* as "information, including a formula, pattern, compilation, program, device, method, technique, or process, that is the subject of efforts that are reasonable under the circumstances to maintain its secrecy." In light of the relative ease with which e-mail communications may be intercepted or misdirected, routine transmission of confidential information through e-mail may undercut an employer's ability to prove reasonable effort to maintain secrecy.

Accordingly, employers that wish to protect trade secrets and other confidential information should adopt policies specifically defining what information may be communicated through internal and external electronic communications systems. As a general rule, information of a sensitive or confidential nature should not be communicated by e-mail. Warning employees of the risks associated with such forms of communication may encourage them to be cautious and help prove that the company took appropriate steps to guard the secrecy of its confidential information.

Copyright Infringement

Another potential risk arising out of the use of electronic communications in the workplace is copyright infringement. Many employees have access to public e-mail networks. As anyone who has "surfed the network" knows, copyright violations are common, creating the impression that users can post and use any information. For example, many users erroneously assume that it is permissible to post newspaper articles and other types of information. Although this activity is usually harmless, employers may face potential claims of copyright infringement if employees post copyrighted information on company computers, especially if the employers know of and approve of this posting. In addition, printing material that has been posted by others and distributing that material within the office or publishing it outside the office may also constitute copyright infringement.

Accordingly, the best strategy to protect an employer from potential liability for copyright infringement is to adopt and enforce written guidelines concerning the posting of information. Even if a written policy does not completely prevent unlawful posting by employees, the mere existence of such a policy may provide a defense for employers accused of copyright infringement. Employers should advise employees not to post information unless they or the employer have created the information or own the rights to it. If there is any doubt regarding the copyright status of a particular publication, employees should refrain from posting the information or distributing it to others.

Union Solicitation by Electronic Communication

Electronic communication may provide labor organizations with a potent method of organizing a company's employees, allowing union sympathizers to send messages to an entire workforce via e-mail or voicemail. Because most of the doctrines developed under the National Labor Relations Act concerning solicitation of employees, distribution of literature, and the use of traditional bulletin boards do not consider the electronic workplace, employers may find it difficult to oppose the use of company e-mail or voicemail systems for organizational purposes without a carefully drafted policy.

Section 8(a)(1) of the NLRA makes it an unfair labor practice for an employer "to interfere with, restrain, or coerce employees in the exercise" of their collective bargaining rights. The Supreme Court has held that an employer's policy prohibiting union solicitation of employees outside work time on company property is an unreasonable obstacle to self-organization and therefore discriminatory in the absence of evidence that special circumstances make the rule necessary to maintain production or discipline. In contrast, enforcement of a no-solicitation rule during working hours will be presumed to be valid in the absence of evidence that it was adopted for discriminatory purposes. The basis of this distinction is that while working time is for work, time outside of working hours is an employee's time to use as he or she wishes without reasonable restraint, even though the employee is on company property.

In contrast to the freedom allowed for oral solicitation, the NLRB has held that employers may forbid distribution of literature in work areas, even if the distribution takes place during non-working hours. The prohibition on distributing written materials is justified since literature could litter an employer's premises and raise a hazard to production whenever it was distributed. Although an employer may prohibit the distribution of literature in work areas even during non-working hours, the NLRB has consistently required employers to first adopt a no-distribution policy.

Even in the face of a written no-solicitation or no-distribution policy, the employer may commit an unfair labor practice if its adoption or enforcement of the policy reveals a discriminatory purpose. Thus, an employer may not selectively enforce such a policy against solicitation and distribution by unions while simultaneously allowing other groups or individuals to solicit employees or distribute literature for other purposes. Furthermore, implementing or strictly enforcing a no-solicitation rule during the height of union organizational activities may make a no-solicitation/no-distribution policy void.

The NLRB and the courts have developed similar guidelines for the use of corporate bulletin boards. Although the NLRB has recognized that the NLRA does not generally grant employees a statutory right to use an employer's bulletin board, an employer that allows employees to use a bulletin board for general purposes must grant labor unions a similar right to post notices on the board.

Although the NLRB has yet to rule on an employer's ability to limit the use of company e-mail or voicemail systems in the context of a union organizing drive, the board found an employer's selective enforcement of a rule prohibiting the use of e-mail for union purposes was unlawful. In addition, the NLRB's general counsel has taken the position that where an e-mail communication can reasonably be expected to occasion a spontaneous response, or initiate conversation, it may be treated as solicitation. In that case, a rule prohibiting all non-business use of e-mail would be presumed unlawful. Until the NLRB and the courts provide further guidance for the use of e-mail and voicemail systems by unions for organizational purposes, the employers should review their policies in light of the general counsel's position on this issue.

Discovery of Stored Communication

As the use of e-mail and other electronic communications grows, the cost of storing the communications grows as well. Moreover, a large volume of stored e-mail can cause significant problems for employer's networks. Many information systems consultants recommend that companies restrict the storage of e-mail and other electronic communications for purely technical reasons and employers should implement an electronic document retention policy.

Many employers have not implemented a consistent electronic document retention policy and there is a perception that e-mail or other electronic documents may provide damaging evidence in employment or other cases. However, employees often erroneously believe that once an email is deleted it will be removed permanently from the system. This mistaken belief encourages employees to recklessly send e-mail messages that they would ordinarily not communicate through other means.

Given the potential value of stored electronic communications, plaintiffs' employment attorneys have begun to focus on discovery of stored e-mail, voicemail, and other electronic communications that may confirm the existence of sexual or racial harassment or other types of discrimination. Businesses now exist that actually specialize in locating computer files that companies once thought were destroyed.

Complying with electronic discovery requests can cost employers thousands of dollars and courts have been reluctant to shift that cost to the party requesting such information. In light of the technical problems associated with retaining e-mails and other electronic communications, as well as the economic costs of complying with electronic fishing expeditions, companies should adopt a preventive policy designed to limit the use of the company's e-mail system and define procedures for its use. Employers should inform employees at all levels of the company's storage practices and the company's ability to retrieve communications. Employers should also be familiar with how their electronic communication systems operate and they may wish to alter those operations so as to ensure that communications are actually destroyed when deleted.

An Effective Company Policy
Benefits

Well-designed company policies will significantly limit the risks associated with e-mail and voicemail communications. In particular, such a policy, by reducing employees' expectations of privacy, may limit an employer's liability for monitoring e-mail and voicemail messages. The existence of such a policy may also indicate whether employees have consented to the interception of their electronic communications, thus constituting an exception to federal and state wiretapping statutes.

An effective electronic communications policy can also have other benefits:

- It can reduce the potential for on-line defamation and harassment caused by misuse of electronic communications.

- It can lessen the risk of disclosure of confidential information.

- It can reduce the possibility of copyright infringement.

- It can moderate the tactical use of e-mail and voicemail systems by unions.

- It can protect against the future discovery of stored communications and the use of these communications in litigation.

- It may allow an employer to take needed disciplinary action against employees who misuse electronic communications.

Characteristics

In order to provide all possible benefits, a company policy on electronic communications should do the following:

- Clearly communicate to employees that the security of e-mail and voicemail communications is not guaranteed. The policy should inform employees that the employer may override individual passwords and codes and may require employees to disclose all passwords and codes to the employer to facilitate such access.

- Explain the employer's monitoring procedures and how they will be used.

- Provide for limited, authorized access to e-mail and voicemail communications, defining the scope of authorization.

- Stipulate that electronic and telephone communications—including e-mail and voicemail communications and the contents of an employee's computer—are the sole property of the employer.

- Identify the reasons for surveillance and the specific business purposes to be achieved. These could include preventing excessive personal use of the company's systems, monitoring employees' service and their effectiveness with clients and customers, assuring compliance with company policies, and investigating conduct or behavior that may be illegal or that may adversely affect the employer or the welfare of the employees.

- Stipulate that by using the employer's e-mail and voicemail systems and other equipment, including company computers, an employee knowingly and voluntarily consents to being monitored and acknowledges the employer's right to conduct such monitoring. It is also advisable to obtain from each employee a signed acknowledgment for indicating the employee's consent to such monitoring.

- Prohibit use of the employer's e-mail or voicemail system for personal messages, solicitation of employees, or distribution of information not related to the employer's business, with the exception of short informational messages or information posted on a designated computer "bulletin board."

- Prohibit communications that may constitute verbal abuse, slander, defamation, or trade disparagement of employees, customers, clients, vendors, competitors, or others.

- Prohibit offensive, harassing, vulgar, obscene, or threatening communications, including disparagement of others based on race, national origin, marital status, sex, sexual orientation, age, disability, pregnancy, religious or political beliefs, or any other characteristic protected under federal, state, or local law.

- Prohibit employees from creating, distributing, or soliciting sexually oriented messages or images, unwelcome sexual advances, requests for sexual favors, or other unwelcome conduct of a sexual nature.

- Prohibit the distribution or printing of copyrighted materials, including articles and software, in violation of copyright laws.

- Prohibit the exchange of trade secrets, exclusive/private information, or any other confidential information via e-mail. Communications that may be privileged (for example, communications to in-house counsel that may be subject to attorney-client privilege) should be clearly identified as such.

- Prohibit employees from accessing or attempting to access the e-mail or voicemail system of another user or from transmitting messages from a co-worker's e-mail or voicemail system.

- Explain the significance of the "Delete" and "Wastebasket" functions and describe procedures for ensuring the permanent destruction of e-mail and voicemail communications when desired.

- Inform employees of the potential discovery of stored e-mail and voicemail communications, including the use of such messages for litigation against the company. Simply by promoting this understanding, employers may encourage the cautious and appropriate use of e-mail and voicemail systems.

- Explain to employees that any e-mail messages sent externally that could be interpreted as stating a company position, policy, or viewpoint must be approved in advance, by the appropriate company official.

Conclusion

The widespread use of e-mail and voicemail systems in the workplace has raised many complicated and unanticipated legal issues for employers. Unfortunately, many of the existing statutory, regulatory, and common law rules and principles have not adequately kept pace with advancements in electronic communication technology. Most significantly, current legislation does not define the boundaries of appropriate monitoring of employees' e-mail and voicemail communications.

Although state and federal legislation intended to correct some of these problems is likely, further regulation will undoubtedly raise even more complicated issues concerning the use of electronic communications in the workplace. Given the changing nature of the situation, adopting defensive policies and procedures is the best way for employers to reduce their potential liability and risks while taking advantage of technology designed to improve the efficiency, responsiveness, and effectiveness of companies in this century.

E-mail and Voicemail Systems

Chapter 39
Telecommuting

Introduction

A growing number of employers are allowing their employees to choose whether to work at home or from an alternative worksite. Because the practice often involves computer and telecommunications technology, it is known as *telecommuting*. Reports indicate that almost 11.1 million employees telecommuted in 1997. More than two-thirds of Fortune 1000 companies have telecommuting programs in place. The volume of telecommuters is expected to double over the next 10 years.

Before implementing a telecommuting policy, management should consider the benefits for and concerns of both the employer and the potential telecommuting employee. In addition, the legal consequences of telecommuting must be considered. Companies should formulate policies or guidelines that define criteria for evaluating positions eligible for telecommuting. Obviously, some employees will always be needed in an office to support co-workers or coordinate telecommuters in the field. Clear criteria can help employers determine whether telecommuting is right for them and distinguish which positions are suitable for home performance and which should remain traditional office or workplace jobs.

Benefits for Employers

Based on a number of recent studies and surveys, an employer considering telecommuting as a workplace option might expect the following benefits:

- Cost savings in fixed expenses such as office rental, utilities, and employee parking.
- Increased productivity.
- Increased job satisfaction.
- Improved employee morale.
- Reduced absenteeism.
- Reduced employee turnover.
- Reduced employee stress and related medical expenses.
- Improved work quality.

Jobs Adaptable to Telecommuting

Employers should consider their own circumstances and requirements to determine the likelihood of successfully implementing telecommuting in their company. What job categories would be appropriate for telecommuting? What job functions or tasks can be accomplished away from the office? As a general rule of thumb, if an employee can close his or her office door for up to eight hours and effectively accomplish his or her job without the need for face-to-face contact with other employees, that employee's job is adaptable for telecommuting.

Job tasks that have been proven to be suited to telecommuting include:

- Tasks that are easily measured. Jobs that have countable or observable output with obvious beginning and ending points are a better choice than those that are not as clearly defined. This would include unit-oriented jobs such as data entry jobs, as well as project-oriented jobs such as accounting, auditing, designing, and writing.

- Tasks that require very little unscheduled face-to-face contact. Most of the employee's contacts can be done via telephone or electronic mail or can occur at scheduled meetings. The job should require few, if any, critical face-to-face meetings.

- Tasks that do not require frequent access to files, equipment, or supplies that can't easily or economically be moved to the employee's home or other telecommuting site.

Concerns About Telecommuting

In addition to the benefits derived from telecommuting, employers and employees must also address various concerns, including legal ones, which are discussed in this section.

Employee Concerns

The benefits to employees able to telecommute are easily identified. Telecommuting can decrease their commute time, work expenses, and stress. In addition, it can increase the flexibility of their work and family schedules, improve their work environment, and give them a feeling of more control or autonomy.

Nevertheless, many employees have concerns regarding telecommuting. Employees often enjoy the social aspect of their jobs and fear the isolation of working at home. Not every employee can cope with the reduction of personal interaction. In addition, based on the principle of "out of sight, out of mind" some good candidates for telecommuting may opt to stay in the office because they fear that their work will not be appreciated and they will become expendable. Further, they fear that telecommuting will reduce their chances for advancement.

Employer Concerns

The primary concern most employers have entering into telecommuting arrangements is maintaining appropriate control over the employee. Executives are often reluctant to give up control and face-to-face contact. These concerns and others should be addressed at the outset by establishing exactly what the employer and employee expect. The following issues should be considered:

- **Hours of work.**
  Although flexibility is an advantage to telecommuting, employers have a right to be able to reach employees on a regular basis. It may be appropriate to establish set hours during which the employee is available.

- **Days in office and days at home.**
  The parties should plan from the start how many days the employee will be working out of his or her home and how many days he or she will be at the office or workplace. This information will be helpful for scheduling meetings and addressing office space requirements. Employers may find it appropriate to eliminate individual offices and have several telecommuters share an office based on their in-office schedules.

- **Expenses.**
  The employer and the telecommuting employee should resolve how various expenses will be handled. For example, the employee should know in advance whether the employer is going to pay for any alterations necessary to make the employee's home suitable for work, such as increased wiring or additional telephone lines. Incidental expenses, such as long-distance charges, should be discussed and procedures established for the handling of such expenses.

- **Use of employer property.**
  Equipment supplied by the company in order to make telecommuting possible, such as computers, fax machines, and photocopiers can be used for both commercial and personal reasons. Employers should address with the telecommuter the issue of the appropriate use of company equipment and establish specific guidelines and procedures that must be followed.

- **Vacations, leaves, personal days, and sick days.**
  While telecommuters face the same risks of sickness or accident as other office or workplace workers and have the same need to get away from work on periodic vacations, the mechanics of how to handle time off must be considered. Solutions will vary with employers and telecommuters. The job functions of some employees can allow for day-to-day flexibility as long as fixed deadlines are met. However, other jobs require set hours. The time-off issues for these two types of employees will vary. Applicable policies and procedures should be discussed and agreed to before beginning telecommuting. If the employee is subject to a labor contract, care must be taken to ensure that the contract requirements are met.

Legal Concerns Regarding Telecommuting

Telecommuting raises a number of legal issues that an employer should consider before implementing a telecommuting policy. A policy should contain guidelines to limit the company's legal risks and the employer should follow the guidelines if telecommuting is put into practice.

Occupational Safety and Health Act

Employers are required by law to maintain a safe workplace for employees, even if it is at home. Based on recent policy announcements, OSHA generally will not inspect, nor require employers to inspect, the home worksites of employees engaged in telecommuting. However, if employees are engaged in manufacturing or other activities at home in the interest of their employers, which may pose safety or health hazards to them (for example, making lead molds), then OSHA may seek to inspect the work areas upon complaint. In any event, employers subject to recordkeeping requirements must record the occupational injuries and illnesses of all home workers and may need to take feasible measures to comply with relevant OSHA standards at least to the extent that they do not involve controlling the worksite.

Workers' Compensation

Employees injured during their employment are often entitled to compensation under state workers' compensation laws. These laws may apply whether the employee is working at the office or at home. As a result, employers should take precautions to both minimize the possibility of injury and protect themselves from fraudulent claims. Inspections as previously discussed for OSHA compliance are also relevant here. In addition to pre-telecommuting and periodic subsequent inspections, the employer should take care to avoid procedures that may cause injury. For example, care should be taken to ensure packages of files or supplies sent to the telecommuter are not too heavy for the employee.

Procedures about how to report work-related injuries occurring at home need to be discussed with employees before they begin telecommuting. When injuries are not witnessed (as would be true for most injuries occurring at the employee's home), there may be a potential for fraudulent claims. The employee should be required to report all injuries immediately. In addition, as part of the pre-telecommuting arrangement, an employer should secure a release from the employee allowing the employer to come in and inspect the employee's worksite immediately after any accident or injury. While such actions will not stop all fraudulent claims, they will help employers to better address such claims.

Fair Labor Standards Act

Telecommuting policies and procedures must remain within acceptable limits of federal and state wage-and-hour laws. The regulations do not contain any unique requirements or exceptions for telecommuters. Wage-and-hour requirements that apply to your on-site employees also apply to your off-site employees. If an employee is not exempt from the Fair Labor Standards Act (FLSA) the employer still has the obligation of maintaining time records for the employee, as minimum wage and overtime restrictions are still applicable. This may be done by having the employees fill out time sheets or log on and off a computer or telephone at the beginning and ending of their work hours. Employers concerned about potential exaggeration of time records should develop methods for verification.

When establishing a system for evaluating the productivity of exempt or salaried employees, employers must take care not to compromise the employees' exempt status under the FLSA. The system should not undermine the fact that they are paid on a salary basis.

Americans with Disabilities Act

The Americans with Disabilities Act (ADA) requires employers to offer reasonable accommodation to otherwise qualified disabled individuals. The law does not directly discuss telecommuting. However, working from home is an accommodation disabled employees increasingly are seeking. As the concept of telecommuting grows and becomes more acceptable, courts are likely to closely consider whether telecommuting is a reasonable accommodation under ADA.

Some courts have already considered the issue. The results have varied. Depending on the circumstances the ADA may force employers to provide telecommuting as a reasonable accommodation. If the essential functions of the job can be performed by the employee at home, there may be an obligation to allow the disabled employee to telecommute, unless the employer can demonstrate that it would create an undue hardship. Therefore, companies must formulate policies or guidelines for determining which positions are eligible for telecommuting. Such policies can help employers distinguish for employees and courts the reasons why some jobs are suitable for home performance and others must remain a traditional office or workplace job.

Insurance and General Liability Issues

Before implementing a telecommuting policy, an employer must determine how to handle certain insurance issues. Work injuries and workers' compensation have already been discussed. The employer and the telecommuter should consider other insurance and liability issues before telecommuting begins. For example, it needs to be determined who will be responsible for theft or damage to equipment. Will it be the employee's obligation to provide insurance coverage for such incidents, or will the company provide the insurance coverage?

Likewise, who shall provide insurance coverage if third parties are injured at the telecommuter's home? It is unlikely that injuries to individuals at the telecommuter's home for social or personal reasons will be the employer's responsibility. However, injuries that are related to the telecommuter's work or equipment may be found to be the employer's responsibility. Preventive steps should be taken to lessen the chance of such problems. The employer and the employee should understand from the beginning where the liability of each begins and ends.

Zoning

Local zoning codes may prohibit home-based work at the telecommuter's home. Zoning is highly variable and changes from city to city, so two telecommuters may face very different situations in regards to zoning restrictions. An employer should work with its telecommuters to find out if there are any restrictions and, if so, develop a strategy for dealing with them.

Telecommuting Written Agreement

To clarify expectations and obligations, employers and employees should enter into written agreements covering telecommuting arrangements. Important subjects for such an agreement would include:

- The employee's coverage by workers' compensation while working at the alternative job site.
- The employer's (or employee's) provision of necessary equipment.
- The maintenance of the employee's alternative workspace to the same standards as required for the onsite office. The employer may retain the right, subject to reasonable notice, to inspect the alternative worksite during scheduled work hours.
- The employee's responsibility to secure any equipment provided by the employer.
- Responsibility for the cost of utilities.
- Clarification of the employer's policy regarding dependent care during work hours.
- The employee's accessibility for and the location of business or client meetings.
- The employee's duty to make reports to the employer's office or to report in, periodically.

Conclusion

More employers are coming to recognize that telecommuting offers a unique opportunity to cut costs and retain valuable employees. Management support is essential for a program to succeed. Managers must be trained to supervise telecommuting employees and policies and procedures must be developed to accommodate the telecommuter while limiting the risks to the employer. Clearly defined procedures and guidelines not only allow both employers and employees to know what is expected of them, but also reduce the likelihood of unexpected employment issues or lawsuits.

Telecommuting

Chapter 40
Posting and Recordkeeping Requirements

Introduction

State and federal laws vary with regard to the requirements for an employer to display informational posters and retain company records. The following charts are designed to acquaint the employer with these requirements and to provide information about posting, and recordkeeping functions.

The following charts outline many of the employer's responsibilities with regard to recordkeeping and posting requirements and defining the procedures for employers covered under particular laws. This guide also provides suggestions for employers who merely wish to establish compliance but are not mandated to do so under any federal regulation.

This chapter reviews federal policy concerning retaining employment records as enforced under a variety of federal acts. It then reviews any state requirements for handling employment records. Each state's labor and employment laws have their own recordkeeping requirements, sometimes requiring retention for lengthy periods of time (for example, six years.) As always, the laws themselves should be consulted to ensure your company is in compliance.

Federal Recordkeeping

Table of Applicable Federal Laws

- Age Discrimination in Employment Act (ADEA)
- Americans with Disabilities Act (ADA)
- Consolidated Omnibus Budget Reconciliation Act of 1985 (COBRA)
- Employee Polygraph Protection Act (EPPA)
- Employee Retirement Income Security Act of 1974 (ERISA)
- Employment Tax Laws—Federal Insurance Contribution Act (FICA)
- Employment Tax Laws—Federal Unemployment Tax Act (FUTA)
- Equal Pay Act (EPA)
- Fair Credit Reporting Act (FCRA)
- Fair Labor Standards Act (FLSA)
- Family and Medical Leave Act of 1993 (FMLA)
- Health Insurance Portability and Accountability Act (HIPAA)
- Immigration Reform & Control Act (IRCA)
- Mental Health Parity Act (MHPA)
- Newborns' and Mothers' Health Protection Act (NMHPA)
- Occupational Safety & Health Act (OSH Act)
- Title VII Civil Rights Act of 1964
- Vietnam Era Veterans' Readjustment Assistance Act (VEVRAA)
- Women's Health and Cancer Rights Act (WHCRA)

Age Discrimination in Employment Act (ADEA)

Mandatory Recordkeeping

Record	Description	Duration
Payroll records	▸ This includes employee's name, address, date of birth, occupation, rate of pay, and compensation earned per week	▸ 3 years
Personnel records	▸ This includes records used in hiring (for example, applications, résumés, responses to job ads, etc.), records pertaining to employment decisions (for example, termination, demotion, promotion, transfer, layoff, recall, selection for training, etc.), results from employment tests, job advertisements, and training records	▸ 1 year from the date of the personnel action **Note:** If enforcement action is brought against employer, records must be kept until final disposition of action
Employee benefits	▸ Benefit plans, written seniority systems, and written merit plan (if such a plan or system is not in writing, then a summary memorandum is to be kept)	▸ 1 year after termination of the plan or system

Americans With Disabilities Act (ADA)

Mandatory Recordkeeping

Record	Description	Duration
Personnel records (I)	▶ This includes general personnel records including application forms, promotion, transfers, discharges, tests, training, rates of pay, requests for reasonable accommodations, etc.	▶ 1 year from the date of the personnel action or the date personnel action is actually taken, whichever is later
Personnel records (II)	▶ All personnel records relating to a charge filed with the EEOC, including records related to similarly situated employees	▶ Until disposition of the charge or action
Apprenticeship programs (I)	▶ This includes a chronological list of the names, addresses, sex, race of all applicants, and date of application	▶ 2 years from the date of application, or the length of apprentice ship, whichever is longer
Apprenticeship programs (II)	▶ All records made solely for completion of EEO-2 report	▶ 1 year from due date of report

Consolidated Omnibus Budget Reconciliation Act of 1985 (COBRA)

Mandatory Recordkeeping
- There are no federally mandated record retention requirements under COBRA.

Optional Recordkeeping
- List of employees covered by your group health plan
- Records of terminations, reductions in hours, leaves of absence, and/or deaths of employees covered by the group's health plan
- The Medicare eligibility of covered employees
- Disability status of covered employees
- List of retirees covered by group health plan
- Current addresses of employees
- Copies of letters sent to employees advising them of their COBRA rights
- Written acknowledgements from employees and qualified beneficiaries that they received notice of their COBRA rights
- Current addresses of anyone receiving COBRA benefits
- Record of COBRA premium payments made by employees
- Record of any changes made to your group health plan
- List of employees denied COBRA coverage, along with reasons why they were denied coverage
- Method used to calculate COBRA premiums

Employee Polygraph Protection Act (EPPA)

Mandatory Recordkeeping

Record	Description	Duration
Investigation materials	▶ An explanation provided to the employee being investigated of the specific incident or activity of economic loss that is under investigation	▶ 3 years from the date the polygraph is conducted, or from the date the polygraph test is requested if no examination is conducted
Subject of the investigation	▶ An explanation of the specific loss or injury involved with the investigation of criminal or other misconduct, involving, or potentially involving, loss or injury to manufacture, distribution, or dispensing of a controlled substance as well as the nature of the employee's access to particular person or property	▶ 3 years from the date the polygraph is conducted, or from the date the polygraph test is requested if no examination is conducted
A written statement	▶ A statement informing the employee of the time and place of the test, and stating the employee's rights to consult with counsel	▶ 3 years from the date the polygraph is conducted, or from the date the polygraph test is requested if no examination is conducted
A copy of the notice to the examiner	▶ A notice identifying which employees are to be examined	▶ 3 years from the date the polygraph is conducted, or from the date the polygraph test is requested if no examination is conducted
Copies	▶ All opinions, reports, or other records given to the employer by the examiner	▶ 3 years from the date the polygraph is conducted, or from the date the polygraph test is requested if no examination is conducted

Employee Retirement Income Security Act of 1974 (ERISA)

Mandatory Recordkeeping

Record	Description	Duration
Data	▸ All data used to support summary plan descriptions and other records supporting plans or reports, including vouchers, worksheets, receipts, and applicable resolutions	▸ 6 years after the filing date of the documents
Employee/beneficiary records	▸ Relevant to benefits due or which may become due	▸ Kept for as long as relevant

Employment Tax Laws—Federal Insurance Contribution Act (FICA)

Mandatory Recordkeeping

Record	Description	Duration
The amount of each wage	▸ Payment which is separately subject to Social Security and Medicare taxes	▸ 4 years after the tax due date or the date tax is paid, whichever is later
The amount of FICA Tax collected	▸ For each wage payment and the date collected	▸ 4 years after the tax due date or the date tax is paid, whichever is later
Wage payment	▸ The reason why the total wage payment is more than the taxable amount	▸ 4 years after the tax due date or the date tax is paid, whichever is later
Employees' receipts	▸ Copies of employees' receipts, if you refunded over-withheld FICA tax to them	▸ 4 years after the tax due date or the date tax is paid, whichever is later

Note: Additional recordkeeping requirements are found in 26 CFR §31.6001-2.

Employment Tax Laws—Federal Unemployment Tax Act (FUTA)

Mandatory Recordkeeping

Record	Description	Duration
Wages paid to each employee	▸ Total wages paid to each employee, including withholding	▸ 4 years after the tax due date or the date tax is paid, whichever is later
Amount of pay subject to FUTA	▸ The amount of pay subject to FUTA, and the reason if this amount is not equal to total compensation	▸ 4 years after the tax due date or the date tax is paid, whichever is later
The amount paid into any state unemployment fund	▸ The amount paid into any state unemployment fund, including any amounts deducted or to be deducted from employee pay	▸ 4 years after the tax due date or the date tax is paid, whichever is later
Other information	▸ Any other information required to be shown on the FUTA tax return (FORM 940 or 940-EZ), and the amount of the tax	▸ 4 years after the tax due date or the date tax is paid, whichever is later

Note: Additional recordkeeping requirements are found in 26 CFR §31.6001.4.

Optional Recordkeeping

- ▸ Your employer identification number
- ▸ Copies of all filed tax returns (941s, 940s, 940-EZs, W-2s, and 1099s)
- ▸ The original W-2, and the envelope in which you mailed it, if an employee's W-2 is undeliverable
- ▸ Copies of cancelled checks, deposit coupons, and ACH confirmation numbers, if you deposit taxes via electronic funds transfer using ACH debit option
- ▸ The dates and amounts of your tax deposits
- ▸ Records of taxable fringe benefits, plus your substantiation of the taxable amounts
- ▸ Records of employees' substantiations of travel and entertainment expenses
- ▸ Correspondence from the IRS regarding any employee's withholding

Equal Pay Act (EPA)

Mandatory Recordkeeping

Record	Description	Duration
Workweek definition (I)	▸ Number of hours each employee works, pay rates, total wages, and total deductions	▸ 3 years after the last date of entry
Workweek definition (II)	▸ Time cards and sheets, records explaining any wage differentials between employees of the opposite sex (job descriptions, job evaluations, merit, incentive, and seniority systems, etc.) and wage rate tables	▸ 2 years from the date the record is made
Collective bargaining	▸ Benefit plans, written seniority systems, and written merit plans	▸ 3 years

Note: In addition, the EPA incorporates by reference the recordkeeping requirements of the FLSA.

Fair Credit Reporting Act (FCRA)

Mandatory Recordkeeping

▸ There are no federally mandated recordkeeping requirements under the FCRA. However, the statute of limitations for employee FCRA claims is 2 years.

Fair Labor Standards Act (FLSA)

Mandatory Recordkeeping

Record	Description	Duration
Personal information (I)	▸ Employee's name, address, and zip code	▸ 3 years after the last date of entry
Personal information (II)	▸ Employee's date of birth (if the employee is under 19 years of age)	▸ 3 years after the last date of entry
Gender	▸ Sex of employee, and occupation he or she holds	▸ 3 years after the last date of entry
Employee schedule (I)	▸ Time of day and the day of the week the employee's workweek begins (if the employee is part of a workforce where all employees' workweeks begin at the same day/time, then a single notation of the day and the time all employees' workweeks begin is sufficient)	▸ 3 years after the last date of entry
Employee schedule (II)	▸ Employee's daily and weekly hours worked	▸ 3 years after the last date of entry
Overtime	▸ Total wages paid for overtime	▸ 3 years after the last date of entry
Additions and deductions	▸ Total additions to and deductions from employee's pay each pay period	▸ 3 years after the last date of entry
Salary	▸ Total wages paid each pay period	▸ 3 years after the last date of entry
Pay period	▸ Date of payment, as well as the pay period covered by the payment	▸ 3 years after the last date of entry
Supplementary records	▸ Time cards; work time schedules; order, shipping, and billing records; wage rate tables, additions and deductions from wages, etc.	▸ 2 years after the record is made

Record	Description	Duration
Payroll records	▶ Payroll records, including: ▶ Full name, identification number, home address, date of birth (if under age 19), gender, occupation, day and time workweek begins, hours worked each day and week, total daily or weekly earnings, overtime compensation, basis of overtime computation, total wages for each pay period, and payment date for certificates, agreements, plans, notice, etc.	▶ 3 years after the record is made ▶ 3 years from last effective date for certificates, agreements, plans, notices, etc.
Certificates of age	▶ N/A	▶ Must be kept until termination of employment
Written training agreements	▶ N/A	▶ Must be kept for the duration of the training program

I (Tipped Employees)

Record	Description	Duration
Identification	▶ A symbol or letter which identifies the employee as a tipped employee	▶ 3 years after the last date of entry
Tipped hours	▶ The actual number of hours worked each workday in a tipped position	▶ 3 years after the last date of entry
Non-tipped hours	▶ The total hours worked each workday in a non-tipped position	▶ 3 years after the last date of entry
Separated daily and weekly earnings	▶ The total daily or weekly straight-time earnings separated by: time paid for hours worked each workday in a tipped position, time paid for hours worked each workday in a non-tipped position, and tips received and accounted for or turned over by the employee to the employer in a weekly or monthly amount	▶ 3 years after the last date of entry

Record	Description	Duration
Wages increased by tips	▸ Amount by which the wages of each tipped employee have been deemed to be increased by tips or determined by the employer (not in excess of 40% of the applicable statutory minimum wage) The amount per hour that the employer takes as a tip credit shall be reported to the employer in writing each time it is changed from the amount per hour taken in the preceding week	▸ 3 years after the record is made

II (Trainees)

Record	Description	Duration
Payroll records	▸ In addition to the general recordkeeping requirements, an employer's payroll records must segregate trainees, learners, and apprentices, and indicate their status using a code or symbol	▸ 3 years after the record is made

III (Students)

Record	Description	Duration
School information	▸ When the student is hired, information from the school that he or she receives primarily daytime instruction at the physical location of the school. If he or she changes schools, another certificate from the new school that he or she is accepted as a full time student and receives primary daytime instruction	▸ 3 years after the record is made
Student's work hours	▸ Monthly records of the student's work hours, and the total hours worked by all employees during the month	▸ 3 years after the record is made

Note: See 29 CFR §516 for recordkeeping requirements for employees of various classifications.

Family and Medical Leave Act of 1993 (FMLA)

Mandatory Recordkeeping

Record	Description	Duration
Basic payroll and identifying employee data	▸ This information includes employees' names, addresses, and occupations, their rates or bases of pay and terms of compensation, daily and weekly hours worked for each pay period, additions to or deductions from wages, and total compensation paid	▸ 3 years after the last date the record is made
Dates FMLA leave is taken by eligible employees	▸ This information can be in the form of time records, employees' request for leave, etc. The leave time must be designated as FMLA leave in the records, and may not include leave required under state law or employer plans that are not also covered by the FMLA. If leave is taken in increments of less than one full day, you must record the hours of leave	▸ 3 years after the last date the record is made
Copies of employee notices of leave furnished to the employee under the FMLA, if in writing	▸ Copies of general and specific written notices given to employees as required by the FMLA are to be kept, as well	▸ 3 years after the last date the record is made
Any documents which describe employee benefits or employer policies and practices related to the taking of paid and unpaid leaves	▸ This includes written and electronic records. Also, records of premium payments of employee benefits must be maintained	▸ 3 years after the last date the record is made
Records of any dispute between the employer and an eligible employee regarding the designation of leave as FMLA Leave	▸ This includes any written statements from the employer or employee relating to the reasons for the designation and/or the dispute	▸ 3 years after the last date the record is made

Note: The FMLA also mandates that records, which relate to medical certifications and medical histories, must be maintained in separate files and treated as confidential records.

Health Insurance Portability and Accountability Act (HIPAA)

Mandatory Recordkeeping
▸ There are no federally mandated recordkeeping requirements under HIPAA.

Immigration Reform and Control Act (IRCA)

Mandatory Recordkeeping

Record	Description	Duration
Employee identification forms (I-9 Form)	▸ Used when an employee is hired to verify the applicant's employment eligibility	▸ 3 years from the date of hire or one year after termination, whichever is later

Mental Health Parity Act (MHPA)

Mandatory Recordkeeping
▸ There are no federally mandated recordkeeping requirements under the MHPA.

Optional Recordkeeping
▸ A summary of the aggregate data and computation supporting the increased cost exemption.

Newborns' and Mothers' Health Protection Act

Mandatory Recordkeeping
▸ There are no federally mandated recordkeeping requirements under the NMHPA.

Occupational Safety and Health Act (OSHA)

Mandatory Recordkeeping

Record	Description	Duration
Form 200—*Log and Summary of Occupational Injuries and Illnesses* Effective January 1, 2002, this form will be replaced by Form 300, titled *Log of Work-related Injuries and Illnesses*	▸ Work-related injuries which result in the loss of a workday, require medical treatment beyond first aid, involve a loss of consciousness, restriction of motion, or transfer to another job, must be recorded in OSHA Form 200	▸ 5 years from the end of the calendar year to which the record relates (form must be updated during this period) ▸ After January 1, 2002, Form 300 must be kept for 5 years following the year to which the form relates
Form 101—*Supplementary Record of Occupational Injuries and Illnesses* Effective January 1, 2002, this form will be replaced by Form 301, titled *Injury and Illness Incident Report*	▸ Used to record details about a workplace injury or illness, including the employer's address, a description of the incident, description and cause of injury or illness, and the name of the treating doctor or hospital	▸ 5 years from the end of the calendar year to which the record relates ▸ After January 1, 2002, Form 301 must be kept for 5 years following the year to which the form relates
Form 300A—*Summary of Work-related Injuries and Illnesses* (effective January 1, 2002)	▸ Used to simplify calculation of incidence rates	▸ 5 years from end of the calendar year to which the record relates
Employee exposure records	▸ Exposure records and medical records for all employees working in areas that may expose them to toxic substances or harmful physical agents	▸ Generally, 30 years, except biological monitoring results described as exposure records by a specific standard must be maintained as per the standard

Posting and Recordkeeping Requirements

Record	Description	Duration
Material safety data sheets (MSDSs)	▸ Contain detailed information about hazardous chemicals	▸ Must be maintained and made accessible to employees in their work area during each shift; must be kept for 30 years (deemed an exposure record)
Employee medical records	▸ Records concerning the health status of an employee which is made or maintained by a physician, nurse, or other healthcare professional or technician	▸ Duration of employment PLUS 30 years
Records	▸ Medical removal records	▸ At least to the duration of the person's employment

Note: Employers in many industries are exempt from OSHA's basic injury and illness recordkeeping requirements. However, they still may be required to maintain records pursuant to specific applicable OSHA standards (for example, asbestos). (See 29 CFR §1904 et. Seq.) Moreover, all employers must report fatalities in the workplace or the hospitalization of three or more employees resulting from a workplace incident.

Title VII of the Civil Rights Act of 1964

Mandatory Recordkeeping

Record	Description	Duration
Personnel records (I)	▶ This includes general personnel records including application forms, promotions, demotions, transfers, discharges, tests, training, rates of pay, etc.	▶ 1 year from the date of the personnel action or the date of making the record, whichever is longer
Personnel records (II)	▶ All personnel records relating to a charge filed with the EEOC or ACRD, including records related to similarly situated employees	▶ Until disposition of the charge or action
Personnel records (III)	▶ Employee requests for reasonable accommodation	▶ 1 year from the date of the personnel action
Apprenticeship programs (I)	▶ This includes a chronological list of the names, addresses, sex, race of all applicants, and date of application	▶ 2 years from the date of application, or the length of apprenticeship, whichever is longer
Apprenticeship programs (II)	▶ All records made solely for completion of EEO-2 report	▶ 1 year from due date of report
EEO-1 (*Employer Information Report*)	▶ Report shows numbers of minority and female employees compared to employer's total workforce in different job categories	▶ A copy of the most recent report filed must be retained

Note: Employers with 100 or more employees must file an EEO-1 report by September 30 of each year.

Vietnam Era Veterans' Readjustment Assistance Act (VEVRAA)

Mandatory Recordkeeping

Record	Description	Duration
Records (I)	▸ Records regarding complaints about discrimination against disabled veterans	▸ 1 year

Women's Health and Cancer Rights Act (WHCRA)

Mandatory Recordkeeping
▸ There are no federally mandated recordkeeping requirements under the WHCRA.

Federal Posting Requirements

Table of Federal Posters

Required

Private Employers, State and Local Governments, and Educational Institutions

- Age Discrimination in Employment Act (ADEA
- Americans with Disabilities (ADA)
- Employee Polygraph Protection Act (EPPA)
- Fair Labor Standards Act (FLSA)
- Family and Medical Leave Act (FMLA)
- Occupational Safety & Health Act (OSHA)
- Title VII Civil Rights Act of 1964

Government Contractors

- Davis–Bacon Act
- Drug-Free Workplace Act
- Executive Order 11246
- Section 503 of the Rehabilitation Act
- Service Contract Act
- Vietnam Era Veterans' Readjustment Assistance Act (VEVRAA)
- Walsh–Healy Public Contract Act

Recommended

- Civil Rights Act of 1991
- Consolidated Omnibus Budget Reconciliation Act (COBRA)
- Consumer Credit Protection Act, Title III
- Employee Retirement Income Security Act of 1974 (ERISA)
- Fair Credit Reporting Act (FCRA)
- Federal Military Selective Service Act
- Immigration Reform and Control Act (IRCA)
- Jury Service and Selection Act of 1968
- Uniformed Services Employment and Re-employment Rights Act (USERRA)
- Worker Adjustment and Retraining Notification Act (WARN)

Private Employers, State and Local Governments, and Educational Institutions

Statute	Minimum Employees	Poster	Necessary Language
Age Discrimination in Employment Act (ADEA)	20	"Equal Employment Opportunity is the Law"	"The (ADEA) of 1967, as amended, protects applicants and employees 40 years of age or older from discrimination on the basis of age in hiring, promotion, discharge, compensation, terms, conditions, or privileges of employment."
Americans with Disabilities Act (ADA)	15	"Equal Employment Opportunity is the Law"	"The (ADA) of 1990, as amended, protects qualified applicants and employees with disabilities from discrimination in hiring, promotion, discharge, pay, job training, fringe benefits, classification, referral, and other aspects of employment on the basis of disability. The law also requires that covered entities provide qualified applicants and employees with disabilities with reasonable accommodations that do not impose undue hardship."
Equal Pay Act (EPA)	No minimum	"Equal Employment Opportunity is the Law"	"In addition to sex discrimination prohibited by Title VII of the Civil Rights Act, the EPA of 1963, as amended, prohibits sex discrimination in payment of wages to women and men performing substantially equal work in the same establishment."
Family and Medical Leave Act (FMLA)	50	"Your Rights Under the Family and Medical Leave Act of 1993"	Poster must inform workers that they are entitled to 12 weeks of unpaid, but job-protected leave for family medical reasons.

Posting and Recordkeeping Requirements

Statute	Minimum Employees	Poster	Necessary Language
Fair Labor Standards Act (FLSA)	No minimum	"Fair Labor Standards Act"	Poster must inform workers of their rights under the FLSA, including minimum wage and overtime compensation. **Note:** If a significant portion of the employer's workforce is not literate in English, the employer must post another copy of the poster in the language the employees can understand.
Employee Polygraph Protection Act (EPPA)	No minimum	"Notice of Employee Polygraph Protection Act"	Poster must inform workers of their rights regarding lie-detector tests in an area where the notice may be easily seen by both applicants and employees.
Occupational Safety and Health Act (OSHA)	No minimum	"Job Safety and Health Protection Act" "You Have a Right to a Safe and Healthful Workplace"	Poster must inform workers of their rights regarding what compliance is required of employers and employees; describe worksite inspection, complaint, and citation procedures; describe penalties; voluntary safety guidelines; and describe methods of consulting with OSHA.
Title VII of the Civil Rights Act of 1964	15	"Equal Employment Opportunity is the Law"	Title VII of the Civil Rights Act of 1964, as amended, prohibits discrimination in hiring, promotion, discharge, pay, fringe benefits, job training, classification, referral, and other aspects of employment, on the basis of race, color, religion, sex, or national origin.

Note: Compliance with above-referenced posting requirements can be maintained by displaying an updated EEOC "Federal 5-in-1 Labor Law Poster" in a conspicuous place for convenient viewing by all employees and applicants.

Government Contractors

Amount of Contract	Minimum Employees	Act/Order	Poster	Necessary Language
$2,000	No minimum	Davis–Bacon Act	"Notice to all Employees Working on Federally Financed Construction Projects"	Poster must inform workers of their rights regarding minimum hourly rates, which must be paid by the employer
$25,000	No minimum	Drug-Free Workplace Act	"Notice to all Employees Working on Federally Financed Construction Projects"	Poster must inform workers with information concerning drug abuse and awareness programs
$10,000	No minimum	Executive Order 11246	"Notice to all Employees Working on Federally Financed Construction Projects"	"Executive Order 11246, as amended, prohibits job discrimination on the basis of race, color, religion, sex, or national origin, and requires affirmative action to ensure equality of opportunity in all aspects of employment"
$10,000	No minimum	Walsh–Healy Public Contract Act	"Agricultural Employees" "Notice to Employees Working on Government Contracts"	Poster must inform workers with information concerning that the employer must pay the prevailing minimum wage, as well as time and a half for hours worked exceeding 40 hours per week

Amount of Contract	Minimum Employees	Act/Order	Poster	Necessary Language
$2,500	No minimum	Section 503 of the Rehabilitation Act	"Equal Employment Opportunity is the Law"	Poster must inform workers with information detailing the prohibition of discrimination against handicapped persons
$2,500	50	Section 503 of the Rehabilitation Act	"Equal Employment Opportunity is the Law"	Poster must inform employees that the employer is required to have an affirmative action program
$2,500	No minimum	Service Contract Act	"Notice to All Employees Working on Government Contracts"	Poster must be displayed in its entirety
$25,000	No minimum	Vietnam Era Veterans' Readjustment Assistance Act	"Equal Employment Opportunity is the Law"	"38 USC 4212 of the Vietnam Era Veterans' Readjustment Assistance Act of 1974 prohibits job discrimination and requires affirmative action to employ and advance in employment qualified Vietnam-era veterans and qualified disabled veterans"

Recommended Posters

Civil Rights Act of 1991	▸ This poster informs workers of amended Title VII and ADA rules permitting jury trials in intentional discrimination claims, and that punitive damages may be awarded
Consolidated Omnibus Budget Reconciliation Act (COBRA)	▸ This poster informs workers that employers must extend the option of continued health insurance to employees, their spouses, and dependants who otherwise would lose this coverage as a consequence of termination
Consumer Credit Protection Act, Title III	▸ This poster informs workers that garnishment withholding of more than 25% of disposable income is prohibited
Employee Retirement Income Security Act of 1974 (ERISA)	▸ This poster informs workers of pension and welfare information relative to employee participation in certain programs
Fair Credit Reporting Act (FCRA)	▸ This poster informs workers of an employer's intention to research and use employee credit reports in hiring or other employment processes
Federal Military Selective Service Act	▸ This poster informs workers that their employer must give those employees returning from military service the same wages, benefits, and rights as the employee would have received if they had not left
Immigration Reform and Control Act of 1986 (IRCA)	▸ This poster informs workers that their employer must verify the employment authorization of new hires. It also states that discrimination based upon national origin or citizenship status is prohibited in all hiring and firing
Jury Service and Selection Act of 1968	▸ This poster informs workers that employers must grant "time-off" for jury service as a leave of absence. It also informs workers that these employees must be reinstated without a loss in wages, benefits, seniority, and/or other employment conditions
Uniformed Services Employment and Re-employment Rights Act (USERRA)	▸ This poster informs workers that they cannot be discriminated against for being members of the armed services, which includes the National Guard
Worker Adjustment and Retraining Notification Act (WARN)	▸ This poster informs workers that their employer must give them no less than 60 days' notice if a closing or layoff of at least 50 workers is expected

Massachusetts State Recordkeeping Requirements

Table of Affected Subjects

Benefits
- Unemployment Insurance
- Workers' Compensation

Discrimination
- Age Discrimination
- Fair Employment Practices Act
- Personnel Records Statute

Hiring
- New-Hire Reporting

Leave
- Small Necessities Leave Act

Pay
- Child Labor
- Home Workers
- Income Tax Withholding
- Public Works
- Wage & Hour

Safety and Health
- Smoking

Benefits

Topic	Description	Duration
Unemployment Insurance	▸ Copies of Forms 0001 and WR-1, *Employer's Quarterly Report of Wages Paid* ▸ Copies of Forms 0209, *Low Earnings Report* ▸ Copies of all correspondence related to the benefits eligibility of former employees ▸ Rates Notices ▸ Copies of 0590-A, *Separation Reports*	▸ 4 Years after a return is filed or required to be filed
Unemployment Insurance	▸ Copies of Form 1110-A, *Employer Status Report*	▸ As long as the employer is in business in the state
Workers' Compensation	▸ Copies of Form 101 for all injuries that cause and employee to be disabled for five or more days	▸ As long as the employer is in business in the state

Discrimination

Topic	Description	Duration
Age Discrimination	▸ Employers must keep accurate records of all employees' age	▸ 1 year from date of personnel action
Fair Employment Practices Act	▸ This applies to all employers with six or more employees, and requires that those employers must keep records relating to race, color and national origin	▸ 1 year from date of personnel action
Massachusetts Personnel Records Statute	▸ This applies to employers with 20 or more employees	▸ 3 years after termination of employment

Hiring

Topic	Description	Duration
New-hire Reporting	▸ Employers must keep information on: • Newly hired workers • Rehired workers • Contractors hired to perform services for the employer • Employees who retire and receive retirement pay • Employees who file workers' compensation claims	▸ Employers have a continuing obligation to keep records of new-hires ▸ These records need not be kept more than 3 years after creation of the record

Leave

Topic	Description	Duration
Small Necessities Leave Act	▸ All employers, who are governed by the Family Medical Leave Act, must keep copies of certification forms provided by employees under the Act	▸ 2 years

Pay

Topic	Description	Duration
Child Labor	▸ Employers must keep a list of minors employed as well as their educational certificates showing: • Age • Whether they meet the 6th grade requirement in the town of employment	▸ As long as the child is employed

Pay (cont)

Topic	Description	Duration
Income Tax Withholding (General)	Copies of: - Form M-941W, *Employer's Weekly Payment of Income Taxes Withheld* - Form M-942, *Employer's Monthly Return of Income Taxes Withheld* - Form M-941-Q, *Employer's Quarterly Return of Income Taxes Withheld* - Form M-941-A, *Employer's Annual Return of Income Taxes Withheld* - Form M-941D, *Quarterly Return of Incomes Taxes Withheld for Employers Weekly Payment of Income Taxes Withheld*	▶ 3 Years after a return is filed or required to be filed
Income Tax Withholding (General)	- Form M-3M, *Reconciliation of Massachusetts Income Taxes Withheld* - Form M-3 W1R, *Reconciliation of Massachusetts Income Taxes Withheld for Quarterly Filers* - Employees' Forms W-2 - All federal Forms 1099 and 1096 - Acknowledgments of electronic funds transfer tax deposits - Copies of canceled checks	▶ 3 Years after a return is filed or required to be filed

Pay (cont)

Topic	Description	Duration
Income Tax Withholding (Books and Accounts)	▸ The amounts and dates of all wages paid and taxes withheld ▸ Employees' names, addresses, Social Security numbers, occupations, and dates of employment ▸ Amount and pay rate of personal injury and sick leave payments ▸ Employees' requests for cumulative withholding	▸ 3 Years after a return is filed or required to be filed
Income Tax Withholding (Books and Accounts)	▸ Employer's federal employer identification number	▸ 3 Years after a return is filed or required to be filed
Income Tax Withholding (Certificates)	▸ Forms W-4 and W-2 ▸ Form M-4, *Massachusetts Employee's Withholding Exemption Certificate* ▸ Form M-4P, *Massachusetts Withholding Exemption Certificate for Pension, Annuity and Other Periodic Payments and Nonperiodic Payments* ▸ Employees' statements of tips received	▸ Employees' state withholding certificates must be kept as long as they're active inactive ▸ Certificates should be retained for at least 3 years after new certificates are filed or employees terminate
Income Tax Withholding (Other Forms)	▸ Application for Electronic Funds Transfer or Application for Mass-Debt Tax Payment ▸ Form TA-1, *Application for Original Registration*	▸ As long as the employer is in business in the state

Public Works

Topic	Description	Duration
General Records	▸ Contractors and subcontractors must keep employee information: • Employees' names and addresses • Trades (crafts) • Hours worked and rates	▸ 3 Years
Wage & Hour	▸ Employers must keep employee information: • Employees' names • Addresses • Social Security numbers • Occupations • Rates of pay • Times and days workweeks • Begin • Hours worked daily and weekly • Total and daily or weekly straight time wages (including overtime)	▸ 3 Years

Safety and Health

Topic	Description	Duration
General Records	▸ Employers must retain material safety and data sheets (MSDS)	▸ 30 Years

Massachusetts State Posting Requirements

- Unemployment Insurance Notice.
- State Workers' Compensation Notice.
- Fair Employment Practices Act.
- Employee Rights Regarding Sexual Harassment (15 employee minimum).
- State Whistleblowers' Protection Law.
- State's Maternity Leave Provisions (if company employs females).
- Child Labor Laws (meal allowances, number of hours they can work, etc.).
- Minimum Wage Rates and Provisions.
- Employees' Rights Relating to Hazardous Substances.
- Smoking and Non-Smoking Area Designations.
- Healthcare Whistleblower Law (if a healthcare employer).

Index

Numbers

401(k) 236
403(b) 237

A

absenteeism. *See also* discipline 135
    Americans with Disabilities Act, covered by 137
    attendance policy, establishment of 135
    calculating 136
    chronic 136
    discipline 137
    Family and Medical Leave Act, covered by 137
    incentive plans 135
    physician certificates 136
    policy, establishment of 135
    return-to-work physicals 136
advertising
    discrimination in 89
    guidelines 13
Age Discrimination in Employment Act (ADEA). *See also* federal law 83, 396
AIDS/communicable diseases 309
    Americans with Disabilities Act 309
    commonly asked questions and answers 313
    confidentiality 311
    Family and Medical Leave Act 312
    health insurance benefits 311
    information resources 313
    medical examinations 310
    policy considerations 312
    policy statements on transmission risk 310
    pre-employment inquiries 309
    protection for applicants and employees under ADA 310
    reasonable accommodation 311
    workplace safety 312
alcoholism. *See* drug and alcohol testing 109
alternative dispute resolution (ADR) 285
    arbitration 287
        advantages 287
        clauses, terms of 288

Index

  disadvantages ... 287
  mandatory ... 26
  to avoid civil litigation ... 288
 internal mediation ... 286
 ombudsman ... 286
 open-door policies ... 285
 peer review ... 286
Americans with Disabilities Act (ADA). *See also* federal law ... 83, 309, 315, 396
 contingent employees ... 302
anti-discrimination. *See* discrimination ... 81
attendance policy. *See also* absenteeism ... 135

B

background checks ... 29
 information sources ... 29
  consumer reports ... 30
  credit checks ... 31
  criminal record ... 31
  disclosure to applicants ... 30
  references ... 31
  reports ... 29
benefits
 employee leave. *See* Family and Medical Leave Act ... 225
 fringe benefits, taxable as ... 176
 healthcare. *See* healthcare plans ... 187
 Pension and Welfare Benefits Administration ... 198, 209
 retirement. *See* ERISA and retirement plans ... 219
 unemployment compensation ... 160
breaks
 minors ... 73

C

casual employees. *See* contingent employment ... 301
child support payments ... 60
Civil Rights Act of 1866 (Section 1981) ... 83
Civil Rights Act of 1964. *See also* federal law ... 396
COBRA ... 187
 benefits ... 189
 coverage
  during election period ... 195
  length of ... 193
  loss of ... 191
  nature of ... 192
  termination of ... 194
 covered employees ... 190
 covered employers ... 189
 covered plans ... 190
 disability extensions ... 193

election period 195
employee
    moves 193
    revocation/reinstatement 196
    terminated for cause 192
Family Medical Leave Act, and 198
HIPAA, under 197
multiple beneficiaries 196
notices of rights 195
payments 196
qualified beneficiary 191
qualifying events 191
reduction in hours 192
when a business is sold 198
Consolidated Omnibus Budget Reconciliation Act of 1985. *See* COBRA, federal law 187, 396
contingent employment 301
    contract workers 301
    definitions 301
    discrimination 302
    employment laws 302
    Fair Labor Standards Act (FLSA) 304
    Family and Medical Leave Act (FMLA) 303
    Immigration Reform and Control Act (IRCA) 304
    independent contractors 302
    leased employees 302
    National Labor Relations Act (NLRA) 305
    Occupational Safety and Health Act (OSH Act) 305
    outsourced employees 301
    part-time employees 301
    taxes and withholding 305
    temporary employees 301
    Workers Adjustment and Retraining Notification (WARN) 303
credit reports 31

D

defamation suits. *See* termination 153
defined benefit plans. *See* retirement plans 235
defined contribution plans. *See* retirement plans 236
disability 2, 9, 13, 178, 386
    AIDS/communicable diseases 309, 310, 311, 312, 313
    Americans with Disabilities Act (ADA) 315, 414
    COBRA 192, 194, 196, 197, 399
    discrimination 9, 10, 11, 82, 83, 88, 97
        harassment 88, 382
    drug and alcohol testing
        Americans with Disabilities Act (ADA) 110, 111
    employee leave 231
    ERISA 220, 221
    HIPAA 214

Index

- recordkeeping ... 399
- recruiting and hiring ... 11, 13, 18, 32
- smoking in the workplace ... 315, 316, 319
- termination ... 160
- workplace violence ... 324

discipline ... 131
- absenteeism ... 135
  - physician certificates ... 136
  - return-to-work physicals ... 136
- appeal process ... 134
- Disciplinary Action Form ... 138
- documentation ... 134
- enforcing rules ... 132
  - appeal process ... 134
  - explanation and imposition ... 133
  - investigation ... 132
- establishing rules ... 131
- imposition of ... 131
- progressive ... 146

discrimination ... 81
- age ... 88
- complaint procedure ... 90
- contingent employees and the ADA ... 302
- damage caps ... 91
- discriminatory impact ... 83
- discriminatory treatment ... 82
- disparate impact ... 85
- EEOC investigations ... 90
- employer defenses ... 91
  - bona fide occupational qualifications ... 91
  - bona fide seniority or merit ... 92
  - business necessity ... 92
- enforcement ... 90
- English-only rules ... 85
- federal law ... 81
- forms
  - EEO-1 ... 95
  - EEO-4 ... 95
  - EEO-5 ... 95
  - EEO-6 ... 95
- harassment ... 84, 86, 87, 88, 92
- income withholding order ... 69
- laws prohibiting ... 83
- Massachusetts law ... 95
  - age ... 98
  - criminal records ... 98
  - disability ... 97
  - Equal Rights Act ... 96

430

  health records 98
  prohibitions, general 95
  recordkeeping and reporting 98
  religious discrimination 96
  retaliation 98
  sex discrimination 97
  sexual harassment 97
 national origin 85
 pregnancy 88
 protected conduct 82
 protected status 81
 racial 84
 recordkeeping and reporting requirements 94
 religious 86
 remedies 91
 reverse 85
 sex 86
  equal pay 69
 Title VII of the Civil Rights Act of 1964 83
 typical situations 82
drug and alcohol testing 109, 373
 Americans with Disabilities Act 110, 111
 Department of Defense regulations 115
 Department of Transportation 112
  policy requirement 114
  required alcohol testing 113
  required drug testing 112
  violation of alcohol testing regulations 114
  violation of drug testing regulations 113
 Drug-Free Workplace Act 114
 job applicants 110
 nonunion contract employees 110
 positive test result 118
 prevalence of drug use 119
 private at-will employees 109
 public sector employees 110
 state law considerations 119
 substance abuse performance indicators 120
 substances tested for 117
 testing laboratory 118
 testing limits 109
 testing policy 118
 testing program, implementing 116
 troubled employee, confronting 120
 types of tests 117
 union employees 110
Drug-Free Workplace Act. *See also* drug and alcohol testing, federal law 114
duty of loyalty. *See also* non-competition agreements, trade secrets 44

E

education
    pre-employment questions you may ask regarding ... 15
    programs for workplace violence ... 331
Electronic Communications Privacy Act ... 378
e-mail and voicemail systems ... 377
    company policy
        benefits ... 385
        characteristics ... 385
    copyright infringement ... 383
    defamation, slander, and trade libel ... 381
    Electronic Communications Privacy Act ... 378
        access to stored communication ... 380
        monitoring, existing and proposed legislation ... 381
        restrictions ... 379
            exceptions to ... 379
    federal wiretapping statutes ... 378
    Fourth Amendment protection ... 378
    harassment and discrimination ... 382
    privacy rights ... 377
    trade secrets and confidential information ... 382
    union solicitation ... 383
employee handbooks ... 23, 39
    advantages of ... 40
    at-will status ... 39
    commonly asked questions and answers ... 41
    disadvantages of ... 40
    disclaimer provisions ... 39
    important considerations when making an ... 40
employee leave. *See also* Family and Medical Leave Act (FMLA) ... 225
    Massachusetts law ... 231
        jury duty leave ... 232
        legal holidays ... 232
        maternity leave ... 231
        school and family leave ... 232
        voting leave ... 232
    other federal requirements ... 231
    Pregnancy Discrimination Act ... 231
employee performance evaluations ... 123
    alternative methods ... 127
        computer-assisted ... 128
        multi-rater feedback systems ... 128
    communication ... 123
        confidentiality ... 125
        expectations ... 123
            goals ... 124
            job description ... 123
        honesty ... 124

    interaction 125
        presentation.. 124
   evaluation checklist.. 129
   procedure.. 126
       consistency... 126
       content... 126
       documentation... 127
       self-evaluation... 127
Employee Polygraph Protection Act. *See also* federal law, lie-detector tests............................ 33, 374, 396
Employee Retirement Income Security Act of 1974. *See* ERISA. *See also* federal law 219, 396
employer identification number 180
employment discrimination. *See* discrimination... 81
employment of minors. *See* minors.. 71
employment-at-will 24, 26, 39
Equal Pay Act. *See also* federal law, wages and hours... 62, 84, 396
ERISA.. 219
   annual reports.. 222
   coverage 219
   fiduciary requirements 224
   pension plans... 220
   plan administration.. 223
   plan asset and investment requirements.. 223
   summary plan descriptions 222
   welfare plans... 220
evaluations. *See* employee performance evaluations 123
experience ratings calculations 242

F

Fair Credit Reporting Act. *See also* federal law 374, 396
Fair Labor Standards Act. *See also* federal law, wages and hours 51, 396
   contingent employees... 304
   covered employees... 51
   covered employers 51
   overview... 52
Family and Medical Leave Act (FMLA). *See also* federal law 225, 230, 303, 312, 396
   contingent employees... 303
   covered employers 225
   definitions 226
   eligible employees 225
   employee leave.. 225
   fitness-for-duty reports... 227
   instructional employees 225
   intermittent or reduced-schedule leave 229
   maintenance of health benefits.. 228
   medical certification.. 226
   notification requirements
       for employees.. 227
       for employers 228

Index

    penalties and enforcement 230
    recertification 227
    recordkeeping requirements 230
    requirements 226
    restoration to same or equivalent position 229
        exception 229
    second opinion 227
    serious health condition 226
Federal Insurance Contribution Act (FICA). *See also* federal law, Social Security 396
federal law
    Age Discrimination in Employment Act (ADEA)
        compliance threshold 5
        posting requirements 414
    Americans with Disabilities Act (ADA)
        compliance threshold 5
        optional recordkeeping 398
        posting requirements 414
    Civil Rights Act of 1964
        compliance threshold 5
        mandatory recordkeeping 411
        posting requirements 415
    Civil Rights Act of 1991
        compliance threshold 5
        posting recommendations 418
    COBRA
        compliance threshold 5
        posting recommendations 418
    Consumer Credit Protection Act, Title III
        compliance threshold 5
        posting recommendations 418
    Davis-Bacon Act
        posting requirements 416
    Drug-Free Workplace Act
        compliance threshold 5
        posting requirements 416
    Electronic Communications Privacy Act
        compliance threshold 5
    Employee Polygraph Protection Act (EPPA)
        compliance threshold 5
        mandatory recordkeeping 400
        posting requirements 415
    Employee Retirement Income Security Act (ERISA)
        compliance threshold 5
        mandatory recordkeeping 401
        posting recommendations 418
    Employee Right-to-Know
        compliance threshold 6
    Equal Pay Act (EPA)
        compliance threshold 6

    mandatory recordkeeping ... 403
    posting requirements ... 414
Executive Order 11246 (Affirmative Action) ... 6
    posting requirements ... 416
Fair Credit Reporting Act (FCRA)
    mandatory recordkeeping ... 403
    posting recommendations ... 418
Fair Labor Standards Act (FLSA)
    compliance threshold ... 6
    mandatory recordkeeping ... 404
    posting requirements ... 415
Family and Medical Leave Act (FMLA)
    compliance threshold ... 6
    mandatory recordkeeping ... 407
    posting requirements ... 414
Federal Income Tax Withholding
    compliance threshold ... 6
Federal Insurance Contribution Act (FICA)
    compliance threshold ... 6
    mandatory recordkeeping ... 401
Federal Military Selective Service Act
    posting recommendations ... 418
Federal Unemployment Tax Act (FUTA)
    compliance threshold ... 6
    mandatory recordkeeping ... 402
    optional recordkeeping ... 402
Health Insurance Portability and Accountability Act (HIPAA)
    compliance threshold ... 6
    mandatory recordkeeping ... 408
Immigration and Nationality Act
    compliance threshold ... 6
Immigration Reform and Control Act
    compliance threshold ... 6
    posting recommendations ... 418
Jury Service and Selection Act of 1968
    posting recommendations ... 418
Labor Management Relations Act. *See* National Labor Relations Act
    compliance threshold ... 6
Mental Health Parity Act (MHPA)
    compliance threshold ... 6
    mandatory recordkeeping ... 408
    optional recordkeeping ... 408
Newborns' and Mothers' Health Protection Act
    compliance threshold ... 6
    mandatory recordkeeping ... 408
Occupational Safety and Health Act (OSH Act)
    compliance threshold ... 6
    mandatory recordkeeping ... 409
    posting requirements ... 415

Index

Older Workers Benefit Protection Act
  compliance threshold 6
Personal Responsibility and Work Opportunity Act
  compliance threshold 6
Pregnancy Discrimination Act
  compliance threshold 6
Rehabilitation Act Section 503
  posting requirements 417
Service Contract Act
  posting requirements 417
Uniformed Services Employment and Re-Employment Rights Act
  compliance threshold 6
  posting recommendations 418
Vietnam Era Veterans' Readjustment Assistance Act
  compliance threshold 6
  mandatory recordkeeping 412
Walsh-Healy Public Contract Act
  posting requirements 416
Women's Health and Cancer Rights Act (WHCRA)
  mandatory recordkeeping 412
Worker Adjustment and Retraining Notification Act (WARN)
  compliance threshold 6
  posting recommendations 418
federal minimum wage. *See also* wages and hours 57
Federal Unemployment Tax Act (FUTA). *See also* federal law 396
forms
  Form 1099 .... 173, 297, 402
  Form 1099-MISC 182
  Form 4070 176
  Form 5500 222
  Form 8109 180
  Form 940 182
  Form 940-EZ 182
  Form 941 180
  Form 943 181
  Form SS-4 180
  Form SS-8 .... 171, 295, 297
  Form W-2 182
  Form W-3 182
  Form W-4 175
  Form W-5 178
  Schedule H 182
Fourth Amendment protection 110, 371, 378

G

garnishment. *See also* wages and hours, child support 59
  complying with order 59
  discharging employee 60

gender discrimination. *See* discrimination, sex 86
green card 103

H

harassment 82
    electronic communications 382
    ethnic 86
    racial 84
    sexual 87
        employer defenses against 92
        employer liability 87
        same-sex 88
Health Insurance Portability and Accountability Act. *See* HIPAA, *see also* federal law 205, 396
healthcare plans. *See also* COBRA 187
    Massachusetts law 199
        group insurance policies 199
            continuation coverage 201
            infant health coverage 200
            medical heath coverage 199
            mental health coverage 200
        health maintenance organizations 203
        hospital service contracts 201
            continuation coverage 202
            infant health coverage 201
            medical health coverage 201
            mental health coverage 201
        medical service agreements 202
            continuation coverage 203
            infant health coverage 202
            medical health coverage 202
            mental health coverage 202
        small business healthcare continuation 203
    required benefits and features 188
    state law regulations 188
HIPAA *See also* federal law 205
    certification of prior plan coverage 207
    commonly asked questions and answers 213
    creditable coverage 206
    dependent special enrollment period 208
    disclosure to participants 209
    enforcement provisions 211
    health status 208
    loss of coverage 208
    Mental Health Parity Act (MHPA) 210
    Newborns' and Mothers' Health Protection Act 211
    pre-existing condition exclusion 206
    requirements 205
    special enrollment period 208

hiring. *See* recruiting and hiring ... 13
holiday leave. *See also* employee leave ... 225

I

I-9 Form ... 19
immigration ... 99
    Alien Labor Certification ... 101
    anti-discrimination enforcement ... 99
    documentation requirements ... 99
    E-1 and E-2 status ... 101
    green cards ... 103
    specialty occupation ... 100
    visas
        H-1B ... 100
        H-2B ... 101
        L-1 ... 102
        O ... 103
Immigration and Naturalization Service (INS) ... 99
Immigration Reform & Control Act (IRCA). *See also* federal law ... 396
    contingent employment ... 304
income tax ... 178
independent contractors ... 289
    benefits ... 289
    common-law employee status ... 292
    contingent workers ... 299
    determining employee/contractor status ... 290
        ABC test ... 292
        common-law agency test ... 290
        economic fair realities test ... 291
        IRS 20-factor list ... 293
    discrimination and safety standards ... 298
    employer liability ... 292
    Form 1099 ... 298
    Form SS-8 ... 297
    income tax ... 292
    IRS worker classifications ... 294
        federal tax penalties for workers misclassification ... 295
    legal issues ... 289
    safe haven rule ... 296
    statutory employees ... 295
    untaxed employees ... 296
interviews. *See also* recruiting and hiring ... 18

J

job application. *See* employment application ... 13
job description ... 9
    disability discrimination and protection ... 9
    how to prepare ... 10

    performance standard 10
    wage and hour exemption 10
job interview. *See* interviews, *see also* recruiting and hiring 18
job offer letter 19
jury duty 51, 53, 54, 221
juvenile. *See* minors 71

L

labor unions. *See* National Labor Relations Act 271
leased employees
    payroll taxes and withholding 306
leave. *See* employee leave 225
lie-detector tests 33, 374
    alternatives to 35
    circumstances allowed in 34
    Employee Polygraph Protection Act 33
    enforcement of statutes 35
        waiver 35
    federal law 33
    Massachusetts law 36
        definition 36
        enforcement 37
        notice 36
        provisions 36
    testing procedures 34
lunch. *See* meal periods 55

M

Massachusetts law
    discrimination in employment 95
    employee leave 231
    employment of minors 73
    employee screening and lie-detector tests 36
    healthcare plans 199
    new-hire reporting 108
    payroll taxes and withholding 182
    plant closings and workforce reduction 165
    recordkeeping
        table of affected subjects 419
    smoking in the workplace 320
    unemployment compensation 248
    wages and hours 64
    whistleblower protection 367
    workers' compensation 251
meal periods 55
Mental Health Parity Act (MHPA). *See also* federal law 210, 396
minimum wage. *See also* wages and hours 51
minors 71
    federal laws 71

    hours of employment 73
    Massachusetts law.. 73
        employees covered.. 73
        employment prohibited 74
            exclusions.. 76
            minors under 12 76
            minors under 16 74
            minors under 18 74
            minors under 21 74
            prohibitions, other 76
        hours of employment 77
            exclusions.. 78
            minors between 16 and 18 77
            minors under 16 78
        meal periods 78
        permits... 79
        postings 79
            exceptions 79
        records... 79
    prohibited employment 72
        ages 14 and 15.. 72
        all minors 72
    recordkeeping and posting requirements 73
    required breaks... 73
    wages 73

N

National Labor Relations Act (NLRA). *See also* federal law.. 271
    contingent employees... 305
    elections
        challenges... 275
        conducting... 274
        prohibited pre-election conduct 276
        types of... 274
    enforcement... 283
    Excelsior List 275
    grievance arbitration procedure 282
    hearing 282
    injunction proceedings 282
    jurisdictional limits 271
        nonretail enterprises... 272
        other enterprises 272
        retail enterprises 272
    labor practices
        unfair.. 276
            by employers... 276
            by unions... 280
            case procedure 281
    settlements.. 281
    stip agreement 274

National Labor Relations Board 271
negligent retention 141
    claims 141, 142
    elements of 141
negligent supervision 142
    claims 142
negligent training 143
Newborns' and Mothers' Health Protection Act. *See also* federal law 396, 408
new-hire reporting 107
    Massachussets law 108
        employer obligations 108
        penalties 108
    penalties 108
non-competition agreements 43
    conflict-of-interest clause 48
    definition 45
    enforcement of 46
    hiring a competitor's employees 48
    restrictions on 46
    supplemental agreements 47

O

Occupational Safety and Health Act (OSH Act).
    See also federal law, workplace safety 333, 334, 396
    citation appeals 338
    citations and penalties 337
    compliance officers 334
    consultation services 335
    contingent employment 305
    enforcement 335
    Hazard Communication Standard 339
        enforcement and penalties 341
    inspections 336
        phases of 336
    Personal Protective Equipment Standard 343
    recordkeeping requirements 338
    regulations and standards 335
Occupational Safety and Health Administration (OSHA).
    See also Occupational Safety and Health Act , federal law, workplace safety 334
    contingent employees 305
Older Workers' Benefit Protection Act 84
ombudsman 286
on-call time, what is compensable regarding 60
OSHA. *See* Occupational Safety and Health Administration above 334
overtime. *See also* wages and hours 51, 61
    computing 61
    rate of pay 62
    scheduling 61
    unauthorized 61

P

part-time employees. *See* contingent employment ... 301
payroll taxes and withholding ... 169
    20-factor analysis for determining employee status ... 170
    contingent employees ... 305
    contract employees ... 305
    electronic transfer of funds ... 180
    employees
        common-law status ... 170
        covered by safe haven rule ... 173
        statutory ... 172
        untaxed ... 173
        vs. contract workers ... 169, 172
    employer identification number (EIN) ... 180
    exemptions ... 176
    family members ... 174
    Federal Insurance Contributions Act (FICA) ... 178, 180
    federal tax penalties for misclassification of workers ... 172
    federal taxes ... 180
    Federal Unemployment Tax Act (FUTA) ... 178, 180
    forms
        Form 1099-MISC ... 182
        Form 4070 ... 176
        Form 940 ... 182
        Form 940-EZ ... 182
        Form 941 ... 181
        Form 941c ... 182
        Form SS-4 ... 180
        Form SS-5 ... 175
        Form SS-8 ... 171
        Form W-2 ... 182
        Form W-2c ... 175
        Form W-3 ... 182
        Form W-4 ... 175
        Form W-5 ... 178
        Schedule H ... 182
    income tax ... 178
    leased employees ... 305
    Masschusetts law ... 182
        calculating the tax ... 185
        compensation ... 184
        corrections ... 186
        deadlines ... 185
        definitions
            employee ... 184
            employer ... 183
        filing ... 185
        recordkeeping ... 186
        registering to withhold ... 185

   outsourced employees 305
   recordkeeping requirements 181
   Social Security card 175
   state income taxes 179
   state unemployment tax 179
   temporary employees 305
   tips 176
   wages 176
   withholding period 177
   worker classifications, training materials for 171
pension plans. *See* retirement plans 219
polygraph tests. *See also* lie-detector tests 33
posters
   recommended federal 413, 418
   required federal 413
   required state 425
Pregnancy Discrimination Act. *See also* discrimination, federal law. 88, 231
privacy. *See* workplace privacy 371
promissory estoppel 23
pure consent agreement 274

R

recordkeeping
   table of applicable federal laws 396
recruiting and hiring 13
   advertising guidelines 13
   contracts 20
      at-will 24
      avoiding claims 24
      collective bargaining agreements 21
      express 21
         oral 22
         written 21
      implied 22
         employee handbooks 23
      promissory estoppel 23
   disability 15
   discrimination law, exemptions 16
   employment agreement 25
   I-9 Form 19
   interview questions, allowed and prohibited 14
      age 14
      arrests 15
      education 15
      military service 15
      national origin 14
      organizations 15
      race 14
      references 16

      religion 14
      sex 14
    interviews 18
      forms 19
      things to avoid 19
    job applications 13
    new-hire notification 20
    offer-of-employment letter 19
    pre-employment inquiries 13
    references 16
    suggestions 26
      definite term of employment 26
      employment-at-will 26
      mandatory arbitration 26
      other terms and conditions 27
Rehabilitation Act of 1973 83
restrictive covenants. *See* non-competition agreements 45
retirement plans 235
    401(k) 236
    403(b) 237
    accrual of benefits 238
    defined benefit 235
    defined contribution 236
    hybrid 236
    money-purchase 236
    participation requirements 237
    Pension Benefit Guaranty Corporation (PBGC) 235
    profit sharing 236
    qualified domestic relations order 238
    qualified joint and survivor annuity 238
    qualified preretirement survivor annuity 238
    tax-qualification benefits 239
    top-hat exemption 239
    vesting 237

S

safety in the workplace. *See* workplace safety 333
seasonal employees. *See* contingent employment 301
smoking in the workplace 315
    administrative controls 318
    bans
      partial 318
      total 317
    controlling environmental tobacco smoke 317
    employee screening 319
    engineering controls 318
    federal law
      Americans with Disabilities Act (ADA) 315
      National Labor Relations Act (NLRA) 316
      Occupational Safety and Health Act (OSH Act) 316

    Rehabilitation Act of 1973 316
    workers' compensation 315
  Massachusetts law 320
    employers' requirements 321
    exceptions 320
    penalties 321
    provisions 320
  policy considerations 319
  state and local regulations 317
Social Security 175
  disability extensions in COBRA coverage 193
  employer identification number, obtainment of 180
  new-hire reporting 107
  payroll deduction
    penalties for misclassification of workers 295
  payroll taxes
    age requirements when employing your own children 174
    deduction from pay 58, 169
      business expense reimbursement 176
      FICA 178
      noncash payments 176
      other than full-time employees 178
      retirement plans 239
      tips 176
      when exempt from withholding 178
    deposits by employers 180
    penalties for misclassification of workers 172
    pre-tax salary reduction contributions to 401(k) plans 237
    recordkeeping
      FICA 401
    wages of parents employed by their children 174
  recordkeeping
    forms
      Form 941 181
      W-2 182
    general employment tax records 181
  Social Security card, obtainment of 175
  Social Security number
    employee requirements 175
    new-hire reporting 20
    recordkeeping
      separation notices 246
    verification of number 175
Social Security Act of 1935 241
Social Security Administration 175

T

tangible employment action 87
taxes. *See* payroll taxes and withholding 169
  contingent employees 305

    exemptions 176
    Federal Insurance Contributions Act (FICA) 180
    Federal Unemployment Tax Act (FUTA) 178, 180
    income tax 175, 178
    independent contractors 172
    records 181
    Social Security 175, 178
    state unemployment taxes 179
    taxes and family members 174
    untaxed employees 173
telecommuting 389
    adaptable jobs 390
    concerns
        employee 390
        employer 390
        legal
            Americans with Disabilities Act (ADA) 392
            Fair Labor Standards Act (FLSA) 392
            insurance and liability 392
            OSHA 391
            workers' compensation 391
            zoning 393
    employer benefits 389
    written agreements for 393
temporary employees. *See* contingent employment 301
    payroll taxes and withholding 306
termination. *See also* workers' compensation 145
    at-will employees 145
    avoiding liability for wrongful termination 155
    breach of contract claims 150
    checklist of procedures 158
        for misconduct 158
        for poor performance 158
        legal 159
        procedural 159
    claims 151
    constructive discharge 149
    contractual employees 145
    defamation 153
        absolute privilege 153
        qualified privilege 153
    federal statutes limiting employment-at-will 148
    fraud and negligent misrepresentation 152
    guidelines for 146
    intentional infliction of emotional distress 152
    interference with contractual relationships 150
    invasion of privacy claims 154
    laws and regulations restricting at-will 147
    unavoidable 147

unemployment compensation 160
wrongful discharge 147, 151
tipped employees 405
Title VII of the Civil Rights Act of 1964 (Title VII). *See* discrimination 83
trade secrets 43
   defined 44
   general protections 44
   inevitable disclousure doctrine 47
   legal test 44
   Uniform Trade Secrets Act 44

U

unemployment compensation 241
   controlling costs 243
   employee separations, eliminating 243
   employment separations 245
      documentation 246
      recording 246
      terminology 246
   experience ratings calculations 242
   Federal Unemployment Tax Act (FUTA) 241
      computing FUTA tax 242
   independent contractors 245
   Massachusetts law 248
      benefits and eligibility 250
      disqualification from benefits 250
      employees covered 248
      employers covered 248
      returns and reports 250
      taxes 249
      wages 249
   refusal of suitable employment 245
   state tax accounts 242
Uniform Trade Secrets Act 44
Uniformed Services Employment and Re-employment Rights Act 84
unions. *See* National Labor Relations Act 271

V

vacation
   leave 227
   pay. *See* payroll taxes and withholding 176
vesting. *See also* retirement plans 237
video surveillance 373
Vietnam Era Veterans' Readjustment Assistance Act (VEVRAA). *See also* federal law 396
violence in the workplace. *See* workplace violence 323
visa. *See* immigration 100
voicemail systems. *See* e-mail and voicemail systems 377

W

- wages and hours ... 51
  - child support ... 59, 60
    - complying with order ... 59
  - compensation ... 57
    - minimum wage requirements ... 57
  - deductions from pay ... 58
  - disabled individuals ... 58
  - discrimination ... 62
  - enforcement ... 63
  - exemptions
    - administrative ... 57
    - commonly asked questions and answers ... 52
    - executive ... 56
    - professional ... 56
  - Fair Labor Standards Act (FLSA) ... 51
  - garnishments ... 59
  - hours worked ... 60
  - Massachusetts law ... 64
    - compensation ... 64
      - benefit payments ... 65
      - exceptions ... 65
      - frequency of payment ... 65
      - method of payment ... 65
      - reimbursements ... 65
      - termination ... 65
        - discharged employees ... 65
        - voluntary termination ... 65
    - deductions ... 66
      - garnishment ... 66
      - support orders ... 66
      - wage assignments ... 66
    - discrimination ... 69
    - employees covered ... 64
    - employers covered ... 64
    - hours worked ... 67
    - overtime ... 68
      - exceptions ... 68
      - regular rate of pay ... 68
    - posting ... 69
    - recordkeeping ... 69
    - wage statements ... 65
  - on-call time ... 60
  - overtime
    - compensation ... 61
    - computing ... 61
    - exemptions ... 57
    - rate of pay ... 62
    - unauthorized ... 61

payment timing	58
recordkeeping and posting requirements	63
student learners	58
training time	61
whistleblowing	361
Civil False Claims Act	364
complaints, minimizing	366
environmental acts	365
federal defense contractor whistleblower statute	364
federal law	361
Massachusetts law	367
definitions	367
employer obligation	369
enforcement	368
exclusions	368
Massachusetts Healthcare Whistleblower Law	369
statute	367
protected activities	364
protected employees	362
who participate in an investigation or hearing	363
who refuse to follow an unlawful order	363
who report healthcare services violations	363
who report unlawful activities	363
violation of law, proving	365
wiretapping	
e-mail and computers	373
e-mail and voicemail	378
telephone	372
Women's Health and Cancer Rights Act (WHCRA). *See also* federal law	396
Worker Adjustment and Retraining Notification Act (WARN)	161
affected employees	163
aggregations	162
contingent employees	303
coverage	161
employment loss	162
exceptions to notice requirements	163
legal obligations	161
mass layoff	162
Massachusetts law	165
notification	166
re-employment assistance benefits	166
re-employment assistance programs	167
part-time employees	161
plant closing	162
required notice contents	164
statute of limitations	165
violation penalties	165
workers' compensation	251
advantages and disadvantages	257

Americans with Disabilities Act and workers' compensation ... 263
benefits claims procedures ... 258
   employees' responsibilities ... 258
      Massachusetts administrative procedures ... 258
   employers' responsibilities ... 259
characteristics of coverage ... 252
   coverage provided ... 255
      Massachusetts benefits ... 256
   employer-financed aspect ... 252
      Massachusetts requirements ... 252
      purchase coverage ... 253
      self-insurance ... 253
         self-insurance in Massachusetts ... 254
      state fund ... 253
   no-fault aspect ... 254
      injuries and illnesses covered ... 254
   penalties under Massachusetts law ... 257
developing a policy ... 260
   detailed policy ... 260
   standard policy ... 260
employees affected ... 251
   Massachusetts requirements ... 252
employers affected ... 251
   Massachusetts requirements ... 251
reduction of costs ... 261
workers' compensation and other federal laws ... 269

workplace privacy ... 371
   drug and alcohol testing ... 373
   Electronic Communications Privacy Act ... 373
   Employee Polygraph Protection Act ... 374
   Fair Credit Reporting Act. *See also* federal law ... 374
   Federal Wiretapping Act ... 372
   honesty testing ... 374
   monitoring
      e-mail and computer use ... 373
      telephone conversations ... 372
   polygraph testing ... 374
   recordkeeping ... 375
   searches ... 371
   surveillance ... 372
      video ... 373

workplace safety. *See also* OSH Act and OSHA ... 333
   AIDS ... 333
   employee information and training ... 340
   exposure and medical records, employee access to ... 339
   Federal Bloodborne Pathogen Standard ... 333
   hazard evaluation ... 339
   Hepatitis B ... 333
   labels and other forms of writing ... 340

   material safety data sheets (MSDSs) 340
   National Institute for Occupational Safety and Health 334
   refusals to work 338
   regulations and standards
      AIDS 341
      Hepatitis B 341
   safety and health program 344
      administrator responsibility 346
      benefits of 344
      director/coordinator responsibility 346
      employee involvement 345
      employee responsibility 346
      job descriptions, importance of 346
      management leadership 344
      need for 344
      program evaluation 358
      providing ample resources 347
      supervisor responsibility 346
      ten steps to implementation 348
      written policy statement 347
   trade secrets 341
   violence 343
   written programs 339
workplace violence 323
   aftermath training 332
   anti-discrimination laws 324
   anti-violence policy 330
   federal protections 324
   negligent hiring 328
   negligent retention 328
   negligent supervision 328
   OSHA requirements 326
   potentially dangerous work environments 327
   pre-employment screening 331
   publications, OSHA 326
   state law issues 325
   statistics 323
   threat-assessment team 332
   trouble, anticipating 329
   troubled environment, signs of 328
   violence, avoiding incidents 330
   workers' compensation 324